THE BATTLESHIP *DREADNOUGHT*

THE BATTLESHIP
DREADNOUGHT

John Roberts

CONWAY.

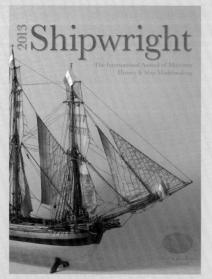

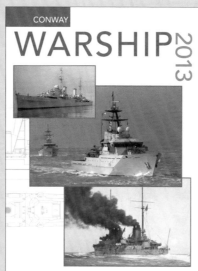

Frontispiece: *Dreadnought* leaving Valetta harbour, Malta, in November 1913. Note that the main topmast had been removed. (Richard Ellis)

© John Roberts 1992, 2001
First published in Great Britain in 1992 by Conway Maritime Press.
Revised edition first published in 2001.
Reprinted 2002, 2004

This first paperback edition published in 2013 by Conway
an imprint of Anova Books Ltd
10 Southcombe Street
London W14 0RA
www.conwaypublishing.com

ISBN 9781844862061

Printed and bound by IP Softcom, China

VISIT THE CONWAY PUBLISHING WEBSITE
The ultimate destination for all warship enthusiasts

- Up-to-the-minute book news, author interviews, special offers and competitions

- A number of scale plans from the Anatomy of the Ship series are available for purchase and download

- Latest information and previews of all books, including the Warship and Shipwright annuals

- Premium access to special offers and limited editions of Conway books

- Purchase all Conway books, including the new range of ebooks

www.conwaypublishing.com

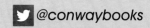 @conwaybooks

CONTENTS

ACKNOWLEDGEMENTS 6

INTRODUCTION 7
The gunnery revolution 7
A question of Speed 8
Design 9
Construction 13
The experimental cruise/Operational history 17
Summary of service 18
Hull, weights and stability 23
Machinery 24
Steering gear 26
Electrical machinery/Ventilation 27
Accommodation/Armament 28
Fire control equipment 30
Armour 31
Compasses 32
Wireless/Telephone system/Modifications 33

NOTES 36

SOURCES 37

The PHOTOGRAPHS 39

The DRAWINGS 69
A. General arrangement 70
B. Lines and constructional details 94
C. Machinery 147
D. Accommodation 191
E. Superstructure 195
F. Rig 206
G. Armament 217
H. Fire control 238
I. Fittings 244
J. Ground tackle 252
K. Boats 254

ACKNOWLEDGEMENTS

Acknowledgements

The author would like to thank the following organisations and individuals for their help in gathering material for the preparation of this book: the National Maritime Museum; the Public Record Office; the Ministry of Defence Library (Naval Section); the Cumbria County Council Archive Service; David Lyon, Graham Slatter and David Topliss of the National Maritime Museum; Fred Lake of the MoD Library; Susan Benson of the Cumbria Archive Service; David Brown, RCNC, Ray Burt, John Campbell and Brian King.

INTRODUCTION

On 10 February 1906 the hull of the first all-big-gun battleship, HMS *Dreadnought*, was launched at Portsmouth Dockyard. Over 6000 tons of mater-ial had been built into her since her laying down just nineteen weeks beforehand. Eight months later she went to sea for the first time for her preliminary steam trials and, although this did not mark her final completion, the production of a seagoing warship of 18,000 tons, and of a new type, in such a short period of time was a remarkable achievement. The speed with which she was built was the product of the need to evaluate her qualities at the earliest opportunity and, more importantly, to steal a march on foreign navies for her revolutionary design would, if successful, render existing battleship designs obsolete. She was, indeed, a great success and marked the beginning of a new era in battleship development; she gave her name to all subsequent vessels of the type, which became known as dreadnought battleships, or simply 'dreadnoughts'.

This British coup was unusual for, in theory at least, the Royal Navy, with its enormous fleet, had the most to lose from the premature obsolescence of its battleships and had a tradition of not initiating revolutionary ideas for this very reason. That this was not the case on this occasion was due to the foresight of the recently appointed First Sea Lord, the dynamic Admiral Sir John Fisher. He knew that other countries, in particular the United States, were progressing toward the all-big-gun concept and that such a ship would be built sooner rather than later. Another consideration was the general improvement in the building times in foreign yards, particularly in Germany, which threatened to undermine Britain's ability – enjoyed throughout the 1890s – to outbuild her rivals using the superior efficiency of her shipyards. Under these circumstances the development of a new type abroad could have seriously weakened the Royal Navy's dominant position; but if Britain took the lead it would at least provide a chance to begin rebuilding the battlefleet while others were still catching up. In fact, a substantial breathing space was obtained and Britain was to lay down a further three dreadnoughts before Germany laid down her first in June 1907. Even so, Germany was to complete thirteen against Britain's twenty by the outbreak of war in 1914 leaving a margin of superiority well below that enjoyed in the pre-dreadnought period.

Although Fisher can be credited with the initiation of *Dreadnought*'s construction and her outline requirements, particularly her speed which was to be greater than that of contemporary battleships, the all-big-gun concept was not his but the product of an evolutionary process that began around 1900. The concept had been suggested at various times before 1905, but not taken up because of its radical nature, although the United States and Japan decided on a uniform big-gun armament for their future battleships at about the same time as *Dreadnought* was being designed. *Dreadnought* was the product of many minds for which Fisher provided a focus; and he had the forceful character necessary to push the idea into existence. Subsequently, Fisher became more interested in the armoured cruiser contemporaries of *Dreadnought*, the three large 12in-gun ships of the *Invincible* class (the first battle cruisers) which he regarded as the capital ships of the future – the 'new testament' ships, to use his own colourful language. These ships reflected his particular obsession with high speed and gunpower at the expense of protection. However, gaining acceptance for *Dreadnought* herself was difficult enough: asking for an abandonment of battleship construction in favour of big armoured cruisers would have been impossible.

The gunnery revolution

British battleships of the 1890s carried an armament of four 12in and twelve 6in guns and were expected to fight at a maximum range of around 2000yds. Heavy guns did, however, have a maximum range well beyond this distance and they were steadily improving in accuracy and rate of fire. Battle ranges were limited by the inadequacy of sighting and control methods which did not allow for any certainty of hitting a target at longer ranges other than by luck. The initial drive to improve this capability came from the increasing power and range of the torpedo, which made it necessary to set a battle range beyond the reach of such weapons. The first experimental long-range firing practices were carried out by the Mediterranean Fleet in 1898 and these were continued under Fisher during his period as C-in-C (1899–1902). Long-range practices became standard throughout the Navy in 1901 and two years later the official fighting range had increased to 3000yds.

The early Mediterranean experiments, which were carried out at ranges of between 5000 and 6000yds, developed 'spotting' to control the fire of the guns – that is, observing the fall of shot and then correcting the elevation and training of the guns to bring them to bear on the target. This system employed rangefinders to give an initial indication of range, and required an initial slow and deliberate fire. It was controlled centrally from a position high on the superstructure – later from mast platforms – and it demonstrated the need for improved communication between the control position and the guns, in the form of fire control instruments, for transmitting range and deflection. In September 1903 two committees, one in the Mediterranean Fleet and one in the Channel Fleet, were set up to investigate the problems of long-range fire control and experiments were carried out onboard the battleships *Venerable* (Mediterranean Fleet) and *Victorious* (Channel Fleet). These committees produced a joint report on 30 May 1904 which stated that guns could, with spotting and suitable fire control instruments, be effective up to 8000yds under ideal conditions (*ie* in clear weather and with the target on a steady course at a constant speed). From this point on, the provision of a fire control system and the necessary instrumentation in all British battleships and armoured cruisers was made a high priority and battle practice up to 8000yds was included in the standard range of exercises.

This increase in range, however, created fresh problems. The secondary batteries of 6in guns were considerably less effective at longer ranges, and it was soon realised that the spotting system would be more efficient with larger numbers of uniform calibre guns. The initial solution was to provide a larger calibre secondary battery, but the fall of shot with a two-calibre armament was difficult to distinguish. The ideal solution was a uniform-calibre armament. A number of proposals were made around 1903–4 for ships with uniform-calibre main armament but, while the need to increase gunpower was widely understood, the difficulties of mixed-calibre fire control were not and the Admiralty rejected these suggestions.

In Italy Colonel (later General) Vittorio Cuniberti, chief constructor for the Italian Navy, also proposed the construction of a ship with a uniform armament of 12in guns. His project was turned down by the naval authorities but he was allowed to publish the results of his work. This duly appeared in the 1903 edition of *Jane's Fighting Ships* under the heading 'An Ideal Battleship for the British Navy' and it proposed a 17,000-ton, 24kt ship with an armament of twelve 12in guns, and protected by 12in armour. Cuniberti's ship was not intended to answer the problems of fire control at long range but simply combined the tactical advantage of speed with the ability to out-gun a potential adversary – a concept very close to that later adopted by Fisher. Cuniberti's proposal was received with interest in Britain but was also criticised as being extravagant, and it is possible that the reaction against this design contributed to the Admiralty's reluctance to adopt a single-calibre armament.

The first vessels to reflect the desire for increased gun power were the two ships of the *Lord Nelson class, Lord Nelson* and *Agamemnon*. The design of these ships was begun in 1902 and was based on an investigation into the possibility of constructing battleships which were individually superior to foreign designs. This investigation indicated that the destructive power of the 12in gun – on a rate of fire to hits ratio – was much greater than that of the 6in gun; that the secondary armament was likely to be completely disabled by heavy shells before the range was sufficiently reduced for it to become effective; and that a general improvement in the thickness and extent of armour was required. A number of outline designs were produced during 1902–3, mostly for ships with a 9.2in secondary armament, but two of the sketches were for ships mounting a uniform armament of twelve 10in guns. This was a new Armstrong 50cal

gun of substantial power and with a high rate of fire, which appeared to offer considerable advantages over the heavier, slower firing 12in; but having a lighter shell it still could not match the larger gun's destructive effect. Designs with sixteen 10in guns were also discussed, and in September 1903 Constructor J H Narbeth suggested to the DNC that twelve 12in 45cal guns could, with a small increase in size, provide a substitute armament for these designs. His outline plan for six twin turrets, one forward, one aft and two on each beam amidships, was rejected as too ambitious, but the basic layout was to reappear in the preliminary sketch designs for *Dreadnought* and proved to be the penultimate layout of that chosen. The uniform armament was greatly favoured in the Constructors' Department. The DNC himself preferred the 10in-gun designs, but in the end the Board accepted the more standard arrangement with four 12in and a heavier secondary battery of ten 9.2in, all mounted in turrets. Despite the guarded approach to a change, *Lord Nelson* showed a marked improvement over earlier ships in both armament and protection but for various reasons, including the extended debate on the final details, the two ships of the class were not laid down until May 1905.

A question of speed

In the late 1890s the form of battle tactics employed in a fleet action was the subject of much debate but by the early 1900s the single 'line-ahead' of the old sailing navy was emerging as the ideal battleship formation. It had the advantage of being easier to control than independently manoeuvring divisions, and it gave all the ships in the line clear broadside arcs of fire. Fisher was among the leading proponents of these tactics and from his own experience concluded that when employing line-ahead formation a fleet with a speed advantage would have the greatest chance of success. Initially, these tactics evolved around the manoeuvre of placing the battle line across the line of advance of the enemy – 'crossing his T'. In this way the full broadside of all the ships could fire on the enemy fleet which could only reply with the forward guns of its leading ships. This tactic created the opportunity for destroying the enemy's van and throwing his entire fleet into confusion. Speed could be used either to gain this advantage at the outset, with a suitable mixture of luck and judgement, or, when fighting broadside-to-broadside, to move ahead and turn across the enemy's bow. The latter manoeuvre became less feasible as battle ranges increased and permitted a slower fleet to turn away, exploiting its position closer to the centre of the turning circle. Fisher, however, discovered other advantages in higher speeds, which were in part a consequence of the latest developments in gunnery. The main advantages of the use of salvo firing of heavy guns were achieved at long range, and to exploit this effectively it was necessary to be able to close to the most advantageous range and maintain it by moving away or closing the target as required. To be able to dictate the range in this fashion required a margin of speed over the enemy.

While C-in-C Mediterranean Fisher began to consider the outline requirements for future ships in relation to the latest developments in gunnery and tactics, and during the following years this evolved into a full set of outline designs. His ideas crystallised during his period as C-in-C Portsmouth where he was assisted and advised by a group of like-minded naval officers, and provided with technical assistance by W H Gard, the Chief Constructor of Portsmouth Dockyard, and Alexander Gracie, the Managing Director of the Fairfield Shipbuilding Co. It is not clear at what point Fisher opted for a uniform armament for the battleship designs but in about 1903 he favoured an outline design mounting sixteen 10in guns. This design was the last of a series said to have originated with Armstrong Whitworth although whether these were submitted direct to Fisher (he was a friend of Sir Andrew Noble, the Chairman of the company), or to the Admiralty is not clear.[1] Details of this design were circulated among a select group of Fisher's supporters, and Captains Madden, Jackson and Bacon commented that they would prefer to see a uniform 12in-gun armament. Fisher was particularly impressed by Bacon's arguments on this point and he asked Gard to produce a modified design mounting eight 12in guns. These two designs, together with a detailed appreciation of their relative merits and the arguments in favour of the all-big-gun armament and high speed, were used to gain acceptance for his proposals when he became First Sea Lord in October 1904. The apparent ease with which this approval was obtained, from both the Board of Admiralty and the Government, was in part due to reports of the first naval battles of the Russo-Japanese War (1904–5) which confirmed the greater effectiveness of heavy guns and the importance of long-range gunfire. Intelligence had also been received of the American plans to construct battleships with a uniform 12in-gun armament, and of the intention of Japan and Russia to produce similar vessels as a result of their recent war experiences.[2]

Design

The proposed designs presented by Fisher in October had the following basic particulars:

	A	B
Displacement	c16,000 tons	c16,000 tons
Armament	16–10in (8 × 2)	8–12in (4 × 2)
Speed	21kts	21kts
IHP	30,000	30,000
Main belt	10in	12in
Upper belt	7in	9in
Barbettes	10in	12in
Decks	2in–1in	2in–1in

The description given by Fisher indicates that the 12in-gun design had its turrets placed one forward, one aft and one on each beam, while the 10in-gun design had one forward, one aft and three on each beam. He also indicated that the ships were comparatively long and of shallow draught to help generate the required speed. Judging by subsequent designs, however, the horsepower necessary was greatly over-estimated.[3]

The 12in gun was taken as the preferred weapon almost immediately and all subsequent work concentrated on the production of designs for an

TABLE 1: **Narbeth Fast Battleship Outline Designs, November 1904**

Eight 12in guns in pairs with protection practically as *Lord Nelson*.
A1 – 20kts, 425ft × 83ft × 27ft, 16,000tons, 19,000ihp.
A2 – 21kts, 440ft × 83ft × 27ft, 16,500tons, 22,000ihp.

Twelve 12in guns in pairs with protection practically as *Lord Nelson*.
B1 – 20kts, 475ft × 83ft × 27ft, 18,000tons, 19,000ihp.
B2 – 21kts, 495ft × 83ft × 27ft, 18,800tons, 22,000ihp.

NOTE: Later A1 became B, A2 became A, and B2 became D.

armament of this calibre. The DNC's Department began its development of the battleship design in early November 1904 but the particulars differed markedly from those given above. This would indicate that the initial design work had been fairly elementary and that other minds were now at work on the requirements set by Fisher. Records of the deliberations that took place during November and December are sparse but it is possible to draw some conclusions from those which remain. In November Narbeth, who was responsible for the production of sketch designs and later the design of *Dreadnought* herself, produced four sets of outline particulars for alternative 20kt and 21kt ships armed with either eight or twelve 12in guns (see Table 1). In submitting these he pointed out that they 'could be produced by a little squeezing and a few innovations, the chief being obtaining 10 percent more power out of the machinery with weight and space as at present, this having been done in *Swiftsure* and *Triumph* and in the *Monmouth* class, and much exceeded in *Beneditto Brin*'. He also mentioned the need to provide an improved hull form to give '… . better results than any yet adopted for battleships as regards to IHP.'[4] These comments obviously refer to the need to keep the displacement within acceptable limits, which was difficult in the face of the desire for a heavier armament *and* increased speed. This led to the suggestion of adopting turbine machinery which would save weight in both the machinery and the hull; as a result several of the later sketch designs were worked out for both turbine and reciprocating engines.

On 26 November Narbeth submitted a further series of outline designs (see Table 2), all with eight 12in guns, of various speeds and with alternative reciprocating or turbine machinery arrangements. All subsequent sketch designs were for ships with twelve or, in one case, ten 12in guns; one (design 'D') originated from Narbeth and the remainder from Gard and Fisher. The designs, which had been prepared by the end of December, were designated 'A' to 'F', the letters apparently indicating the various armament layouts, rather than the particulars (see Table 3). The twelve-gun designs fulfilled the need for increasing the number of guns on the broadside for efficient salvo firing (the minimum requirement being for eight), while at the same time maintaining a good end-on fire – a particular requirement of Fisher. The slower designs, 'B' and 'C', were soon removed from those under consideration, leaving only' A' and 'D' to 'F', but it is not possible to match the designations of the three eight-gun arrangements with their respective armament layouts.

It was realised that the radical nature of the proposed designs, including those for the armoured cruiser, would be the subject of criticism both

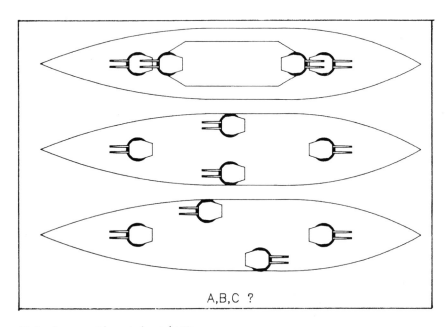

A,B,C ?

Fig 1 Armament layouts for eight 12in guns. It is possible that these were alternatives for all three of the A, B and C designs; unfortunately it is not known which layout belongs to which designation.

Fig 3 Armament layouts for the Narbeth design 'D' and its later modifications leading to the chosen design 'H'.

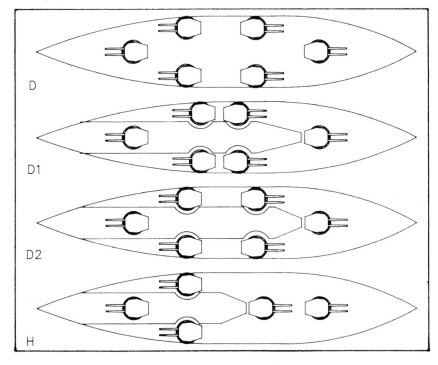

D

D1

D2

H

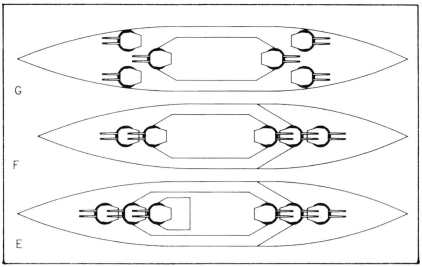

G

F

E

Fig 2 Armament layouts for the Fisher/ Gard designs.

within and outside the service. In order to limit the force of any such criticism the Board decided on the formation of a Committee on Designs to investigate the new proposals. This Committee was to be composed of leading authorities in the field whose opinions could not lightly be ignored. They were also to be chosen from among those who were in close agreement with Fisher's ideas. The Committee was not formed to consider the basic concept of the designs but to study the various alternatives and make recommendations on the general layouts and the detailed design of the new ships. In effect, the Committee took over the normal function of the Board and its advisors, thereby diverting much of the responsibility for the end result upon itself. The First Lord, the Earl of Selbourne, reported the Board's decision on 6 December and the Committee members were appointed on the 22nd; these were:

> Admiral Sir John Fisher (First Sea Lord and President of the Committee)
> Rear Admiral Prince Louis of Battenberg (Director of Naval Intelligence)
> Engineer Rear Admiral Sir John Durston (Engineer in Chief of the Fleet)
> Rear Admiral Alfred L Winsloe (Commander of Torpedo and Submarine Craft Flotillas)

TABLE 2: **Preliminary Design for Fast Battleships, 26 November 1904**

	A	B	C
Length (pp) (ft)	460	425	410
Beam (moulded) (ft in)	81 6	826	83
Displacement (VE)	16,500	15,750	15,000
Displacement (Tu)	16,000	15,350	14,700
Speed	21	20	19

All designs have eight 12in guns.
VE = Vertical triple expansion engines.
Tu = Turbines.
There were three alternatives to the above – A1, B1 and C1. A1 was 250 tons lighter than A and B1 80 tons lighter than B; all other figures were as given above – the differences otherwise are not known.

Captain Henry B Jackson (Controller of the Navy)
Captain John R Jellicoe (Director of Naval Ordnance)
Captain Charles E Madden (Naval Assistant to the Controller)
Captain Reginald H S Bacon (Naval Assistant to the First Sea Lord)
Phillip Watts (Director of Naval Construction)
Lord Kelvin
Professor J H Biles (Glasgow University)
Sir John Thornycroft
Alexander Gracie (Fairfield Shipbuilding Co)
R E Froude (Superintendent of the Admiralty Experimental Works, Haslar)
W H Gard (Chief Constructor)
Commander W Henderson (Committee Secretary)
E H Mitchell (Assistant Constructor and Committee Assistant Secretary)

In addition, Narbeth continued his responsibilities for providing sketch designs and acted as secretary to the DNC. According to Oscar Parkes, Fisher was not a member of the Committee and only acted as Chairman, but Selbourne in his Statement on the Naval Estimates for 1905–6 included him in the list of Committee members.

The first meeting of the Committee on Designs took place on 3 January 1905 and, after Fisher's opening remarks, started its deliberations by considering the available outline designs for battleships. Design 'E', with three superfiring turrets mounted on the centreline fore and aft, was intended to meet Fisher's desire to achieve maximum end-on fire combined with a good broadside. It was, however, rather large and to reduce the dimensions one of the forward turrets was omitted in the alternative design 'F'.[5] Jellicoe pointed out that blast effect would make the lower turrets unworkable over a wide arc of fire fore and aft which would negate the purpose of the whole arrangement, but this view was mistaken, as evidenced by the general adoption of superfiring turrets in all navies within a few years of *Dreadnought's* completion. At the time, however, there was little experience of the arrangement and those that had been tried were generally reported as unsuccessful.

A third Fisher-Gard type, design 'G', was prepared for the following day. In this the forward and after groups were rearranged to give a slightly wider spacing between the turrets at the expense of reducing the broadside fire to eight guns. However, the close grouping of the 12in turrets in all three designs was objected to on the grounds that a single hit might disable several guns, and so the designs were dropped. The Committee's thoughts on design 'A' and its armament distribution are not known, but it was probably passed over because it had an insufficient broadside or, if it had superfiring guns, because of the danger of blast effects.

This left only Narbeth's design 'D' which was basically the same as that which he had proposed for the *Lord Nelson* design in 1903. There were three variants: 'D' with reciprocating machinery, 'D2' as 'D' with turbine machinery and 'D1' as '02' but with the wing turrets placed closer together. The design had a comparatively low freeboard, which was not suited to high speed nor to the working of the foremost turret in a seaway, and it was requested that the turbine design be modified to include a raised forecastle with the fore turret mounted on it. The secondary battery was also to be modified to twelve 4in guns in place of the mixed

TABLE 3: Sketch Designs, 4 January 1905

	F	E	D1 & D2	D	A
Length (pp) (ft)	530	550	500	520	460
Beam (moulded) (ft)	82	85	83	84	81.5
Draught (ft)	26	27	27	27	25.5
Displacement	19,000	21,000	18,000	19,000	16,500
Hp	25,000	27,500	23,000	23,500	23,000
Speed (kts)	21	21	21	21	21
Armament	10 12in	12 12in	12 12in	12 12in	8 12in
	16 4in	16 4in	35 12pdr	35 12pdr	35 12pdr
			& 3pdr	& 3pdr	& 3pdr
Torpedo tubes	6	6	5	5	
Weights					
General equipment	600	600	575	600	560
Armament	3280	3860	3775	3775	2615
Machinery	2300	2500	1700	2200	2150
Coal	900	900	900	900	900
Armour	5620	6400	4700	4875	4275
Hull	6100	6540	6250	6450	5,800
Board margin	200	200	100	200	200
TOTAL	19,000	21,000	18,000	19,000	16,500

All designs had armour on a similar scale to Lord *Nelson*, ie 12in belt, barbettes and gunhouses.
All the above had vertical engines except D1/D2 which was for turbine machinery.
Design A with turbine machinery was 500 tons lighter but otherwise as above.
There was also a modified E design at this time (4 January) with twenty 4in guns and 200 tons transferred from the armour to the hull weight – in other respects the particulars were as given above.
Design G, had the same particulars as E.
A turbine version of Design F was 700 tons lighter and 20ft shorter (hull 5900 tons, armour S470 tons, machinery 1950 tons) but was otherwise as given for F above.
The A and D designs above date from 14 December (although at that time D had a secondary armament of twelve 12pdr, and ten 3pdr); the exact original dates for the others are not known.

12pdr and 3pdr gun battery. These alterations increased the displacement to 18,500 tons (150 tons added to the hull weight, 250 tons to the armour and 100 tons to the armament), while the beam was increased to 84ft to compensate for the additional topweight. On 4 January the Committee decided that it preferred design 'D1' but asked for the preparation of an alternative arrangement with the two after wing turrets replaced by a single centreline turret placed between the engine and boiler rooms. This reduced the number of guns to ten but provided the same number for all arcs of fire as the twelve-gun design while at the same time saving a substantial amount of weight. This modified design, designated 'H', was discussed by the naval members of the Committee on 13 January and it was decided that the new arrangement was preferable to design 'D' and that it should be recommended for adoption. They requested the preparation of fuller details, for both turbine and reciprocating machinery, and a model for the next full meeting of the Committee on 18 January. They also stated that the ship was to be arranged with the officers' accommodation forward and that the drawings of the ship should show the arrangements for this and the crew accommodation.

At the meeting on the 18th design 'H' was duly approved and the turbine version, which saved 1100 tons in displacement, was chosen, after a lengthy debate, as that which should be developed for the new ship. The particulars provided for the committee are shown in Table 4. The full Committee, in meetings on 25 January and 21 February, concentrated, as far as the battleship design was concerned, on the discussion of the best form of the machinery layout and the number of shafts to be adopted. The naval members, during a number of sub-committee meetings, decided on a number of design matters, listed below.

Table 4: Design 'H', 18 January 1905

Machinery type	Turbine		Vertical
Length (pp) (ft)	490		500
Beam (moulded) (ft)	83		84
Hp	23,000		23,500
Speed (kts)	21		21
Armament	10 12in		10 12in
	14 4in		14 4in
Armour			
Main belt		12in	
Bulkheads		8in	
Barbettes		12in	
Gun shields		12in sides, 3in roof	
Conning tower		12in	
Communication tube		6in	
Main deck		1.75in	
Middle deck		1in–2in flat, 3.25in slope	
Lower deck		1in–3in	
Weights (tons)			
General equipment	600		600
Armament	3300		3300
Machinery	1700		2400
Armour	5000		5200
Hull	6150		6350
Coal	900		900
Board margin	100		100
TOTAL	17,750		18,670

Torpedo protection. It was decided to provide longitudinal protective bulkheads abreast the magazines and shell rooms as defence against underwater explosions. To provide for these without increasing the displacement the main belt, barbette and turret armour was reduced from 12in to 11in thickness.

Mast and boat arrangements. The cramped superstructure, a direct result of the armament arrangement, made the provision of suitable stowage and handling arrangements for the boats difficult. The matter was settled by a sub-committee of Jackson, Jellicoe and Madden who chose to place the principal boats on skid beams over the main superstructure served by a derrick on the foremast. Unfortunately, this arrangement involved placing the foremast abaft the fore funnel where the fore top was liable to interference by smoke and heat. As the top was to be the primary control position for the main armament this was a serious error. The masts themselves were of heavy tripod construction to avoid the use of shrouds, and provide a rigid structure, reasonably free from vibration, for fire control purposes.

Watertight sub-division. The main transverse bulkheads below the main deck were to be as numerous as possible and were to be kept intact, pierced only for power pipes (steam and hydraulic) and electricity cables. Each of the main compartments was to have its own pumping and ventilation systems. Vertical voice pipes were acceptable but no horizontal voice pipes were to be fitted, telephones and a central exchange being provided instead. These decisions were taken on 23 January. In fact, the ship herself had watertight doors in all the watertight bulkheads abaft the engine room and in the bulkheads at stations 32, 58 and 142 – a matter of convenience of access to the steering and torpedo compartments, the coal bunkers abreast 'X' turret and 'A' magazine, and small access doors to the engineers' stores abreast 'Y' magazine.

Anti-torpedo-boat armament. The Admiralty members concluded that the 12pdr, 18cwt gun would be more effective than the 4in QF, an odd decision presumably based on the 12pdr's higher rate of fire and the fact that more could be carried (although the real problem here was one of space rather than weight). It was therefore decided, on 23 January, to replace the existing fourteen 4in of design 'H' with twenty 12pdrs – five to be mounted on the turret roofs, six in the superstructure and the remainder on the weather decks. It is interesting to note that the designs said to have come from Fisher/Gard had an anti-torpedo boat armament of 4in guns while those from Narbeth originally had 12pdr and 3pdr guns.

Stem. It was decided at an early date that the ram was no longer a viable weapon, particularly so when given the change in expected battle ranges, and all the sketch designs had clipper bows. Fisher, however, preferred the appearance of the ram form and to meet his wishes design 'H' was given a stem of blunt ram shape, which was to remain a standard feature of all British capital ships until the construction of the battlecruiser *Hood*.

Construction. The ship was to be laid down at the earliest possible date and constructed in the shortest possible time in order to evaluate its qualities with the minimum of delay. Until the ship had been fully tried no further battleships were to be laid down.

The Committee on Designs completed its deliberations on 22 February, leaving the Admiralty to continue the discussions of the details of the new ship and the DNC's department to complete the design. The design approved by the Committee was modified to include the alterations mentioned above and went through various minor weight adjustments to accommodate the machinery (the initial figures were rough estimates) and the armour and armament changes, much of which seems to have been intended to keep the displacement to the original figure. In March, however, it became necessary to add 2ft to the length of the engine room to accommodate the fitting of cruising turbines which, together with the associated increase in the length of protection and the addition of oil-fuel fittings, added 50 tons to the displacement. At the same time the hull form was refined and after an initial increase in the length to 500ft both the length and beam were reduced. The details of the final legend are given in Table 5.

Construction

To expedite the construction of *Dreadnought* Portsmouth Dockyard, which, at this time, could outbuild any shipyard in the world, was chosen. It also had the advantages of being familiar to Fisher, who had recently completed fourteen months as C-in-C Portsmouth, and in having Thomas Mitchell as its Chief Constructor. Mitchell had been appointed to this post in place of Gard on 23 December 1904, while Gard stayed in London initially for 'temporary service' but eventually to become Assistant DNC. In 1905 Mitchell's title, along with all the other dockyard chiefs, was changed to Manager Constructive Department (MCD) as a result of a dockyard reorganisation; later he was knighted in recognition of his contribution to *Dreadnought's* rapid construction. A great deal of effort by both the Admiralty and Portsmouth construction staffs was put into the reduction of the building time which Fisher wanted to be kept to one year. Special care was taken over the provision of the simplest form of hull construction and in limiting the number of steel sections and plate thicknesses employed, using standard sizes as much as possible. Careful attention was also paid to weight saving, a process that had been steadily improving in British warship design since 1890, with the result that *Dreadnought's* designed hull weight was only 450 tons above that of *Majestic*, a battleship of 3000 tons less displacement built in 1894–5.

Work began early at Portsmouth; materials were ordered and a good deal of prefabrication was carried out well in advance of the ship's official commencement. In the well-known series of photographs of the ship under construction, those taken on 2 October 1905, the day the ship was laid down, show the areas on both sides of the slipway covered with completed transverse frames, longitudinal sections and much other material ready for the construction of the double bottom framing. By this

time there were already 1100 men employed on *Dreadnought* and this quickly increased to 3000, working eleven and a half hours a day, six days a week.[6] It has often been implied that it was hardly surprising that, given these conditions, *Dreadnought* was built so quickly, but this underestimates the extensive organisational problems which were involved. Men and material had to be available at the right time and in the right place: simply throwing steel and man hours into the system would not have worked. The problems in managing this high-speed operation, involving

TABLE 5: HMS *Dreadnought*, Legend 12 May 1905

Length	490ft (pp), 526ft (oa)
Beam	82ft moulded
Mean draught	26ft 6in (norma]), 29ft (deep)
TPJ*	70
Freeboard at load draught	28ft (for' d), 16ft 6in (amid'), 18ft (aft)
Depth from underside of keel to top of deck at sides amidships	43ft
Shp	23000
Speed	21kts
Complement	657
Armament	10 12in
	18 12pdr
	5 torpedo tubes

Armour	
Belt	11–4in
Bulkheads	8in
Barbettes	11–4in
Gun shields	11in
Protective bulkheads to magazines	2–3in
Conning tower	11in
Signal tower	8in
Communication tube	5–4in
Main deck	0.75in
Middle deck	1.75in flat, 2.75–4in slopes
Lower deck	1.5–3in

Weights (tons)		
General equipment		
Water for 10 days	60	
Provisions, spirits, etc for 4 weeks (incl tare)	40	
Officers' stores and slops (incl tare)	42	
Officers, men and effects	82	
Masts, yards, spare rig etc	113	
Cables (475 fathoms of 2 11/16th) and anchors	115	
Boats	48	
WO's stores for 3 months	90	
Torpedo net defence	60	
Total for equipment	650 tons	650
Armament		3100
Machinery		1990
Engineers' stores		60
Coal		900
Hull		6100
Armour and backing		
Vertical armour on side and citadel	1940	
Protective bulkheads to magazines	250	
Protective decks and gratings	1350	
Backing	100	
Barbettes	1260	
CT	100	
Total for armour and backing	5000 tons	5000
Board margin		100
TOTAL		17,900 tons

*Tons per inch immersion – the amount of weight required to change the draught 1in at the load waterplane.

TABLE 6: Dimensions, Weights and Stability

Dimensions

Length: 490ft (pp), 520ft (wl), 526ft (oa)
Beam, extreme: 82ft (as designed), 82ft 1in (as built)
Beam, moulded: 81ft 10.25in (as designed), 81ft 11.25in (as built)
Depth from outer keel to upper deck at side amidships: 43ft 1.25in (as designed), 43ft 2.25in (as built)
Draught: based on inclining of 8 Sept 1908 – 26ft 0.625in (fore), 26ft 11.625in (aft) at load displacement/29ft 4.5in (fore), 29ft 10.625in (aft) at deep displacement/30ft 7.75in (fore), 31ft 5.375in (aft) at extra deep
    displacement/24ft 3.625in (fore), 26ft 0.125in (aft) at light displacement.
TPI: 70.4

Estimates of load displacement (tons)

	August 1906	June 1907	November 1907
Fresh water for 10 days	60	60	60
Provisions	40	40	40
Officers' stores	42	42	27
Officers, men & effects	84	86	88
Anchors and cables	115	118.7	116.8
Boats	48	46	43
Masts and rig	112	119.8	119.8
WO's stores for 3 months	90	75.8	116.2
Net defence	50	60.4	60.4
Total for equipment	641	648.7	671.2
Armament	3140	3102	3105
Machinery	2035	1980	2147
Engineers' stores	60	–	–
Coal	900	900	900
Vertical armour	3430	–	–
Protective decks	1445	–	–
Protective bulkheads	254	–	–
Total for armour	5129	5160	5160
Hull	6215	6400	6400
TOTAL	18,120 tons	18,191 tons	18,383 tons

Stability calculated from inclining experiment of 8 September 1906

	Mean draught	GM	Max GZ	Angle of maximum stability	Angle at which stability vanishes
A – Load, 360 tons in upper, 540 tons in lower coal bunkers.	26ft 6in	5.07ft	3.06ft	33	66
B – Deep, with FW, RFW tanks and bunkers full, 2900 tons coal.	29ft 7.5in	5.6ft		32	65
C – Extra deep with 1120 tons oil and 122 tons patent fuel.	31ft 1.5in	6.7ft		32	72
D – Light with boilers full to working height, engines, condensers and feed tanks full to working height. Water (incl RFW), provisions, officers' stores and half WOs' and engineers' stores consumed.	25ft 2in	4.7ft		33	61

Estimate of displacement and weight based on inclining 8 Sept 1906

	Normal load displacement: 18,122 tons	Deep displacement: 20,735 tons	Extra deep displacement: 21,977 tons
Fresh water	60	70	
Provisions	40	75	
Officers' stores	42	15	
Hydraulic pumping water	20	61.3	
Feed water	15	15	
Reserve food water		233.5	
Coal	900	2100.8	
Oil fuel			1120
Patent fuel			122
Powder		31.3	
Shell		35.1	
Boats		8.6	
Crew		2.3	
Total additions	–	2612.9	1242

Light displacement = 17,012 tons

so many men and such a wide variety of mutually interdependent processes, must have been formidable.

Dreadnought was launched by King Edward VII on 10 February 1906 and then moved to No 5 Basin to begin fitting-out, a process that included some time in dry dock.[7] Captain Bacon, whose advice had converted Fisher to the 12in gun armament, was appointed as her first captain on 2 July and he officially joined the ship on 1 September when she was commissioned with a nucleus crew in preparation for her steam trials.[8] Bacon was an ideal candidate who was appointed because of his close association with *Dreadnought's* design, his belief in the importance of the ship's success, and because he was technically competent to deal with any problems that arose. It was his job to take her through her trials and initial service, and to report on any defects or other problems and suggest improvements that could be made in both *Dreadnought* and later ships of the same type. Initially, there were two major concerns among those responsible for the ship's design and construction: first, that her turbine machinery, the most powerful yet installed in any ship, would not function adequately, and second that the ship's structure could be damaged by the firing of a broadside of eight 12in guns, particularly in the areas around the wing turrets where it was difficult to maintain the continuity of the upper hull structure. Everyone was quite satisfied that they had done everything possible to ensure the ship's success but there was always that remote chance of the unforeseen circumstance, particularly as, with such a major change in design, the value of previous experience was limited. In Captain Bacon's words, 'had we had an accident, the ungodly would have at once raised a hue and cry against the ship, her designers and her design'.[9]

The main machinery was brought up to working condition well before the ship was completely fitted out and it was decided to run her steam trials immediately. Basin trials were carried out on 17 September and the ship was docked for a hull inspection between the 24th and 28th. On 1 October, just one day under a year after she was laid down, she raised steam for 13kts and, at 11.40am proceeded out of the harbour and anchored off Spithead where her compass was adjusted and a preliminary steering trial carried out. On the following day *Dreadnought* tested her engines up to 19kts and, no serious problems having been encountered, she sailed for Devonport on 3 October, running her 30-hour low-power trial on route. She arrived at her destination on the 5th and between then and the 9th, when she returned to Portsmouth, carried out her full range of steam trials which, much to everyone's relief, were highly successful, though she did require a much higher power to reach her designed speed than anticipated. During this time she carried two large water measuring tanks abreast the mainmast on the upper deck, a temporary installation fitted to measure her loss of feed water during the trials. This was to become a standard feature of early dreadnought trials.

On her return to Spithead, further steering trials were carried out on 10 October and she then returned to the dockyard for the removal of the measuring tanks and the continuation of her fitting out. *Dreadnought* sailed again on 17 October for her gun and torpedo trials, her armament

TABLE 7: **Particulars of Steam Trials**

Steam trials of 1–9 October 1906
Last undocked 28 Sept 1906, bottom clean, wind force 3–4, sea strength 2.

1 and 2 October 1906: preliminary trials
Six trial runs made at 4647.7/7715/11,086/12,736/16,318 and 22,196shp.

3 and 4 October 1906: 30-hour low power trial

No of boilers in use	Nine
Draught at start	25ft 9in forward, 27ft 6in aft
Displacement at start	c18,225 tons
Average gauge pressure	220psi at boilers, 210psi at engines
Condenser vacuum	27.7in starboard, 27.57in port
Pressure in stokehold	0.56in wg
Rpm	193.51 mean (205 inner shafts, 182 outer shafts)
Shp	5013.34 (3418.9 inner shafts, 1594.44 outer shafts)
Speed	13.02kts by log, 13.3kts by bearing
Coal consumption	5.78 tons/hr = 2.58lbs/shp/hr
Feed water lost	31 tons

4 October 1906: four progressive trials

Shp	Duration hours	Steam consumption lbs/shp/hour	Auxiliary exhaust to:
1303	2	58.5	Auxiliary condenser
1748	1	41.6	Turbines
3423	1	32.3	Turbines
2771	2	49.7	Auxiliary condenser
11,301	1	19.9	Auxiliary condenser
13,092	2	18.6	Turbines
15,875	2	16.6	Turbines
13,748	1	18.9	Auxiliary condenser

Note economy from using exhaust steam on turbines at low power. All these trials were with cruising turbines in use.

6 and 7 October 1906: 30-hour max continuous (three-fifths power)

No of boilers in use	Eighteen
Draught at start	25ft 11in forward, 27ft 7in aft
Displacement at start	c18,120 tons
Average gauge pressure	232psi at boilers
Condenser vacuum	27.5in starboard, 27.9in port
Pressure in stokehold	0.9in wg
Rpm	291.3 mean (296.4 inner shafts, 286.15 wing shafts)
Shp	16,931 (10,080 inner shafts, 6850 wing shafts)
Speed	19.3kts by log
Coal consumption	12.86 tons/hr = 1.7lbs/shp/hr
Feed water lost	54.03 tons

Note: First 10 hours without closed exhaust, next 6 hours with closed exhaust on turbines and auxiliary condenser, last 14 hours with closed exhaust on turbines and evaporators.

9 October 1906: 8-hour full power contractor's trial at Polperro

No of boilers in use	Eighteen
Draught at start	25ft 6in forward, 27ft 1.5in aft
Displacement at start	c17,750 tons
Average gauge pressure	241psi at boilers, 221.5psi at engines
Condenser vacuum	27in starboard, 27.4in port
Pressure in stoke hold	1.2in wg
Rpm	328.4 mean (335.3 inner shafts, 321.9 wing shafts)
Shp	24,712 (14,877 inner shafts, 9835 wing shafts)
Speed	21.05kts
Coal consumption	16.66 tons/hr = 1.51lbs/shp/hr
Steam consumption for all purposes	15.3lbs/shp/hr
Feed water lost	25.06 tons

Trial run with hand picked Welsh coal

continued overleaf

9 October 1906: measured mile trial at Polperro

Speed	21.78/21.45/21.78/21.39kts = 21.6kts mean of four runs
Average gauge pressure	250psi at boilers
Shp	27,899/27,333/26,728/26,112 = 27,018 mean of four runs
Rpm	inner shafts 348.5/352.3/347.9/340.8 = 347.4 mean
	wing shafts 322.8/330.8/327.6/327.8 = 327.3 mean
	mean of all shafts = 337.4

1–2 December 1906: 24-hour acceptance trial in English Channel

Draught at start	25ft 3in forward, 27ft 9in aft
Displacement at start	c18,120 tons
Shp	not calculable – the port torsion meter was not fitted and the starboard torsion meter was set for astern reading only.
Speed	16kts by log, 17kts by bearing (average for last 12 hours of trial

5 june 1907: propeller trials at Polperro

Last undocked 1 June 1907, bottom clean, wind force 2–3

Shp on inner shafts	5580	12,624	16,890+
Shp on wing shafts	1440	5416	9460
Shp total	7020	18,040	26,350
Rpm on inner shafts	235.5	310.7	342.2
Rpm on wing shafts	196.3	277.3	318.1
Rpm mean	215.9	294	330.15
Mean speed	14.63kts	18.97kts	20.76kts
No of runs	6	6	4
Pressure at boilers (psi)	233.5	234.3	228
Pressure at engines (psi)	221.3	222.2	206
Starboard engine only	4 runs, 11,519shp = 15.53kts		
Port engine only	2 runs, 12,547shp = 15.05kts		
Port engine only	2 runs, 7047shp = 12.98kts		
Starboard engine only	2 runs, 6453shp = 11.97kts		

† Note that the figures for this trial have in the past been confused with those of the ship's measured mile trial in 1906.

11 November 1907: propeller trails at Polperro

Last undocked 25 Oct 1907, bottom clean, sea smooth

Duration	3 hours	4 hours	4 hours
Pressure at boilers (psi)	245	242	242
Pressure at engines (psi)	219	224	224
Rpm	338.07	281.9	246.05
Shp	26,452	16,276	10,451
Speed	20.73kts	18.14kts	15.83kts

Draught at start of above trials 27ft 6in (fore), 28ft 3.5in (aft);. draught at finish 27ft 3in (fore), 28ft1in (aft)– approx mean displacement 19,000 tons.

6 April 1908: steam trial in North Sea

Last undocked 25 October 1907 – bottom foul, sea smooth

	Full power	Three-fifths power
Draught at start (fore)	28ft 5in	28ft 4.5in
Draught at start (aft)	29ft 7.5in	29ft 7in
Displacement at start	c20,000 tons	c19,950 tons
Rpm	328.8	292.4
Shp	25,177	18,667
Speed	20.3kts	18.2kts

29 August 1908: steam trials

	Full power	Three-fifths power
Draught at start (fore)	29ft 5in	29ft 0.5in
Draught at start (aft)	30ft 3in	30ft 2.5in
Displacement at start	c20,700 tons	c20,570 tons
Rpm	314	287.75
Shp	23,545	19,640
Speed	18.25kts	16.8kts

NOTE: did not reach required speed due to displacement and very foul bottom.

3 April 1914: 8-hour full power steam trial on route Gibraltar–Portsmouth

Last undocked 30 April 1913, bottom foul, wind force 3–4 NE, sea state 3–4.

Draught at start	29ft (fore), 30ft 2in (aft)
Displacement at start	c20,500 tons
Draught at end	28ft 2in (fore), 29ft 8in (aft)
Displacement at end	c19,930 tons
Average gauge pressure	206.4psi at boilers,191.4psi at engines
Condenser vacuum	27in wg starboard, 26.7in wg port
Rpm	306.2 mean (228.4 stb outer, 330.7 stb inner, 324.8 port outer, 287.2 port inner)
Shp	22,642 (11,240 stb, 11,410 port)
Speed	18kts
Coal consumption	1.95lbs/shp/hour
Feed water lost	27 tons

17 November 1915: full power steam trial on route to Scapa Flow

Last undocked 17 Nov 1915, bottom clean, wind force 3, sea NE, slight swell.

Draught at start	30ft (fore), 30ft 3in (aft)
Displacement at start	c21,100 tons
Average gauge pressure	213psi at boilers, 206psi at engines
Condenser vacuum	28in wg starboard, 27.5in wg port
SHP	22,920
Speed	20.04kts over the ground, actual estimated 19.5kts
Coal consumption	1.84/shp/hour
Feed water lost	6 tons

April 1918: steam trial at full and three-fifths power

Displacement at start	17,900 tons	17,900 tons
Shp	24,712	16,100
Speed	20.9kts	18.9kts

having been brought up to an almost completed state, though some of her instrumentation and other details were still incomplete. These again proved successful and she returned once more to the dockyard for final fitting out and a detailed inspection of her machinery which was completed on 28 November. A second basin trial took place on the following day and her acceptance trials were run on 1–2 December 1906, again without any serious problems. On 3 December, while passing through the Fountain Lake entrance into No 4 Basin, *Dreadnought* was driven out of the middle line of the entrance by the tide and struck the sill, damaging one of her bilge keels and the outer bottom plating. She was docked in No 15 dock during 10–17 December for repairs and some final tidying-up and actually completed at the end of the month.

The completion date for *Dreadnought* has been the subject of much comment and discussion. Whether or not she was completed within a year depends to a great extent on how 'completion' is defined. The usual quoted construction time is 'a year and a day' – that is, completion on 3 October, the day she sailed from Spithead for her steam trials, and this seems to have originated from the publicity that accompanied the first appearance of the ship. Her official completion date was 11 December – the day she commissioned to full complement and hence became a part of the fleet. In fact, because of her accident she was not fully functional until at least the 17th when she was undocked. Her final fitting out was also delayed a little by minor alterations carried out as a result of suggestions by Bacon and as a result of her trials. In the end, however, it is not particularly relevant; even fifteen months was a remarkable and very creditable construction time.

TABLE 8: Steering trials, 10 October 1906

East of Isle of Wight, wind force 2–3, SE, sea smooth, clean bottom.

Power	Full	Full	12kts	12kts	1 ahead/1 astern
Direction of turn	Stb	Port	Stb	Port	Stb
Angle of helm (degrees)	35	35	35	35	
Time to put helm					
Full over (seconds)	17	15	13	12	13
First 4pts turned in (seconds)	40	36	50	48	53
First 8pts turned in (seconds)	61	61	85	80	96
Advance (yards)	508	470	480	427	483
Tactical diameter (yards)	466	460	442	443	443
Rpm at helm over	281.5	253	182.5	190.5	173.5
Speed at helm over	c19kts	c19kts	c12kts	c12kts	

Rudder area	170sq ft each
Axis of rudder from fore edge	5ft 4in
Centre of area from fore edge	7ft 6in
Diameter of rudder heads	16.5in

The experimental cruise

As soon as *Dreadnought* was ready she was sent on an experimental cruise in order to test her armament thoroughly, and to gain as much information as possible for the future development of the type. On 5 January 1907 she sailed from Portsmouth for Arosa Bay (Spain) whence she sailed to Gibraltar, Sardinia and then back to Gibraltar before setting out for Port of Spain, Trinidad, where she arrived on 5 February. This remote location had been chosen to enable *Dreadnought* to be fully worked-up well away from the eyes of both critics and foreign observers. For the next six weeks, operating out of Port of Spain, she carried out an extensive programme of evolutions and exercises. Much of this concentrated on the training of the gun crews, the calibration of the armament and a programme of gun trials; these trials also included searchlight exercises and experiments, exercising the torpedo net defence, torpedo practice, steering trials and so on. By the time she sailed for her return journey to Portsmouth on 18 March, Bacon must have had a very efficient ship and a well-trained crew. *Dreadnought* arrived at Spithead on 23 March after a record trip at an average speed of 17kts, a speed that would have been higher had it not been for a damaged rudder.

Bacon's report on the experimental cruise was extensive and contained many criticisms of the details of the ship, particularly her ventilation arrangements, and it made a number of suggestions for the improvement of *Dreadnought* and other vessels of similar design. However, in general he found the ship very satisfactory and pointed out that she had steamed 11,000 miles without any serious machinery problems and that 'no member of the Committee on Designs . . dared to hope that all the innovations introduced would have turned out as successfully as had been the case'.[10] The satisfaction with the design can best be judged by the fact that the next six battleships to be built for the Royal Navy were of substantially the same design, although this must be tempered with the realisation that the officers involved, particularly Bacon, were biased towards the need for her to be successful; that it was necessary to build more battleships of the same type as quickly as possible, which militated against a major design change; and that there were as yet no foreign contemporaries with which to compare her.

It was as well that *Dreadnought* quickly proved herself successful because, though she attracted a great deal of popular support, there was strong adverse reaction from many naval officers, naval writers, politicians and other commentators. One criticism was that her construction had unnecessarily rendered the existing battlefleet prematurely obsolete and placed Britain in a position of having to build a completely new fleet of excessively large and expensive ships. She was also criticised for her lack of an intermediate armament, and much debate took place as to the relative merits of uniform- and mixed-calibre armaments. However, most of this debate assumed close-range action, and the critical developments in long-range gunnery and fire control, which lay behind *Dreadnought's* construction and which Fisher in particular regarded as 'secret', were not publicly revealed. This left the Admiralty defending itself without being able to use its most valuable and conclusive argument. In any event, *Dreadnought* was by then a *fait accompli*. Her success, as well as the construction of similar vessels abroad, meant there could be no turning back and the Board of Admiralty, and Fisher in particular, managed to ride out the storm without loss of position or reputation.

Operational history

Shortly after her return from the experimental cruise *Dreadnought* was commissioned as flagship of the Nore Division of the newly formed Home Fleet (formerly the Channel Fleet) and in April hoisted the flag of the C-in-C, Vice Admiral F C B Bridgeman. She remained flagship of the Home Fleet until 1911 when she became a private ship in the 1st Division until transferred to the 4th Battle Squadron, as flagship, at the end of 1912. She remained in the 4th Battle Squadron, first with the Home Fleet, then on the outbreak of war with the Grand Fleet until July 1916 when she was sent south as a reinforcement for the 3rd Battle Squadron at Sheerness. She returned to Scapa Flow and the 4th Battle Squadron in May 1918.

She spent almost her entire service career in home waters apart from the occasional fleet exercises on the Atlantic coast of Spain and brief visits to the Mediterranean in 1907 and 1913. Even during the war her service was comparatively uneventful; she was under refit at the time of Jutland and she never fired her main armament at an enemy. She did, however, have one claim to fame in being the only battleship to sink a submarine. On 18 March 1915, having just completed strategic exercises with the Grand Fleet, the 4th Battle Squadron was detached to proceed to Cromarty, which had just been established as a relief base. At 12.28pm as they were moving away from the main fleet, Lieutenant Commander Piercy of *Dreadnought* sighted a periscope about 1500yds away just off the ship's bow. *Dreadnought* altered course toward the submarine, which was steering a slightly erratic course across the battleship's bow from port to starboard, and increased speed to 17.5kts. As the U-boat does not appear to have made an attempt to dive it seems likely she was not aware of the battleship's approach, at least not until it was too late. When the range was down to 600yds one of *Dreadnought's* 12pdr guns was fired, but with only a periscope to aim at the shot missed. At 12.35pm, with the submarine still moving to starboard and *Dreadnought* turning in the same direction, the U-boat was rammed in the starboard quarter. The bow of the enemy vessel rose up out of the water at a steep angle and passed down *Dreadnought's* side before sinking. On the submarine's bow, in raised but overpainted lettering, was seen the number U29. Her commander was Otto Weddigen who, while commanding the U9 in 1914, had sunk the cruisers *Aboukir*, *Cressy*, *Hogue* and *Hawke*. *Dreadnought's* only other actions were against enemy aircraft. She fired her AA weapons on several occasions during 1917–18 when German air raids took place against Chatham or passed over on route to London.

When the war ended *Dreadnought* was undergoing an extensive refit at Rosyth which included the fitting of aircraft flying-off platforms on 'A' and 'Y' turrets. The work, which was partially incomplete, stopped at the end of 1918 and she was soon reduced to reserve. On 31 March 1920 she was ordered to be paid off and placed on the sale list and shortly afterwards the ship which had started a new era in warship construction and had cost £1,785,683 to build was sold to the shipbreakers T W Ward for £44,750.

Summary of service
Built by Portsmouth Dockyard.
2 Oct 1905: Laid down.

1906
10 Feb: Launched by King Edward VII.
7 Mar–23 May: Docked.
2 July: Captain R H S Bacon appointed.
17 Aug–5 Sept: Docked.
1 Sept: Commissioned in reserve with nucleus crew at Portsmouth in preparation for trials.
8 Sept: Inclining experiment.
12 & 13 Sept: Preliminary hydraulic trials.
17 Sept: Basin trials.
24–28 Sept: Docked for hull inspection.
29 Sept: Naval crew and navigation party joined ship.
1 Oct: Left dockyard and anchored off Spithead.
2 Oct: Preliminary steam trial (19kts).
3 & 4 Oct: 30hr low power steam trials on route to Devonport.
5 Oct: Plymouth Sound.
6–9 Oct: Steam trials.
9 Oct: Portsmouth.
10 Oct: Turning trials E of Isle of Wight.
11–17 Oct: Portsmouth preparing for gun trials.
17–18 Oct: Gun and torpedo trials.
19 Oct: Portsmouth Dockyard – No 5 Basin.
28 Nov: Machinery inspection completed.
29 Nov: Second basin trial.
1–2 Dec: 24hr acceptance trial.

3 Dec: Returned No 5 Basin.
10–17 Dec: Docked, No 15 dock.
11 Dec: Special Service Home Fleet, commissioned to full complement at Portsmouth for experimental cruise.

1907
Jan–Mar: Experimental cruise.
5 Jan: Sailed from Portsmouth on experimental cruise, calling at Arosa Bay, Spain (7–8 Jan), Gibraltar 10–14 Jan), Golfo d' Aranci, Sardinia (17–21 Jan), Gibraltar (24–28 Jan) before sailing for Trinidad.
5 Feb–18 Mar: Exercises, trials and working-up while based at Port of Spain, Trinidad.
23 Mar: Arrived Portsmouth.
27 Mar: Spithead. Commissioned for service as flagship of Nore Division, Home Fleet.
28 Mar–7 May: Portsmouth (under refit 9–30 Apr).
Apr: Hoisted flag of Vice Admiral F C B Bridgeman, C-in-C Home Fleet.
9–30 Apr: In hand at Portsmouth.
7–16 May: S coast cruise with Home Fleet, calling at Bournemouth (7–9 May), Torquay (9–13 May), Falmouth (13–15 May) and returning to Portsmouth via Bournemouth on 16th.
17 May–17 June: Under refit at Portsmouth (docked 25 May – 1 June).
3 June: Sailed for Devonport for steam trials.
6–17 June: Portsmouth.
18 June: Sailed from Spithead with Nore Division for visit to coast of Norway, staying at Bergen (21–27 June) before sailing for Invergordon where she arrived on 29th.
29 June–11 July: Invergordon and Cromarty, cruising in Cromarty Firth.
12 July: Sailed for Portsmouth.
14–23 July: Portsmouth.
23 July: Sailed for test mobilisation of Home Fleet and cruise to Torbay and Cowes. Visited Torquay (23–25 July) and Bournemouth (26–27 and 28–30 July), cruised off the Isle of Wight (27–28 July) and arrived at Cowes on 30th.
3 Aug: Fleet Review off Cowes by King Edward VII followed by two days of exercises.
5 Aug: Ship visited by King Edward VII & Queen Alexandra at Spithead, Royal party taken for short trip to SW of the Isle of Wight and back.
4–8 Aug: Fleet manoeuvres.
12 Aug: Captain C E Madden appointed.
12 Aug–9 Nov: Under refit at Portsmouth (docked 12 – 25 Oct).
9 Nov: Sailed for Devonport.
10–13 Nov: Devonport (steam trials at Polperro on 11th).
13 Nov: Sailed for fleet cruise and exercises in Mediterranean calling at Bantry Bay (14–16 Nov), Gibralter (19–22 Nov), Aranci Bay, Sardinia (25 Nov–20 Dec), Gibraltar (22–24 Dec) arriving back at Portsmouth on 28 Dec.

1908

31 Dec–3 Feb: Under refit at Portsmouth.

3 Feb: Sailed for Sheerness.

4 Feb–9 Mar: Under refit at Sheerness (docked 25 Feb–7 Mar).

9 Mar: Sailed for Cromarty for fleet exercises.

12 Mar–3 Apr: Based at Cromarty (cruising in Moray Firth 24–27 Mar).

4–6 Apr: Rosyth.

6 Apr: Sailed for Portland. Steam trials.

8–9 Apr: Portland.

10–12 Apr: Devonport.

13–30 Apr: Portsmouth.

30 Apr: Sailed for the Nore.

1 May–2 June: Based at the Nore, alternating between anchorages at the Nore and Barrow Deep but also visited Margate (5–6 May) and Sheerness (22–25 May).

2 June–2 July: Sheerness (under refit 6–25 June) – left Sheerness for firing practice at the Nore during 17–19 June.

2 July: Sailed for the Downs where Home Fleet assembled for annual exercises.

4 July: Fleet sailed for Queensferry.

7–15 July: Queensferry.

15 July: Sailed for exercises.

16–21 July: Strategic exercises in North Sea with Atlantic Fleet and Nore Division (Home Fleet, based in Firth of Forth, patrolled North Sea during daylight).

21 July–3 Aug: Queensferry.

3 Aug: Sailed for Portsmouth.

5 Aug: Arrived Spithead.

6–25 Aug: Portsmouth.

25 Aug: Sailed for Queensferry.

27–29 Aug: Queensferry.

29 Aug–10 Oct: Based at Cromarty, cruising in Moray Firth.

10 Oct: Sailed from Nairn to Cromarty and then to Queensferry.

11–26 Oct: Queensferry.

28–29 Oct: The Nore.

29 Oct–11 Nov: Sheerness.

12–21 Nov: Spithead.

22–24 Nov: Off Harwich.

24 Nov–16 Dec: Sheerness.

1 Dec: Captain A G H W Moore appointed.

1909

17 Dec–20 Feb: Portsmouth (under refit 19 Dec–15 Feb, docked 20 Jan–8 Feb).

20 Feb: Sailed to Spithead.

21 Feb: Sailed to Sheerness.

22–28 Feb: Sheerness.

28 Feb: Sailed for Queensferry.

3–10 Mar: Queensferry.

11–14 Mar: Sheerness.

15–16 Mar: Plymouth.

17 Mar–Apr: Portsmouth, under refit 18–31 Mar.

23 Mar 1909: Paid off.

24 Mar 1909: Recommissioned as flagship of Admiral Sir W May, C-in-C Home Fleet.

1 Apr: Sailed for Queensferry for annual manoeuvres. On passage with *Invincible*.

3–7 Apr: Queensferry.

7 Apr: Sailed with fleet for tactical exercises.

10–15 Apr: Cromarty.

17 Apr–5 May: Scapa Flow.

6–7 May: Lerwick.

8–12 May: Scapa Flow.

12–24 May: Cromarty, firing in Moray Firth on 14th and 18th.

24 May: Sailed for Portsmouth.

26 May: During full speed trial steam pipe to fan in 'A' boiler room burst, several men collapsed in attempt to close auxiliary steam valve. Fire drawn in boiler room.

27 May–9 June: Portsmouth.

10–16 June: Spithead.

12 June: Imperial Conference Review at Spithead, delegates aboard *Dreadnought*.

16 June: Sailed for Berehaven.

17–30 June: At Berehaven.

30 June–8 July: Annual manoeuvres with Nore Division, Atlantic and Mediterranean Fleets in Atlantic.

8–14 July: Berehaven.

16–17 July: Anchored in the Downs.

17–24 July: Visited Southend with other units of Home and Atlantic Fleets.

24–28 July: Off Deal.

29 July–3 Aug: Cowes.

30 July: Captain H W Richmond appointed.

31 July: Review of Home Fleet by King Edward VII during visit by Tsar of Russia.

Aug: Nore Division became 1st Division, Home Fleet.

3–17 Aug: Portsmouth.

19 Aug–8 Oct: Cromarty (visited Brora on 10 Sept).

9–27 Oct: Queensferry (visited St Andrews Bay 21–22 Oct).

27 Oct: Sailed for Portland.

30 Oct 1909–22 Feb 1910: Operating with fleet from Portland. Carried out series of tactical exercises in Channel. At Spithead on 14–16 Nov, 16 Dec–8 Jan, 15–18 Jan.

1910

22 Feb: Sailed from Portland.

24 Feb: Arrived Spithead.

25 Feb–12 Apr: Under refit Portsmouth (docked No 15 dock 26 Feb–14 Mar).

16 Apr: Sailed to Portland.

16–18 Apr: Portland.

18 Apr: Sailed for Cromarty for tactical exercises with the Home and Atlantic Fleets.

22–25 Apr: Cromarty.

28 Apr–3 May: Scapa Flow.

4–30 May: With Fleet operating from Campbeltown. (Fleet moved to Kingston during 19–23 May so that representatives from fleet could take part in memorial service at Dublin following death of the King on 6 May).

30 May: Sailed for Portland.

31 May–9 July: Portland (battle practice at sea 7 June and 14 June).

9 July: Sailed for Berehaven for combined manoeuvres off W coast of Scotland with Atlantic and Mediterranean Fleets.

11–13 July: Berehaven.

13–20 July: At sea on manoeuvres.

20–25 July: Mounts Bay.

25–29 July: With Home Fleet at Torbay for visit of King George V.

29 July–19 Sept: Portland and Weymouth Bay.

19 Sept: Sailed for Cromarty.

21 Sept–12 Oct: Based Cromarty (Dornoch Firth on 5–7 and 11–12 Oct).

13–25 Oct: Queensferry.

25–26 Oct: Nairn.

26–31 Oct: Invergordon.

31 Oct: Sailed for Portland via Blacksod Bay (1–2 Nov).

5–28 Nov: Portland.

28 Nov: Sailed for tactical manoeuvres (anchored off Abbotsbury 1–2 Dec).

2–3 Dec: Portland.

3–8 Dec: Spithead.

8 Dec–16 Jan: Portland.

1911

16 Jan: Sailed for combined exercises of Home, Atlantic and Mediterranean Fleets off NW coast of Spain.

19–24 Jan: Arosa Bay.

24–27 Jan: At sea off Arosa Bay with combined fleets.

27–30 Jan: Arosa Bay.

30 Jan–1 Feb: Cruised off Arosa Bay.

1–2 Feb: Pontevedra Bay.

3 Feb: Arosa Bay.

11–15 Feb: Ferrol.

17 Feb–23 Mar: Portland (Channel cruise 6–8 Mar).

23 Mar: Sailed to Portsmouth.

27 Mar: Paid off for refit.

28 Mar: Recommissioned with nucleus crew by Capt S R Fremantle on transfer of flag (to *Neptune*), for service in 1st Division Home Fleet.

29 Mar–10 June: Under refit at Portsmouth.

6 June: Completed crew for service in 1st Division Home Fleet as private Ship. Proceeded to Berehaven to work-up prior to rejoining Fleet.

15 June: Spithead.

24 June: Coronation Review for King George V at Spithead.

June–July: Combined exercises with 1st Division Home Fleet, Atlantic Fleet and 4th Cruiser Squadron off SW coast of England and Ireland.

July: Exercises with combined Fleets in North Sea.

1912

Mar: With Home and Atlantic Fleets returned to Portland and Torbay after trip to Arosa Bay. Fleet visited by Churchill in *Enchantress*.

16 Mar–29 May: Under refit at Portsmouth (docked 3–21 May).

1 May: 1st Div. became 1st Battle Squadron of 1st Fleet (Home Fleet).

17 June–July: Portsmouth.

9 July: Parliamentary review of Home Fleet at Spithead followed by annual manoeuvres with 1st and 2nd Fleets and parts of 3rd and Mediterranean Fleets.

Oct: Tactical exercises with Home Fleet for three days following end of manoeuvres. With *Indefatigable, St Vincent, Monarch, Irresistible* and *Orion* joined *Thunderer* at Bantry Bay, for competitive trials of new director system between *Thunderer* (with director) and *Orion*. *Dreadnought* served as target tug for these trials. Trials delayed by bad weather.

14 Oct: Preliminary trials outside Berehaven.

13 Nov: Final trials.

16 Dec: Transferred to 4th Battle Squadron (ex Mediterranean Fleet) Home Fleet as flagship. Vice Admiral Sir C Briggs and Captain W S Nicholson appointed.

1913

1–8 Jan: Portland.

9–17 Jan: Torbay.

17 Jan–7 Feb: Portland (at sea cruising on 4 and 5 Feb).

8 Feb–2 May: Portsmouth.

12 Feb–30 Apr: Under refit at Portsmouth (docked 5 Mar–30 Apr).

3–5 May: Portland.

6–7 May: Weymouth Bay.

8–21 May: Portland (trials and exercises at sea 15–16 May).

21 May: Sailed for Stornoway.

24–28 May: Stornoway.

28 May–4 June: Portree.

4–9 June: Loch-na-Keal.

10–26 June: Lamlash.

26 June: Sailed for Portsmouth.

28 June–28 Aug: Portsmouth.

30 June: Paid off.

30 June–8 July: Under refit at Portsmouth.

1 July: Recommissioned at Portsmouth for same service.

End July: Manoeuvres with 1st, 2nd and part of 3rd Fleets.

1–3 Aug: At sea.

3–6 Aug: Spithead.

6–27 Aug: Portsmouth (under refit 9–23 Aug).

28 Aug: Sailed to Weymouth Bay.

29 Aug: Sailed for Glengariff.

31 Aug–1 Sept: Off Glengariff.

2–11 Sept: Anchored off Whiddy Isle, Bantry Bay.

11–12 Sept: Queenstown.

13–22 Sept: Portland.

22 Sept: Sailed for Gibraltar.

27 Sept–28 Oct: Gibraltar.

28 Oct: Sailed for Malta for manoeuvres with 4th Battle Squadron, 1st Battle Squadron and 3rd Cruiser Squadron.

1–7 Nov: Malta.

7–11 Nov: Exercises at sea and cruising.

11–19 Nov: Malta.

23–27 Nov: Algiers.

29 Nov–12 Dec: Gibraltar.

12 Dec: Sailed for Portsmouth.

17 Dec: Arrived Spithead where stayed until at least 31 Dec.

1914

26 Feb–2 Apr: Under refit at Gibraltar (docked 5 Mar).

3 Apr: Steam trials on route Gibraltar – Portsmouth.

June: Fleet regatta at Invergordon.

10 June: Captain W J S Alderson appointed.

23 June: Weymouth Bay.

24 June: Torpedo exercises off Portland.

25–26 June: Weymouth Bay.

26 June–6 July: Portsmouth.

1 July: Vice Admiral Sir D Gamble replaced Vice Admiral Briggs.

6–16 July: Portland.

16 July: Left Portland for Spithead with 1st Fleet.

17–20 July: Spithead. Test mobilisation and Fleet Review.

21–26 July: Weymouth Bay (tactical exercises at sea 21–22 July and anchored in Lyme Bay 22–23 July).

27–29 July: Portland (due for refit at Portsmouth but owing to outbreak of war this was cancelled).

29 July: With 1st Fleet sailed from Portland for Scapa Flow.

31 July–4 Aug: Scapa Flow.

War service 1914

4 Aug: Flagship 4th Battle Squadron. Grand Fleet, Scapa Flow. 8.30am proceeded to sea with Fleet.

4–7 Aug: Cruising in northern North Sea.

7 Aug: Scapa Flow, sailed same day.

8–13 Aug: Exercises and cruising with Grand Fleet. *Dreadnought* sighted periscope on the 8th, and opened fire on what was assumed to be submarine attacking *Monarch* (off Scapa).

13 Aug: Scapa Flow, sailed same day.

14 Aug: Exercises with Fleet.

15–18 Aug: North Sea sweep.

18–20 Aug: Loch Ewe.

21 Aug: Target practice W of the Orkneys.

22–25 Aug: Cruising and exercises in North Sea.

26–27 Aug: Scapa Flow.

28 Aug: With 4th Battle Squadron joined 1st and 3rd Battle Squadrons at sea SE of the Orkneys.

28–30 Aug: Cruising and exercises in North Sea.

31 Aug–1 Sept: Scapa Flow.

2–5 Sept: Cruising between Scotland and Norway, exercises and gunnery practice.

5–7 Sept: Loch Ewe.

7 Sept: Fleet sailed from Loch Ewe. 4th Battle Squadron joined by *Agincourt* at sea.

8–13 Sept: Fleet exercises and North Sea sweep.

13–17 Sept: Loch Ewe.

18–23 Sept: Cruising and exercises in North Sea.

24–25 Sept: Scapa Flow.

25–26 Sept: Cruising with 4th Battle Squadron and *Iron Duke* W of Orkneys.

27–28 Sept: Cruising E and S of Orkneys with Grand Fleet.

29 Sept – 2 Oct: Scapa Flow.

3–11 Oct: Cruising between Scotland and Norway.

12–16 Oct: At Scapa Flow with 4th and 1st Battle Squadrons.

16–22 Oct: Cruising and exercises.

22 Oct: Arrived Lough Swilly with *Iron Duke*, 1st and 4th Battle squadrons.

22 Oct–3 Nov: With 4th Battle Squadron temporarily based at Lough Swilly.

3 Nov: Sailed from Lough Swilly with 1st, 2nd and 4th Battle Squadrons.

4–7 Nov: Target practice off Bills Rocks, Galway, then cruised between Hebrides, Faroes and Shetlands.

8–9 Nov: Cruising with *Iron Duke* and 4th Battle Squadron.

9–20 Nov: Scapa Flow.

20–27 Nov: Cruising and North Sea sweep.

27 Nov–16 Dec: Scapa Flow.

10 Dec: *Benbow* and *Emperor of India* arrived Scapa to join 4th Battle Squadron. *Dreadnought* relieved as squadron flagship by *Benbow*.

16–19 Dec: Cruising and exercises E of Orkney.

19–23 Dec: Scapa Flow.

23–27 Dec: Exercises and North Sea sweep.

27 Dec–5 Jan: Scapa Flow.

1915

6–11 Jan: Cromarty (docked 9 Jan).

12–23 Jan: Scapa Flow.

23–26 Jan: North Sea sweep.

26 Jan–7 Mar: Scapa Flow.

7–10 Mar: Cruise and exercises with Fleet in northern North Sea.
10–15 Mar: Scapa Flow.
16–18 Mar: Cruise and exercises with Fleet in northern North Sea.
18 Mar: Sank U29.
19 Mar: Cruising with 4th Battle Squadron.
20–29 Mar: Cromarty.
29–30 Mar: Cruising with 4th Battle Squadron.
30 Mar–11 Apr: Cromarty.
11–14 Apr: Cruising with 4th Battle Squadron and Grand Fleet.
14–17 Apr: Scapa Flow.
17–21 Apr: Sweep of southern North Sea and exercises.
21 Apr: Scapa Flow.
21–23 Apr: Sweep towards Danish coast with Grand Fleet.
23 Apr–17 May: Scapa Flow.
17–19 May: Cruising with Grand Fleet, swept central North Sea.
19–22 May: Scapa Flow.
22 May: Sailed for Portsmouth.
27 May–7 June: Under refit at Portsmouth.
8 June: Sailed for Scapa.
12 June–11 July: Scapa Flow.
11–13 July: Cruise and exercises with Grand Fleet in vicinity of Shetlands.
13 July–3 Aug: Scapa Flow.
4–24 Aug: With 4th Battle Squadron based at Cromarty. 4th Battle Squadron carried out target practice in Moray Firth and cruised independently of main fleet.
24 Aug–2 Sept: Scapa Flow.
3–5 Sept: Cruised northern North Sea with 4th Battle Squadron.
5–24 Sept: Scapa Flow.
24 Sept: Manoeuvres with 4th Battle Squadron.
25 Sept–13 Oct: Scapa Flow.
14–15 Oct: Cruising with Grand Fleet.
15 Oct–1 Nov: Scapa Flow.
2–5 Nov: Cruise and exercises to W of Orkneys with Grand Fleet.
5–11 Nov: Scapa Flow.
11–17 Nov: Cromarty.
17–23 Nov: Scapa Flow.
23 Nov: Cruise with 4th Battle Squadron and gunnery exercises.
24 Nov–1 Dec: Scapa Flow.
1–4 Dec: Cruise to W of Orkneys and battle practice with Grand Fleet.
4–17 Dec: Scapa Flow.
17 Dec–10 Jan: Based Cromarty.
20 Dec: 4th Battle Squadron, 2nd Cruiser Squadron and *Iron Duke* carried out gunnery practice in Moray Firth. Returned Cromarty same day.
30 Dec: At Cromarty when cruiser *Natal* blew up.

1916

11 Jan–10 Feb: Scapa Flow (at sea on 9 Feb).
10–12 Feb: At sea with Grand Fleet.
12–25 Feb: Scapa Flow.

26–28 Feb: Cruise and exercises with Grand Fleet in northern North Sea.
28 Feb–13 Mar: Scapa Flow.
14 Mar–15 Apr: Based at Invergordon, at sea on 26–27 Mar and 30–31 Mar.
16–17 Apr: Scapa Flow.
18 Apr–22 June: Under refit at Rosyth (docked 20–27 Apr and 5–25 May).
24 June–8 July: Scapa Flow.
8 July: Sailed for Sheerness.
9 July: Joined 3rd Battle Squadron at Sheerness as flagship of Vice Admiral Sir E Bradford.
July 1916–Apr 1918: During her service with the 3rd Battle Squadron *Dreadnought* spent practically her entire time alternating between No 2 Buoy at Sheerness and an anchorage in the Swin (in the Thames Estuary) where she stayed for about two or three days at a time. The exceptions to this pattern are noted below.
20 July: Vice Admiral Bradford relieved by Vice Admiral Sir J de Robeck.
25 Aug: Sailed for Portland.
25 Aug–18 Sept: *Dreadnought* and 3rd Battle Squadron at Portland for gunnery and torpedo exercises.
Dec: Vice Admiral de Robeck relieved by Admiral H L Heath.

1917

16–27 Jan: Under refit at Chatham.
13 Feb: At sea.
8–24 Feb: Under refit at Chatham.
8 Mar: At sea.
12 Mar: At sea.
4 Apr: Sailed from Sheerness and at sea.
5 Apr: In the Swin and under way.
6 Apr: At sea and returned Sheerness.
5 June: Engaged enemy aircraft at Sheerness.
16 July: Sailed to Portsmouth.
23 July–19 Aug: Under refit at Portsmouth.
24 Aug: Left Portsmouth Dockyard for Spithead and Stokes Bay.
25 Aug: Sailed for Sheerness.
26 Aug: Arrived Sheerness.
10 Sept: Admiral Heath relieved by Vice Admiral Sir Dudley de Chair.
18–21 Sept: Anchored in the Warp.
29 Sept, 30 Sept and 1st Oct: Fired on enemy aircraft at Sheerness.
10–11 Oct: Carried out tactical exercises, torpedo practice and sub calibre firing.
31 Oct: Fired on enemy aircraft at Sheerness.
15 Nov: Exercises.
1 Dec: Fired on enemy aircraft at Sheerness.
18 Dec: Sailed from Sheerness for gunnery exercises, anchored in Swin in evening, fired on enemy aircraft.

1918

1 Jan: Fired on enemy aircraft at Sheerness.
8–10 Jan: Anchored in the Warp.

23 Jan: Cruising and returned Sheerness.

16 Feb, 17 Feb and night of 7–8 Mar: Fired on enemy aircraft at Sheerness.

Mar: 3rd Battle Squadron decommissioned and *Dreadnought* officially returned to 4th Battle Squadron, Grand Fleet.

1–3 Apr: The Swin.

3–28 Apr: Sheerness.

28 Apr–2 May: Anchored in the Warp off Mouse Light Vessel.

2 May: Sailed from the Warp to Yarmouth, night 2–3 May, anchored Yarmouth Roads.

4–15 May: Rosyth.

15 May: Sailed for gunnery exercises, anchored off Rosyth.

19–22 May: At sea with 4th Battle Squadron.

22–24 May: Scapa Flow.

25 May: Arrived Cromarty, then moved to No 1 dock Invergordon.

25 May–1 June: Docked in No 1 dock Invergordon. Bottom cleaned.

1 June–6 July: Scapa Flow (exercises at sea on 12 June).

7–8 July: Exercises with Grand Fleet.

8–10 July: Scapa Flow.

10–12 July: Cruise and exercises.

12–14 July: Scapa Flow.

14–16 July: Cruising in North Sea.

16–21 July: Scapa Flow.

21 July: Sailed for Rosyth with 4th Battle Squadron.

22 July–2 Aug: Burntisland Roads.

2 Aug: Sailed to Rosyth Dockyard.

5 Aug–31 Dec: Under refit at Rosyth (docked 22 Oct – 6 Nov).

7 Aug: Paid off, to be recommissioned for further service in 4th Battle Squadron but this cancelled owing to end of the Wwar.

1919

12 Jan: Reduced to reserve commission at Rosyth. Recommissioned with 3rd Fleet crew from Chatham under C-in-C Rosyth.

25 Feb: Transferred to Reserve Fleet at Rosyth and recommissioned as tender to *Hercules* (flagship of Rear Admiral reserve fleet, Rosyth).

31 Mar 1920: Ordered to be paid off and placed on sale list.

3 May 1920: Transferred to Dockyard control.

9 May 1921: Sold at Rosyth to T W Ward for £44,750.

2 Jan 1923: Arrived Inverkeithing for scrapping.

NOTE: *Dreadnought's* Logs for mid-1911 to the end of 1912 and for the first six months of 1914 are missing.

Hull, weights and stability

Although *Dreadnought* was larger than earlier battleships and great care was required in the preparation of her lines to accommodate the higher speed, the general structural arrangements and midship section followed closely that of previous ships. When the *Lord Nelson* class was designed a squarer midships section was adopted to provide for the displacement and a good set of lines without increasing the overall dimensions beyond existing docking limits. This pattern was followed in *Dreadnought* which had a slightly squarer form than *Lord Nelson*, with a large flat bottom and almost vertical sides amidships. The flat bottom in the area of 'A' boiler room extended slightly beyond the natural curve of the bilge producing a knuckle-line in the outer bottom plating in this area.

Dreadnought did, however, differ from previous ships in the form of her bow and stern and in having a raised forecastle deck. The stem was of a smoothly curved shape rather than the sharply pointed ram of the pre-dreadnoughts while the stern had a lengthy cut-up to accommodate the propeller and rudder arrangements – a feature brought about by the adoption of turbines. The fuller hull section assisted in damping the ship's roll which was slightly faster than in earlier battleships due to an increased level of stability.

Dreadnought was inclined on 8 September 1906 from which the stability figures given in Table 6 were calculated. At this time the load displacement was 320 tons above the designed figures given in Table 5 (excluding the board margin), this being made up of 40 tons added to the armament, 45 tons to the machinery, 128 tons to the armour and 115 tons to the hull, less a 9-ton reduction in the equipment weights. These figures were a combination of weights added to the design (*eg* additional 12pdr guns, shaft holding gear, etc) and the refinement of the original calculations as the construction progressed. The extreme deep displacement had increased even more but this was principally because the calculations were based on the extreme full stowage of stores and fuel rather than the arbitrary allowance made in the design calculations. It is worth noting that the full load was somewhat variable, particularly in the case of coal which varied according to how well the bunkers were filled and on the weight per unit volume (the calculations assumed that the coal was 43cu ft/ton but this varied according to coal type and its condition).

In June 1907 Portsmouth Dockyard sent in an estimate of *Dreadnought's* weights which appeared to indicate that some unapproved additions were being made to her equipment. A further return was therefore requested, which was prepared following a refit in November 1907. Calculations, taking account of the draught of the ship and the weights on board, showed her extreme deep displacement to have risen by 762 tons since she was first completed. As this represented an 11in increase in draught it was viewed with some concern, particularly as there was a 240-ton discrepancy between the displacement estimated from the ship's draught at the time and the weights reported to be on board; this seemed to suggest that this unrecorded addition was in the ship's structure.

These anomalies were not resolved until February 1909 when constructor M P Payne carried out a detailed investigation of the ship's condition while she was in No 15 dock at Portsmouth. At the time the draught indicated a displacement of 17,980 tons and she was estimated to be carrying a load of 1888 tons, leaving 16,092 tons for the bare hull, armour, armament and machinery. This was only 81 tons above the recorded figures of which 64 tons was accounted for by approved additions. Subsequent calculations showed that her extreme deep displacement, with the weights allowed, had increased by only 106 tons since completion, of which 80 tons was accounted for by approved additions. It was concluded that the reported increases of 1907 were a combination of excess weights of stores, etc, above those allowed for, and incorrect estimates of the weights on board by the ship's officers.

Machinery

Fisher's desire for high speed was one of the weaker arguments in his proposal for the *Dreadnought* design. While there were obvious advantages when set against existing ships – which he exploited to the full – he does not seem to have considered the probability that any foreign answer to *Dreadnought* would match her speed as well as her armament. The tactical advantage would, therefore, eventually be lost although, in the meantime, the speed advantage would ensure that *Dreadnought* could keep her distance from the destructive effects of the secondary armament of pre-dreadnoughts – barring a surprise encounter at close quarters in poor visibility. By chance, the introduction of the turbine actually allowed an increase in speed without a serious disruption of the overall balance of the design and it is safe to assume that this method of propulsion would, in any case, have led to the adoption of higher speeds. In fact, the turbine was as much a part of the revolutionary nature of *Dreadnought's* design as was her armament.

The Committee on Designs spent much time deciding between reciprocating and turbine engines. Briefly the advantages of the turbine were:

1. Reduced weight.
2. Reduced cost.
3. Quieter, cleaner and easier operation.
4. Reduced liability to breakdowns.
5. Smaller engine room complement.
6. Improved fuel economy at high speeds.
7. Reduced height of machinery which was therefore easier to accommodate below the waterline where it was better protected.

Against these advantages was the fact that turbines only ran efficiently at comparatively high speeds, although they could be run slower if a large diameter of rotor was adopted. The latter, however, also meant accepting an increase in size and ultimately a balance had to be struck between machinery weight and the propeller design. High-speed propellers required a relatively large blade area and a small diameter in order to avoid excessive cavitation and loss of efficiency which, in turn, required an increase in the number of propellers in order to transmit the required power. The overall effect was less economy at low power and reduced manoeuvring and astern power when compared to the standard twin screw reciprocating engines of existing battleships. In addition to this, the turbine system was relatively new and had only recently been applied experimentally to a few destroyers and one cruiser, the latter

TABLE 9: **Particulars of Machinery**

Main machinery	Two sets Parsons direct drive turbines driving four shafts.
Rotor drums	HP ahead – 5ft 8in diameter × 8ft 7.5in long, 72 blade rows, 6 expansions, mean diameter at blade centres 70.9in
	HP astern – 5ft 8in diameter × 3ft 1.5in long
	LP ahead and astern – 7ft 8in diameter × 6ft 6in long, 36 blade rows, 6 expansions, mean diameter at blade centres 99.2in
	Cruising – 5ft 8in diameter × 8ft 6.375in long
Designed shp	23,000
Designed speed	21kts
Designed rpm	320 – all shafts
Boilers	Eighteen Babcock and Wilcox water tube; normal working pressure 250psi, reducing to 185psi at turbines; total heating surface – 55,400sq ft; total grate area – 1599sq ft; six fuel oil sprayers per boiler giving 960lbs oil/boiler/hour at 150psi; height of funnel above fire bars 85ft.
Main machinery auxiliaries	For each turbine set –
	One cylindrical surface condenser (cooling surface – 26,000sq ft)
	Two twin cylinder Weir wet air pumps.
	One twin cylinder Weir dry air pump.
	Two steam driven centrifugal circulating pumps.
	Two steam driven forced lubrication pumps.
	One water service pump (for oil coolers).
Auxiliary machinery	
Auxiliary condensers	Two surface condensers (cooling surface 6000sq ft). Electricity power plant: Four Siemens dynamos supplying 1000amps max at 100–105v DC, two driven by Brotherhood steam engines and two by Mirrlees diesel engines (one diesel replaced by steam engine plant in 1908).
Distilling machinery	Two Kilkaldy evaporator plants, each consisting of two evaporators, one distilling condenser, one brine pump and one distiller pump.
Pumping and flooding machinery	Four Weir 75-ton fire and bilge pumps in engine rooms, three Weir 50-ton fire and bilge pumps in boiler rooms, seven 50-ton electrically driven centrifugal service pumps outside main machinery spaces, total pumping capacity = 800 tons/hour, in addition the main condenser circulating pumps could be used to pump out the engine room bilges in an emergency.
Feed pumps	Nine Weir, one main and two auxiliary in each boiler room.
Fresh water pumps	Two electrically driven centrifugal, one Downton hand pump.
Sanitary pumps	Two electrically driven centrifugal.
Oil fuel pumps	Five Weir, one in each main machinery compartment.
Hydraulic machinery	Three steam-driven hydraulic pumping engines built by Vickers, hydraulic boat hoisting machinery built by Armstrong Whitworth.
Refrigerating machinery	Electrically driven Haslam dry-air refrigeration plant. Pulsometer Ammonia-compression ice making machinery.
Electric lifts	Five (one in each main machinery space) built by Laurance-Scott.
Electric coaling winches	Eight
Steering	Napier steam engines, screw type steering gear.
Air compressors	Seven (four fitted in dynamo rooms, one in each boiler room), built by General Engine and boiler company.
Main machinery ventilation	Twenty-four 81in steam driven supply fans for boiler rooms; four 30in electrically-driven supply fans and four 35in electrically driven exhaust fans for engine rooms.

Machinery weights, August 1906 (tons)

Engines and shafting to after engine room bulkhead and all fittings, including spare gear in engine room	700
Weight of auxiliary machinery for which separate prices quoted	38.1
Water in condensers, pumps, pipes and feed tanks when hall full	38.65
Screw propellers, stern fittings, shafting and fans forward of after engine room bulkhead and all fittings in connection	62

Boilers, funnel casings, pipes and spare gear and all fittings in boiler rooms	927	
Hot fresh water in boilers at working level	74.25	
Weight of spare gear	34	
Lifting and shaft holding gear	16	
TOTAL	1890 tons	

Coal capacity

	Cubic feet*	Tons‡
Upper bunkers	38,070†	885
Lower bunkers	52,995	1232.4
Wing bunkers	25,842	600.9
Cross bunkers	11,130	258.8
Total	126,887	2977.1

* These are taken from the ship's 'as fitted' drawings, the weight being calculated at the nominal rate of 43cub ft/ton.
† This figure reduced to 36,900 when part of one of the bunkers was converted for use as a compartment for the magazine cooling machinery during 1907–8, giving a total maximum stowage of 2950 tons.
‡ Probably as a result of practical experience the nominal maximum capacity accepted in service was 2868 tons, reducing to 2834 tons after the loss of part of the upper bunker stowage.
The design capacity in June 1906 was estimated at 129,035cu ft = 3000.8 tons, this figure being used by Attwood in his estimate of the deep displacement following the ship's inclining.

Patent fuel capacity 146 tons (43 tons in each wing bunker abreast P and Q magazine and 30 tons in each wing bunker abreast X magazine). This was carried mainly for protective purposes but also provided fuel for the galleys and stoves.

Oil fuel capacity 1120 tons

Endurance

Shp	Coal consumption tons/24hrs	Speed (knots)	Radius of coal	action (naut miles) coal and oil
18,400	360	19.5	3230	4890
16,100§	336	18.9	3240	4910
9200	246	16	3800	5760
4600	100	12.9	4700	7110
2220	127	10	4340	6620

§ = maximum continuous sea going full power.

Water tank capacities (tons)

Feed water	30.0 (15 + 15)
Reserve feed water	237.8 (61.8 + 91.3 + 84.7)
Overflow feed water	80.4 (40.2 + 40.2)
Fresh (drinking) water	124.4 (32.5 + 47.3 + 44.6)
Hydraulic pumping water	56.3 (29.3 aft + 13.5 + 13.5 fore)
Trimming tanks	20.4 aft, 52.4 fore

representing the highest power yet installed at 12,000shp, less than half that required for the new battleship. [11]

Initially, the naval members of the Committee were reluctant to adopt the turbine, conscious as they were of its limitations for manoeuvring, but Rear Admiral Durston, Watts and Froude were in favour and after receiving evidence from Sir Charles Parsons, the British inventor of the turbine, it was decided that the advantages of the turbine far outweighed the small chance of failure. The fact that this form of machinery would save a substantial amount of weight worked strongly in favour of the turbine. It was estimated that about 500 tons, as a result of the lighter machinery, and about 1000 tons in all, due to the subsequent reduction in armour and hull weight, would be saved.

On 21 January the Committee considered the arrangement of the turbines and how best to distribute the required 23,000shp. Three-, four-, five- and six-shaft arrangements were discussed, all with three engine rooms. On the 25 January the five-shaft arrangement, with one turbine in the centre engine room and two in each of the wing engine rooms, was recommended for adoption. However, this arrangement required a number of cross connections through the longitudinal bulkheads and it was later decided that two independent sets of turbines in two engine rooms, separated by a middle-line bulkhead, would be preferable; four shafts, running at 320rpm, was the arrangement finally chosen.

There was still concern about the poor economy at low power which, as warships normally operated at economic cruising speeds, affected the cost of running the ship substantially. This led to a proposal to fit the ship with cruising turbines specifically designed to provide economic use of steam at cruising speeds. These high-pressure turbines, fitted to the forward ends of the inner: shafts, were designed to develop 6000shp in combination with the main turbines and provide an economic speed of around 14kts. In practice, the cruising turbines proved to be more trouble than they were worth, principally because they were only in use at cruising speeds. For the remainder of the time they idled, and placed drag on the shafts to which they were coupled. This intermittent use led to difficulties in maintaining the turbines' temperature, which had to be carefully controlled to avoid uneven expansion and subsequent damage. On 6 November 1907, *Dreadnought's* port cruising turbine was opened up and it was discovered that a large number of blades had been stripped from the second and third expansion stages. Further trouble was later experienced with cracked casings, which resulted in loss of vacuum when the main turbines were running, and further increased the drag on the inner shaft. Experience with the turbine soon showed that good economy could be obtained without the use of separate cruising elements and these were eventually disconnected. *Dreadnought's* cruising turbines thus became no more than dead weight which she was to carry for the rest of her career. Work did begin on dismantling them during her last refit at the end of 1918 but this was never to be completed.

The letter inviting tenders for the main machinery was sent out on 18 May 1905 and on 24 June that from Vickers (dated 12 June) for £252,553 was accepted. At this time, however, Vickers did not manufacture turbines and these were subcontracted to Parsons who constructed them at their Wallsend works. In general, the design of the turbines followed earlier practice but some changes were made to improve accessibility for servicing and to provide for more even expansion when warming them through. In addition, the rotor spindles were coupled directly to the shafts instead of via loose couplings as in earlier designs. The turbines were fitted in the ship during May and June 1906.

The results of *Dreadnought's* steam trials in October 1906 are given in Table 7. The most notable feature of these, apart from the fact that she achieved well over her design power, is that the shp on the inner shafts was much higher than that on the outer shafts. This was because of the difficulty of accurately dividing a turbine set between two shafts – the high-pressure turbine on the outer and the low-pressure on the inner shaft being effectively a single unit divided into two casings. It is possible that this contributed to the increased power needed, over that designed, for her to reach 21kts, although her length was set at a particularly sensitive point in relation to this speed.[12]

It was hoped that some further improvement in performance might be obtained by modifying the propellers to suit the different shaft powers. During May and June 1907 her original three-bladed propellers, which were 8ft 10in diameter with an 8ft 4½in pitch and a blade area of 33sq ft, were replaced with ones with blade areas of 40sq ft for the inner shafts and 28sq ft for the outer shafts. The number of blades, diameter and pitch remained the same. Trials were run at Polperro on 5 June 1907. Despite allowance being made for the ship being 1100 tons heavier than during the 1906 trials, the new propellers proved to be slightly less efficient, giving a gradual reduction in speed from 0 at 15kts to 0.5kts at full speed. Further trials were carried out at Polperro on 11 November 1907, this time with the pitch of the inner propellers altered to 8ft 8in. The results were almost identical to those produced in June.

Despite this, her machinery installation proved highly efficient as demonstrated during the experimental cruise. On the 3430-mile trip from Gibraltar to Trinidad, and on the return journey of 3980 miles to Portsmouth, her average speed was 17kts. In fact, the return average should have been higher as she started the journey at 19kts but, although the engine revolutions were not reduced, the speed dropped to 16kts for about two days and then increased to 20kts as she entered the English Channel. On docking the ship in May 1907, it was found that the plating of the port rudder had opened up at the forward end and that the fore part of the frame had carried away, further damaging the plating as it went. This had added to the ship's resistance until the plating, or whatever had caused the damage, cleared itself as the ship approached the end of her journey. Although some vibration was noticed in the port inner shaft, there was no discernible effect apart from the drop in speed. It was assumed that the damage had been caused by floating wreckage.

On opening up the turbines after the trial cruise they were found to be in perfect condition. A ship driven by reciprocating engines could not have matched this performance, as it was impossible to run such machinery at high speeds for extended periods without it requiring adjustment or risking the danger of breakdown. Although the turbine was to be further developed and improved, principally by the introduction of gearing to reduce the propeller speed, *Dreadnought* established this form of propulsion as the ideal for warships, and it remained as such for a further sixty years.

Steering gear

To forestall the manoeuvring problems inherent in the use of small high-speed propellers, *Dreadnought* was designed with twin balanced rudders, one placed immediately behind each of the inner propellers. This greatly increased the rudder area available compared with the single rudders used in earlier battleships and gave the ship exceptionally good man-

oeuvring powers at speeds above about 10kts. Below this speed, however, the problems foreseen by the naval members of the Committee on Designs – lack of astern power, difficulty in steering – began to manifest themselves. Bacon seems to have ignored these deficiencies, stating rather that she was possessed of 'perfect' manoeuvring qualities and was 'quick to answer her helm, quick and steady, steady on a course in a seaway, [has a] small turning circle, starts turning quickly from rest, turns well under her propellers, stern does not come up to the wind with a sternway, can be kept straight with engines reversed and headway on, can be steered slightly with stern way on, or can be kept absolutely straight'.[13] However, he did admit she had less astern power than other battleships and requested that no reduction in the stopping power should be accepted for later ships. These remarks contrast markedly with those of Captain S R Fremantle (*Dreadnought's* Commander in 1911–12) who said 'The *Dreadnought* was not an easy ship to handle. She would not steer at any speed under ten knots, at lower speeds if the helm was put over nothing would stop her from turning like a saucer, though at higher speeds she steered beautifully ... It was almost impossible to turn her at rest and her astern power was very small'.[14] However, once commanders had become used to these characteristics at low speed and had adjusted their methods accordingly, they were not an embarrassment. In August 1908 her Captain for the previous year, C E Madden, said she was a very handy ship, which steered very straight and steady and that there were no difficulties in operating in company with earlier classes of battleship. He added that the best helm for manoeuvring in company was 15°, as at greater angles she lost speed rapidly which made it necessary to increase speed to keep station. At 15° the tactical diameter was 625 yards, much larger than *Dreadnought* was capable of but similar to that found in pre-dreadnoughts.

After a preliminary trial to test the operation of the steering gear on 1 October 1906, *Dreadnought* carried out her full turning trials east of the Isle of Wight on 10 October 1906 (see Table 8). While the results were generally satisfactory, it was found that when turning at speed the rudders were slow in responding to the steering engine when returning to a straight course. Eventually, while carrying out a full-speed turn, with the rudder hard-over at 35°, the steering gear jammed and would not bring the rudders back to less than 25° until the ship's speed had dropped substantially. It was noticed that the gears on the control shafting from the steering engine to the steering gear tended to move laterally and lock. Stronger supporting brackets were fitted to the gears which seemed to cure this problem, but the steering difficulties remained and restrictions were placed on the amount of helm that could be employed. She sailed on her experimental cruise in this condition, mainly to avoid the delays which would have resulted from attempting to locate and correct the fault. The gear was to jam again on a number of occasions including once in the restricted waters of the Straits of Bonifacio at the northern tip of Sardinia.[15]

The trouble was eventually traced to the rudders themselves which had been deliberately over-balanced to reduce the load on the rudder head when going astern. As a result, when going forward with the helm over, the forces on the rudder forward of the axis were substantially higher than those abaft the axis, and under certain conditions the steering gear was not strong enough to overcome the differential. This problem was compounded by the arrangement of the control shafts between the steering engines in the engine room and the steering gear itself. Due to the difficulty of finding suitable positions for these engines, they had been placed low down on the after engine room bulkhead which necessitated several changes in direction in the routes of the control shafts via a skew (helical) gear in the starboard engine room and several bevel gears which redirected the drive from the hold to the platform deck. The high loads transmitted through these gears eventually began to distort the teeth, which made the problem worse.[16] After investigations were carried out during the summer of 1907 it was decided to fit the ship with more powerful steering engines. In addition, the after ends of the engine rooms were modified so that these engines could be fitted higher to allow a more direct drive from the engine room to the steering compartments. These alterations were carried out during her refit of August–November 1907 and no further problems were encountered.

Electrical machinery

Dreadnought's electricity installation followed closely that provided in the *Lord Nelson* class except that it was less extensive, with four dynamos instead of five. It was originally intended to fit the ship with a 220-volt ring main but there was insufficient time to prepare the design and it was not adopted until the *Bellerophon* class were built. She had four Siemens dynamos with a total power of 410kW supplying current at 1000 amps and connected in parallel to a Cowan switchboard from which the 100-volt DC circuits were distributed on the branch system. Two of the dynamos were driven by Brotherhood steam piston engines and two by Mirrlees diesel engines. The latter provided the ship with a power source independent of the main machinery plant to allow equipment to be run even if the boilers were out of use, and to give a source of emergency power in case of action damage to the steam supply. Almost all the auxiliaries outside the main machinery spaces, including the pumps, were driven by electric motors; the only exceptions were the main capstan and the hydraulic pumping engines. The engine room ventilation fans were also electrically driven and the whole system helped to reduce the number of steam pipes that passed through watertight bulkheads and decks.

Some difficulties were experienced with the diesel engines which suffered from excessive vibration and a number of breakdowns. The port engine eventually broke down completely and was removed in December 1905 and replaced by a steam piston engine. The deck under the starboard engine was fitted with additional stiffening to reduce the vibration and apparently worked satisfactorily for the remainder of *Dreadnought's* service.

The ship's low-power system consisted of a number of motor generators to supply 15-volt DC circuits via two switchboards – one in the main switchboard room and one in 'X' turret working space. These supplied the fire control instruments, gun firing circuits and other communication devices. Later, a third lower-power switchboard was fitted in the 12pdr working space on the lower deck, the gun circuits being separated from the cabin bell, revolution indicator and other minor circuits which were run entirely off the board in the main switchboard room. In addition to these a separate motor generator was fitted for the telephone exchange, and motor alternators (DC–AC converters) were provided for the wireless transmitters and turret danger signals. The low-power system was extensive compared with that in ships prior to the *Lord Nelson* design and was representative of a move away from batteries for low power supplies. Batteries were, however, carried for emergency use in case of failure of the low power supply, and were employed for the telephones.

Ventilation

The requirement to provide the ship with unpierced bulkheads below the protective deck meant that each main compartment had its own ventilation system. These consisted of supply trunks with electric fans and natural exhaust outlets via hatches, trunks and skylights. Bacon found much to criticise in this system, particularly with regard to the supply of air to the auxiliary machinery rooms which were ' . . . far too hot, the reason is that it is nobody's business to keep them cool. The contractors are allowed a free hand in running steam pipes and so long as the floor space is sufficient no one gives two pence about the poor devils who have to work there'.[17] These problems were discussed by Bacon and officers of the Engineer-in-Chief's department on the *Dreadnought's* return from the experimental cruise, and it was agreed to fit exhaust fans to the escape trunks of the dynamo rooms and the forward hydraulic engine rooms (the after hydraulic engine room was considered satisfactory). These alterations were carried out between August and November 1907, when a 25in electrically-driven exhaust fan was fitted on the main deck to each of the three escape trunks concerned.

Another major concern was the inadequate ventilation of the magazines, which at times during the experimental cruise reached a temperature of 100°F. Although this was not surprising in a hot climate, it presented a major problem in that the ballistic performance of cordite varied according to its temperature. As *Dreadnought* was intended to use her guns for controlled long-range fire, this was an undesirable feature. Indeed, it was one of several which came to light during the initial development of modern fire control which required improvements in order to maintain consistency in the calibration of guns. The solution in this case was to fit the magazines with cooling systems intended to maintain the temperature at a steady 80°F. This work was carried out in *Dreadnought* during 1907–8. A ventilation system and cooler was fitted to each magazine and two steam-driven carbon dioxide plants provided to supply the cooling medium. One of these plants was fitted in part of one of the wing coal bunkers on the port side of the middle deck, which reduced the coal stowage by about 25 tons.

Accommodation

At a meeting of the naval members of the Committee on Designs on 13 January 1905 it was decided that because of the length of the ship the officers were to be berthed forward and the men aft in order to position the officers nearer their command positions. This reversal of the normal arrangement was not generally popular with the ship's officers partly because of the loss of the quarterdeck as the officers' preserve – it was replaced by the less spacious areas on each side of the upper deck forward – and partly because conditions forward were less comfortable at sea. Lionel Dawson (a lieutenant aboard *Dreadnought* during 1913–15) regarded her as a very uncomfortable ship. On the whole though, senior officers seemed to prefer the new arrangement. Bacon considered it an 'unqualified success' and Fremantle thought that any disadvantages were outweighed by the advantages. One of the main objections for many officers was the proximity of the cabins to the diesel dynamos, hydraulic pumping engines and the refrigeration plant, all of which were noisy. This must have been particularly galling as the turbine machinery had produced a ship which was comparatively free of vibration and noise from the propellers. The system survived for a number of years but eventually, with the design of the *King George V* class of the 1910 Estimates, tradition won and the old arrangement was reverted to.

Armament

The ship's 12in MkX guns were a new 45cal weapon designed by Vickers which the *Lord Nelson* class would have been the first to carry but for the intervention of *Dreadnought*. They were powerful guns which gave a substantial improvement in performance and penetrating power compared with the previous 40cal MkIX; indeed, they were probably the best British 12in guns of the period as the later 50cal MkXI was not an unqualified success. The twin mountings were also designed by Vickers but they built only 'X' and 'Y' mountings; the other three were constructed by Armstrong. Tenders for the mountings were received in July 1905 and were £70,092 per mounting from Armstrong and £69,860 from Vickers. This, and the fact that the *Lord Nelson* and *Agamemnon* were not laid down until May 1905, casts some doubt on the common assertion that the guns and mountings ordered for the *Lord Nelson* class were transferred to *Dreadnought* as a time-saving measure. Although guns and mountings took a long time to construct, and were normally ordered in advance of the ships into which they were to be fitted, there could not have been that much progress on the construction of the mountings prior to the date on which this decision is said to have been made in January 1905. It seems more likely that the manufacturers were requested to give priority to the *Dreadnought* order and to transfer any material thus far prepared to the new ship. There was certainly no shortage of capacity for during the next three years twenty-seven of these mountings were constructed, excluding those for *Dreadnought* herself.

The layout of the 12in mountings gave a full broadside of eight guns from 60° before to 50° abaft the beam. Beyond these limits six guns could be fired aft and four guns forward, except for a small arc of fire of 1° on either side of the bow which allowed six guns to fire directly ahead. In practice, the firing of the wing turrets directly forward or aft would have caused blast damage to the superstructure but it is not known if this was ever attempted. A better layout would have resulted from mounting a pair of superfiring turrets fore and aft, as the Americans did in *South Carolina*. This arrangement would have given much the same arcs of fire, saved the weight of a turret and avoided the need to strengthen the structure for the wing turrets. This is, however, written with the considerable advantage of hindsight and, taking account of the expected dangers of blast effects and the generally accepted layout of ships prior to *Dreadnought*, the chosen arrangement is difficult to criticise.

The ship's gun trials were carried out off the Isle of Wight on 18 October 1906 and were described as 'generally satisfactory'. No particular problems seem to have been experienced with either the guns or the mountings, and they gave excellent service throughout the ship's career. *Dreadnought* originally carried an outfit of 2crh (the radius of a shell head in calibres) shells but these were replaced by 4crh shells during 1915 or 1916. These gave improved accuracy (they were manufactured to tighter dimensional limits) and increased the range of the guns by over 2000yds. In 1918 the gun mountings were fitted with pneumatic run-out gear.

TABLE 10: **Particulars of Armament**

Main armament	Ten 12in MkX BL, five twin BVIII mountings
Secondary armament	12pdr, 18cwt QF MkI, single PIV* mountings
	As built – twenty-seven
	1907–16 – twenty-four
	1916–17 – twenty-two
	1917–19 – eighteen
AA armament	1915–16 – two 6pdr QF, single HA MkIc mountings
	1916–17 – two 3in, 20cwt MkI, single HA MkII mountings
	1917–19 – two 3in, 20cwt MkI, single HA MkII mountings
	two 12pdr, 18cwt QF, single HA MkIV*c mountings
Small arms	Five 0.303 Maxim machine guns
Torpedo tubes	Five 18in submerged torpedo tubes Type B, four broadside, one stern (removed 1917)
	Six 14in torpedoes carried for steam picket boats
Ammunition stowage	12in – 80rpg (forty steel common, forty APC) plus eight practice
	12pdr – 200rpg (with twenty-seven guns) steel common plus 1016 (total) practice.
	0.303 – 5000rpg
	18in torpedoes – twenty-three Fiume MkIII* (Sept 1906)
	14in torpedoes – six RGF Mk1*
Fire control system	As built – Vickers dial instruments for range and deflection, Barr and Stroud rate instruments added 1908–9. Telaupad for night defence
	*c*1913 Dreyer Fire Control Table MkI
	1916 – Fitted with geared type director on tripod mounting
Rangefinders	1906–12 – Two FQ2 on MP2 mountings in control positions
	1912–15 – One FQ2 on MP2 mounting in aft control
	One FQ2 on Argo mounting in fore top
	One FT8 on MG3 turret mounting in 'A' turret
	One FQ2 on MNI mounting on compass platform
	1915–18 – One FQ2 on Argo mounting in fore top
	One FQ2 on MNI mounting on compass platform
	Five FT8 on MG3 turret mountings in turrets
	1918 – FT24 fitted in 'A' turret in place of FT8

All these rangefinders were of 9ft base and all except the Argo mounting were manufactured by Barr and Stroud

Searchlights	1906–17 – Twelve 36in, one 24in (removed 1910)
	1917–19 – Six 36in, two 24in signalling

TABLE 11: Particulars of Guns

12in, 45mi, BL MkX

Construction	Steel, wire wound; nickel steel inner 'A' tube and 'A' tube
Calibre	12in
Nominal weight	58 tons
Length oa	556.5in
Bore length	540.9in = 45cal
Chamber: Diameter	19in max, 13in min
Length	81in
Capacity	18,000in^3
Weight without BM	56 tons 16cwt 1qtr
Weight of BM	17cwt
Breech mechanism	Welin stepped screw block, 'pure couple' mechanism hydraulic or hand operation
Rifling: Type	Plain Section MkI
No of grooves	60
Length	453.193in
Twist	Uniform 1-in-30
Cordite type	MD45 cordite
Full charge	260lbs
Reduced charge	195lbs
Average weight of shell	850lbs
Shell type	2crh APC and CP, replaced by 4crh APC, CPC and possibly HE c1915–16
Weight of burster§	83.25lbs powder for Mk IV* or MkV 2crh CP
	80lbs Lyddite for Mk VIIa 4crh CPC
	112lbs 3oz for MkIa 4crh HE
	113lbs 4oz for MkI 4crh HE
	17lbs powder for MkIVa 2crh APC
	26lbs 6oz Lyddite for MkVa 4crh APC
	27lbs 4oz Lyddite for MkVIa 4crh APC
Chamber pressure	18tons/in^2 (designed)
Muzzle velocity	2725fps (2311fps with reduced charge)
Muzzle energy	44,431ft-tons
Range	16,450yds (2crh shell)
	18,850yds (4crh shell)
Perforation of KC armour	2crh shell = 10.4in at 6000yds
	8.6in at 9000yds
	4crh shell = 11.6in at 6000yds
	10.1in at 9000 yds
Barrel life, approx	280efc
Mounting	Twin BVIII
Max elevation	13.5°
Max depression	5°
Inside diameter of barbette	27ft
Crew	44 (18 turret, 13 magazine, 13 shell room)

§ The weights given are for various shell Marks. It is not known which were carried by *Dreadnought*.

12pdr, 18cwt, QF MkI

Consriuction	Steel/wire wound
Calibre	3in
Nominal weight	18cwt
Weight with fittings	18cwt 2qtrs 6lbs
Length oa	154.7in
Bore length	150in – 50cal
Chamber: Diameter	4in max, 3.24in min
Length	20.6in
Capacity	186in^3
Rifling: Type	Modified Plain section MkI
No of grooves	20
Length	128.162in
Twist	Uniform 1-in-30cal
Charge type	MD11 cordite
Full charge	2lbs 12.125ozs
Average weight of shell	12.5lbs common MkII, Lyddite MkIII and IV (fitted for tracer)
Weight of burster	1lb 1oz powder for MkII shell, 1lb 5oz Lyddite for MkIII and 12oz Lyddite for MkIV
Chamber pressure	17tons/sq in (designed)
Muzzle velocity	2660fps
Muzzle energy	630ft-tons
Barrel life, approx	1200efc
Mounting	Single pedestal PIV*
Weight of cradle	7.5cwt
Weight of carriage	6.75cwt
Weight of pedestal	5.25cwt
Max elevation	20 degrees
Max depression	10 degrees
Rate of fire	20rpm
Crew	6

3in, 20cwt, QF MkI

Construction	Steel, wire wound
Calibre	3in
Nominal weight	20cwt 1qtr
Length oa	140.1in
Bore length	135in – 45cal
Weight incl BM	20cwt 10lbs
Rifling: Type	Plain section MkI
No of grooves	20
Length	117.385in
Twist	Uniform 1-in-30
Charge type	MD11 cordite
Full charge	2lbs 8.625ozs with 12.5lbs shell
	2lbs 2.625ozs with 16lbs shell
Average weight of shell	12.5lbs or 16lbs
Chamber pressure	17tons/in^2 with 2lbs 10oz charge and 12.5lbs shell
Muzzle velocity	2517fps with 12.5lbs shell
	2100fps with 16lbs shell
Range	23,500ft height with 12.5lbs shell
Rate of fire	29rpm at 50 degrees elevation
Mounting	Single HA MkII
Max elevation	90 degrees
Max depression	10 degrees
Weight of mounting	33cwt 22lbs
Weight of sighting gear	3cwt 1qtr 10lbs
Total weight incl gun	56cwt 2qtr 10lbs
Recoil	11in working, 12in max

6pdr, 8cwt, Hotchkiss, QF MkI

Calibre	2.244in (57mm)
Nominal weight	8cwt
Length oa	97.63in
Bore length	89.76in – 40cal
Weight incl BM	7cwt 1qtr 9lbs
Rifling: Type	Plain section MkI
No of grooves	24
Length	76.807in
Twist	increasing from 1-in-180cal at breech to 1-in-29.89cal 9.98in from muzzle then uniform
Charge type	Size 5 Mark I cordite
Full charge	8.6875ozs
Average weight of shell	6lbs Lyddite common MkI
Weight of burster	10.5ozs
Chamber pressure	16tons/in^2 (designed)
Muzzle velocity	1735fps
Muzzle energy	125.1ft-tons
Barrel life, approx	6000efc
Mounting	HA MkIc (c = converted)
Max elevation	60 degrees
Max depression	8 degrees

The 12pdr, 18cwt guns were also of a new type and were also originally specified for the *Lord Nelson* class. They were the last, and most powerful, of a series of 12pdr guns to be produced for the Royal Navy. The gun was of 50cal, had a muzzle velocity of 2660fps and a high rate of fire. Its only disadvantage as an anti-torpedo-boat weapon was the light weight of the shell (12½lbs) compared with the 4in gun (31lbs) which replaced it in the battleships and battlecruisers that followed *Dreadnought*.

Considerable difficulty was found in positioning the 12pdr guns because of the limited size of *Dreadnought's* superstructure and the need to find positions clear of the blast of the 12in guns. Originally, a 12pdr gun had been positioned on each of the 12in turret roofs to serve as a sub-calibre weapon for short-range practice with the 12in guns. However, to obtain an adequate broadside of 12pdrs the number on the wing turret roofs was increased to two, and these were included as part of the anti-torpedo-boat armament. In addition, a compromise arrangement was adopted by placing four guns on the forecastle and four on the quarterdeck which, because of the blast effects from the 12in guns, could only be used when the main armament was not in operation. They were primarily intended as night defence weapons and it was expected that the guns would be dismounted and stowed on chocks on the deck during daylight to avoid their being damaged when the main armament was in use.

When *Dreadnought* first went to sea in October 1906 she carried twenty-seven 12pdrs, ten on the flying deck, two abreast the conning tower, two each on 'P' and 'Q' turrets, one each on 'A', 'X' and 'Y' turrets, four on the forecastle and four on the quarterdeck. During gun trials at the beginning of December it was found that the forecastle and quarterdeck guns were difficult to mount and dismount quickly and as the mountings and gun-sights were liable to damage during this operation, it was considered doubtful if the arrangement would ever be satisfactory. Bacon suggested a number of alternative arrangements, in particular the fitting of a second gun on 'A', 'X' and 'Y' turrets thereby providing all the 12in guns with a 12pdr for practice firing. During December the two port mountings on the forecastle, and the outer starboard mounting on the quarterdeck, were moved to the turret roofs, and she served with this rather odd arrangement until the end of 1907 when the remaining forecastle guns and the starboard mounting on the quarterdeck were removed thereby reducing the anti-torpedo-boat armament to twenty-four guns. The 12pdrs on 'A' turret and the remaining 12pdrs on the quarterdeck were provided with portable blast screens although it seems these were seldom rigged. In 1911 a fixed blast screen was fitted on 'A' turret but this was removed temporarily during 1912–13 when the turret was modified to take a rangefinder.

During her refit at Portsmouth during May and June 1915 the 12pdr guns on 'A' turret were removed and refitted in the original quarterdeck positions on the starboard side. In the following year during her April–May refit at Rosyth the 12pdrs at the after end of the flying deck were removed, giving her a 12pdr outfit of twenty-two guns. In 1917 two of the four quarterdeck mountings were converted to AA weapons and the two guns mounted abreast the conning tower on the boat deck were removed.

In 1915 two 6pdr HA MkIc mountings were fitted on the quarterdeck but these were replaced by two 3in HA in 1916. It is probable that the latter is why *Dreadnought* has been described as having four 12pdr AA guns at the end of the war as the 12pdr gun was also a 3in-calibre weapon.

Dreadnought was the first ship to be fitted with a new type of submerged torpedo tube known as the 'B' type. It was similar to the earlier design but had a 'chopper' rear door in place of a hinged door, which could be opened at the same time as the side door so speeding up the loading process. In addition, the bar (which prevented the torpedoes jamming in the broadside tubes as they were launched) was run-out by an electric motor instead of hydro-pneumatically. The stern tube (which did not have a bar) was removed in 1917 and the after torpedo-head magazine was converted into a magazine for the HA guns. The torpedo room itself was also converted to a HA magazine in 1918.

Fire control equipment

Although *Dreadnought* was built to take advantage of the latest developments in fire control, the system was in its infancy when the ship first went to sea. Suitable instruments for the transmission of information, and an organisation for the control of the guns as a group had been developed, but there were still many problems to overcome. It was found that the accurate ranging of guns required the control of cordite temperature, more accurate shell dimensions, corrections to allow for the wear of the gun and any misalignment of the turret roller paths and so on. The control system itself similarly required many corrections and it was not until just before the outbreak of war in 1914 that a full fire control system, including director firing and a central calculating station, had been developed to a reasonable level of efficiency.

Dreadnought's main control positions were the fore top and a platform on the roof of the signal tower. Either of these could be connected to the main TS (Transmitting Station) in the lower conning tower or the secondary TS in the lower signal tower. Each turret could be connected to either of the TSs so that any or all of the turrets could be connected to either control position through either TS. The system was designed to separate the circuits for the control positions from those of the guns to avoid damage to the control positions causing a breakdown of the whole system. Vickers' fire control instruments were provided for transmitting ranges and deflection corrections, while navyphones (telephones) and voice pipes (from TSs to control positions only) were fitted for voice communication. Each control position was fitted with a 9ft Barr and Stroud rangefinder.

The two TSs were on the middle deck and were thus above the protective deck and, although provided with protective bulkheads, vulnerable to shells passing over the top of the side armour. This point was criticised by Bacon who suggested that the main TS be moved to the deck below. This work was carried out during 1908–9, the 12pdr ammunition working space on the lower deck being reduced to accommodate the new position. At the same time the original main TS was converted to a plotting station, while a secondary plotting station was built on the port side of the lower signal tower. She was also fitted with Barr and Stroud rate-of-change instruments (communicating between the control positions and the TS and the plotting stations) and range indicators (for transmitting range information to ships in company) on the forward and after sides of the fore top. The latter were removed in 1910-11.

During 1912-13 the turrets were equipped for local control, whereby the sightsetting receivers could be operated from the officer's position at the rear of the turret, and 'A' and 'Y' turrets were equipped to serve as secondary control positions for all or part of the main armament. The latter involved the provision of additional fire control instruments, navy-phones and voice pipes to communicate between the TSs and the controlling turrets. During the same period the ship was fitted with a new fore top to carry a gyro-stabilised Argo rangefinder, and new rangefinders were fitted in 'A' turret and on the compass platform. She was also fitted with Evershed bearing indicators in the fore top during 1913-14.

Being the oldest dreadnought, she was one of the last to receive a director system although preparatory work for this began during her refit during May and June 1915. At this time the fore top was rebuilt to take the director tower, rangefinders were fitted in 'P', 'Q', 'X' and 'Y' turrets and the after control position was removed. It is not known exactly when she received her director, particularly as it was not unusual for work to be carried out in ships while they were at Scapa Flow or Cromarty. However, whatever the preparatory work, it had been completed by the end of 1915 and it seems likely that the system was finally fitted at Rosyth during April and May 1916. This consisted of a standard tripod type director in a tower on the fore top roof, together with the necessary follow-the-pointer elevation and training receivers at the guns. In director firing the guns could be controlled from either the director or from 'Y' turret and could not be split into separate groups. The director system was separate from the existing Vickers instruments which remained as a back-up-system. In 1917 the upper 12pdr magazine was converted to a TS, the lower position on the platform deck being more secure from action damage. During the same period that the director was installed a Dreyer Fire Control Table Mkl was fitted in the main TS. The last known modification to the fire control system was the fitting of Henderson gyro-stabilised firing gear to the director during 1917-18.

For Control of the anti-torpedo-boat armament, the 12pdr guns were divided into groups, each group being controlled from the fore or main tops. Communication was by means of what was referred to as telaupad control gear. In effect this was simply telephone communication, the telaupad being what we would now call earphones. The control officer was provided with a navyphone which communicated directly with the telaupads worn by the sightsetters at each gun of the group he was controlling, and also with the navyphone of a group officer positioned close to the guns. The system was simple and effective and was also used for the control of searchlights (from the compass platform) and as a secondary means of control for the main armament. The gear was portable and battery powered.

Armour

When Fisher gave the Committee on Designs its brief he stated that the uniform armament of 12in guns and the speed of 21kts had been fixed and that the armour should be 'adequate'. This clearly reflected his own lack of interest in armour protection, which he regarded as a restriction on a ship's speed. Although the implication was that armour could be provided on whatever scale was possible once the other elements of the design had been fixed, the DNC's department actually provided armour on the same scale as that fitted in *Lord Nelson*, which was substantially heavier than that of previous classes. However, the need to save weight resulted in the omission of side armour between the main and upper decks and, later, in the 1in reduction of thickness for the main belt, barbettes and turrets. In the *Lord Nelson* design the upper 8in armour provided protection to the bases of the 9.2in turrets as well as protecting the upper part of the hull whereas *Dreadnought's* 12in mountings had their own barbette protection and, presumably, the risk of damage to the upper hull was considered acceptable. Given the range at which she was expected to fight, the worst possibilities were damage to the funnel bases, a weakening of the structure around the wing turrets and the possibility of shells detonating closer to the protective deck. To reduce the last mentioned effect, the protective deck was made 0.75in thicker than that of Lord Nelson.

When Narbeth presented his paper on the designs of *King Edward VII*, *Lord Nelson* and *Dreadnought* to the Institution of Naval Architects in 1922 he stated that *Dreadnought's* protection was considered quite adequate and had not been reduced to save displacement. However, this was not accepted by Sir William Smith (Vice President of the Institution) who said the design was limited by financial and political considerations and that better protection would have been provided had it not been for this situation. This view was endorsed by Sir John Biles (one of the members of the Committee on Designs) who added that Phillip Watts himself was not entirely happy about her armour arrangements. Narbeth, however, argued that there was no secondary battery to protect; that the deck protection had been improved; and that openings were required in the side of the ship for the adequate provision of natural light and ventilation to the main deck. Given that *Dreadnought* was intended to fight, the latter seems a particularly weak argument and it would seem, therefore, that the balance was in favour of the views of Sir William Smith.

More serious was the general arrangement of the side armour that was provided. At normal load the top of the 11in main belt was only 2ft above the waterline and at ordinary deep displacement it was submerged over 1ft below it, leaving only a narrow strip of 8in armour to protect the waterline. In fact, the 11in armour was level with the waterline at about 20,000 tons, 2000 tons below her extreme deep displacement. A better arrangement would have resulted from a uniform belt thickness, although the maximum that could have been provided without increasing the displacement would have been 9.5in. Alternatively, the belt could have been raised to a higher level, but this would have altered the stability and may well have involved an undesirable increase in beam. It

TABLE 12: **Particulars of Protection**

Armour

Main belt (KC)	11in amidships (9in abreast 'A' barbette) tapering to 7in at lower edge
Upper belt (KC)	8in
Belt forward (KC)	6in
Belt aft (KC)	4in
Aft bulkhead (KC)	8in
Barbettes (KC)	11in/8in/4in
Turrets (KC)	11in sides, 13in back
Turret roofs (KNC)	3in
Conning tower (KC)	11in sides
Conning tower roof (KNC)	3in
Conning tower floor (KNC)	4in
Communication tube (mild steel)	8in
Signal tower (KC)	8in sides
Signal tower roof (KNC)	3in
Signal tower floor (KNC)	4in
Communication tube (mild steel)	4in

Protective plating

Protective bulkheads	2in to A, X and Y magazines and lower conning and signal towers, 4in to P and Q magazines
Main deck	0.75in, 1in over lower conning and signal towers
Middle deck	1.75in flat, 2.75in slope, 3in over A and Y magazines (slope and flat)
Lower deck	1.5in forward with 4in slope forward of A barbette, 2in aft with 4in slope abaft Y barbette and 3in slopes over steering gear

Armour weights (tons)

Side armour (incl fittings)	1876.33
After bulkhead (incl fittings)	110.86
A barbette	355.5
A barbette fittings	23.96
P and Q barbettes	429.74
P and Q barbette fittings	21.36
X barbette	185.38
X barbette fittings	9.66
Y barbette	196.33
Y barbette fittings	10.05
Conning tower (incl fittings)	52.97
Signal tower (incl fittings)	46.73
TOTAL	3324.87

does not seem that the armour arrangement was seen at the time as particularly inadequate, as the same basic arrangement was followed in all the later British 12in-gun battleships, although a number of detail improvements were made, including increasing the depth of the main belt.

One odd aspect of the arrangement of the side armour was the reduction of the main belt to 9in thickness abreast 'A' turret. This was also adopted from the *Lord Nelson* design and was repeated in the *Bellerophon* class though not thereafter. As it only saved about 15 tons in weight it cannot have been introduced as a weight-saving measure; protection of the machinery was obviously perceived as the prime requirement of the 11in belt. The after magazines were even less well protected as the 11in belt stopped at about the centre of 'Y' barbette, abaft which there was only the 4in side armour, although the decks in this area were substantially thicker. Another weakness, common to all British ships of the

period, was the reduction of the barbette armour below the level of the belt and away from the engaged side. *Dreadnought*, however, was designed to give protection against horizontal gunfire. Nobody at this time could have predicted the extreme ranges at which battles were to be fought during the First World War and the consequent dangers of plunging fire that were to result. Following the experiences of this at the Battle of Jutland, additional 0.75in–1in plating was fitted on the protective deck over the magazines (January 1917) and in 1918 new 4in armour roofs were fitted to the 12in turrets.

Dreadnought's deck protection was, in fact, a substantial improvement on that of earlier ships as it was both thicker and the material of improved quality. Earlier ships employed mild steel for the protective decks but with those of *Dreadnought* the upper thicknesses on the slopes of the protective deck amidships and on the thick sections of the protective deck fore and aft of the citadel were of KNC plating. In the *Bellerophon* classes and later ships this was taken a stage further and all the main protective decks were constructed of nickel steel.

Two further improvements were made on the *Lord Nelson* scheme of protection. First, the 6in lower and 4in upper belts at the forward end were altered to a uniform 6in thickness, and second, longitudinal protective bulkheads were fitted abreast the magazines and shell rooms as protection against underwater attack by mines and torpedoes. These consisted of layered plates of mild steel with a total thickness of 2in except abreast the wing turrets, where, to compensate for the closeness of the magazines to the ship's side, they were increased to 4in. Again this was taken further in the *Bellerophon* class where full-length protective bulkheads were provided.

Compasses

The ship's standard compasses, on the bridge and compass platform, proved difficult to correct because of the large masses of steel in the turrets that surrounded them and the close proximity of the funnel. In December 1906 a third compass was fitted on a raised platform on the quarterdeck, well away from the centre of the ship, from which more reliable readings might be taken. During the experimental cruise the initial correction problems were cured but, on Bacon's recommendation, the after compass was retained in case any further difficulty arose, and it was not removed until 1909.

Dreadnought was the first and only Royal Navy ship to be fitted with an electric compass. This, again, was provided to meet the changing conditions brought about by the introduction of fire control which required an immediate indication of the ship's' course and any alterations thereto close to the TS. This compass had been developed by Siemens and consisted of a magnetic master compass with an electrical device which could transmit the compass reading to remote electrically-operated compass repeaters. The master was positioned in the lower signal tower and the repeat compasses in the lower conning tower and after hand steering compartment. In practice, the gear proved difficult to maintain in a working condition and the system was not adopted. It was replaced with an

Anschultz gyro-compass in about 1911 and this was in turn replaced by a Sperry gyro compass during 1917–18.

Wireless

Dreadnought was originally fitted with a long-range Tune C, Mk II wireless set, with the wireless office on the flying deck just forward of the second funnel. In early 1910 this set was replaced by a more modern version, the Standard Installation Mk II, which was soon redesignated as Type 1. At the same time she was fitted with a short-range Type 3 set with an office in the lower conning tower. These sets were supplemented by a Type 16 auxiliary set and a Type 13 after-action set in 1917, and a Type 31 fire control set in 1918. The type 16 set was fitted in what was the lamp room (on the middle deck between 'P' and 'Q' barbettes).1t was intended that this should become the main WIT office and the Type 1 set be moved to this position, but the work was never carried out. The Type 13 set was fitted in a new office built next to the diving gear room (on the middle deck, starboard side of 'X' turret) and the Type 31 office replaced the upper 12pdr shell room on the platform deck (next to the new TS).

Telephone system

A central telephone exchange was provided on the lower deck for an extensive internal communication system linking the machinery compartments, senior officers' cabins, navigation platforms, wireless office, signal platform, conning and signal towers, capstan, torpedo rooms, etc. In total, there were forty-six connections on the exchange (excluding three extensions). The exchange lamps and call bells were supplied with power from a motor-generator but the speaking circuits were powered by batteries. This was an interim design, fitted only in *Dreadnought*, and in later ships the exchanges were all powered by motor-generators; *Dreadnought* herself was brought up to this standard in 1910.

In addition to this system, a large number of direct navyphone lines were fitted for the important communications concerned with the navigating and fighting of the ship. These included all those for the fire control system, connections between the main machinery compartments and the control positions, and from the signal tower to each torpedo tube. All this equipment was supplied by Alfred Graham and Co. Note should be made here that the principal difference between a telephone (usually fitted in cabins, etc) and a navyphone was that the latter was contained in a watertight box.

Modifications

Oct-Nov 1906: 24in searchlight fitted under fore top; pipes added to scuppers on ship's side; rangefinder platform fitted on roof of signal tower.

Dec 1906: Two port 12pdr mountings on forecastle and extreme starboard mounting on quarterdeck relocated on roofs of 'A', 'X' and 'Y' turrets; 12pdr gun port doors removed except for those in forward screen bulkhead; Kelvin Pattern 23 compass fitted on platform on quarterdeck.

TABLE 13: Boats

As designed: 11 Sept 1905
Two 50ft motor pinnaces*
One 40ft launch
One 36ft pinnace
Three 32ft cutters
Two 27ft whalers
One 30ft gig
For Admiral:
One 40ft steam pinnace
One 32ft galley
*It was hoped to fit motor-driven pinnaces. but no suitable design could be obtained.

As completed: Jan 1907
Two 45ft steam pinnaces
One 40ft steam barge
One 42ft launch
One 36ft pinnace
Three 32ft cutters
One 32ft galley
One 30ft gig
Three 27ft whalers
One 16ft dinghy
One 13ft 6in balsa raft
By 1909 one of the 45ft steam pinnaces had been replaced by a 50ft steam pinnace and the 32ft galley had been replaced by a second 30ft gig. By 1913 the number of whalers had been reduced to two and by 1917 one of the gigs had been landed. The outfit carried at the end of the war was as follows:

Sept 1918
One 50ft steam pinnace
Two 45ft steam pinnaces
One 42ft motor sailing launch
One 36ft pinnace
Two 32ft cutters
Two 27ft whalers
One 30ft gig
One 16ft dinghy
One 10ft balsa raft

TABLE 14: Complement

Complement

January 1907	692 (incl 69 marines)
January 1910	733 (incl 70 marines)
April 1910	798 (incl 83 marines)
December 1914	770
July 1916	810
September 1918	830

Make-up of complement for Mar-June 1913

Officers	50
Seamen	294
Boys	38
Marines	95
Engineering personnel	220
Other non ex rates	73
TOTAL	780

9–30 Apr 1907, refit at Portsmouth: Flagstaff added to fore topmast; flag deck moved to position abreast foremast*; semaphores fitted abreast each strut of foremast*; midship boats restowed fore and aft, and boats abreast forefunnel removed (area plated over) as a result of modified arrangement of signal platform*; portable blast screens provided for 12pdr guns on 'A' turret*; canvas ash chute at aft end of quarterdeck replaced by

Hull	£ 381,208	
Armour	£ 471,516	
Machinery	£ 319,585	
Gun mountings and shields	£ 382,205	
Incidental charges	£ 117,969	
Guns	£ 111,400	
TOTAL	£1,783,883	

Machinery tenders

24 June 1905	Vickers for main propelling machinery	£252,553
	Vickers for auxiliary machinery	£ 3,348
22 July 1905	Napier Bros for steering engines	£ 1,700
	General Engine & Boiler Co for air compressing machinery	£ 2,925
	Brotherhood for steam-driven dynamos	£ 1,850
	Haslam Foundry Co for refrigeration machinery	£ 790
	Pulsometer for ice making machinery	£ 350
18 August 1905	Mirrlees Watson Co for Diesel Dynamos	£ 7,230
29 September 1905	Armstrong Whitworth for hydraulic boat hoist machinery	£ 5,480

fixed internal chute*; pipes to scuppers on ship's sides removed and replaced by small lips on outlets*.

17 May–17 June 1907, refit at Portsmouth: Two small booms added at extreme after end for ship's boats*; new propellers fitted; rudders repaired.

19 Aug–9 Nov 1907, refit at Portsmouth: 12pdr guns on forecastle and on starboard sice of quarterdeck removed*; portable blast screen provided for 12pdrs on port side of quarterdeck*; name on stern raised by one deck; modified steering gear and new steering engines fitted; cowls over boiler room vents on flying deck removed and gratings fitted in lieu*; torpedo net shelves fitted abreast 'P' and 'Q' barbettes*; Sergeant of marines' mess and CPOs' mess on main deck extended*; stokers' wash places modified*; escape and vent added to fore end of engine room hatch; exhaust ventilation fans fitted to dynamo rooms and forward hydraulic engine rooms*; work started on fitting magazine cooling machinery*; sirens moved from fore funnel to searchlight platform on fore mast*; flag signal platform enlarged and signal lockers rearranged outboard of platform; boat booms on foremast struts removed; lower booms abreast 'P' and 'Q' barbettes moved forward to positions abreast 'A' barbette; blacksmiths' forge moved from starboard side of 'X' turret depression rail to quarterdeck.

31 Dec 1907–3 Feb 1908, in hand at Portsmouth: Aft low-power switchboard moved to clear cooling fan and ventilation trunk to 'X' magazine.

25 Feb–7 Mar 1908, docked at Sheerness: Completed fitting of magazine cooling machinery.

6–25 June 1908, docked at Sheerness: Platform and semaphore fitted on starboard side of compass platform; semaphores on signal deck removed.

Apr 1908–Feb 1909: Modifications spread over this period. Work started on replacing port diesel-driven dynamo with steam dynamo; main transmitting station moved to lower deck*; fire control plotting stations pro-

vided in lower conning tower and at port side of lower signal tower on middle deck; cabin accommodation modified; additional stiffening fitted under starboard diesel dynamo; corticine on decks in galleys, bathrooms, wash places, etc, replaced with tiles*; metal edge strips added to corticine on superstructure.

c1908: Stowed position for coaling derricks abreast bridge and on mainmast altered from vertical to horizontal.

19 Dec 1908–15 Feb 1909, refit at Portsmouth: Replacement of port diesel dynamo completed; work begun on fitting additional fire control instruments.

18–31 Mar 1909, in hand at Portsmouth: Admiral's shelter enlarged and converted to sea cabin, with Admiral's bridge on roof and new signal house built onto port side; cabin arrangements modified.

June–July 1909: Range indicator drum fitted on fore top roof and range indicator board on rear of fore top; on or before this date compass platform on quarterdeck removed.

25 Feb–12 April 1910, refit at Portsmouth: Torpedo stowing positions altered to take ten heater torpedoes; officers' lookout periscopes fitted to 12in turrets; submarine sound signalling gear fitted in provision room in hold forward; Type 1 W/T set replaced original main W/T and main W/T office enlarged; Type 3 short-range W/T fitted in lower conning tower; main guest-warp booms raised above level of net shelf; additional motor generator fitted for telephone exchange; additional fire control instruments fitted; range indicator drum moved from roof to front of fore top; 24in searchlight on foremast removed; steaming light post added to front of bridge; starboard 12pdr gun on quarterdeck removed.

Autumn 1910: Roof added to secondary control position on signal tower; range indicator on fore top removed (after the fitting of roof to secondary control position).

29 Mar–10 June 1911, refit at Portsmouth: Work begun on fitting Forbes speed indicator; fitted fixed blast screen to rear of 12pdr guns on 'A' turret.

16 Mar–29 May 1912, refit at Portsmouth: Began work on fitting 9ft rangefinder in 'A' turret which entailed the temporary removal of the blast screen on the turret roof (the turret was fitted with a temporary unarmoured hood for the rangefinder as the armoured hood was not yet available); began work on fitting range transmitters and receivers be-

*Modifications made as a result of Captain Bacon's recommendations following the experimental cruise.

tween transmitting stations and rangefinder in 'A' turret; fitted with new fore-aft fore top for Argo rangefinder; WOs' mess enlarged; coaling derricks on mainmast repositioned further forward and stowed vertically.

12 Feb–30 Apr 1913, refit at Portsmouth: Work on rangefinder installation in 'A' turret completed and blast screen replaced; bilge keels enlarged; 9 ft rangefinder fitted on compass platform; fixed blast screen fitted abaft 'Y' turret on starboard side to protect after 12pdr guns; painted draught marks amidships.

30 June–8 July 1913, in hand at Portsmouth: Main topmast was removed at about this time but it is not known on exactly what date - the work was, however, carried out before the following alterations.

9–23 Aug 1913, in hand at Portsmouth: Work begun on fitting Evershed bearing indicators in fore top; steaming light arm added on foremast below fore top.

26 Feb–2 Apr 1914, refit at Gibraltar: Fitting of Evershed bearing indicators continued.

7 May–7 June 1915, refit at Portsmouth: Control top rebuilt in preparation for fitting of director tower; platforms for 36in searchlight fitted on foremast struts; 9ft rangefinders fitted in roofs of 'P', 'Q', 'X' and 'Y' turrets; bridge wings removed; began fitting searchlight control gear; officers' lookout slot in rangefinder hood of 'A' turret enlarged, wind baffle fitted under slot; open sights fitted to all turrets refitted with rangefinders; control platform on signal tower removed; 12pdr guns and blast screen on 'A' turret removed; two additional 12pdr guns and two 6pdr HA guns fitted on quarterdeck.

Mid 1915–mid 1916: torpedo nets removed; fore part of navigating platform removed; director fitted on roof of fore top; fitted with Dreyer Fire Control Table MkI; aftermost pair of 12pdr guns on flying deck removed; third coaling derrick fitted on mainmast. It is probable that most of this work was done during her refit at Rosyth between 20 April and 25 May 1916.

Late 1916: Two 6pdr HA replaced by two 3in HA.

16–27 Jan 1917, in hand at Chatham: Additional 0.75in–1in protective plating fitted on middle deck over magazines; eye plates and fairleads fitted for paravanes.

23 July–19 Aug 1917, refit as Portsmouth: Fitted with anti-flash scuttles to magazine doors; lamp room converted into W/T room for Type 16 W/T set; searchlights arrangements modofied – all original positions (except platforms on for mast struts) being renoved, new searchlight platform, with four 36in searchlights, replacing maintop. Manipulating positions for new searchlights provided below searchlight platforms; stern torpedo tube removed; engine room lifts removed; sluice valve fitted on middle line engine room bulkhead; upper 12pdr magazine converted to transmitting station; fitted after-action W/T station outside diving gear room (on middle deck, port side of 'Y' turret); distributing office built in space available under supports of fore bridge on signal deck; after torpedo warhead magazine converted to 3in HA magazine; two of 12pdr guns on quarterdeck converted to HA mountings; pedestals for Evershed bearing indicators fitted on fore bridge; two 24in signalling searchlights fitted on signal deck; fitted bearing indicators to 3in and 12pdr HA guns; began work on fitting Henderson gun director gear and Sperry gyro compass.

1917: Deflection scales painted on 'X and 'Y' turrets.

1917–18: Fore topmast reduced in height; semaphore on bridge removed.

25 May–1 June 1918, refit at Invergordon: Upper 12pdr magazine converted to W/T room and Type 31 W/T fitted.

5 Aug–31 Dec 1918, refit at Rosyth: Glass shutters fitted in for top and a wind screen around the director tower; open director sights fitted in 12in turrets; open trainer's sight fitted to canopy of main director tower; pneumatic run-out gear fitted to 12in turrets; new 9ft FT24 rangefinder mounted in 'A' turret; fitting of Henderson director control gear completed; new 4in armour roofs fitted to 12in turrets; new control cabinets fitted in 12in turrets; fitting of Sperry gyro compass gear completed; Argo rangefinder moved to after end of fore top which was modified and enlarged to allow it to train round above the level of the foretop roof; wind deflectors fitted to officer of turret lookout hoods; paravane stowage modified; new 36in searchlights fitted; stern torpedo tube compartment converted to HA magazine; upper bridge fitted with canvas shelter and portable glass sashes at front and sides; improved flash protection provided for 12in turrets; aircraft flying off platforms fitted on 'A' and 'Y' turrets; stanchions and stays for hangar fitted on after platform and partially fitted on forward platform; work begun on removal of cruising turbines (not completed); a proposed fitting of turbo bilge pumps in all boiler rooms was never implemented.

Notes

1. See Oscar Parkes, *British Battleships*, p468. It seems unlikely that the DNC's Department was not aware of these designs given that Phillip Watts was a long-standing friend of Fisher. It is also worth noting the submission of designs with uniform 10in gun armaments (including one with sixteen such weapons) among those discussed for the *Lord Nelson* design and the fact that these were favoured by Watts, particularly as Fisher was at the Admiralty as Second Sea Lord from 1902 until the end of August 1903 when much of the early discussion of the *Lord Nelson* design was taking place.

2. The two US ships were the 16,000-ton *South Carolina* and *Michigall*, which were authorised in March 1905. The design was begun early in 1904 but it was not until the following year that a uniform big-gun armament was finally decided upon. The design was not completed until 1906 and they were laid down at the same time as *Dreadnought* was completing, in December 1906. Compared with *Dreadnought*, they had fewer guns but as all eight of their 12in were on the centreline (they had superfiring turrets fore and aft), the broadside fire was equal to the British ship while the reduction in end on fire was largely theoretical. In fact, they would have compared very well but for the fact that they lacked *Dreadllought*'s speed, having been designed for a fairly standard 18.5kts.

   The Japanese planned to construct two large battleships with twelve 12in guns but owing to difficulties in the supply of these weapons actually opted for four 12in and twelve 10in. The first of these ships, *Satsuma*, was laid down in May 1905 and completed in 1910. The second, *Aki*, was modified for turbine machinery which gave her a speed of 20kts compared with *Satsuma*'s 18kts.

   The Russian ships *Imperator Pavel* and *Andrey Pervozvannyy*, were designed before the Russo-Japanese War but were greatly modified as a result of war experience. They were never intended as all-big-gun ships although it is not known if the Russians considered this for new designs. They carried an armament of four 12in and fourteen 8in and, like the Japanese ships mentioned above, were equivalents of the British *Lord Nelson* class.

3. See Oscar Parkes, *British Battleships*, p468–71.

4. Ship's Covers. *Beneditto Brin* was an Italian battleship completed in 1905, capable of 20kts. It is interesting to note that Narbeth referred to these early designs as for 'Fast Battleships' indicating that he, at least, saw the principal novelty in the speed rather than the armament.

5. Given Fisher's original proposal for a ship of around 16,000 tons and the subsequent efforts to keep *Dreadnought's* displacement below 18,000 tons, it is not clear how it was thought that a 21,000-ton ship would be acceptable. One possible answer is a story related by Oscar Parkes (*British Battleships*, p473) that certain weights had been erroneously omitted from the original calculations for design 'E', producing a 3000-ton error – a fact revealed when the figures were checked by the DNC's department. However, it is difficult to believe that it would not have been realised that there was something seriously wrong.

6. See D K Brown, *A Century of Naval Construction*, p91. The normal working hours in Portsmouth Dockyard were eight and a half hours a day, five days a week, and five hours on Saturday.

7. What is at present No 3 Basin at Portsmouth Dockyard was, at the time of *Dreadnought's* construction, three separate basins – Nos 3, 4 and 5.

8. According to his memoirs, *From 1900 Onward*, Bacon joined the ship in June but it is possible this early date is mistaken as there are several minor errors, presumably of memory, in this book. For example, *Dreadnought* is said to have stuck in the entrance to the basin when leaving on her steam trials when this did, in fact, occur several weeks later when returning to the basin, and he actually states the *Dreadnought* had three propeller shafts when she had four.

9. Bacon, *From 1900 Onward*.

10. ADM116/1059, Report on Experimental Cruise.

11. The cruiser was HMS *Amethyst*, the destroyers were *Viper, Cobra, Velox* and *Eden*.

12. See D K Brown, *A Century of Naval Construction*, p87.

13. ADM116/1059, Report on Experimental Cruise.

14. Fremantle, *My Naval Career*, p161.

15. This probably occurred on 21 January when *Dreadnought* was returning to Gibraltar from Aranci Bay. Neither this incident, nor any other rudder jamming, is mentioned in Bacon's report on the experimental cruise but in the programme of events the phrase 'Read collision and grounding stations' appears under this date. Bacon does mention these incidents in *From 1900 Onward* and says he did not report them for fear of the ship being recalled.

16. Narbeth stated in *Three Steps in Naval Construction* that the skew gearing became deformed but this was the gear in the engine room which only had a slight helical angle on it. It seems more likely that the problem was with the bevel gears which had to redirect the shafting through a 90-degree angle, especially as this type of gearing is more prone to load problems. It is possible that in using the term skew, Narbeth was simply referring to gears providing a change in the direction of drive.

17. Ship's Covers.

Sources

PUBLISHED

Attwood, E L, MINA, RCNC, *War–Ships*, Longmans 1912

Babcock & Wilcox Ltd, *Patent Water Tube Marine Boilers*, 1907

Bacon, Admiral Sir Reginald, KCB, KCVO, DSO, *From 1900 Onward*, Hutchinson, 1940

Brown, D K, RCNC, *A Century of Naval Construction*, Conway Maritime Press, 1983

— 'The Design and Construction of the Battleship *Dreadnought*', *Warship*, Vol IV, Conway Maritime Press, 1980

Burt, R A, *British Battleships of World War One*, Arms and Armour Press, 1986

Dawson, Capt L, Flotillas, Rich & Cowan, 1935

Fremantle, Admiral Sir S R, GCB, MVO, *My Naval Career 1880–1928*, Hutchinson

Jellicoe, Admiral Viscount J of Scapa, GCB, OM, GCVO, *The Grand Fleet 1914–16*, Cassell, 1919

Marder, A J, *The Anatomy of British Sea Power*, Frank Cass, 1964

— *Portrait of an Admiral*, Harvard University Press, 1952

Narbeth, J H, CBE, MVO, RCNC, *Three Steps in Naval Construction*, Transactions of the Institute of Naval Architects, 1922

The Naval Annual, Edited by T A Brassey, Griffen, 1906, 1907, 1908

Parkes, Oscar, OBE, AINA, *British Battleships*, Seeley Service, 1966

Richardson, Alex, AINA, 'The Evolution of the Parsons Steam Turbine', *Engineering*, 1911

Sennett, R and Oram, H J, *The Marine Steam Engine*, Longmans, 1909

Southern, J W M, MIES, MIME, *The Marine Steam Turbine*, James Munro & Co Ltd, 1919

UNPUBLISHED

PRO = Public Record Office, NMM = National Maritime Museum, MOD = Ministry of Defence Library, CRO = Cumbria Record Office

Admiralty design and 'as fitted' drawings for HMS *Dreadnought* (NMM)

Vickers machinery drawings (NMM)

Vickers gun mounting drawings (CRO)

E L Attwood's Calculation Book (NMM)

Specification Book for the *Bellerophon* Class (*Dreadnought*'s is missing) (NMM)

Ship's Covers (NMM)

Ship's Books, ADM136/7. (PRO)

Dreadnought, Ship's logs, ADM53/19805–19812, 40179–40193 (PRO)

Report on Experimental Cruise, 1907, ADM116/1059 (PRO)

HM Ships and Armaments, various editions 1907–1921, ADMI86/–(PRO)

HM Ships Designs 1903–4, ADM116/964 (PRO)

ADMIRALTY HANDBOOKS

Torpedo Manual for HM Fleet Vol 1, 1911

Torpedo Manual for HM Fleet Vol 3, 1909 ADM186/365 (PRO)

Torpedo Drill Book, 1908, 1912 and 1914

Handbook for 12pdr QF Guns, 1913

Handbook for Fire Control Instruments, 1909

Handbook for Fire Control Instruments, 1914, ADM186/191 (PRO)

Director Firing Handbook, 1917, ADM186/227 (PRO)

Handbook of Naval Ordnance, 1907

Gunnery Manual Vol 1, 1915

Handbook for Barr and Stroud Naval Rangefinders, 1916, ADM186/205 (PRO)

Naval rangefinders and mountings, 1921, ADM186/253 and 254 (PRO)

Handbook of Captain F C Dreyer's Fire Control Tables, 1918 (MOD)

THE PHOTOGRAPHS

The *Dreadnought* is eased into dry dock at
Portsmouth in mid 1907. In the
left background Britain's second dreadnought, the
Bellerophon, is under construction. *(CPL)*

Dreadnought's double bottom framing was well advanced early in October 1905. The plate down the centre is the inner keel and the parallel lines immediately to the left and right of it are the first and second longitudinals. The flat plate on the extreme left is the 5th longitudinal abreast the forward magazines. This view was taken from forward looking aft. (*R A Burt*)

A close-up of the inner bottom and double bottom framing, looking aft. The station numbers are written (upside down) on some of the frames; the nearest is 82. (*R A Burt*)

Looking aft from amidships. A start has been made on fitting the inner bottom plating and the middle deck beams. Note the change in the form of the framing abreast the engine rooms. (*R A Burt*)

Looking forward from the starboard side. The vertical plating on the left is the middle line longitudinal bulkhead between the two engine rooms. (*R A Burt*)

The view from aft on 7 October 1905. The nearest bulkhead is that at station 206, at the after end of the after submerged torpedo room. (*R A Burt*)

The protective deck on 14 October 1905. The first layer of plating on the slope of the deck has been bolted into position ready for riveting. (*R A Burt*)

The forward end on 21 October 1905 showing the stem casting and contour plate in position. (*R A Burt*)

The protective deck on 28 October 1905 looking aft. The circular hole in the foreground is for the trunk of 'A' turret. (*R A Burt*)

Looking forward, the beams of the main deck being fitted in place. The designation on the nearest beam indicates station 162 main deck. Note that the beams have not yet been cut away from the circular opening for the trunk of 'X' turret in the protective deck. (*R A Burt*)

Dreadnought on her first day out of Portsmouth Dockyard, anchored at Spithead on 1 October 1906, 364 days after being laid down. She carries water measuring tanks abreast the mainmast, a temporary installation for measuring the loss of feedwater during her steam trials. (*Author's collection*)

The bridge and foremast at the time of *Dreadnought's* steam trials in October 1906. The 24in searchlight is not yet fitted to the platform under the foretop. (*NMM*)

Dreadnought's after funnel early in October 1906. The 12pdr gunport doors were removed in December. (*NMM*)

A close-up of *Dreadnought*'s forward superstructure early in October 1906. The after control platform above the signal tower has not yet been fitted. Note the 32ft cutter stowed athwartships, and the cowl top to the ventilator shaft abreast the after end of 'A' turret. The latter was replaced by a hinged cover before completion. (*NMM*)

BRIDGE & TRIPOD MAST OF H.M.S. DREADNOUGHT.

The forward superstructure, October 1906. (*NMM*)

Dreadnought at the time of her gun trials, 17–19 October 1906. There is a stack of cordite cases on the upper deck abreast 'A' turret. The only visible alteration since early October is the removal of the water measuring tanks. (*IWM*)

Another view, this time from the starboard
quarter, taken at the time of the October
gun trials. (*IWM*)

Dreadnought entering Portsmouth harbour after her acceptance trials in early December 1906. She was effectively complete but was to be further delayed by an accident while entering No 4 dock. Note that the 24in searchlight on the foremast and the control platform (less rangefinder) above the signal tower are fitted but she still carries the single 12pdr guns on 'A', 'X' and 'Y' turrets. (*IWM*)

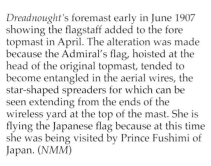

Dreadnought's foremast early in June 1907 showing the flagstaff added to the fore topmast in April. The alteration was made because the Admiral's flag, hoisted at the head of the original topmast, tended to become entangled in the aerial wires, the star-shaped spreaders for which can be seen extending from the ends of the wireless yard at the top of the mast. She is flying the Japanese flag because at this time she was being visited by Prince Fushimi of Japan. (*NMM*)

This rare photograph is of *Dreadnought*'s gun room on the upper deck forward, looking from port to starboard. Note the longitudinal girder to the deckhead and the two supporting pillars, the stove (in the centre against the forecastle side) and the gramophone on the table to the left. (*R A Burt*)

Dreadnought in mid 1907 with her portable
blast screen for the 12pdrs on 'A' turret
rigged. Note the new semaphore at the side
of the fore tripod strut. (*IWM*)

Dreadnought coaling in mid 1907. (*R A Burt*)

Dreadnought at the Fleet Review off Cowes
on 3 August 1907. (*IWM*)

Dreadnought in January 1905 just prior to sailing on her experimental cruise. A comparison of this view with a standard pre-dreadnought will give some idea of the impact *Dreadnought* must have had on the Edwardian public. Note the compass platform on the quarterdeck. (*PRO*)

Dreadnought in April 1908. (*NMM*)

A close-up of the bridge and 'A' turret during 1908–9. Note the additional semaphore on the compass platform (added in June 1908) and the new stowed position for the coaling derrick abreast the bridge. There is a signalling shutter over the nearest 36in searchlight on the boat deck. (*NMM*)

'X' and 'Y' turrets viewed from the port side of the funnel. The decks are cleared for gunnery practice, the awning stanchions and guard rails having been laid flat on the deck, and the mirrors and arc lamps removed from the searchlights. (*Author's collection*)

This view, taken at the same time as the previous photograph, shows the 12pdr guns and sighting hoods on the roof of 'X' turret. The 12pdr guns were linked directly to the 12in guns for short-range practice. The connecting rod for the nearest gun is just visible between the pedestal and the breach. (*Author's collection*)

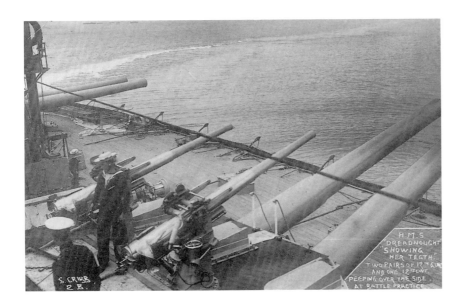

The forecastle and compass platform viewed from the foretop in about 1909. A number of canvas strips are laid out on the deck. (*Author's collection*)

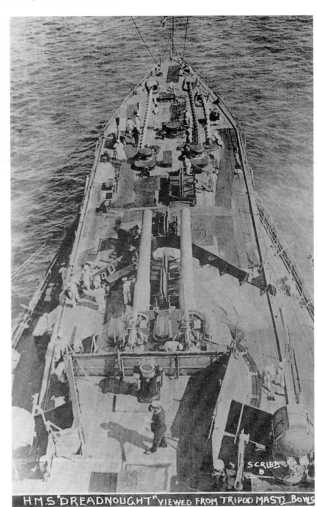

57

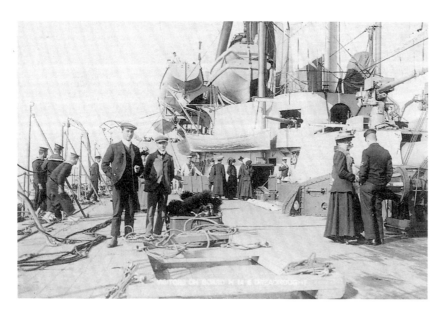

Members of the public viewing the ship in about 1909. This view is taken from the port side of the mainmast looking forward. To the right of the group on the right is one of the ship's coaling winches and to their left can be seen the port end of the depression rail for 'X' turret. Above them, on 'X' turret roof, the 12pdr guns have boxes fitted over their sighting gear to protect the gear from damage and the weather. Below the nearest whaler, on the side of the superstructure, is an open skylight and beyond that the open hatch cover to a mess deck ladderway. (*Author's collection*)

'A' turret and the bridge viewed from the forecastle during a visit by the ship to Southend during 17–24 July 1909. Note the recently added range indicator drum on the foretop roof. (*IWM*)

Dreadnought in the latter half of 1909.
(*IWM*)

Dreadnought at Portland following her major refit carried out between February and April 1910. The range indicator drum has been moved to the face of the foretop and the 24in searchlight on the foremast removed. (*Author's collection*)

Dreadnought during 1911–12 following the initial fitting of a fixed blast screen to the 12pdrs on 'A' turret. A roof has been fitted over the secondary control position and the range indicator removed. (*IWM*)

Dreadnought in 1912 following the fitting of her new foretop and Argo rangefinder. The blast screen on 'A' turret has been temporarily removed during the fitting of a 9ft rangefinder to the rear of the turret. (*NMM*)

Dreadnought in 1913 flying the flag of Vice Admiral Sir C Briggs, Commander of the 4th Battle Squadron. (*NMM*)

Dreadnought in the summer of 1914 following her last peacetime refit. The extensions on the sides of the foretop are for Evershed bearing indicators. Note the framework extending forward from below the foretop which was the final arrangement adopted to keep the steaming light clear of funnel smoke – the lamp was placed at the extreme forward end of the arm. The light was originally fitted on the front of the foretop but was later moved to the top of a post fitted on the front of the bridge before the arrangement shown here was adopted. (*IWM*)

Following the Spithead Review of July 1914 the fleet sails for exercises prior to the ships dispersing to their home ports. A few days later the entire fleet was to move north to take up its war station at Scapa Flow. *Dreadnought* is closest to the camera. (*MoD*)

Dreadnought undergoing a refit at Rosyth during April and May 1916. She has four 12pdr guns and two 6pdr HA mountings on the quarterdeck. The starboard mountings are clearly visible, under canvas covers, but the port mountings are largely hidden. Note the searchlight platform on the foremast strut, the director on the foretop, the absence of torpedo net booms and the additional coaling boom, the 30ft gig and the flagstaff on the mainmast. (*IWM*)

This view is taken from the port side of 'Y' turret looking forward. Note the removal of the 12pdr guns from the after end of the flying deck and the reduction of the size of the empty gunport. On the right can be seen the mushroom top vent to the after dynamo room and a closed skylight. (*IWM*)

'A' turret, the bridge and foremast from the forecastle in 1916. Note the cut-back navigating platform and the new supports for the compass platform. This view was taken at the same time as the previous photograph. (*IWM*)

Dreadnought in 1916–17. (*IWM*)

Dreadnought following her refit of July-August 1917. The maintop has been replaced by a searchlight platform and training scales painted on 'A' and 'Y' turrets. (*IWM*)

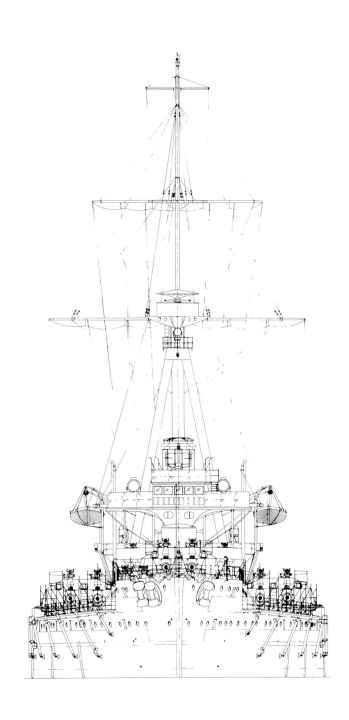

A General arrangement

A1   GENERAL ARRANGEMENT

A1/1   *External profile – as built, January 1907*
       (scale ¹/₃₂in = 1ft)

A1/1

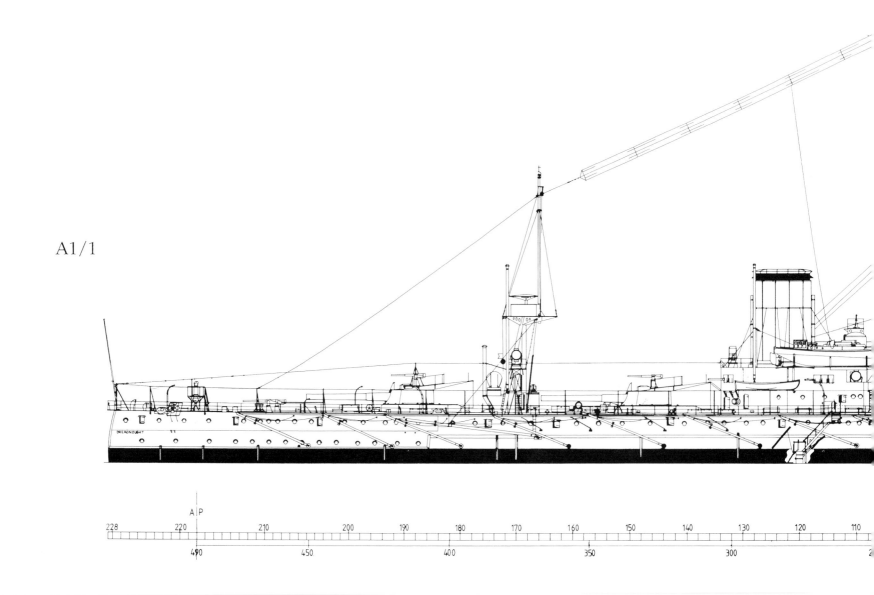

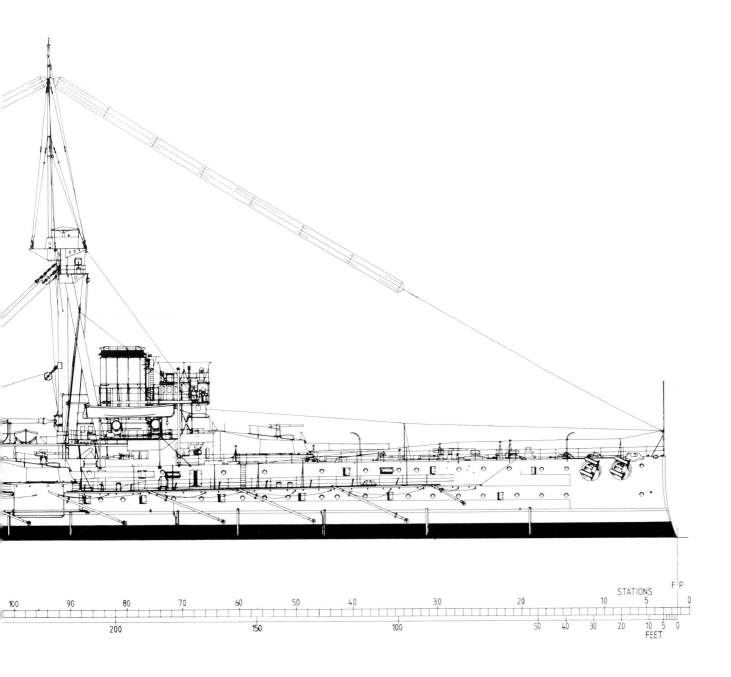

STATIONS

F P

| 100 | 90 | 80 | 70 | 60 | 50 | 40 | 30 | 20 | 10 | 5 | 0 |

| 200 | 150 | 100 | 50 40 30 20 10 5 0 |

FEET

A   General arrangement

A1/2   *View from forward, January 1907 (scale $1/8 in = 1 ft$)*

Note that parts of the superstructure abaft the foremast which would be visible have been omitted for clarity.

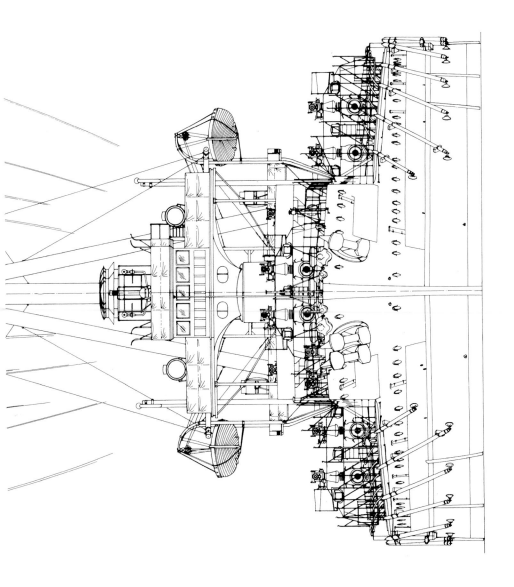

A1/2

A General arrangement

A2 HULL SECTIONS

A2/1   Longitudinal section – as built, January 1907 (scale ⅟₃₂in = 1ft)

1   Watertight compartment
2   Oil fuel tank
3   Reserve feed-water tank
4   Air space
5   Engine room vent
6   Boiler room vent
7   Escape trunk
8   Seamen's head
9   Mess space
10   Paint store
11   Reading room
12   Tiller and stem torpedo tube compartment
13   After capstan
14   CPOs' and 1st class POs' WCs
15   Fresh water tank
16   Hand steering compartment
17   Torpedo head magazine
18   Trimming tank
19   Torpedo lobby
20   Lime store
21   Submerged torpedo room
22   Engineers' stores
23   Shell room
24   'Y' turret
25   Gunners' stores
26   Working space for 12in ammunition
27   12in magazine
28   Handing room
29   Engine room
30   Electric lift
31   Ice making compartment
32   Issue room
33   Engineers' workshop
34   'X' turret
35   Meat house
36   Boiler room
37   Fan chamber
38   Bakery
39   Flour store
40   W IT office
41   Signal house
42   Signal tower
43   Ash hoist
44   Distributing station
45   Admiral's sea cabin
46   12pdr dredger hoist
47   Chief of staff's office
48   Lower signal tower
49   Officer's cabin
50   Lamp room
51   Lower conning tower
52   Switchboard room
53   Coal bunker
54   12pdr shell room
55   12pdr magazine
56   Lower 12pdr shell room
57   Lower 12pdr magazine
58   Central telephone exchange (port side)
59   'A' turret
60   Chart house

61   Conning tower
62   Lobby to lower conning tower
63   Wardroom
64   Skylight trunk to lobby
65   Gun room
66   Medical distributing station
67   Torpedo lobby
68   Refrigeration machinery compartment
69   Space for spare armatures
70   Cable lockers
71   Lobby
72   Torpedo head and dry guncotton magazine
73   Bread room
74   Submarine mine store
75   Capstan

76   Hawse pipe
77   Admiral's domestic's mess
78   Domestics' mess
79   Boatswain's store
80   Admiral's store
81   Ward room store
82   Access to small arms store
83   Capstan engine room
84   Small arms magazine
85   Provision room

v   vent
AP   After perpendicular
FP   Forward perpendicular
WTB   Watertight bulkhead
WTF   Watertight frame

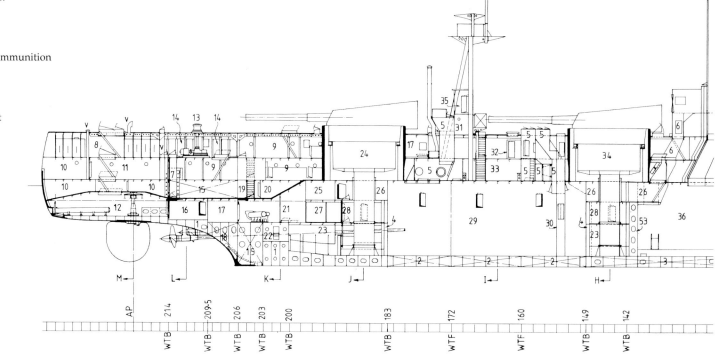

A2/1

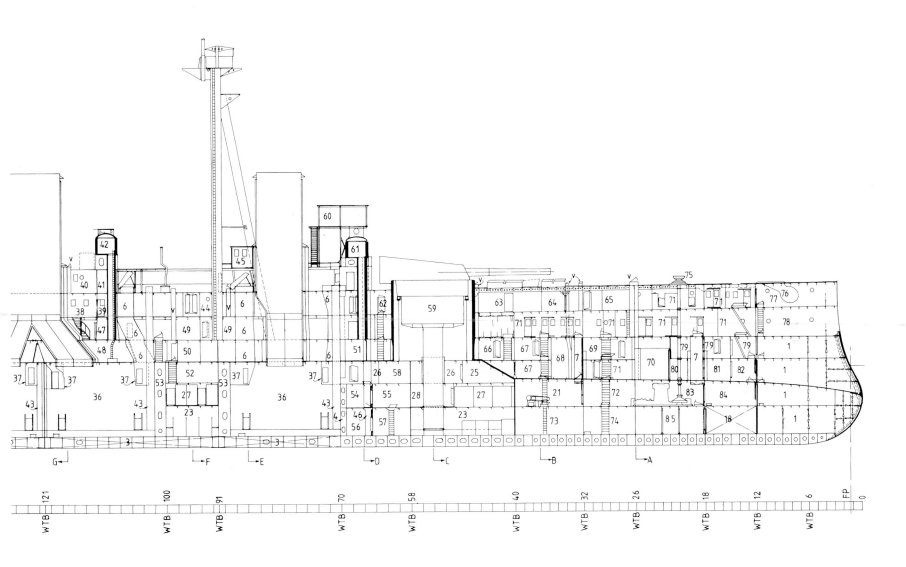

A General arrangement

A2/2 *Transverse sections – as built, January 1907 (scale ¹/₃₂in = 1ft)*

A   Flying (forecastle) deck
B   Upper deck
C   Main deck
D   Middle deck
E   Lower deck
F   Platform deck
G   Hold
v   vent

1   Watertight compartment
2   12in shell room
3   12in magazine
4   12in handing room
5   Reserve feed tank
6   Coal bunker
7   Oil fuel
8   Officers' smoking room
9   Cabin
10 Ward room galley
11 Cable locker
12 Capstan engine room
13 Provision room
14 Bread room
15 Spirit room
16 Submerged torpedo room
17 Torpedo lobby
18 Refrigeration chamber
19 Electrical store and acid room
20 Marines' slops
21 Chart and chronometer room
22 Passage
23 Ward room
24 Skylight and vent
25 'A' barbette
26 Flour store
27 Working space for 12in ammunition
28 Captain's store
29 Ward room stores
30 Admiral's sleeping cabin
31 Conning tower
32 12pdr dredger hoists
33 Admiral's saloon
34 Admiral's dining cabin
35 Lower conning tower
36 Admiral's store
37 Working space for 12pdr ammunition
38 Hydraulic machinery room
39 Hydraulic tank
40 Dynamo room
41 Store
42 12pdr shell room
43 Electric light store
44 Engineer's store
45 Admiral's sea cabin
46 Boiler room vent
47 Gun room commissioned officers' bath room
48 Hydraulic boat hoisting machinery
49 Fan chamber
50 Platform
51 Boiler room
52 'P' barbette
53 'Q' barbette
54 Lamp room
55 Switchboard room
56 Space for steam pipes
57 Patent fuel
58 Bakery
59 Officers' WCs

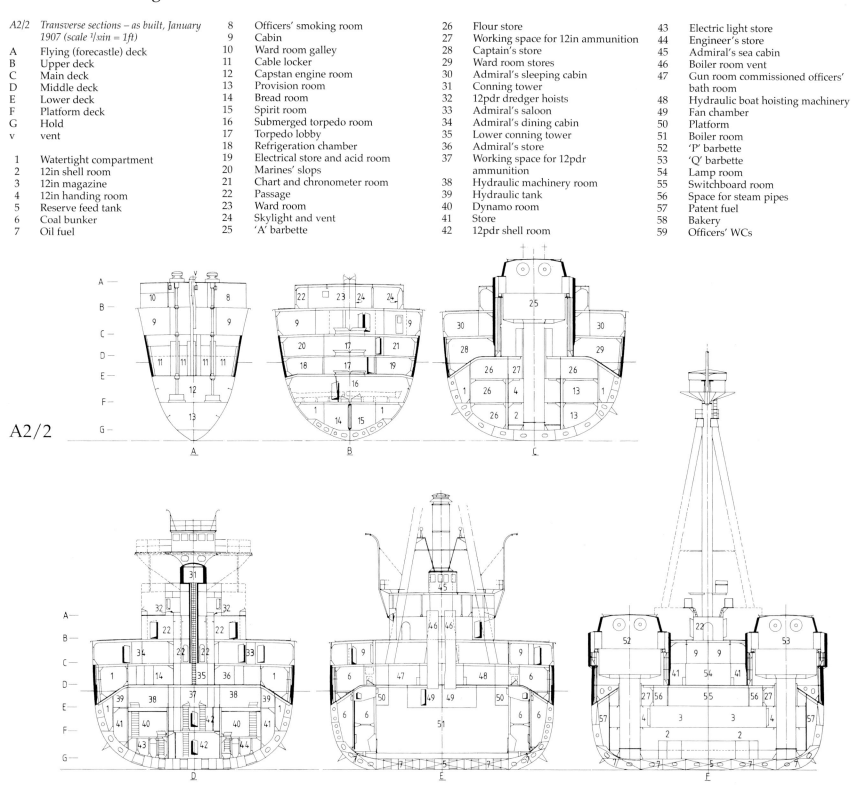

A2/2

60 Armament office
61 Police office
62 Gunner's store
63 Carpenter's store
64 'X' barbette
65 Seamen's wash place
66 Stokers' wash place
67 Engine room
68 Mess space
69 Sick bay
70 ERAs' mess
71 Engineer's workshop
72 Engineer's store
73 'Y' barbette
74 Sergeants of marines' mess
75 Cooks' kitchen
76 Diving gear
77 Electricians' and armourers'
   workshop
78 Ready use bread room

79 Canvas and cordage room
80 Canteen store
81 Compressed air reservoirs
82 Dry canteen
83 First class POs' mess
84 Sand store
85 Lime store
86 Escape trunk
87 Prison
88 Chief and first class POs' WCs
89 Ship's corporals
90 Fresh water tank
91 Boatswain's store
92 Hand steering compartment
93 Seamen's head
94 Reading room
95 Paint store
96 Stern torpedo tube and tiller
   compartment

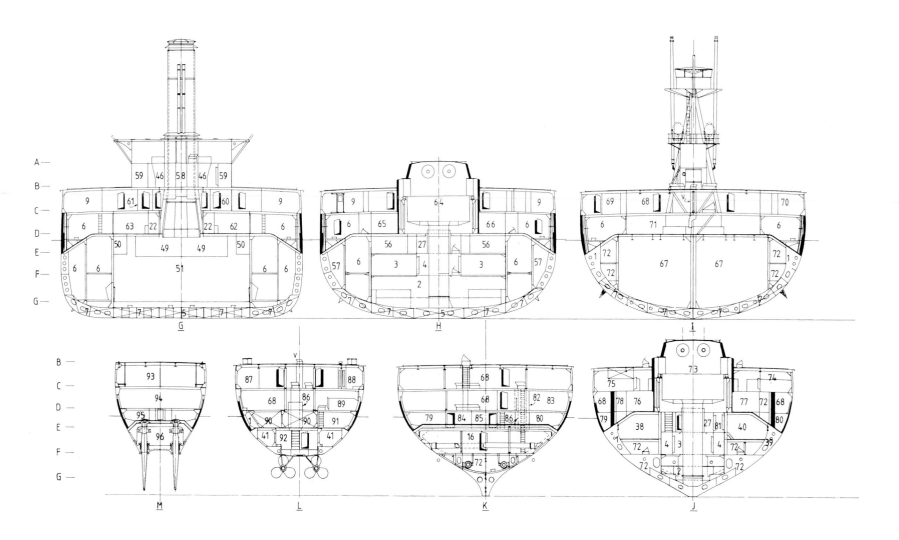

A General arrangement

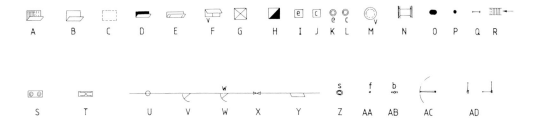

KEY TO A3 PLAN VIEWS

A   Hatch (ladderway)
B   Hatch (t = torpedo hatch, a = ammunition embarkation hatch)
C   Hatch (over)
D   Skylight (light and vent)
E   Wash deck locker
F   Vent trunk top
G   Vent trunk
H   Escape and access trunk
I   Escape from coal bunkers
J   Coal shoot
K   Escape trunk scuttle
L   Coal scuttle
M   Mushroom top vent
N   Hawser reel
O   Manhole
P   Vent pipe
Q   Vertical ladder
R   Ladder (arrow indicates bottom)
S   Bollard
T   Fairlead
U   Side scuttle
V   Door
W   Side port
X   Opening in bulkhead
Y   Opening in bulkhead with horizontally hinged cover
Z   Scupper
AA   Stove funnel
AB   Davit bollard
AC   Davit
AD   Awning stanchions

*A3/1   Boat deck, bridge, tops etc – as built,
January 1907 (scale ¹/₃₂in = 1ft)*

A3/1

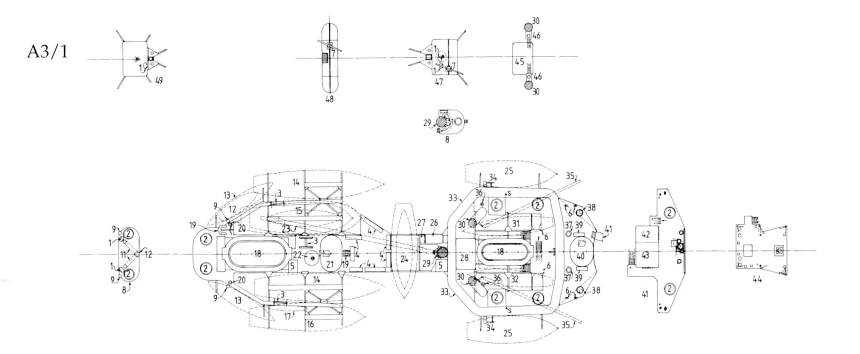

1	Manhole	15	42ft launch/ 36ft pinnace/ 27ft whaler
2	Searchlight	16	40ft steam barge (Admiral's barge)
3	Hawser reel	17	13ft 6in balsa raft (under)
4	Signal (flag) locker	18	funnel
5	Sanitary tank	19	Anchor
6	Pillar	20	Stump mast
7	Rangefinder	21	Signal tower
8	Searchlight platform	22	Main W/T aerial and screen
9	Coaling derrick	23	Main derrick (over)
10	Mainmast	24	32ft cutter / 27ft whaler
11	Mainmast strut	25	32ft (life) cutter
12	16ft dinghy (under)	26	Casing over hydraulic gear for operating main derrick
13	27ft whaler (under)		
14	45ft steam pinnace		

27	Hinged plate	41	Navigating platform
28	Admiral's shelter	42	Captain's sea cabin
29	Foremast	43	Chart house
30	Foremast strut	44	Compass platform
31	32ft galley	45	Roof of Admiral's shelter
32	30ft gig	46	Engine room telegraph tell-tale on platform (over)
33	Admiral's walk		
34	Bow light	47	Fore top
35	Boat derrick	48	Rangefinder platform over signal tower
36	Hole for boat hoist wires		
37	12pdr hand-up	49	Main top
38	12pdr gun mounting		
39	Searchlight locker		
40	Conning tower		

A   General arrangement

A3/2   Flying (forecastle) deck – as built, January 1907 (scale 1/32in = 1ft)

1   Coaling derrick
2   12pdr gun mounting
3   Boiler room vent
4   Ash hoist
5   Electric coaling winch
6   Engine room vent
7   Pillar
8   Mainmast
9   Stopper
10   Stump mast for coaling derrick
11   Mainmast strut
12   Meat house
13   Top of sanitary tank
14   Funnel
15   W/T office
16   Signal house
17   Communication tube
18   Searchlight
19   Expansion joint
20   Boat hoist fairleads
21   Foremast
22   Foremast strut
23   12pdr dredger hoist
24   Silencer to diesel dynamo exhaust
25   Stowage for torpedo dropping gear
     (for boats)
26   Seaboat davits (port and starboard)
27   'A' barbette
28   Breakwater
29   Ribbed deck plate
30   Deck plate
31   Capstan
32   Cable holder
33   Deck pipes
34   Hawse pipes
35   Net defence fairlead
36   Cathead
37   Platform
38   12pdr hand-up
39   Chocks for stowage of forecastle
     12pdr guns
40   Riding bitt (vent through centre)

A3/2

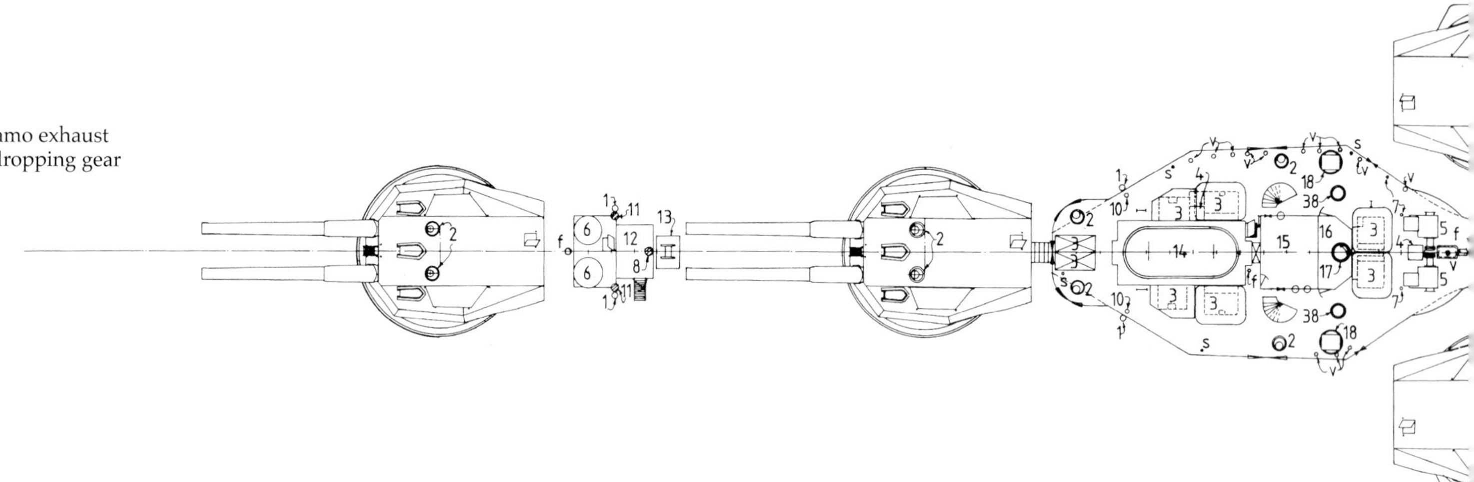

A3/3

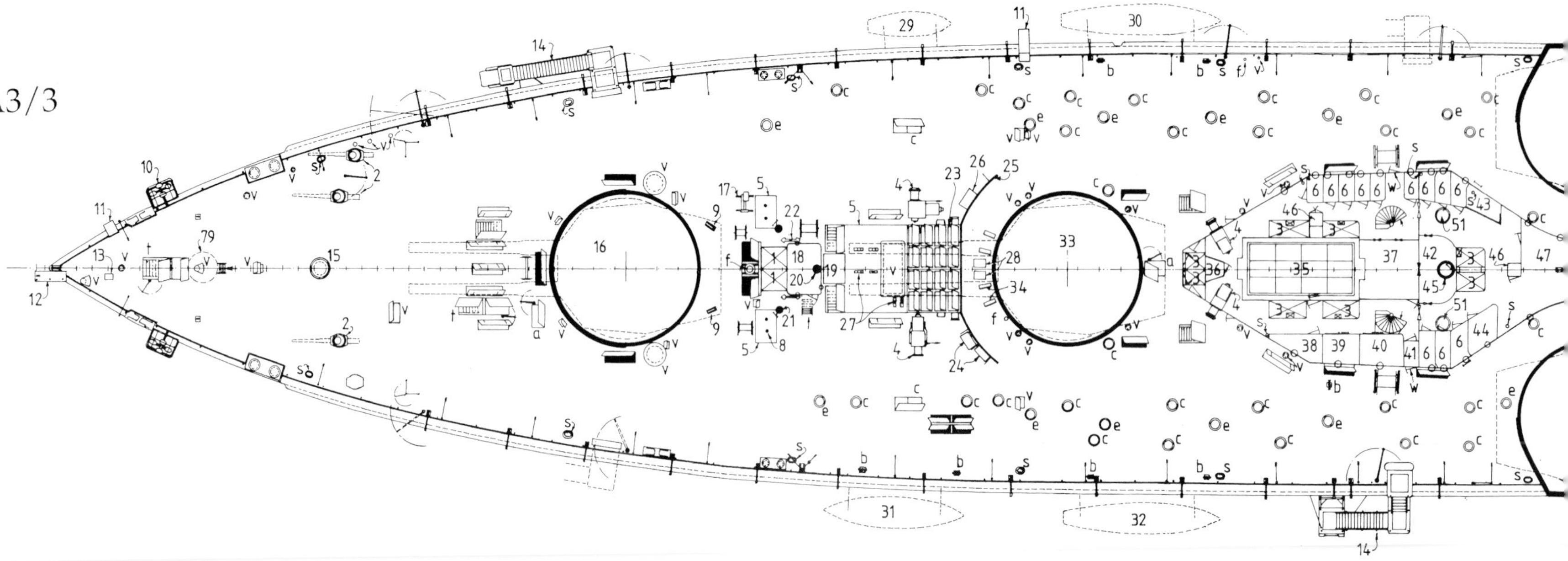

A3/3 *Upper deck – as built, January 1907*
(scale ¹/₃₂in = 1ft)

1 Engine room vent
2 12pdr gun mounting
3 Boiler room vent
4 Electric coaling winch
5 Ribbed deck plate
6 WC
7 Pillar
8 Oil fuel filling connections, port and starboard
9 Stopper
10 Night life buoy, port and starboard
11 Rubbish chute
12 Leadsman's platform
13 Sounding machine
14 Accommodation ladder (alternative position other side of ship)
15 After capstan
16 'Y' barbette
17 Loading teacher
18 Ice making machinery
19 Sanitary tank
20 Mainmast
21 Mainmast strut
22 Admiralty pattern kedge anchor, port and starboard
23 Engine hatch and engine room vent
24 Stowage for blacksmith's forge
25 Depression rail
26 Tank
27 Chocks for stowage of aft 12pdr guns
28 Electric lift
29 Harbour position for 16ft dinghy
30 Harbour position for 20ft gig
31 Harbour position for 27ft whaler
32 Harbour position for 32ft galley
33 'X' barbette
34 Chocks for stowage of collision mats
35 Funnel hatch
36 Metal locker
37 Bakery
38 Painted-canvas room
39 Boatswain's ready-use store
40 Carpenters' ready-use store
41 Bread store
42 Flour store
43 Officers' urinal
44 Gunners' ready-use store
45 Communication tube
46 Ash hoist
47 WOs' galley
48 Foremast
49 Distributing station
50 Passage
51 Hand-up for 12pdr ammunition
52 'P' barbette
53 'Q' barbette
54 Boat hoist leads
55 Quartermaster's locker
56 Admiral's lobby
57 Admiral's galley
58 Foremast strut
59 12in ammunition embarkation trunk
60 'A' barbette
61 Breakwater
62 Lobby to lower conning tower
63 Ward room ante-room
64 Ward room
65 Ward room pantry
66 Gun room
67 Gun room pantry
68 Ward room galley
69 Gun room galley
70 Deck pipe
71 Cable holder spindle
72 Capstan spindle
73 Officers' smoking room
74 Admiral's stewards' cabin
75 Admiral's cooks' cabin
76 Ward room stewards' cabin
77 Admiral's domestics' mess
78 12pdr dredger-hoist
79 Compass platform (over)

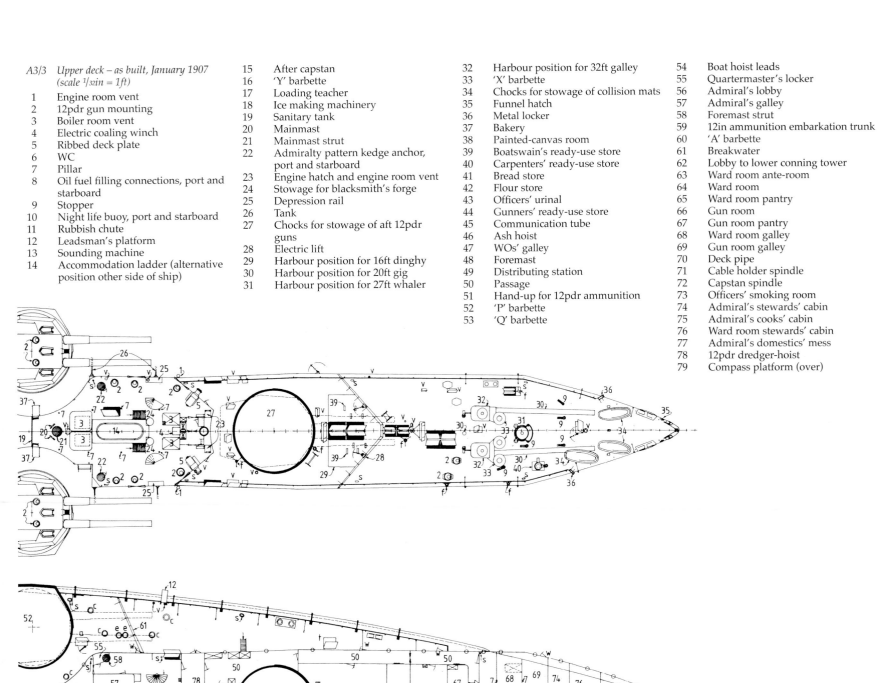

A General arrangement

A3/4 Main deck – as built, January 1907
(scale 1/32in = 1ft)

1 Prisons
2 Pillars
3 Boiler room vent
4 Ash hoist
5 Electric lift
6 Funnel hatch
7 Officers' cabin
8 Seamen's head
9 Spiral ladderway
10 Chief and first class POs' WCs
11 Electric capstan motor
12 Mess space
13 'Y' barbette
14 Sergeants of marines' mess
15 Master at arms' office (surrounded by low wall)
16 Cooks' kitchen
17 Ship's galley (not enclosed)
18 Engine room vent
19 Mainmast
20 Mainmast strut

21 Band instrument room
22 ERAs' mess
23 CPOs' mess
24 Issue room
25 Engine hatch and ventilators
26 Dispensary
27 Sick bay
28 WC
29 'X' barbette
30 WOs' cabin
31 WOs' mess
32 WOs' pantry
33 Engineer lieutenant's cabin
34 Engineer's office
35 Engineer commander's cabin
36 Ship's office
37 Paymaster's cabin
38 Fleet surgeon's cabin
39 Armament office
40 Chief of staff's office
41 Communication tube

42 Chaplain's office
43 Navigating office
44 Commander's cabin
45 Ash ejector
46 'P' barbette
47 'Q' barbette
48 Police office
49 Foremast
50 Foremast strut
51 Tank
52 Chief of staff's day cabin
53 Chief of staffs sleeping cabin
54 Chief of staff's bathroom and WC
55 Passage
56 Captain's day cabin
57 Captain's sleeping cabin
58 Captain's pantry
59 Captain's bath room
60 12in ammunition embarkation trunk
61 Admiral's pantry

62 Admiral's dining cabin
63 12pdr dredger hoist
64 Admiral's saloon
65 Admiral's sleeping cabin
66 Admiral's bathroom and WC
67 Midshipman's study
68 Admiral's Secretary's cabin
69 Secretary's office
70 Flag lieutenant's cabin
71 Lobby
72 Junior officers' bathroom
73 Cable holder spindle
74 Deck pipe for anchor cables
75 Capstan spindle
76 Domestics' mess
77 'A' barbette
78 12pdr hand-up

A3/4

A3/5

A3/5 *Middle deck – as built, January 1907*
(scale ¹/₃₂in = 1ft)

1   Cofferdams
2   Coal bunker
3   Pillar
4   Coaling trunks
5   Paint store
6   Reading room
7   Mess space
8   Dry canteen
9   1st class POs' mess
10 Engineers' stores
11 'Y' barbette
12 Electricians' and armourers' workshop
13 Engine room ventilator space
14 Medical distributing station
15 Diving gear
16 Engineer's workshop
17 Engine hatch and ventilator compartment
18 ERAs' washplace
19 Drying room
20 'X' barbette
21 Stokers' wash place
22 Chief leading stokers' wash place
23 Funnel hatch
24 Boiler room vent
25 Seamen's wash place
26 CPOs' wash place
27 Gunners' store
28 WOs' bathroom
29 Lower signal tower
30 Carpenters' stores
31 'P' barbette
32 'Q' barbette
33 Stores
34 Lamp room
35 Gun-room commissioned officers' bath room
36 Hydraulic boat hoisting machinery compartment
37 Ash hoist
38 Ward room officers' bath room
39 Dredger hoist (12 pdr)
40 Lower conning tower
41 Bread room
42 Admiral's store
43 'A' barbette
44 Captain's store
45 Ward room stores
46 Paymaster's slops
47 Gun room stores
48 Marines' slops
49 Torpedo lobby
50 Vegetable room (extends down to lower deck)
51 Refrigeration machinery compartment (extends down to lower deck)
52 Officers' bedding
53 Spare armature room
54 Space for spare armatures
55 Admiral's stores
56 Cable lockers
57 Cable holder spindle, port and starboard
58 Capstan spindle
59 Boatswain's stores
60 Watertight compartment
61 Ship's corporals
62 Cupboard for shovels
63 Ready-use bread room
64 Space for steam pipes
65 Electric lift
66 12pdr ready-use space
67 Edge of flat
68 Chart and chronometer room

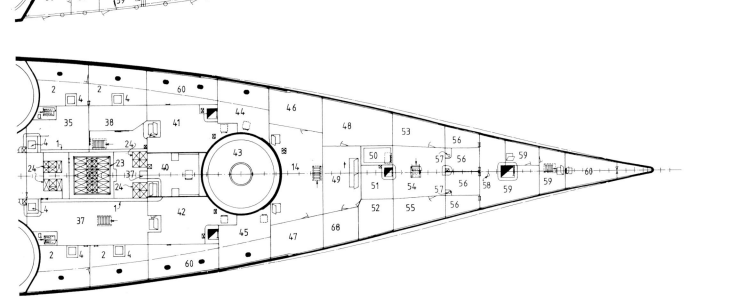

A General arrangement

A3/6 Lower deck – as built, January 1907
(scale ¹/₃₂in = 1ft)

1   Watertight compartment
2   Coal bunker
3   Pillar
4   Coal chute
5   12in ammunition hoist
6   Escape from lower coal bunkers
7   Watertight compartment and patent fuel stowage
8   Watertight hatch over rudder head
9   Engineers' stores
10   Paint store
11   Boatswain's store
12   Fresh water tank
13   Canteen store
14   Torpedo lobby
15   Lime store
16   Sand store
17   Canvas and cordage room
18   Knuckles of after protective deck
19   Lower edge of slope of protective deck (lower deck level)
20   Side at level of middle deck
21   Upper edge of slope of protective deck (middle deck level)
22   Gunners' stores
23   Working space for 12in ammunition
24   Compressed air reservoir storage
25   Dynamo room
26   Hydraulic machinery compartment
27   Steps
28   Hydraulic tank
29   Engine room
30   Electric lift
31   Space for steam pipes
32   Coal break
33   Space for spare hydraulic gear
34   Fan chamber
35   Ash hoist
36   Boiler room
37   Platform (floor is perforated plate)
38   Switchboard room
39   Flour store
40   12pdr dredger hoist, port and starboard
41   Central telephone exchange
42   Working space for 12pdr ammunition
43   Gunners' store
44   Meat room (refrigeration chambers)
45   Vegetable room (refrigeration chambers)
46   Refrigeration machinery
47   Electrical store and acid room
48   Ready use electric light store
49   WOs' mess store
50   Cable lockers
51   Admiral's stores
52   Ward room stores
53   Access to small arms magazine
54   Lobby

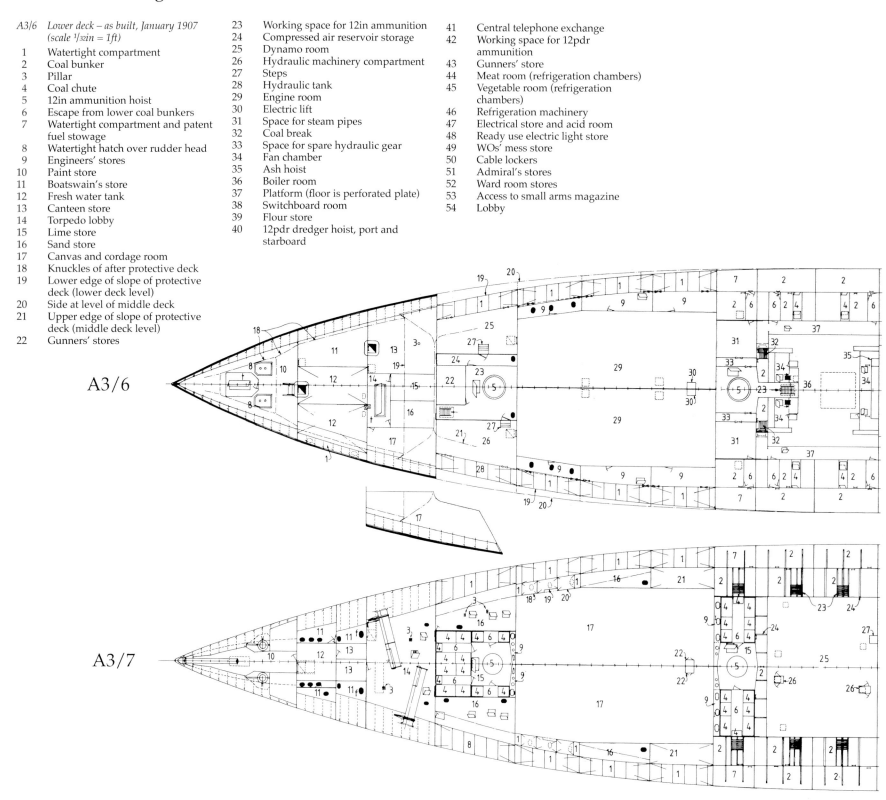

A3/6

A3/7

A3/7 Platforms – as built, January 1907
(scale ¹/₃₂in = 1ft)

1   Watertight compartment
2   Coal bunker
3   Pillar
4   Airtight cases for 12in cordite charges
5   12in ammunition hoist
6   12in magazine
7   Watertight compartment and stowage for patent fuel
8   Hydraulic tank
9   Air space
10 Tiller and stern torpedo tube compartment
11 Store
12 Hand steering compartment
13 Torpedo head magazine
14 Submerged torpedo room
15 Handing room
16 Engineers' store
17 Engine room
18 Olive oil, port and starboard
19 Valvoline oil, port and starboard
20 Mineral oil, port and starboard
21 Feed tank
22 Electric lift
23 Coal breaks
24 Stays
25 Boiler room
26 Air lock
27 Ash hoist
28 Dynamo room
29 12pdr shell room
30 12pdr magazine
31 12pdr dredger hoist
32 12pdr dredger hoist (over), watertight sliding shutter
33 Flour store
34 Torpedo head and dry gun cotton magazine
35 Capstan engine room
36 Small arms magazine

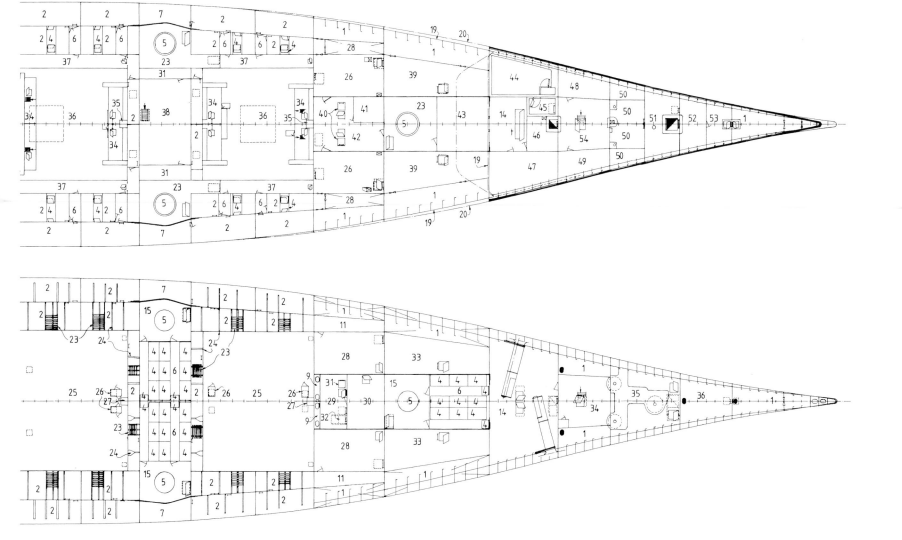

A General arrangement

A3/8 *Hold – as built, January 1907 (scale 1/32 in = 1ft)*

1 Watertight compartment
2 Coal bunker
3 Flat
4 Shell bin
5 12in ammunition hoist
6 Air space
7 Watertight compartment and stowage for patent fuel
8 Frames under torpedo and tiller compartment
9 Double bottom
10 Rudder casting
11 Portable plate (over)
12 Trimming tank (20.4 tons)
13 Fresh water tank (32.5 tons)
14 'A' bracket palms
15 Engineers' store
16 Shaft passage
17 'Y' shell room
18 Engine room
19 Olive oil, port and starboard
20 Valvoline oil, port and starboard
21 Mineral oil, port and starboard
22 Feed tank
23 Boiler room
24 Ash hoist
25 Cavity for ash ejector
26 'X' shell room
27 Pipe space under
28 'P' shell room
29 'Q' shell room
30 'A' shell room
31 Store
32 Lower 12pdr shell room
33 Electric light store
34 Recess for drain suction
35 Cofferdam
36 Lower 12pdr magazine
37 12pdr ammunition trunk with sliding shutter (over)
38 Supports to dynamo
39 Flour store
40 Provision room
41 Spirit room
42 Bread room
43 Submarine mine store
44 Trimming tank (52.4 tons)
45 Pillars
46 Electric lift

A3/8

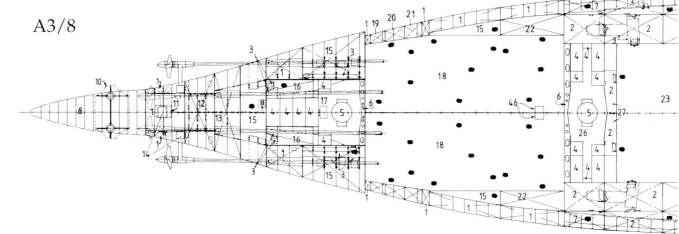

A3/9

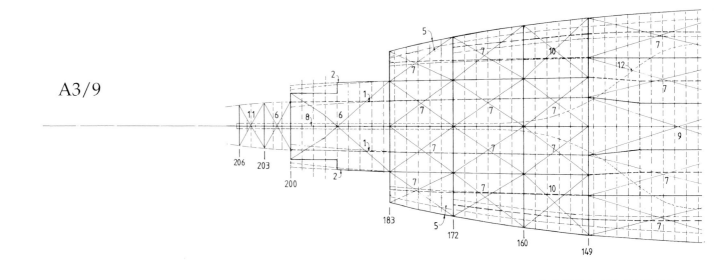

A3/9 *Double bottom (scale ¹/₃₂in = 1ft)*

1   1st longitudinal
2   2nd longitudinal
3   3rd longitudinal
4   4th longitudinal
5   5th longitudinal
6   Watertight compartment
7   Oil fuel tank
8   Keel
9   Reserve feed tank
10   Overflow feed tank
11   Fresh water tank
12   Edge of flat bottom
13   Edge of flat (over)

32–206 Station numbers for watertight frames

Note: Watertight frames and longitudinals are shown in solid line. Non watertight frames and longitudinals are shown in broken line.

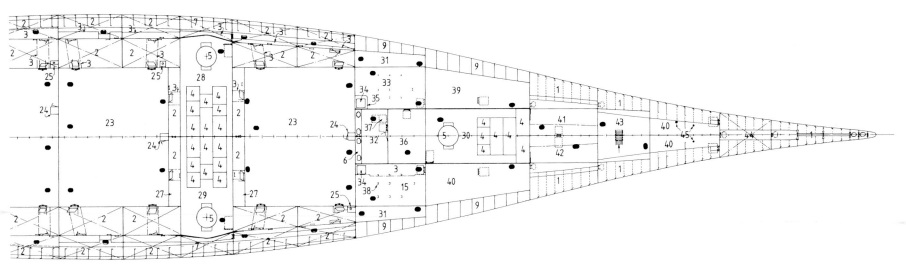

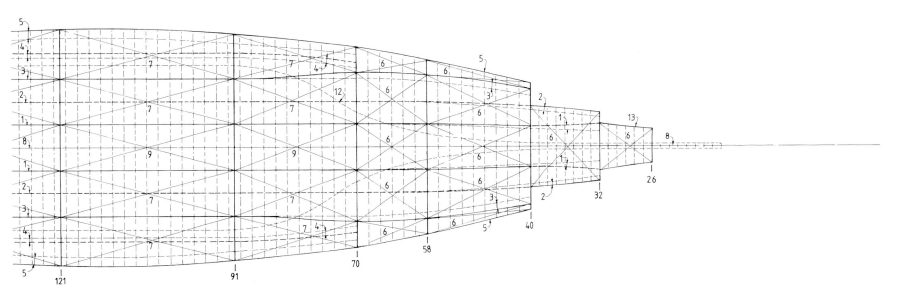

A General arrangement

A4 EXTERNAL PROFILES

A4/1 *External profile – April 1910 (scale $\frac{1}{32}in = 1ft$)*

Visible modifications made to the ship since the experimental cruise of 1907 and the years during which they were made are as follows:

1907: Flagstaff added to fore topmast. 12pdr gunport doors removed. Boat stowage amidships rearranged from athwartships to fore and aft. Portable blast screens added on 'A' turret and on quarterdeck (shown in broken line). 12pdr guns on forecastle and starboard 12pdr gun on quarterdeck removed. Small boat booms added at after end of quarterdeck. Ship's name on stern repositioned. Torpedo net shelf added abreast 'P' and 'Q' barbettes.

1907–8: Sirens moved from fore funnel to searchlight platform on foremast. Flag platform modified with outboard flag lockers (see also A4/2). Boat booms on foremast struts removed. Booms on ship's side abreast 'P' and 'Q' barbettes moved to position abreast 'A' barbette. Blacksmith's forge repositioned on quarterdeck.

1908: Semaphore added on compass platform. Stowed position for coaling derricks abreast bridge and on mainmast modified from vertical to horizontal.

1909: Compass platform on quarterdeck removed and blacksmith's forge relocated further aft.

1910 (to April): Short range wireless fitted (aerial just forward of bridge). Guest warp boom repositioned above net shelf. Range indicator drum fitted to front of foretop (see also A4/3). Pole for steaming light added to front face of bridge. 24in searchlight on foremast removed.

For further details of appearance changes see text and sections on rig and superstructure.

A4/1

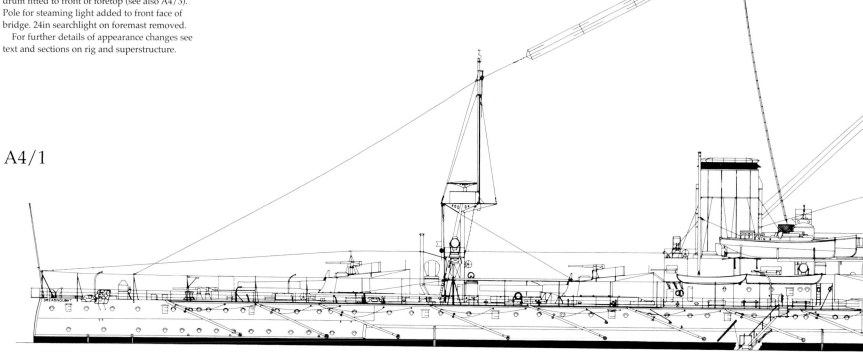

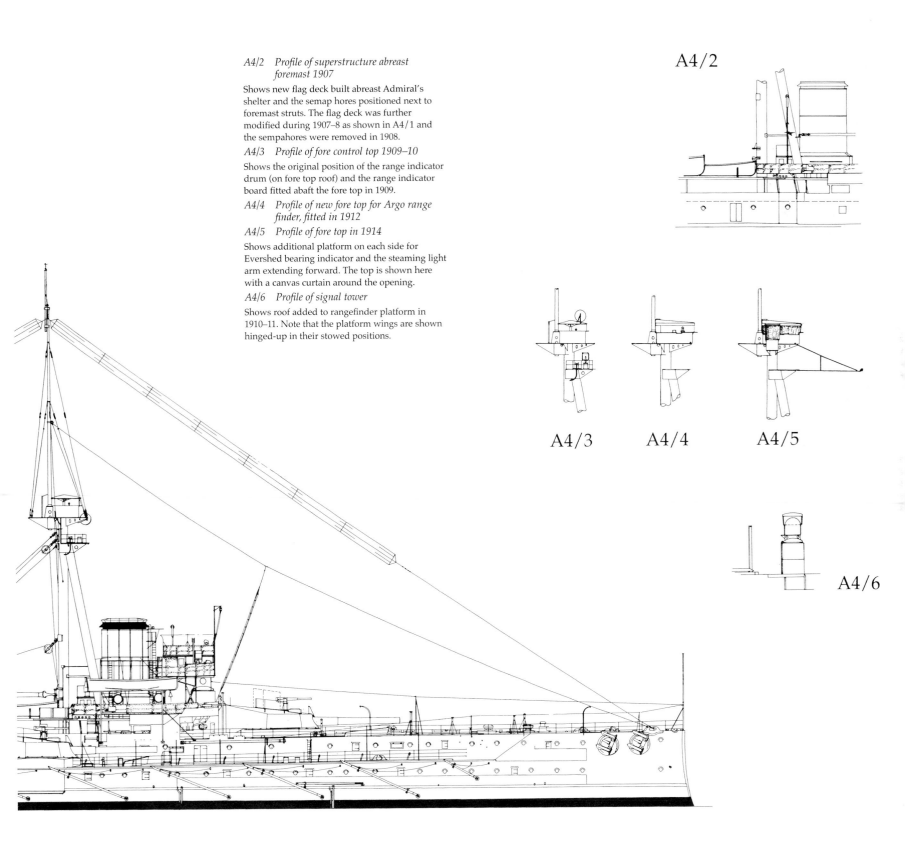

*A4/2   Profile of superstructure abreast
          foremast 1907*

Shows new flag deck built abreast Admiral's
shelter and the semap hores positioned next to
foremast struts. The flag deck was further
modified during 1907–8 as shown in A4/1 and
the sempahores were removed in 1908.

A4/3   Profile of fore control top 1909–10

Shows the original position of the range indicator
drum (on fore top roof) and the range indicator
board fitted abaft the fore top in 1909.

*A4/4   Profile of new fore top for Argo range
          finder, fitted in 1912*

A4/5   Profile of fore top in 1914

Shows additional platform on each side for
Evershed bearing indicator and the steaming light
arm extending forward. The top is shown here
with a canvas curtain around the opening.

A4/6   Profile of signal tower

Shows roof added to rangefinder platform in
1910–11. Note that the platform wings are shown
hinged-up in their stowed positions.

A4/2

A4/3   A4/4   A4/5

A4/6

A General arrangement

A4/7 External profile – June 1915 (scale $^1/_{32}$in = 1ft)

Note that this drawing shows the ship without
awning stanchions and stove pipes, the former
being seldom rigged in wartime and the latter
principally fitted in winter.

Visible modifications made to the ship since
April 1910 and the years during which they were
made are as follows:

1910–11: Range drum removed.

1912: Rangefinder in 'A' gunhouse roof. Coaling
derricks on mainmast repositioned and stowed
vertically.

1913: Rangefinder fitted on compass platform.
Main topmast removed. Steaming light arm
added to top of foremast, extending forward of
siren platform; pole on bridge front removed.

1915 (to June): Fitted with new foretop for
director but director not fitted. Bridge wings
removed and searchlights repositioned on new
platforms on foremast struts. 12pdr guns and
blast screen on 'A' turret removed, guns refitted
on quarterdeck. Two 6pdr HA mountings fitted
on quarterdeck. Rangefinders fitted in 'P', 'Q', 'X'
and 'Y' gunhouses. Rangefinder and platform on
signal tower removed.

For further details of appearance changes see
text and sections on rig and superstructure.

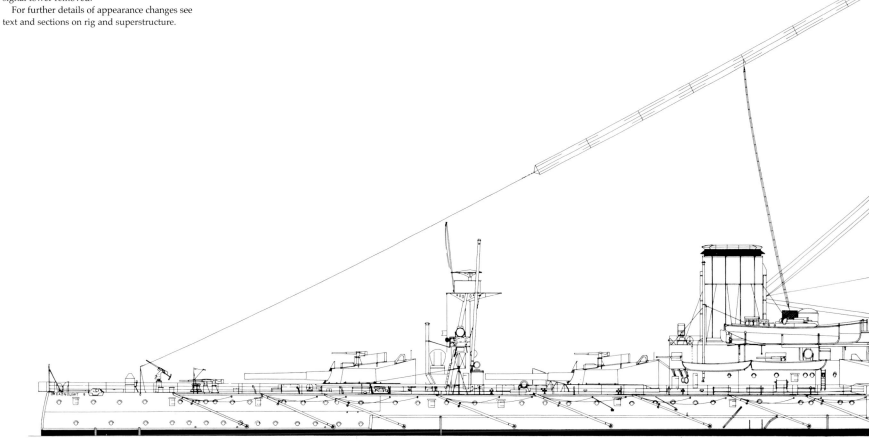

A4/7

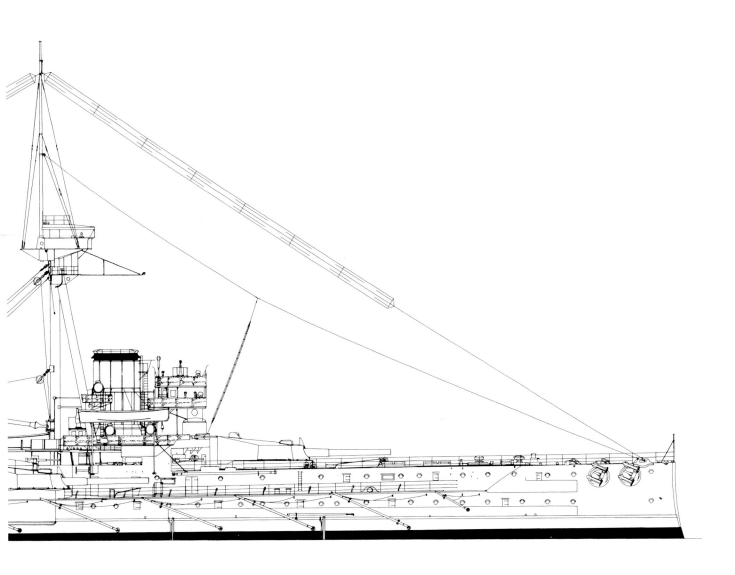

A General arrangement

A4/8 External profile 1918 (scale $^1/_{32}$in = 1ft)

Visible modifications made to ship since June 1915 and the years during which they were made are as follows:

1915–16: Director fitted to foretop. Torpedo nets and booms removed. Third coaling derrick fitted to mainmast. Navigating bridge above conning tower removed. Submarine lookout fitted abreast conning tower. Wireless rig modified.

1916: 6pdr HA mountings on quarterdeck replaced by two 3in HA mountings.

1917: Main top replaced with searchlight platform for four 36in searchlights. Control position for these fitted in place of original searchlight platform on meat house roof. Searchlights on boat deck and flying deck removed, two foremost on boat deck replaced by two 24in signalling searchlights. Two (inner) 12pdr gun mountings on quarterdeck converted to HA. Two 12pdr guns on boat deck removed. Carley rafts added to superstructure.

1917–18: Fore topmast shortened. Carley rafts added to sides of 'X' turret. Semaphore removed from bridge. Whalers abreast after funnel removed.

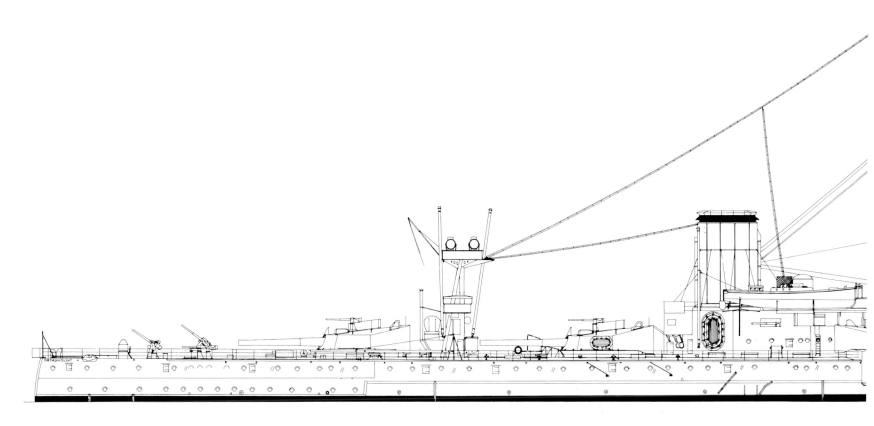

A4/8

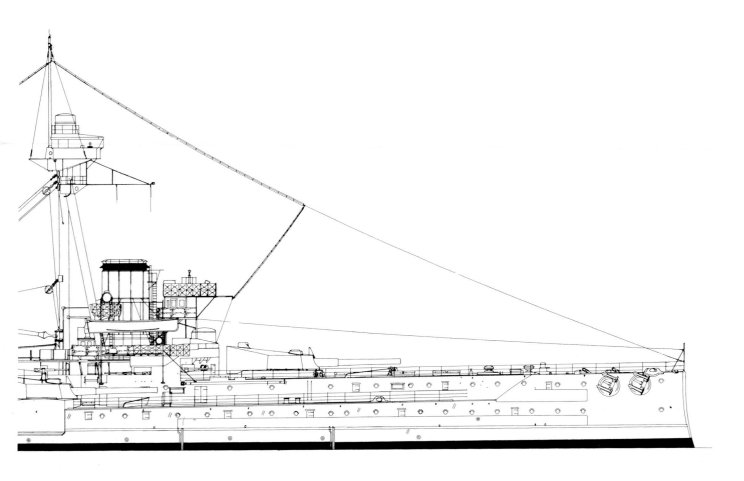

B Lines and constructional details

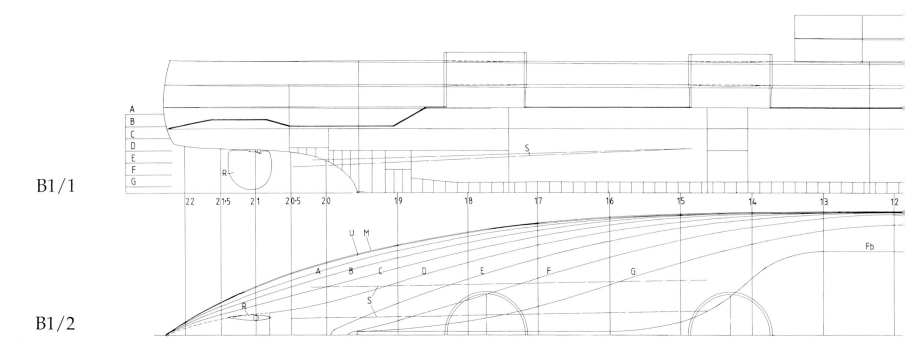

B1/1

B1/2

B1/1   Sheer plan (scale ¹/₃₂in = 1ft)

B1/2   Half breadth plan (scale ¹/₃₂in = 1ft)

B1/3   Body plan (scale ¹/₁₆in = 1ft)

1–22   Body transverse sections

(1 = forward perpendicular, ie the intersection of
the stem with the load water line / 21 = after
perpendicular, ie the centre line of the rudder
axis)

A–G   Water lines

(A = nominal load water line at even keel)

Fb   Flat bottom
FI   Flying deck at side
M   Main deck at side
P   Protective deck at side
Pr   Propellers
R   Rudder
S   Centre lines of propeller shafts
U   Upper deck at side

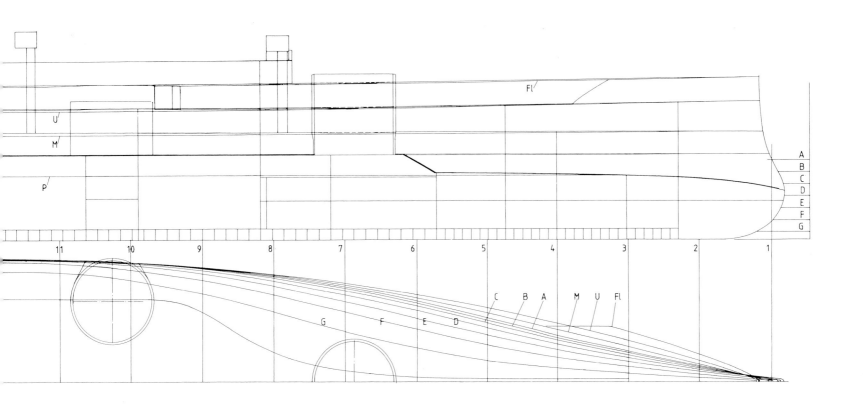

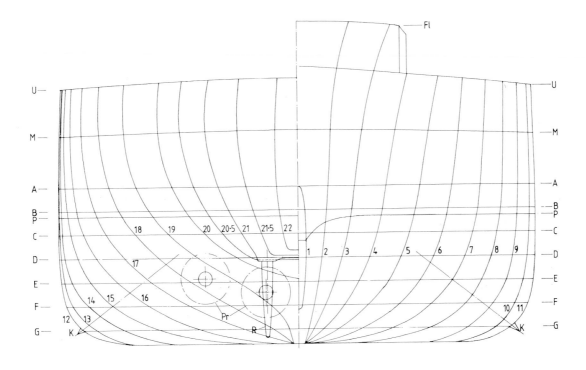

B1/3

B Lines and constructional details

B2 CONSTRUCTIONAL DETAILS

B2/1 Rivet forms

1 Pan head

This was the most common form of rivet. The tapered neck was to accommodate the similarly tapered punched hole in the plates to be joined. Rivets below 0.5in diameter and rivets intended for high tensile plates (which were drilled and not punched) did not have this taper.

2 Countersunk head

Employed in those areas where a flush surface was required on both sides of the assembled plates.

H   Head
N   Neck
S   Shank
P   Point

B2/2 Form after riveting

1 Countersunk point

Used for all areas of important structural strength and / or for watertightness. It also provided for a flush surface to the outer bottom (necessary to reduce skin friction), steel decks, etc.

2 Hammered or boiler point

Used generally for non-watertight internal structure.

3 Snap point

Used generally as 2 but provided for improved appearance in accommodation spaces, etc.

4 Snap point and head

As 3 but with pan head reformed into snap head by the riveting process. Used for minor structure such as cabin bulkheads, etc.

5 Countersunk rivet with countersunk point.

Employed principally to join three thicknesses of steel, the countersunk holes on both sides making it easier to provide for a watertight joint.

B2/3 Caulking arrangements

For watertight plating the butts and edges of plates were caulked by first spliting the edge of the metal, close to the joint, and then forcing the edge of the metal thus formed hard against the adjacent plate. In the drawings the caulking paints are arrowed. Where edge caulking was employed the plate edges had to be machined to give a close fit.

1   Lap caulk
2   Edge caulk

B2/4 Tap rivets

Threaded rivets used for structure that was either blind, as in joining plates to armour or castings, or where the structure had to be portable or there was insufficient access for riveting.

1 Standard form with countersunk head

The projection on top was used to screw the rivet home and was then cut off.

2 Hexagonal head

Used for internal fixing where a flush surface was not required.

3 Standard form with square recess

Used where it might be necessary to dismantle the structure for maintenance or repair.

4 Headless form

Used for securing lining behind armour in occupied areas in order to avoid the danger of flying rivet heads if the armour were struck during action.

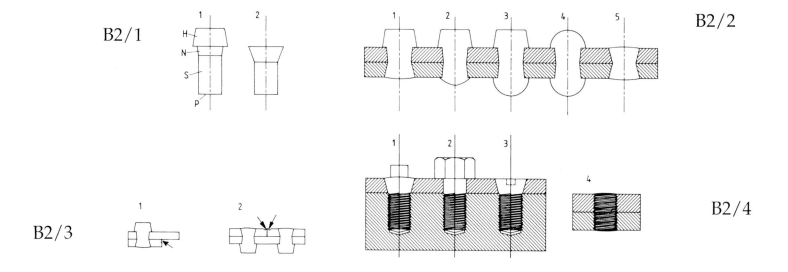

B2/5

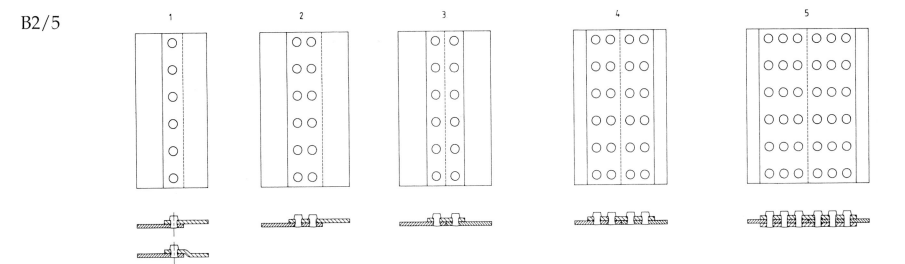

B2/5   Steel plate joints
1   Single riveted lap. Lower section shows a joggled lap
2   Double riveted lap
3   Single riveted, single strap
4   Double riveted, single strap
5   Treble riveted, double strap

B2/6   Rolled steel sections employed in Dreadnought

These sections were designated by size and weight, ie a zed bar 5in × 2.5in × 3in × 12lbs had a 5in centre web, 2.5in and 3in flanges and weighed 12lbs per foot.

1   Angle bar

Used throughout structure in various sizes for joining plates, as stiffening to bulkheads, frames etc. and for light intermediate frames.

2   Angle bulb

Used for deck beams and carlings to all principal decks but not to platforms.

3   Zed bar

Used for beams to platform decks, for stiffening bulkheads and for framing at forward and after ends.

4   Channel bar.

Used for stiffening.

5   Tee bar

Used as internal butt straps in construction of steel masts.

6   H or I bar

Used as stiffeners to principal watertight bulkheads.

7   Flanged plate

This is not a rolled section but a plate with a formed edge. Used principally for the upper edge of longitudinal bulkheads.

8   Half round

Used as a moulding to finish plate edges.

9   Segmental bar

Used as a moulding to finish top edges of hatch coamings, cofferdams etc.

B2/6

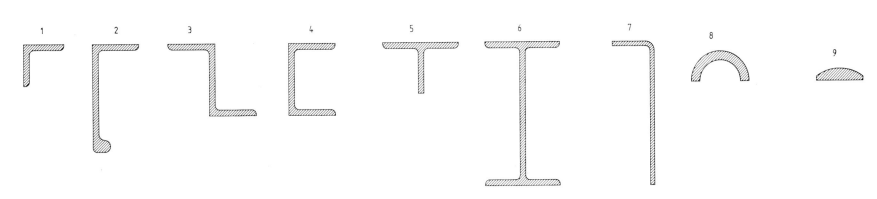

B Lines and constructional details

B3   KEEL (scale ¼in = 1ft)

B3/1   *Section of keel within double bottom – stations 32–200*

B3/2   *Part profile of keel under engine room (oil-tight) – stations 149–183*

Note – details shown for butt strap are the same throughout the keel.

B3/3   *Part profile of keel outside engine room (non watertight) – stations 40–149 and 183–200*

B3/4   *Section of keel forward of double bottom – stations 3–32*

B3/5   *Part profile of keel forward (non watertight) – stations 3–40*

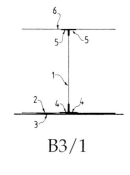

B3/1

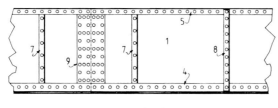

B3/2

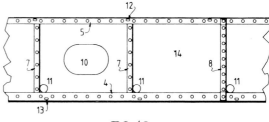

B3/3

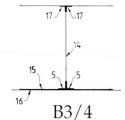

B3/4

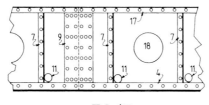

B3/5

1	Vertical keel plate, 25lbs
2	Inner flat keel plate 25lbs
3	Outer flat keel plate 30lbs
4	Angle bar 4.5in × 4.5in × 17lbs
5	Angle bar 4in × 4in × 13lbs
6	Inner bottom 17lbs
7	Angle connections of transverse, non watertight, frames
8	Angle connection of transverse watertight frame
9	Double butt strap to vertical keel plate (36ft intervals)
10	Access and lightening hole, 23in × 15in
11	Drain holes (4in diameter)
12	Air escape holes
13	Drain holes
14	Vertical keel plate, 20lbs
15	Inner flat keel, 20lbs
16	Outer flat keel, 25lbs
17	Angle bar 3in × 3.5in × 8lbs
18	Lightening hole, 15in diameter

B4 LONGITUDINALS INSIDE
DOUBLE BOTTOM (scale ¼in = 1ft)

B4/1 *Section of 3rd longitudinal (docking keel) Stations 79–137*

Note that outside these limits the 3rd longitudinal was of the same construction as that shown at B4/3

B4/2 *Part profile of 3rd longitudinal. Stations 79–137*

B4/3 *Section of longitudinal*

B4/4 *Part profile of watertight longitudinal*

B4/5 *Part profile of non-watertight longitudinal*

B4/6 *Part plan and section of 5th longitudinal. Stations 70–160*

The 5th longitudinal formed the outer edge of the double bottom. Note that from station 160–184 the 5th longitudinal was of the same construction as that shown at B4/3

1	17lbs plate
2	Inner bottom
3	Outer bottom
4	Inner plate, 25lbs
5	Outer plate, 30lbs
6	Angle bar 3.5in × 3.5in × 10lbs
7	Angle bar 4in × 4in × 13lbs
8	Angle bar 3in × 3in × 6.5lbs
9	Angle bar 3in × 3.5in × 8lbs
10	Angle connection of transverse watertight frame
11	Angle connection of transverse non-watertight frame
12	Drain holes (4in diameter)
13	Access and lightening hole, 23in × 15in
14	Treble riveted lap butt
15	Liners, filling space between angle bar and plate created by lap
16	Air escape holes
17	Drain holes
18	Angle to frames
19	Flanged edge to plate to connect with inner bottom
20	20lbs plate

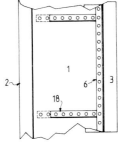

B4/6

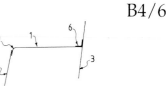

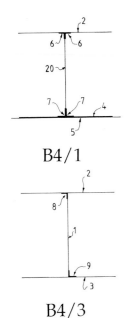

B4/1

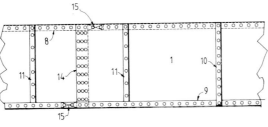

B4/2

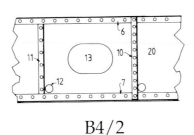

B4/3

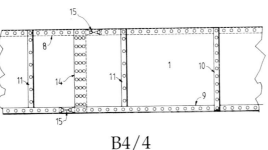

B4/4

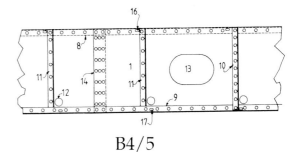

B4/5

B   Lines and constructional details

B5   DOUBLE BOTTOM

B5/1   Perspective view of double bottom, starboard side, forward

B5/2   Perspective view of double bottom, starboard side, aft

The double bottom extended out to the 5th longitudinals from station 40 to station 183 and out to the 2nd longitudinals as far as stations 32 and 200. In the drawing these areas are shown in solid line, the surrounding structure being in broken line except for the frames outside the 5th longitudinal abreast the engine room. This latter area, having both an inner and outer skin, formed a continuation of the double bottom up to the protective deck but was not strictly part of it as the inner bottom plating was worked between the bulkheads and not continuously. The transverse frames were spaced at 4th intervals except for a) the forward section between stations 32 and 40, where the spacing was 3ft, and b) the watertight

frames placed at the half-frame interval (2ft) at stations 91, 121, 149 and 183. The keel and longitudinals were continuous with the frames worked between them (intercostal). The double bottom was 3ft 6in deep generally but reduced slightly at the curve of the bilge, particularly forward and aft. In the drawing the watertight frames are shaded.

1   1st longitudinal
2   2nd longitudinal
3   3rd longitudinal
4   4th longitudinal
5   5th longitudinal
6   6th longitudinal

B5/1

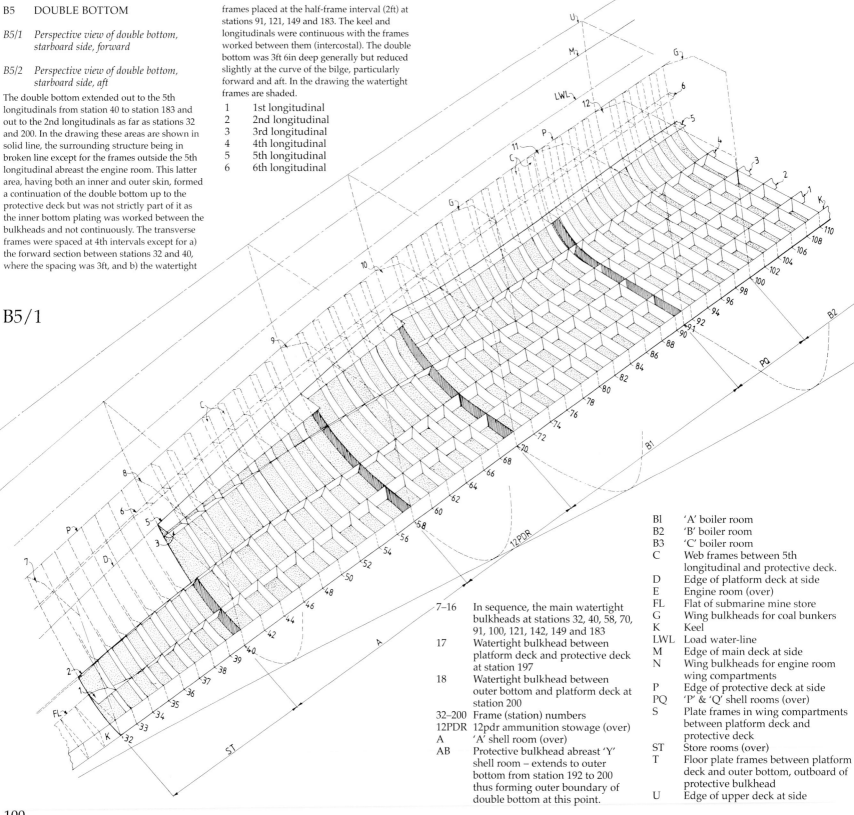

7–16	In sequence, the main watertight bulkheads at stations 32, 40, 58, 70, 91, 100, 121, 142, 149 and 183
17	Watertight bulkhead between platform deck and protective deck at station 197
18	Watertight bulkhead between outer bottom and platform deck at station 200
32–200	Frame (station) numbers
12PDR	12pdr ammunition stowage (over)
A	'A' shell room (over)
AB	Protective bulkhead abreast 'Y' shell room – extends to outer bottom from station 192 to 200 thus forming outer boundary of double bottom at this point.

Bl	'A' boiler room
B2	'B' boiler room
B3	'C' boiler room
C	Web frames between 5th longitudinal and protective deck.
D	Edge of platform deck at side
E	Engine room (over)
FL	Flat of submarine mine store
G	Wing bulkheads for coal bunkers
K	Keel
LWL	Load water-line
M	Edge of main deck at side
N	Wing bulkheads for engine room wing compartments
P	Edge of protective deck at side
PQ	'P' & 'Q' shell rooms (over)
S	Plate frames in wing compartments between platform deck and protective deck
ST	Store rooms (over)
T	Floor plate frames between platform deck and outer bottom, outboard of protective bulkhead
U	Edge of upper deck at side

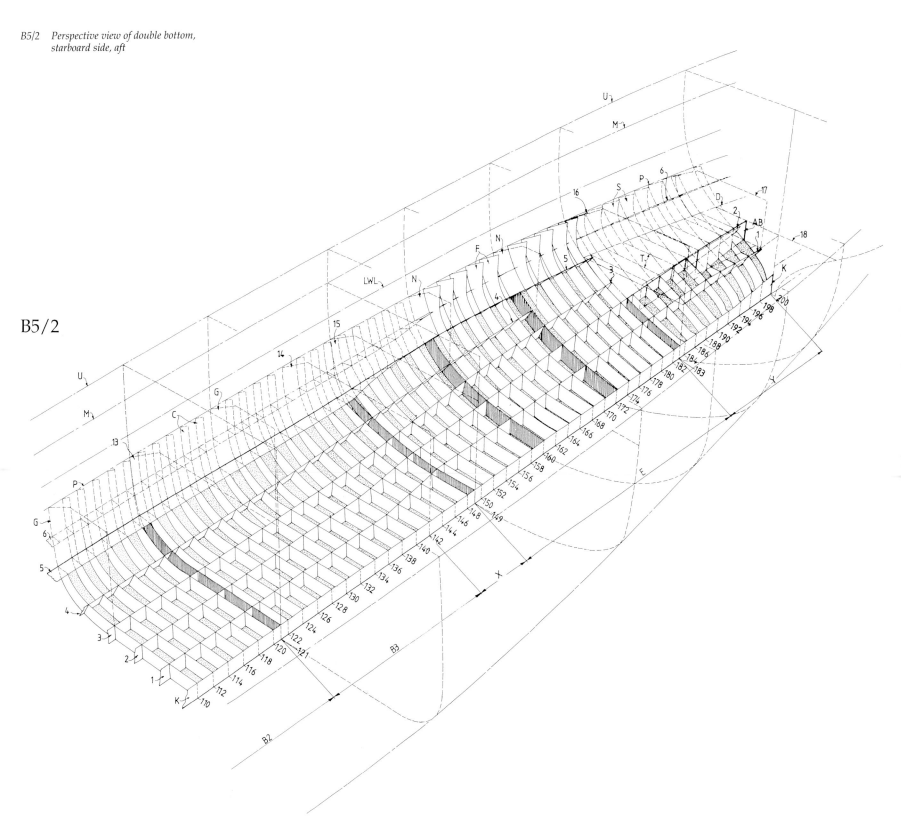

B5/2 *Perspective view of double bottom,*
starboard side, aft

B5/2

101

B Lines and constructional details

B6 FRAMING INSIDE DOUBLE
BOTTOM (scale ¼in = 1ft)

All show starboard side looking forward. The
transverse frames were worked intercostally
between the longitudinals and were of three
types: a) watertight b) lightened plate frames –
fitted below the heavy weights of the engine
rooms, 12in shell rooms and coal bunkers, etc. and
c) bracket frames fitted under the boiler rooms
and 12pdr magazines and shell rooms.

B6/1 Framing at station 37, typical of frames
33 to 39

B6/2 Framing at station 54, typical of frames
42 to 56

B6/3 Framing at station 66, typical of frames
60 to 68

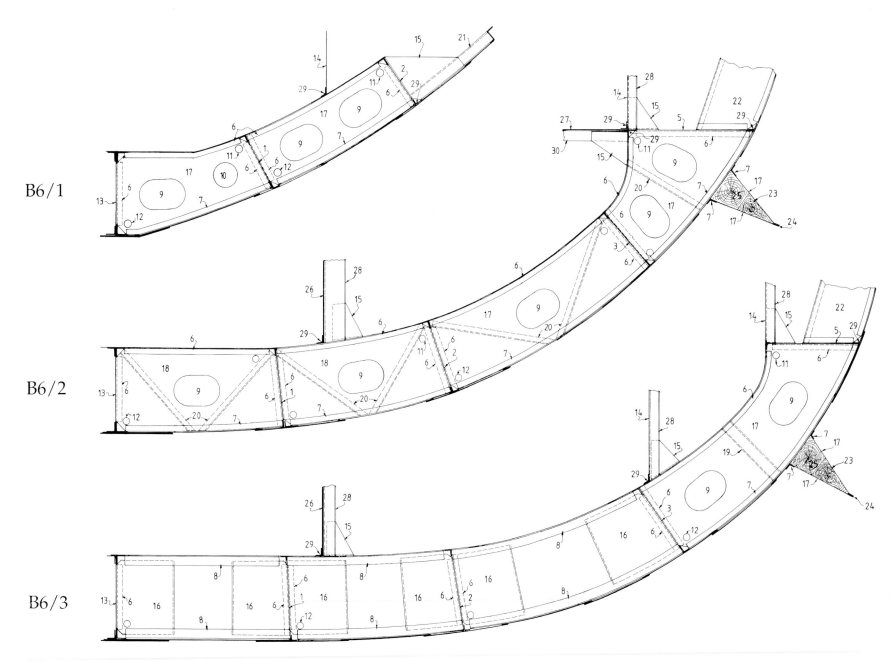

B6/4 Framing at station 95, typical of frames 92 to 100 and 142 to 148

B6/5 Framing at station 187, typical of frames 184 to 192

B6/6 Part detail of frame at station 196. Typical of frames 194 to 198, otherwise similar to B6/5

B6/4

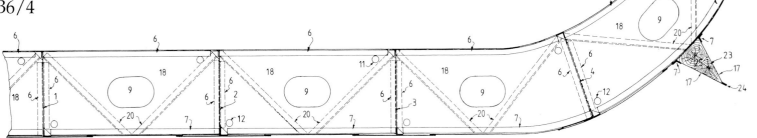

1. 1st longitudinal
2. 2nd longitudinal
3. 3rd longitudinal
4. 4th longitudinal
5. 5th longitudinal
6. Angle bar 3in × 3in × 6.5lbs
7. Angle bar 3in × 3.5in × 8lbs
8. Angle bar 5in × 3.5in × 12lbs
9. Lightening and access hole 23in × 15in
10. Lightening hole
11. Air escape hole
12. Drain hole
13. Keel
14. Longitudinal bulkhead
15. Bracket
16. 17lbs flanged plate
17. 14lbs plate
18. 17lbs plate
19. Channel bar stiffener 6in × 3in × 3in × 15lbs
20. Angle bar stiffener 3in × 3in × 6.5lbs
21. Zed bar frame
22. Bracket frame
23. Bilge keel
24. 1in steel strip fitted between 14lbs plates
25. Wood filling
26. Protective longitudinal bulkhead
27. Platform
28. Zed bar stiffener to bulkhead
29. Angle bar 3.5in × 3.5in × 100bs
30. Zed bar beam
31. 6th longitudinal

B6/5

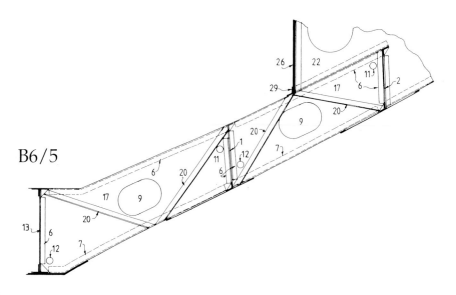

B6/6

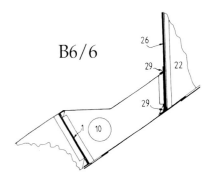

103

B Lines and constructional details

B6/7 *Framing at station 164, typical of frames 150 to 158 and 162 to 170*

Frames 174 to 182 similar but without 4th longitudinal.

B6/8 *Typical watertight framing*

Fitted at stations 40, 58, 70, 91, 121, 149, 172 and 183. Note that at stations 40 and 183 these frames extended to the 2nd longitudinal only, beyond this the end of the double bottom was closed by the watertight bulkheads. The channel bar stiffener was fitted to the frames adjacent to the keel and outboard of the 3rd longitudinal only.

B6/9 *Typical framing below coal bunkers abreast boiler rooms, stations 72–90, 102–120 and 122–140*

B6/10 *Typical framing under boiler room, stations 72–90, 102–120 and 122–140*

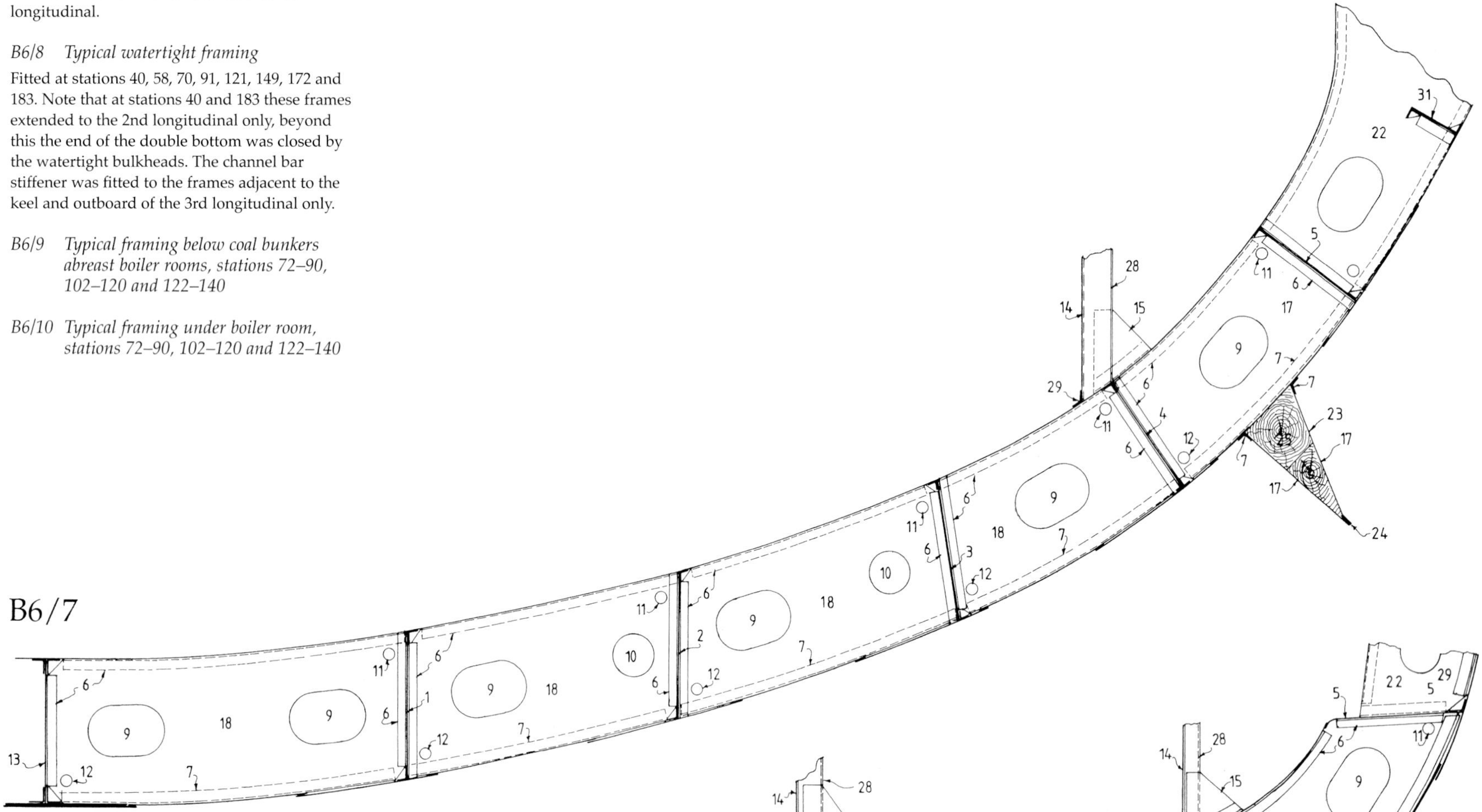

B6/7

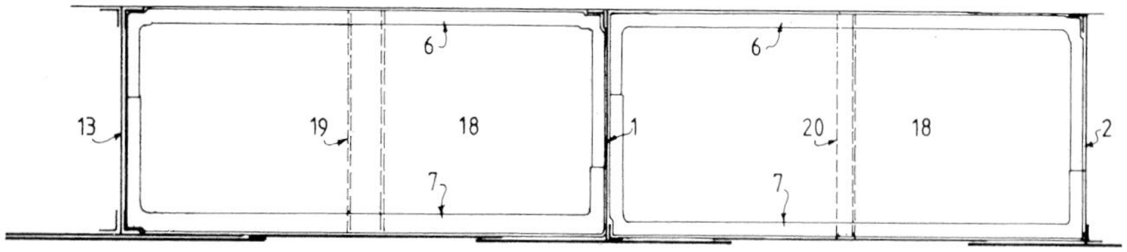

B6/8

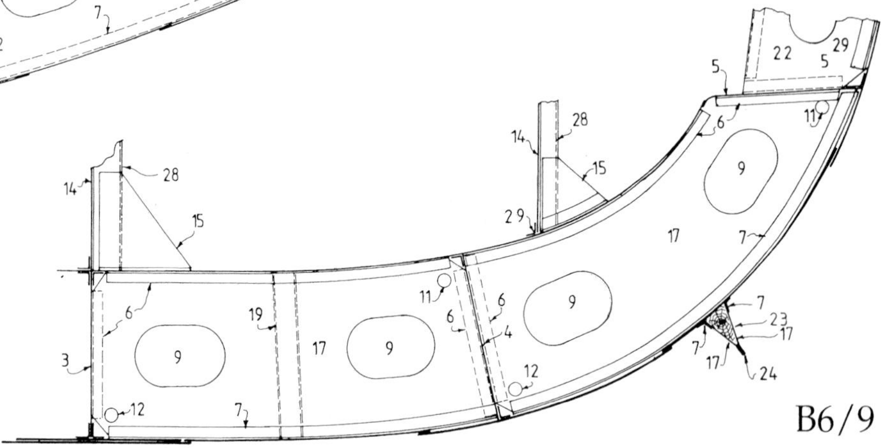

B6/9

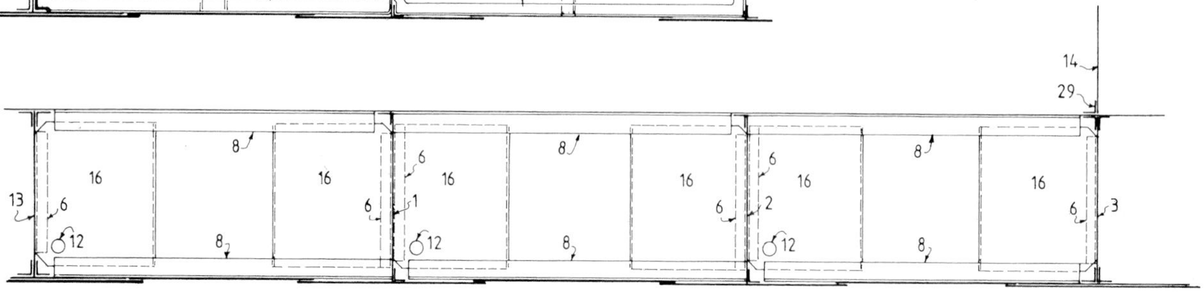

B6/10

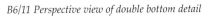

B6/11 Perspective view of double bottom detail

1. 1st longitudinal
2. 2nd longitudinal
3. 3rd longitudinal (docking keel)
4. Keel
5. Bracket frame
6. Plate frame
7. Watertight frame.
8. Inner bottom plating.

This plating was built flush, with double riveted butt straps and single riveted edge strips (double riveted edge strips under engine room). It was constructed of 17lbs plating under the boiler rooms, 20lbs plating under the engine rooms and 14lbs plating elsewhere.

9. Outer bottom plating
10. Butt strap
11. Butt strap to inner flat keel
12. Butt strap to outer flat keel
13. Inner flat keel
14. Outer flat keel
R Raised strake
S Sunken strake
88–96 Frame numbers

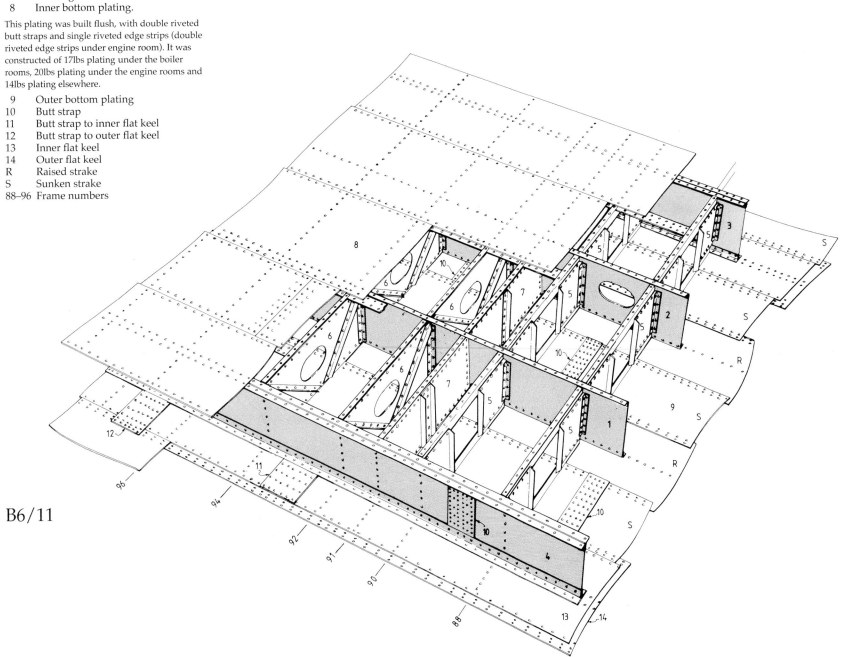

B6/11

105

B7 LONGITUDINALS OUTSIDE DOUBLE BOTTOM

The longitudinals inside the double bottom either terminated within that structure or merged into flats or decks at its ends to maintain the continuity of the structure. The only exception was the 2nd longitudinal which was continued beyond the double bottom at the forward end as far as the stem. Its form beyond the double bottom was the same as that of the 6th longitudinal (see B7/7).

The 6th longitudinal was entirely outside the double bottom. Its form from stations 40 to 160 was similar to that of the longitudinals within the double bottom. The principal difference was that there was no inner bottom on its inboard side. From station 160 to 183 it was of reduced depth but of the same basic construction and between stations 183 and 197 reduced again but changed from continuous to intercostal construction. At the ends, as far as the bulkheads at stations 209.5 aft and station 12 forward it was again reduced, to fit against the Zed frames, and was of intercostal construction.

B7/1 *Plan view of 6th longitudinal at stations 156–164 (scale ¼in = 1ft)*

B7/2 *Plan view of 6th longitudinal at stations 182–188 (scale ¼in = 1ft)*

B7/3 *Plan view of 6th longitudinal at stations 197–202 (scale ¼in = 1ft)*

B7/4 *Plan view of 6th longitudinal at stations 37–44 (scale ¼in = 1ft)*

The gradual tapering-off of the longitudinal from its deep plate construction amidships to the reduced section across the Zed frames was to avoid any sudden changes in the structural strength. The arrangement shown is equally applicable to the 2nd longitudinal where it left the double bottom at station 32.

B7/5 *Sections of 6th longitudinal (scale ¼in = 1ft)*

B7/1

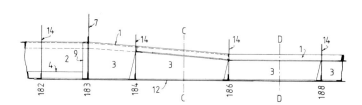

B7/2

B7/3

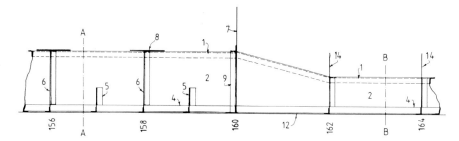

B7/4

B7/5

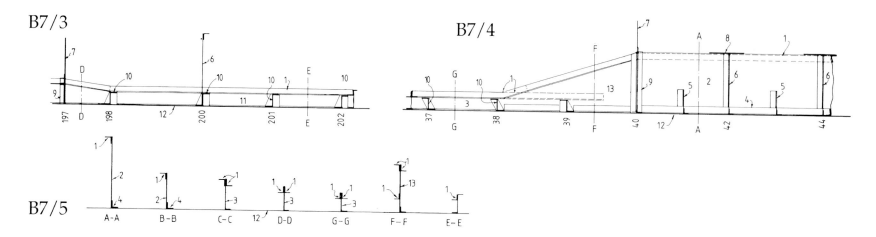

B7/6 *Perspective view of 6th longitudinal amidships*

B7/7 *Perspective view of 6th longitudinal at fore end*

B7/8 *Perspective view of 6th longitudinal at after end*

One frame is shown terminated at the longitudinal to show the arrangement in way of the torpedo tubes where the frames were cut away

1	Continuous angle, 3in × 3in × 6.5lbs
2	17lbs continuous plate
3	17lbs intercostal flanged plate
4	Continuous angle, 3.5in × 3in × 8lbs
5	Heel of intermediate frame
6	Web frame
7	Bulkhead
8	Diamond plate
9	Watertight boundary angle to bulkhead
10	Zed bar frames, 6in × 3.5in × 3in × 14lbs
11	10in Zed bar
12	Outer bottom plating
13	Intercostal 17lbs plate
14	Plate frame

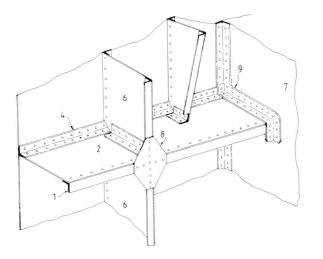

B7/6

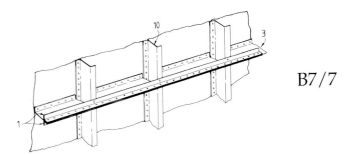

B7/7

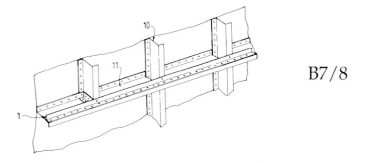

B7/8

B8   FRAMING BETWEEN DOUBLE
      BOTTOM AND PROTECTIVE
      DECK (scale ¼in = 1ft; all shown
      looking forward)

*B8/1   Web frames amidships, fitted abreast
         boiler rooms and 'X' 12in gun
         mounting from stations 102 to 148*

Frames from stations 42 to 90 similar but of
reducing height and therefore with less lightening
holes. (The lower frames from stations 84 to 72
and the upper frames from stations 90 to 72 had
two holes and the remaining frames from station
68 forward one hole each)

B8/2   Intermediate web frame

Fitted intermediately between principal frames as
additional support to armour shelf and outer
edge of protective deck throughout length of
main armour belt from stations 41 to 195

B8/3   Web frame at station 95

Typical of frames from stations 92 to 98 abreast
wing barbettes. Arranged with reduced
lightening holes and added stiffening to support
barbette structure

B8/4   Web frame at station 154

Typical of frames from stations 150 to 158 abreast
forward end of engine rooms

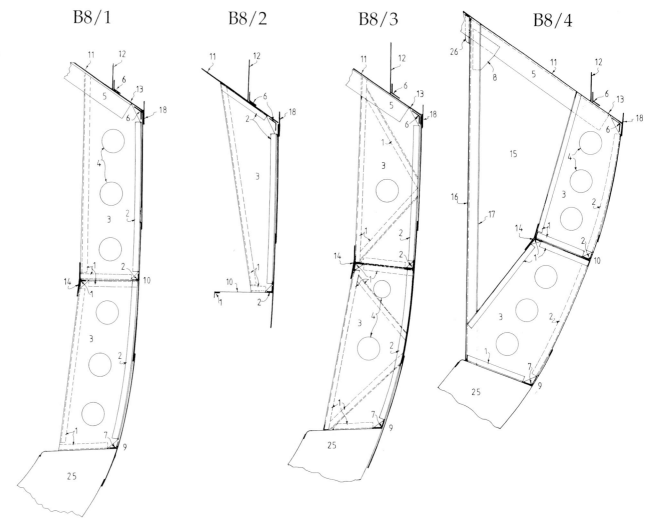

B8/1   B8/2   B8/3   B8/4

B8/5   Plate frame at station 164

Typical of frames from stations 162 to 170 and
stations 174 to 184

B8/6   Plate frames at station 188

Typical of frames from stations 184 to 190. Frames
at stations 192 to 196 similar

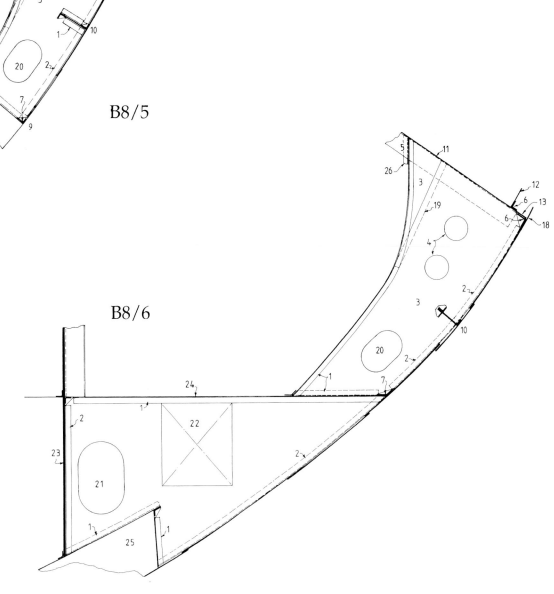

B8/5

B8/6

1   Angle bar 3in × 3in × 6.5lbs
2   Angle bar 3.5in × 3in × 8lbs
3   12lbs plate
4   Lightening holes
5   Deck beam angle bulb 9in × 3.5in ×
    23lbs
6   Angle bar 4.5in × 4.5in × 17lbs
7   Angle bar 3.5in × 3.5in × 10lbs
8   Bracket
9   5th longitudinal
10 6th longitudinal
11 Protective deck
12 Skin plating behind armour
13 Armour shelf
14 Diamond plate (14lbs)
15 Watertight compartment
16 Longitudinal bulkhead
17 Zed bar 5in × 2.5in × 3in × 12lbs
18 Covering plate to lower edge of
    armour belt
19 Lap joint to plates
20 Access and lightening hole, 23in ×
    15in
21 Access hole
22 Opening for propeller shaft
23 Protective bulkhead to 'Y' magazine
    and shell room
24 Flat (platform deck) of engineers'
    store
25 Double bottom
26 Flanged plate

B9   SIDE FRAMING

B9/1   *Perspective view of side structure amidships*

Port side stations 120 to 132 abreast No 3 boiler room. Arrangement shown above protective deck is typical for the full length of the main armour belt from stations 61 to 184 except for that area within the wing barbettes. The arrangement below the protective deck is typical of framing abreast boiler rooms only (see section B8).

1   Upper deck
2   Sheer strake
3   Armour recess
4   Armour shelf
5   Main deck
6   Framing behind armour
7   Longitudinal girder behind armour
8   Stringer (at level of bunker flat – not shown)
9   Protective deck
10 Liner to watertight bulkhead
11 Web frames
12 6th longitudinal
13 5th longitudinal
14 Longitudinal bulkhead to wing bunker
15 Intermediate frame
16 Main transverse bulkhead
17 Double bottom
18 Covering plate to edge of side armour
19 Diamond plate

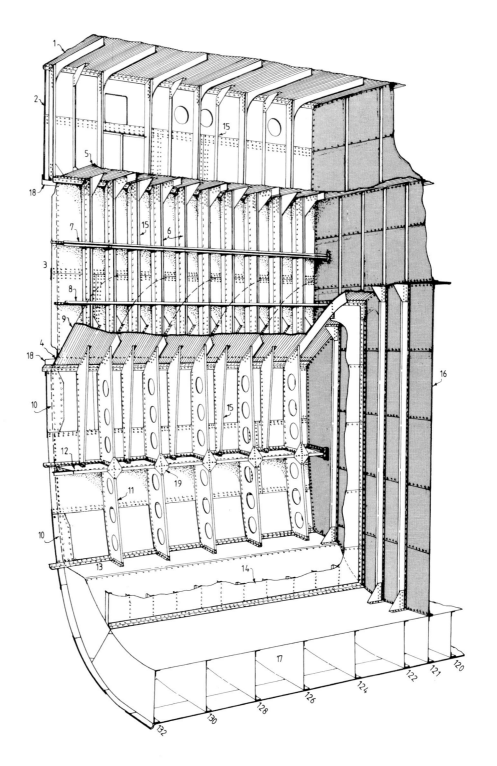

B9/1

B9/2 *Plan view of girder behind armour*

Note that the girder is worked in sections between the frames (intercostal) but that the two angles on the inboard edge run continuously and pass unbroken through the watertight bulkheads. However it did not pass through the wing barbettes which did not have a girder at this level. The girder terminated against the armoured bulkhead aft and at station 46 forward.

B9/3 *Plan view of stringer at level of bunker flat*

Construction is similar to B9/2 except that the inboard angle was continuous between the bulkheads only. It terminated against the armoured bulkhead aft and at station 49 forward.

B9/4 *Transverse section of frames above protective deck (stations 62 to 90 and 102 to 184)*

Note that frames 92 to 99 fall within the wing barbettes and hence vary from the standard arrangement, see B23/6.

B9/5 *Transverse section of intermediate frames above protective deck*

Only the differences from B9/4 are numbered (stations 61 to 89 and 101 to 183).

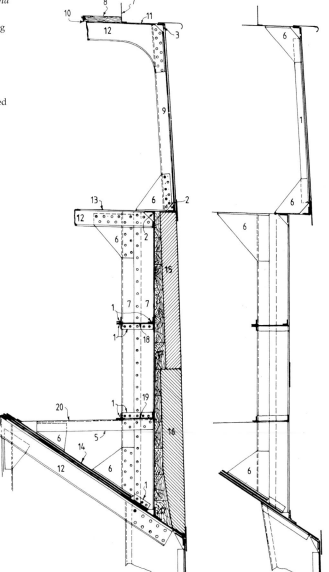

B9/4

B9/5

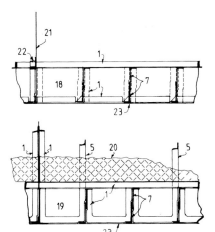

B9/2

B9/3

1	Angle bar 3.5in × 3in × 8lbs	13	Main deck
2	Angle bar 4in × 4in × 13lbs	14	Protective deck
3	Angle bar 3.5in × 3.5in × 10lbs	15	320lbs (8in) armour
4	Angle bar 3in × 3in × 6.5lbs	16	440lbs (11in) armour
5	Angle bar 5in × 3.5in × 12lbs	17	Wood backing to armour (2.5in thick at thinnest point)
6	Bracket		
7	Angle bar 9in × 3.5in × 18lbs	IB	14lbs plate
8	3in thick teak deck planking	19	12lbs stringer plate
9	Zed bar 6in × 3.5in × 3in × 14lbs	20	14lbs chequered plate (bunker flat)
10	Upper deck	21	Bulkhead
11	Torpedo net shelf	22	Watertight collar (3.5in × 3in angle bar)
12	Angle bulb deck beam 9in × 3.5in × 23lbs		
		23	Outer bottom plating

B10 FORWARD HULL STRUCTURE

B10/1 Perspective view of forward hull structure

Note that only the main transverse bulkheads are shown above the main deck, the majority of minor and longitudinal bulkheads etc. being omitted for clarity.

1 Longitudinal bulkhead
2 Pillar
3 Light and vent trunk to main deck
4 Longitudinal girders
5 Opening for vent trunks
6 Watertight compartment
7 Forecastle deck
8 Opening for capstan spindle
9 Upper deck
10 Torpedo hatch
11 Main deck
12 Lower deck
13 Hawse pipe
14 Boatswain's stores
15 Access and escape trunk to capstan engine room
16 Cable locker
17 Longitudinal division to cable lockers (slightly offset to port from centre line)
18 Spare armature space
19 Refrigeration machinery compartment
20 Torpedo lobby
21 Medical distributing station
22 Paymaster's slops
23 Door to marines' slops
24 Access to small arms magazine
25 Ward room stores
26 Admiral's stores
27 Lobby to store rooms
28 Gunners' store
29 Small arms magazine
30 Capstan machinery room
31 Torpedo head and dry guncotton magazine
32 Forward submerged torpedo room
33 Opening for torpedo tube
34 Web frame
35 12in magazine
36 12in shell room
37 Protective longitudinal bulkhead
38 Manhole to double bottom
39 Flour store
40 Spirit room
41 Submarine mine store
42 Provision room
43 Trimming tank
44 Keel
45 Butt strap
46 Breasthook
47 Stem casting
48 Contour plate
49 2nd longitudinal
50 6th longitudinal
51 Skylight to ward room
52 Skylight to main deck
53 Cofferdam
54 Access and escape trunk to submerged torpedo room
55 Slope of protective deck
56 Lower deck
57 Platform deck
58 Watertight liner to bulkhead
59 Double bottom

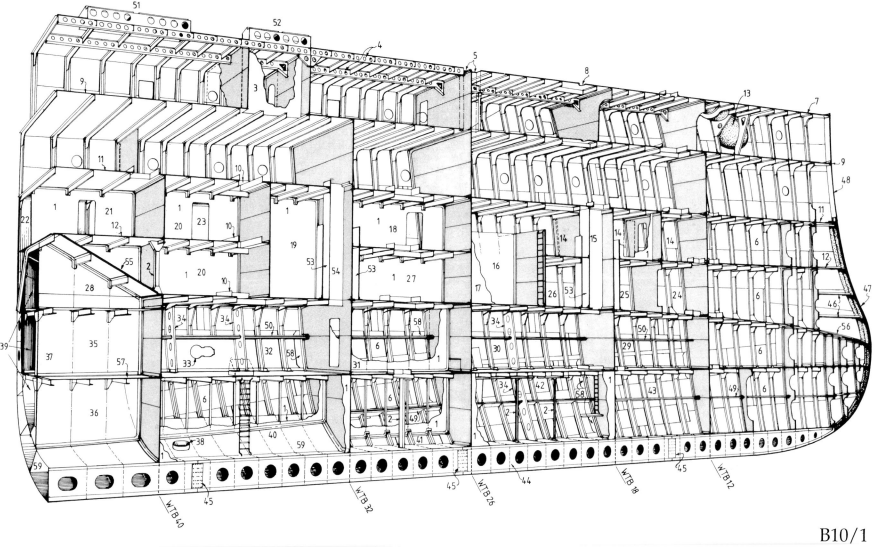

B10/1

B10/2 Transverse section at station 37, looking forward (scale $^1/_8$in = 1ft)

Typical of framing from stations 33 to 39. Above the protective deck this is also typical for frames as far aft as station 60 (*ie* to the start of the main 11in armour belt). Intermediate frames were fitted from stations 41 to 59 which, behind the armour, were identical to the principal frames, except that the brackets were connected directly to the deck head (there being no beams in these positions). Between the main and upper deck the intermediate frames were of the same design as those amidships, see B9/5.

B10/3 Web frames at stations 35 and 38 between the platform and lower decks (scale $^1/_8$in = 1ft)

These frames provided additional support to the ships structure in way of the torpedo tubes.

1	Angle bar 3in × 3in × 6.5lbs
2	Angle bar 3.5in × 3in × 8lbs
3	Angle bar 4in × 4in × 13lbs
4	Angle bar 4.5in × 4.5in × 17lbs
5	Zed bar 6in × 3.5in × 3in × 14lbs
6	Zed bar 8in × 3.5in × 3.5in × 18.2lbs
7	Angle bulb 9in × 3.5in × 23lbs
8	Angle bulb 7in × 3in × 16lbs
9	Bracket
10	Shaded section of frame omitted in way of torpedo tubes at stations 36 and 37 port side and stations 33 and 34 starboard side
11	2.5in thick teak deck planking
12	Longitudinal girder
13	Forecastle deck
14	Upper deck
15	3in thick teak deck planking
16	Angle bar 3.5in × 3.5in × 10lbs
17	Angle bar 9in × 3.5in × 18lbs
18	Torpedo net shelf
19	240lbs (6in) armour belt
20	2½in thick teak backing
21	Main deck
22	Middle deck
23	Lower deck
24	Platform deck
25	Plate frames in double bottom
26	Longitudinal bulkhead
27	Keel
28	1st longitudinal
29	2nd longitudinal
30	6th longitudinal
31	Ward room
32	Lobby
33	Cabin
34	Chart and chronometer room
35	Store
36	Submerged torpedo room
37	Bread room
38	Watertight compartment
39	12lbs floor plate
40	12lbs plate
41	Zed bar 5in × 3in × 2.5in × 12lbs
42	Zed bar flange cut-away where it joins the floor plate
43	Boatswain's stores
44	Admiral's stores
45	Capstan engine room
46	Provision room
47	Angle bar stiffeners to bulkheads 3.5in × 2.5in × 6.5lbs

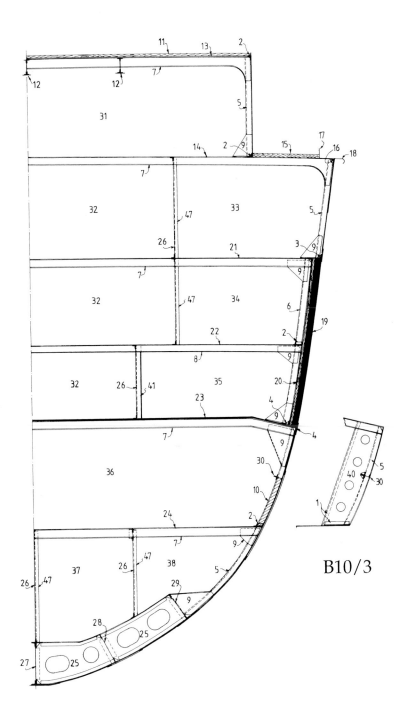

B10/3

B10/2

113

B10/4 Transverse section at station 19, looking forward (scale ⅛ = 1ft)

Typical of framing forward of double bottom ie. from station 31 forward.

B10/5 Web frames at station 22

These frames provided additional support to the heavy weights of the capstan engine and cable lockers.

B10/6 Large brackets at stations 24 and 25

These brackets provided additional support to the weight of the capstan engine on the deck above.

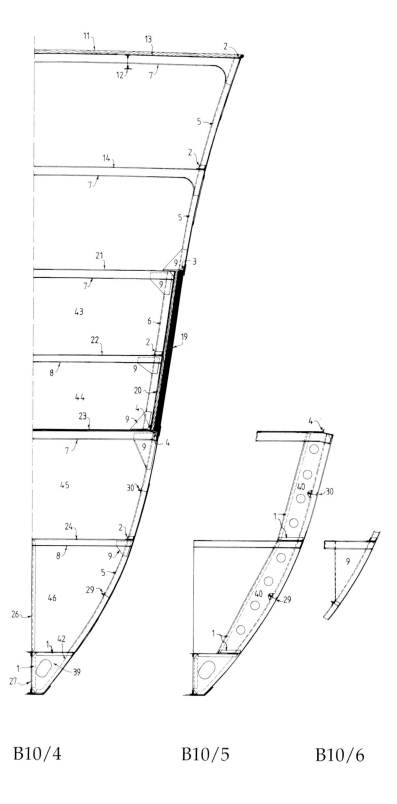

B10/4   B10/5   B10/6

B11/1   Perspective view of after hull structure

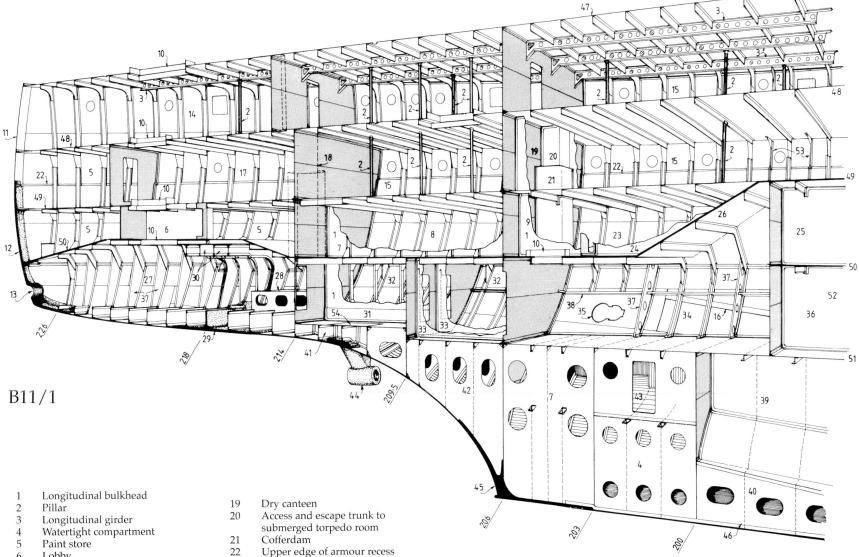

B11/1

1	Longitudinal bulkhead	19	Dry canteen	
2	Pillar	20	Access and escape trunk to	
3	Longitudinal girder		submerged torpedo room	
4	Watertight compartment	21	Cofferdam	
5	Paint store	22	Upper edge of armour recess	
6	Lobby	23	Canteen store	
7	Fresh water tank	24	Lime store	
8	Boatswain's store	25	Gunners' stores	
9	Torpedo lobby	26	Slope of protective deck	
10	Torpedo hatch	27	Stern torpedo tube and tiller	
11	Contour plate		compartment	
12	Stern casting	28	Flat for steering gear	
13	Opening for stern torpedo tube	29	Rudder head casting	
14	Seamen's head	30	Supporting frames for upper rudder	
15	Mess space		bearing.	
16	Edge strip to outer bottom plating			
17	Reading room			
18	Access and escape trunk to steering			
	compartment (shown in broken line			
	– trunk is on starboard side with one			
	edge on middle line)			

31	Hand steering compartment	44	'A' bracket for inner propeller shaft
32	Store	45	Cut-up casting
33	Torpedo head magazine	46	Keel
34	Submerged torpedo room	47	Upper deck
35	Opening for torpedo tube	48	Main deck
36	12in magazine	49	Middle deck
37	Web frame	50	Lower deck
38	6th longitudinal	51	Platform deck
39	12in shell room	52	Longitudinal protective bulkhead
40	Double bottom	53	Intermediate frames
41	Palm compartment	54	Portable plate giving access to palm
42	Trimming tank		compartment
43	Engineers' store		

Note that no beams are fitted between this
structure and the protective deck; this was to
reduce the possibility of any damage to the deck
transmitting itself to the rudder structure and
jamming the steering gear

115

B Lines and constructional details

B11/2 Transverse section of framing at station 201 looking aft (scale ¼in = 1ft)

Below the protective deck this arrangement is typical of the framing at stations 201 and 202. Above the protective deck it is typical for the full length of the after structure from stations 186 to 227, except as noted for the intermediate frames.

B11/3 Transverse section of intermediate frame at station 187, looking aft (scale ¼in = 1ft)

Typical of intermediate frames at stations 187 to 199.

B11/4 Detail of web frames at stations 200 and 203, between platform deck and protective deck (scale ¼in = 1ft)

1   Angle bar 3in × 3in × 6.5lbs
2   Angle bar 3.5in × 3in × 8lbs
3   Angle bar 3.5in × 3.5in × 10lbs
4   Angle bar 4in × 4in × 13lbs
5   Angle bar 4.5in × 4.5in × 17lbs
6   Zed bar 8in × 3.5in × 3.5in × 18.2lbs
7   Zed bar 6in × 3.5in × 3in × 14lbs
8   Angle bulb 7in × 3in × 16lbs
9   Angle bulb 9in × 3.5in × 23lbs
10   6th longitudinal
11   Bracket
12   14lbs plate
13   Centre line bulkhead
14   Longitudinal bulkhead
15   Flat of Engineers' store
16   Structure to support propeller shaft bearing (plummer block)
17   Shaded section of Zed bar omitted in way of torpedo tubes at stations 204 and 205 on port side and stations 207 and 208 on starboard side
18   Hatch
19   Longitudinal girder
20   Carling
21   Torpedo net shelf
22   3in thick teak deck planking
23   Angle bar 9in × 3.5in × 18lbs
24   Upper deck
25   Main deck
26   Middle deck
27   Lower (protective) deck
28   Platform deck
29   Cut-up casting
30   Propeller shaft (inner)
31   Wash plate
32   Shaft recess (free flooding)
33   Rudder head casting
34   160lbs (4in) armour belt
35   2.5in thick teak backing to armour
36   Covering plate
37   Lap joints
38   Flat
39   Floor plate
40   Flanged web frame
41   12lbs plate
42   80lbs plate

(Note there is a clear gap between this plate and the protective deck, which had no beams at this point, to ensure that action damage to the protective deck did not transmit itself to the supporting structure for the rudder)

43   Housing for upper rudder bearing
44   30lbs plate to support frames immediately fore and aft of rudder axis
45   25lbs plate
46   Watertight hatch over rudder head

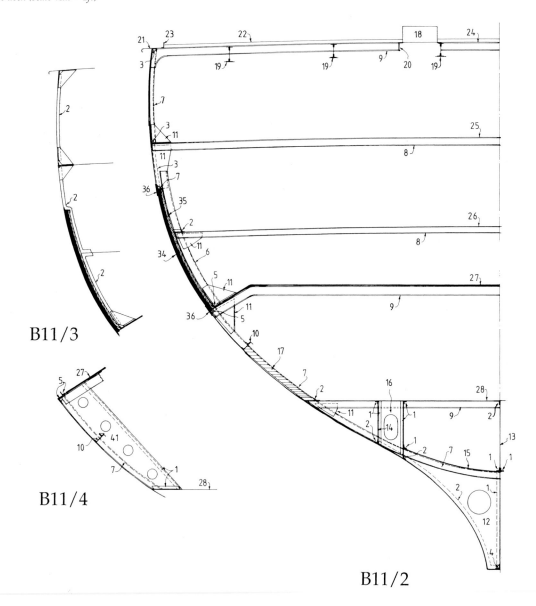

B11/3

B11/4

B11/2

B11/5   Transverse section of framing at
         station 205 below platform deck
         (scale ¼in = 1ft)

Frame at station 204 similar.

B11/6   Transverse section of framing at
         station 204½ (scale ¼in = 1ft)

B11/7   Transverse section of floor plate
         frame at station 208 (scale ¼in =
         1ft)

Frames at station 207 and 209 similar.

B11/8   Transverse section of framing at
         station 222 (scale ¼in = 1ft)

Details shown are typical for frames at stations
215, 216 and 219 to 225.

B11/9   Transverse section of framing at
         station 226 below protective deck
         (scale ¼in = 1ft)

B11/10 Transverse section through centre of
         rudder axis, station 218 (scale ¼in =
         1ft)

B11/11 Transverse section of rudder support
         frame at station 219 (scale ¼in =
         1ft)

Typical for frames at stations 219 and 217.

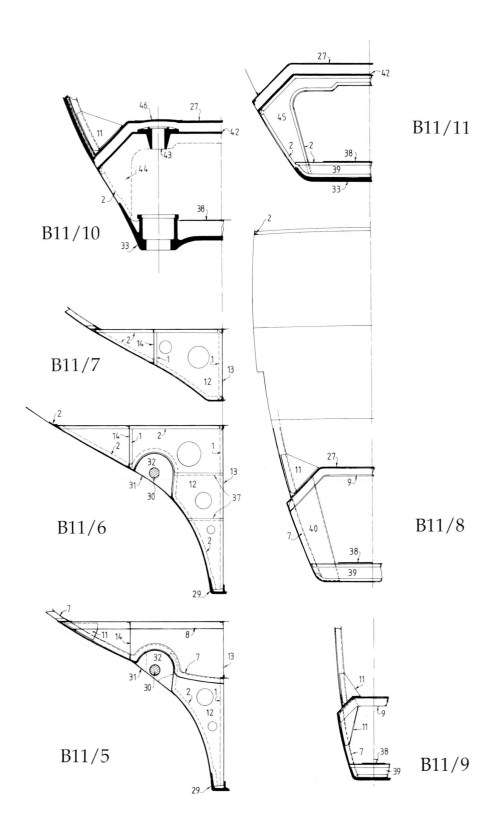

B11/11

B11/10

B11/7

B11/6

B11/8

B11/5

B11/9

B   Lines and constructional details

B11/12   Perspective view of framing below
platform deck, stations 183 to 214

B11/13   Profile of after end

Shaded section indicates area of drawing B11/12

1	Watertight bulkhead
2	Opening for propeller shaft
3	Engineers' store (flat shown cut-away)
4	Inner shaft passage
5	Double bottom
6	'Y' 12in shell room
7	Longitudinal bulkhead
8	Frames formed around shaft recess
9	Supporting structure for shaft bearing (plummer block)
10	2nd longitudinal
11	Longitudinal protective bulkhead
183–214	Station numbers

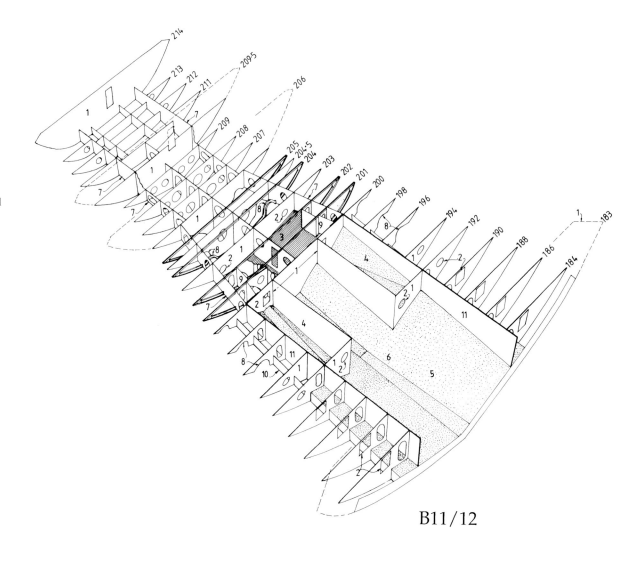

B11/12

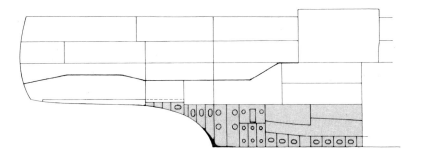

B11/13

B12   FRAMING IN WAY OF
       PROPELLER SHAFT BRACKETS

B12/1 *Perspective view of framing in way of
       propeller shaft brackets*

B12/2 *Profile (scale ¼in = 1ft)*

B12/3 *Plan (scale ¼in = 1ft)*

B12/4 *Section at station 212, looking aft,
       showing inner shaft brackets (scale ¼in
       = 1ft)*

B12/5 *Section at stations 210, looking aft,
       showing outer shaft brackets (scale ¼in
       = 1ft)*

B12/6 *Perspective view of watertight collar
       joining bracket arm and outer bottom*

B12/1

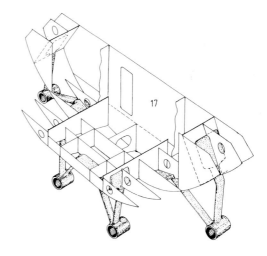

B12/6

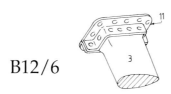

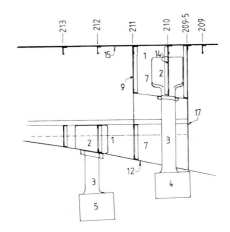

B12/3

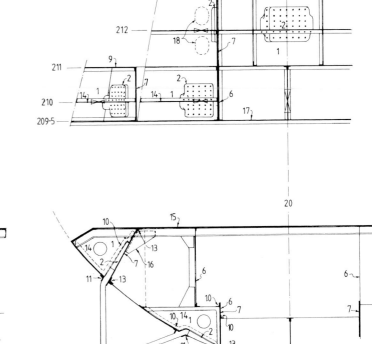

1   Watertight palm compartment
2   Shaft bracket palm
3   Shaft bracket (cast steel)
4   Bearing housing to outer shaft
5   Bearing housing to inner shaft
6   Longitudinal bulkhead
7   40lbs plate
8   Scarph joint between two palms
9   Watertight plate (20lbs)
10 Angle bar 3.5in × 3.5in × 10lbs
11 Angle bar 5in × 4in × 15lbs
12 Outer bottom plating (two
    thicknesses of 30lbs)
13 Angle bar 6in × 6in × 24lbs
14 20lbs plate
15 Lower (protective) deck
16 Bracket
17 Watertight bulkhead at station 209.5
18 Manhole (over)
19 Portable plate giving access to palm
    compartment for maintenance and
    inspection
20 Middle line
209.5–213 Station numbers

B12/4

B12/5

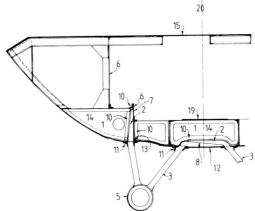

B Lines and constructional details

B13 EXPANSION OF OUTER BOTTOM PLATING

B13/1 Stem, port side only

B13/2 After section

B13/3 Forward section (stem for starboard side only)

The outer bottom plating was constructed with alternate raised and sunken strakes (indicated by R and S respectively on the drawing), the longitudinal lapped edges being double riveted and the butts connected by single and double riveted butt straps. The butts of each strake were alternated, or shifted, in order to avoid any discontinuity of strength created by adjacent joints. On average the outer bottom plates were 24ft long with the butts in adjacent strakes shifted two frame spaces (8ft). Where the strakes came together forward and aft the number was reduced by terminating some strakes and widening others to take their place. The stepped plates, which thus bridged two strakes, were known as 'stealers'. Occasionally this produced adjacent raised strakes which were joined by long edge-straps. In certain areas the plating was in two thicknesses, known as doubling. This was primarily to ensure structural strength but also served, at the forward end, to provide a flush surface in way of the anchors.

The principal areas of doubling were a) the flat keel, b) the strake under the 3rd longitudinal amidships, which served as the docking keel, c) the sheer strake and the strake below it amidships, which provided both for structural strength and compensated for the window and side scuttle openings for the main deck, d) forward, to strengthen the stem, e) the after end around the cut-up which was particularly heavily built in order to cope with the strains created by the rudders and propeller shafts and the overhang of the stern, f) local doubling to compensate for openings in the ships bottom, such as the torpedo tubes.

The doubling plates were shifted in relation to the outer plates and it was not therefore necessary to fit butt straps for this plating.

The principal exception to the above arrangement was the plating behind the armour which was arranged flush, with outer butt straps and edge strips.

The strakes indicated by 'C' on the drawing are clinchers, that is plates that are lapped over the strake below, but connected directly to the frames at the top. The term derives from the same source as 'clinker', used to describe alternate lapped planking in boat construction.

B13/1

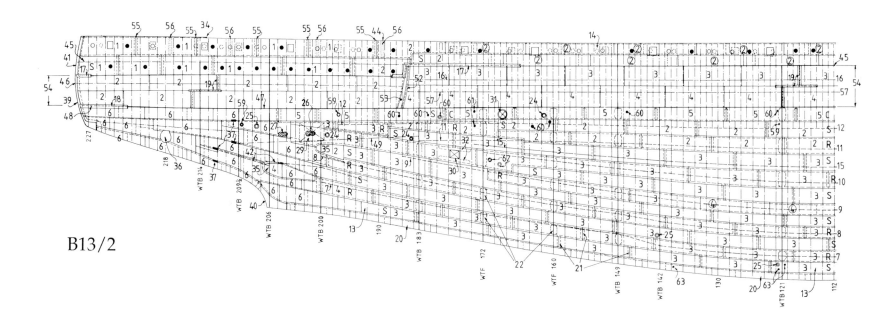

B13/2

1	17lbs plate (circled number indicates doubling with inner 17lbs plate)	18	Covering plate to lower edge of armour belt.	30	Main condenser inlet	53	30lbs angled plate at junction of main belt and armoured bulkhead
2	20lbs plate (circled number indicates doubling with inner 20lbs plate)		20lbs increasing to 30lbs at aft end	31	Main condenser discharge	54	Armour recess
3	25lbs plate	19	External butt and edge straps to all plating behind armour	32	Compensating strips to condenser opening	55	Butts on starboard side only
4	30lbs plate (circled number indicates doubling with inner 25lbs plate)	20	Flat keel	33	120lbs horizontal plate at base of outer edge of wing barbette armour	56	Butts on port side only

1 17lbs plate (circled number indicates doubling with inner 17lbs plate)
2 20lbs plate (circled number indicates doubling with inner 20lbs plate)
3 25lbs plate
4 30lbs plate (circled number indicates doubling with inner 25lbs plate)
5 35lbs plate
6 30lbs outer plate, doubled with 30lbs inner plate
7 1st longitudinal
8 2nd longitudinal
9 3rd longitudinal
10 4th longitudinal
11 5th longitudinal
12 6th longitudinal
13 Garboard strake (1st strake next to keel)
14 Sheer strake
15 Centre line of bilge keel
16 Girder behind armour
17 Covering plate to top edge of armour belt

20lbs amidship reducing to 17lbs at forward and after end

18 Covering plate to lower edge of armour belt.

20lbs increasing to 30lbs at aft end

19 External butt and edge straps to all plating behind armour
20 Flat keel

20lbs inner keel from stem casting to station 27.5, 25lbs inner keel from station 27.5 to cut-up casting, 25lbs outer keel from stem casting to station 29.5, 30lbs outer keel from station 29.5 to cut-up casting

21 Internal butt strap
22 Watertight liners in way of watertight frames
23 Combined watertight liner and butt straps
24 Seacock (port only)
25 Seacock (starboard only)
26 Opening for starboard torpedo tube
27 Opening for port torpedo tube
28 20lbs doubling fitted around torpedo tube opening
29 25lbs doubling fitted to starboard tube only

30 Main condenser inlet
31 Main condenser discharge
32 Compensating strips to condenser opening
33 120lbs horizontal plate at base of outer edge of wing barbette armour
34 End of torpedo net shelf
35 Shaft recess, wash plates not shown
36 Rudder head casting opening
37 Propeller shaft strut
38 Stern casting
39 Stern casting
40 Cut-up casting
41 30lbs contour plate
42 Longitudinal bulkhead
43 Forecastle deck
44 Upper deck
45 Main deck
46 Middle deck
47 Armour shelf
48 Lower deck
49 Platform deck
50 Flat
51 Breasthook
52 30lbs strip

53 30lbs angled plate at junction of main belt and armoured bulkhead
54 Armour recess
55 Butts on starboard side only
56 Butts on port side only
57 Bunker flat
58 Discharge (port only)
59 Discharge (starboard only)
60 Discharge (port and starboard)
61 Suction (lower) and discharge for ice making machinery (port only)
62 Seacock (port and starboard)
63 Boiler blow-down valve
64 Suction (lower) and discharge for refrigeration machinery (starboard only)

WTB Watertight bulkhead
WTF Watertight frame
S Sunken strake
R Raised strake
C Clincher

On the side scuttles and square port those shown solid are on both sides, those shown in broken line are port only, those in continuous line are starboard only.

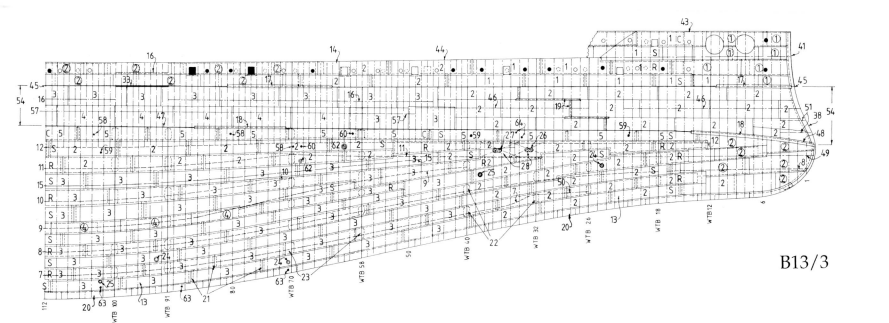

B13/3

121

B Lines and constructional details

B14 DETAILS OF OUTER BOTTOM PLATING

B14/1 Perspective view of typical stealer

B14/2 Perspective view of plating in way of longitudinal

It being undesirable to have a longitudinal or flat diagonally across the lap of adjacent strakes of plating, the plates were arranged to present a square edge to the line of the longitudinal. In this case the plate has been cut away to provide a step at right angles to the longitudinal.

B14/3 Perspective view of playing in way of longitudinal

This is a variation on B14/2 in which the plating strakes have been arranged to produce the desired effect.

1	Watertight frame
2	Non watertight frame
3	Keel
4	1st longitudinal
5	Butt strap to inner flat keel
6	Butt strap to outer flat keel
7	Garboard strake
8	Butt strap
9	Combined butt strap and watertight liner
10	Stealer
11	3rd longitudinal
12	5th longitudinal
13	Edge strip
14	Angle bar of frame or bulkhead
15	Watertight liner
16	Non watertight liner
17	Lightening holes
R	Raised strake
S	Sunken strake

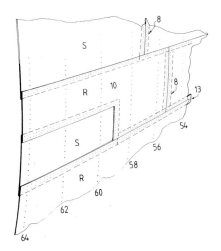

B14/1

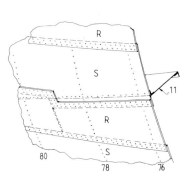

B14/2

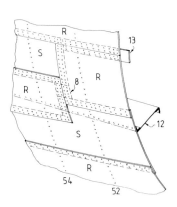

B14/3

B14/4 *Detail of double bottom plating viewed from inboard (scale ¼in = 1ft)*

B14/5 *Perspective view of watertight liner*

These were fitted between the raised strakes and the watertight bulkheads and frames and were intended to compensate for the loss of strength resulting from the closely spaced rivets necessary for watertightness. Where they were close to a butt strap the two features were combined. (See B14/4)

B14/6 *Perspective view of frame liner*

These were fitted between raised strakes and non watertight frames to fill the gap created by the raised plating.

B14/4

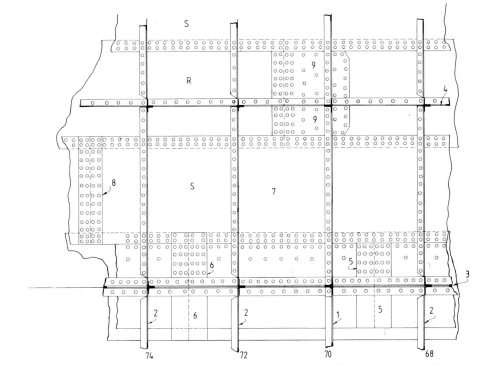

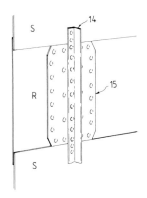

B14/5

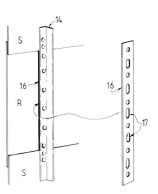

B14/6

123

B Lines and constructional details

B15 ARRANGEMENT OF STEM

*B15/1 Profile of stem and adjacent structure
(scale ¼in = 1ft)*

B15/1

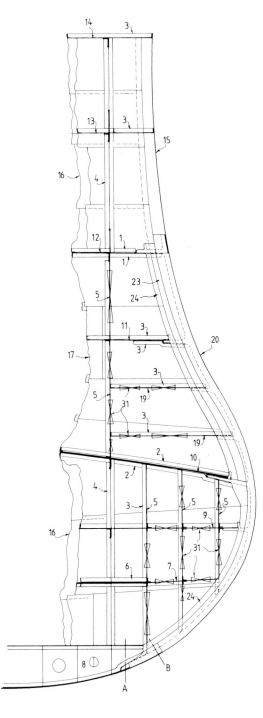

1   Angle bar 4in × 4in × 13lbs
2   Angle bar 4.5in × 4.5in × 17lbs
3   Angle Bar 3in × 3.5in × 8lbs
4   Zed bar frame
5   Plate frame
6   2nd longitudinal
7   Horizontal plate frame at end of 2nd longitudinal
8   Keel
9   Platform deck
10 Lower (protective) deck
11 Middle deck
12 Main deck
13 Upper deck
14 Forecastle (flying) deck
15 Contour plate 30lbs
16 Outer bottom plating (port side)
17 Plating behind armour belt (port side)
18 Covering plate
19 Breasthook
20 Stem (steel) casting
21 Armour belt
22 Wood backing
23 Rabbet for side armour
24 Rabbet for outer bottom plating
25 Rabbet for inner keel plate
26 Rabbet for outer keel plate
27 Outer keel plate
28 Inner keel plate
29 Lug on casting
30 Stop for covering plate
31 Access holes
32 Tap rivet holes for side armour
33 Stop for deck plating

B15/2 Detail of top of stem casting

B15/3 Detail of junction of breasthook and
       stem casting

B15/4 Detail of junction of platform deck and
       stem casting

B15/5 Detail of junction of lower (protective)
       deck and stem casting

B15/6 Section of stem at 'A' (scale ¼in = 1ft)

B15/7 Section of stem at 'B' (scale ¼in = 1ft)

B15/8 Detail of bottom of stem casting

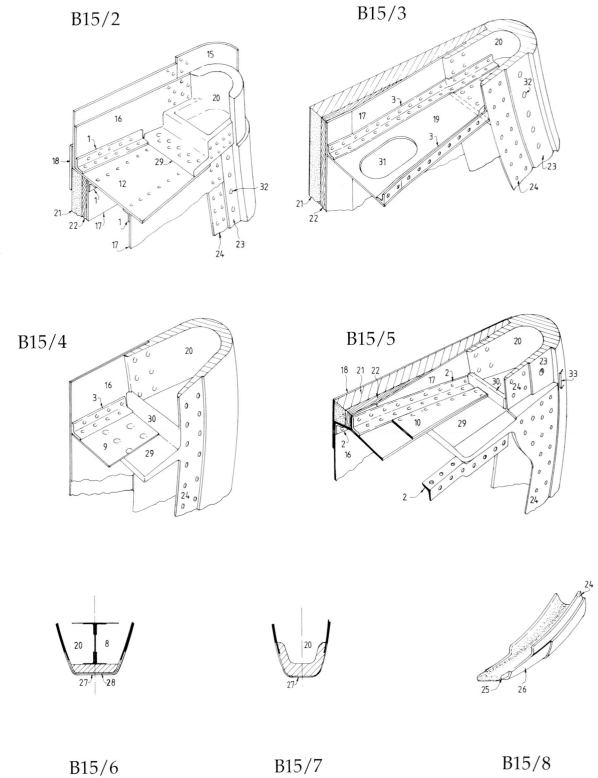

B15/2

B15/3

B15/4

B15/5

B15/6

B15/7

B15/8

B Lines and constructional details

B16 STERN CASTING

B16/1 Perspective view of stern casting

B16/2 Section of stern casting at junction with armour belt (scale ½in = 1ft)

1 Steel stern casting
2 Lug for middle deck
3 Lug for lower deck
4 Rabbet for outer bottom plating
5 Rabbet for armour belt
6 30lbs contour plate
7 Outer bottom plating
8 Opening for stern torpedo tube
9 4in armour belt
10 2.5in teak backing
11 Main deck
12 Lower deck

B17 PERSPECTIVE VIEW OF CUT-UP CASTING

1 Rib for middle line longitudinal bulkhead
2 Lug for transverse bulkhead at station 206
3 Rabbet for outer flat keel
4 Rabbet for inner flat keel
5 Rabbet for outer bottom plating
6 Rabbet for outer bottom plating doubling
7 Rabbet for outer bottom plating and doubling

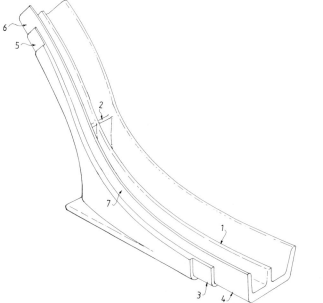

B17

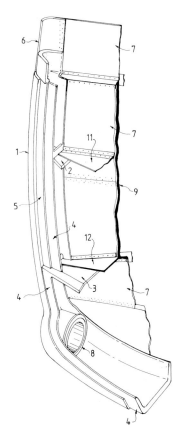

B16/1

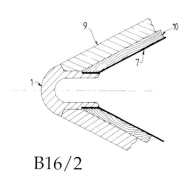

B16/2

B18   DECKS

The upper deck, main deck and protective deck were continuous from stem to stern and unbroken by bulkheads or frames except for the extreme forward end of the upper deck where the frames extended through the deck to the forecastle. The middle deck fore and aft, that is beyond the points where it sloped down to the lower deck level, was also continuous except for the section in way of the cable lockers where no deck was fitted. All the other decks below the protective deck were platforms built between the principal transverse and longitudinal bulkheads and through which, where they extended to the ship's side plating, the frames passed. The flying, or forecastle, deck was part of the hull structure at its forward end and part of the superstructure at its after end. The forecastle, upper and main decks and the middle deck forward and aft were cambered to assist the flow of water off the deck. The camber gave a 12in rise at the maximum beam of the ship, the decks being level at the middle line and curved down to the deck edge.

The upper deck, together with the sheer strake of the side plating, formed the principal strength member of the upper hull girder and for this reason it was made comparatively thick over the majority of its length. Considerable care was necessary in compensating for the loss of strength in this deck resulting from the large openings required for the barbettes, particularly in the case of the wing barbettes where the deck was reduced to 30% of its full width. A longitudinal girder was placed inboard of the wing barbettes on both sides and it is also possible that the plating was doubled in this area (this was the

case with the subsequent *Bellerophon* class). It should also be noted that the ship's side plating passed through the barbette structure unbroken and that the main deck was heavily reinforced in this area by a 3in thick stringer.

The other longitudinal girders fitted under the upper and the forecastle decks were intended to provide support against the blast of the main armament, although those abreast X and Y turrets also served as compensation for the barbette openings in the deck. These girders were in turn supported by the bulkheads or by pillars.

The deck plating was laid in strakes parallel to the middle line, except for the outermost strake, known as the stringer, which for strength purposes followed the line of the deck edge. Those decks which were planked, the forecastle deck and the upper deck outside the superstructure, were of lapped construction, while all other decks were constructed with a flush surface. This surface was achieved by butt straps and edge strips on the underside of the deck except in the case of the majority of the protective deck where the two or three thicknesses of overlapped plating made them unnecessary. The protective deck also differed in that all the strakes on the slope of the deck followed the line of the deck edge and not just the stringer.

All the mess decks, accommodation areas etc were covered with thick linoleum, known as corticene, while elsewhere the decks and platforms were plain steel, hence in both cases, the need for a flush surface. *Platforms* and flats where men worked, such as the torpedo flat,

auxiliary machinery rooms etc were constructed of chequered plating to provide a good foot hold.

The accompanying drawings show the supporting structure under the decks and the location of the principal openings in the decks. Note that for continuity of strength the transverse beams passed across many of these openings in particular the skylights and many of the ventilator trunks. Transverse beams were omitted in positions occupied by the principal transverse bulkheads as the latter provided sufficient support in themselves. Full details of the distribution of the deck plating have not survived and the arrangements shown are based on general practice and photographic evidence and should be regarded as a general guide only.

B18/1   *Flying deck (scale ¹/32in = 1ft)*

1   Beams. Angle bulb 9in × 3.5in × 23lbs (reduced to 7in × 3in × 16lbs abaft 'A' barbette)
2   Bulkheads (under)
3   Carlings
4   Longitudinal girders
5   Additional beams to support 12pdr gun mountings
6   Pillars (under)
7   Expansion joint
8   Longitudinal beam for additional support to fairlead
9   Longitudinal beam for additional support to bollard

10   Longitudinal beam for additional support to riding bitt
11   Longitudinal beams abreast deck pipes

B18/2   *Detail of deck plating at fore end of forecastle (scale ¹/32in = 1ft)*

1   20lbs stringer
2   20lbs plate
3   14lbs plate (20lbs doubling was fitted around the foremast and its struts for a distance of 2ft)
4   Butt strap to stringer

B18/3   *Section of expansion joint*

1   Waterway
2   Flying deck plating
3   Covering plate
4   Angle bar

Note: the side bulkheads of the superstructure were similarly arranged but without the waterway.

B18/4   *Forward section of upper deck (scale ¹/32 in = 1ft)*

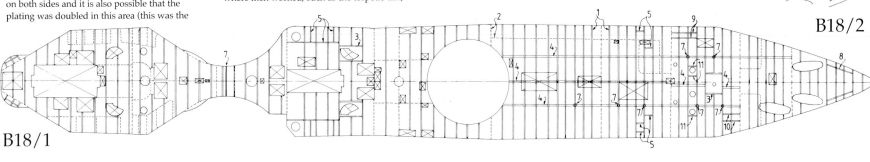

B18/2

B18/1

B18/3

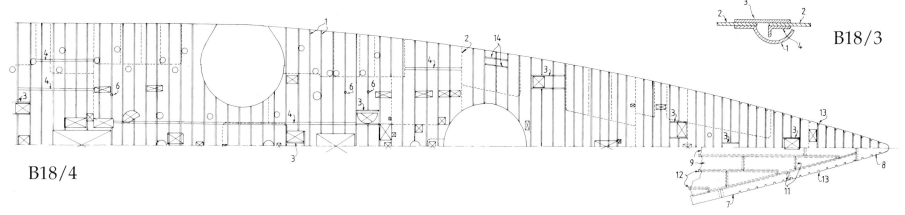

B18/4

127

B   Lines and constructional details

B18/5 *After section of upper deck (scale $^1/_{32}$in = 1ft)*

1   Beams. Angle bulb 9in × 3.5in × 23lbs
2   Bulkheads (under)
3   Carlings
4   Longitudinal girders
5   Additional beams under 12pdr gun mountings
6   Pillars (under)
7   Stringer, 30lbs amidships, 20lbs at ends
8   20lbs plate
9   14lbs plating (at forward and after ends)
10   30lbs plating
11   Butt straps (under)
12   Edge strips
13   Openings for zed frames (see B19/1)
14   Longitudinal beam for additional support to bollard
15   Longitudinal beam for additional support to fairlead

B18/6 *Perspective view of longitudinal girder*

B18/7 *Detail of longitudinal girder (scale ¼in = 1ft)*

1   15lbs intercostal flanged plate
2   Continuous angle bar *
3   Intercostal angle bar *
4   Angle bar *
5   Deck beam
6   Lightening holes
7   Pillar
8   30lbs rider plate (continuous)
9   Rider plate butt strap

*All 3.5in × 3.5in × 10lbs

B18/8 *Perspective view showing typical arrangement of carlings (applicable to all decks)*

1   Carling (of same section as transverse beams)
2   Deck
3   Hatch coaming (note that carlings were also employed abreast other deck openings)
4   Transverse beam
5   Half beam
6   3.5in × 3.5in × 10lbs angle bar

B18/9 *Section of arrangement adjacent to funnel hatches (scale ¼in = 1ft)*

1   20lbs hatch coaming (also known as carlings)
2   Funnel casing
3   Funnel enclosure bulkhead (7.5lbs)
4   Superstructure bulkhead
5   Transverse beam
6   Angle bar 3.5in × 3.5in × 10lbs
7   Angle bar 3in × 3in × 6.5lbs
8   Zed bar
9   Bracket
10   3in teak deck planking
11   30lbs deck plating

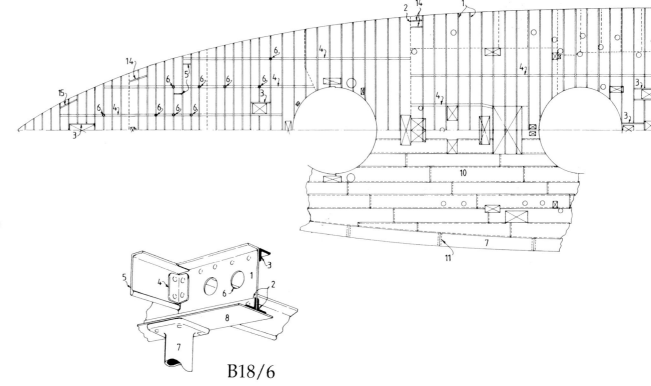

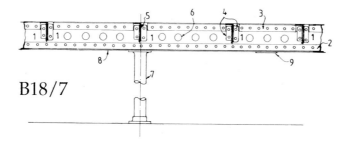

B18/6

B18/7

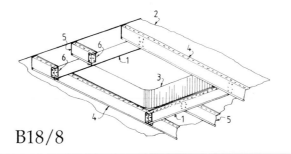

B18/8

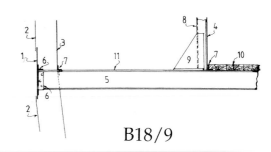

B18/9

B18/10 *Forward section of main deck (scale $^1/_{32}$in = 1ft)*

B18/11 *After section of main deck (scale $^1/_{32}$ in = 1ft)*

B18/12 *Detail of plating abreast wing barbettes (scale $^1/_{32}$in = 1ft)*

1 Beams 9in × 3.5in × 23lbs angle bulb (7in × 3in × 16lbs abaft after armoured bulkhead)
2 Bulkheads (under)
3 Carlings
4 Outer edge of deck
5 Outer bottom plating (under)
6 30lbs deck plating, reducing to 12lbs abaft after armoured bulkhead
7 30lbs stringer, reducing to 20lbs abaft after armoured bulkhead
8 Edge strips (under)
9 Butt straps (under)
10 3.5in × 3in × 8lbs boundary angle to funnel uptakes, ventilator trunks, barbettes etc
11 Pillars (under)
12 Special 120lbs stringer
13 Reversed beam

B18/10

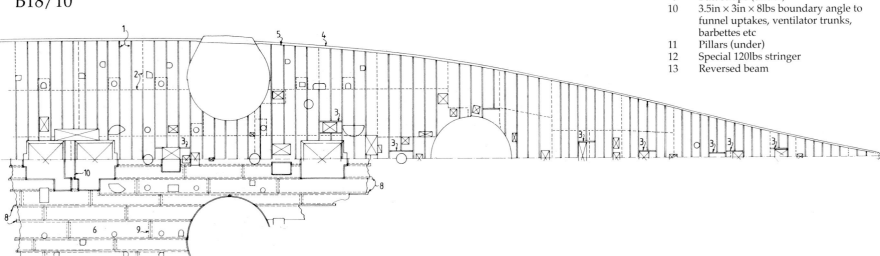

B18/11

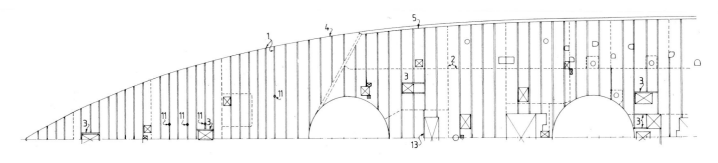

B18/12

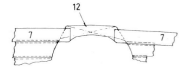

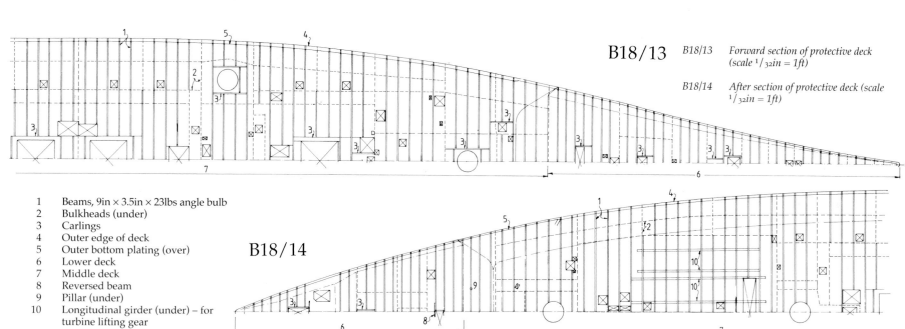

B18/13

B18/13   *Forward section of protective deck (scale $^1/_{32}in$ = 1ft)*

B18/14   *After section of protective deck (scale $^1/_{32}in$ = 1ft)*

1   Beams, 9in × 3.5in × 23lbs angle bulb
2   Bulkheads (under)
3   Carlings
4   Outer edge of deck
5   Outer bottom plating (over)
6   Lower deck
7   Middle deck
8   Reversed beam
9   Pillar (under)
10   Longitudinal girder (under) – for turbine lifting gear

B18/14

B18/15

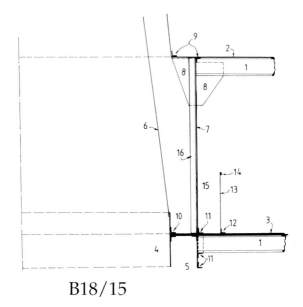

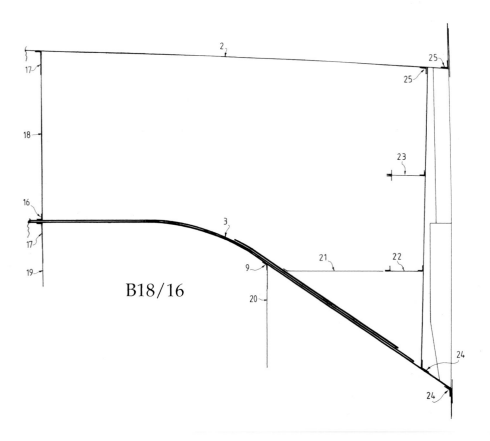

B18/16

130

B18/15   *Transverse section of junction of main and middle decks with funnel hatch (scale ¼in = 1ft)*

B18/16   *Transverse section of main and middle decks at side amidships (scale ¼in = 1ft)*

1	Beams, 9in × 3.5in × 23lbs angle bulb
2	Main deck (30lbs plating)
3	Protective deck (40lbs + 30lbs plating on flat, 40lbs + 30lbs + 40lbs on slope)
4	Funnel hatch coaming (20lbs)
5	Funnel hatch carling

This arrangement is not standard but *Dreadnought's* 'As Fitted' drawings show the beams cut-off at this point; normally the beams extended to the funnel hatch coaming.

6	Funnel uptake
7	Funnel bulkhead (14lbs)
8	Bracket (14lbs)
9	Angle bar, 3.5in × 3in × 8lbs
10	Angle bar, 3.5in × 3.5in × 10lbs
11	Angle bar, 3in × 3in × 6.5lbs
12	Angle bar, 2.5in × 2.5in × 3lbs
13	5lbs plate
14	Segmental bar beading
15	Cofferdam

These were fitted around all the principal openings in the protective deck that would be open in action. In the event of flooding on the deck, the spread of water through any damaged bulkheads to the area below could be stopped or reduced by filling the cofferdam space with canvas, wood, oakum etc.

16	Angle bar stiffener, 3.5in × 2.5in × 6.5lbs
17	Flanged plate (10lbs)
18	Upper bunker bulkhead (10lbs)
19	Lower bunker bulkhead (10lbs)
20	Wing bunker bulkhead (10lbs)
21	Bunker shovelling flat (14lbs chequered plating)
22	Stringer
23	Girder behind side armour
24	Angle bar, 4.5in × 4.5in × 17lbs
25	Angle bar, 4in × 4in × 13lbs

B18/17   *Detail of protective deck plating (scale ⅛in = 1ft)*

Deck is shown in developed form as if completely flat

1	Lower thickness of plating (40lbs)
2	Second thickness of plating (30lbs)
3	Third thickness of plating (40lbs)
4	Butt of third thickness
5	Butt of second thickness
6	Butt of lower thickness
7	Angle bar boundaries to barbette armour
8	Base plate of barbette ring bulkhead
9	Edge strips and butt straps to area under barbette only (single thickness plating)
10	Transverse bulkhead at station 58 (under)
11	Longitudinal bulkheads (under)
12	Escape trunk hatch
13	12pdr dredger hoist
14	Flat of deck
15	Curve of deck
16	Slope of deck
17	Butt strap to single thickness at deck edge
18	Angle bar to plating behind armour
19	Armour shelf

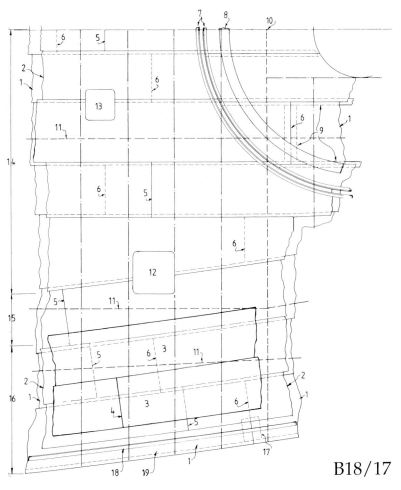

B18/17

B Lines and constructional details

B18/18   *Middle deck aft (scale ¹/32in = 1ft)*

B18/19   *Middle deck forward (scale ¹/32in = 1ft)*

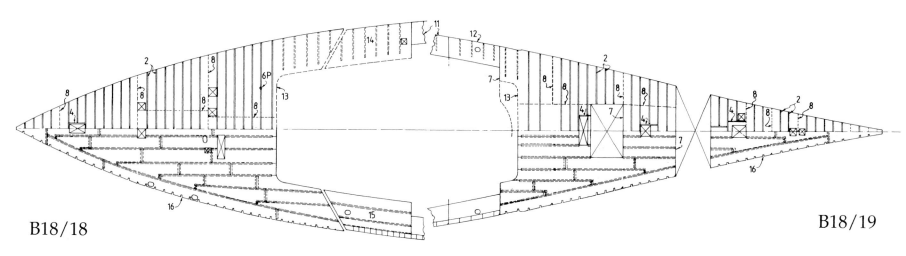

B18/18

B18/19

B18/20   *'Y' magazine and auxiliary machinery flats – lower deck (scale ¹/32in = 1ft)*

B18/21   *'X' magazine flat -lower deck (scale ¹/32in = 1ft)*

B18/22   *'P' and 'Q' magazine flats -lower deck (scale ¹/32in = 1ft)*

B18/23   *'A' magazine, auxiliary machinery, 12pdr magazine and store room flats – lower deck (scale ¹/32in = 1ft)*

B18/20   B18/21   B18/22   B18/23

B18/24   'Y' shell room, torpedo room and engineers' store flats – platform deck (scale 1/32in = 1ft)

B18/25   'X' shell room flat – platform deck (scale 1/32in = 1ft)

B18/26   'P' and 'Q' shell room flats – platform deck (scale 1/32in = 1ft)

B18/27   Platform deck flats forward (scale 1/32in = 1ft)

1   Beam, angle bulb 9in × 3.5in × 23lbs
2   Beam, angle bulb 7in × 3in × 16lbs
3   Beam, zed bar 6in × 3in × 3.5in × 14lbs
4   Carling
5   Longitudinal girder under auxiliary machinery (P = port side only)
6   Pillar (under, P = port side only)
7   Bulkhead (continuous, through deck)
8   Bulkhead (under)
9   Plate frame (under)
10   Beams strengthened under hydraulic pumping engine (see B19/3)
11   Bunker shovelling flat over slope of protective deck
12   Flat over slope of protective deck (watertight compartment)
13   Edge rivetted to top of protective deck
14   Engineers' stores flat (over slope of protective deck)
15   Ready use bread room flat (over slope of protective deck)
16   Openings in deck edge for zed frames (see B19/1)
17   Additional longitudinal angle bar beams under air compressor

Deck plating to middle deck fore and aft was 12lbs with a 20lbs stringer. Lower and platform deck flats were of 14lbs plating under heavy weights and 10lbs plating elsewhere.

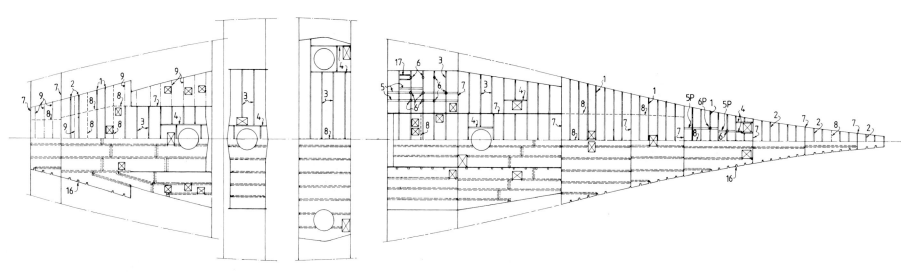

B18/24   B18/25   B18/26   B18/27

B Lines and constructional details

B19 DECK DETAILS

B19/1 *Detail of arrangement for making deck edges watertight to zed frames and bulkhead stiffeners (scale ½in = 1ft)*
1 Angle bar, 3in × 3.5in × 8lbs
2 Deck beam (under)
3 Deck plating
4 Zed frame
5 Liner
6 Outer bottom plating

B19/2 *Detail of arrangement for making deck edges watertight to angle bar intermediate frames and bulkhead stiffeners (scale ½in = 1ft)*
1 Angle bar, 3in × 3.5in × 8lbs
2 Deck beam (under)
3 Deck plating
4 Angle bar frame or stiffener
5 Liner
6 Outer bottom plating

B19/3 *Section at station 66 looking forward, showing supporting structure under auxiliary machinery rooms (scale ⅛in = 1ft)*

1 Girder under hydraulic pumping engine (arrangement for after engine identical)
2 Diesel dynamo room
3 12pdr shell room
4 Engineers' store
5 Electric light store
6 Zed beam
7 Channel bar pillar, (head rivetted to beam) at stations 66, 64 and 62
8 Channel bar pillar at stations 66, 64 and 60
9 Channel bar pillar at stations 66, 64 and 62
10 Tee bar pillar at stations 66, 64 and 62
11 Bracket at stations 66 and 64
12 Longitudinal girder
13 Angle bars between stations 66 and 64 under compressor
14 Watertight angle bar to deck edge
15 Zed bar stiffener to bulkhead
16 Bracket
17 Flanged plate
18 Plate
19 Angle bar

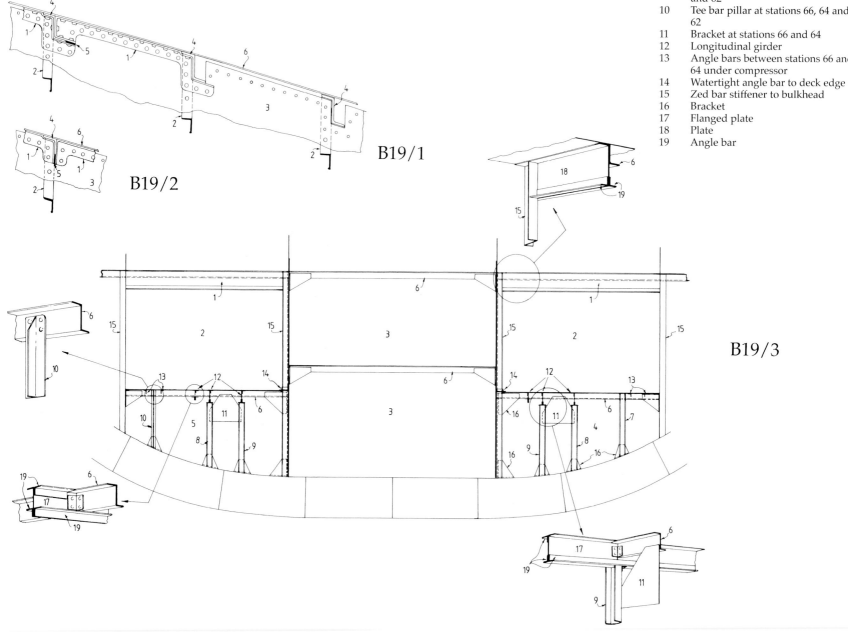

B19/1

B19/2

B19/3

B20 PILLARS

Under heavy weights, such as auxiliary machinery and areas of deck where there was limited support from bulkheads, tubular steel pillars were fitted. (The exception to this arrangement is shown in B19/3.) These were either fitted directly to the beams or under longitudinal girders.

B20/1 *Pillar fitted to angle bulb beam (scale ³/8 in = 1ft)*

B20/2 *Pillar fitted to zed beam (scale ³/8in = 1ft)*

B20/3 *Pillar fitted to longitudinal girder (scale ³/8in = 1ft)*

1 Pillar
2 Angle bulb beam
3 Heel (rivetted to deck and beam below)
4 Zed beam
5 Angle bar
6 Intercostal flanged plate

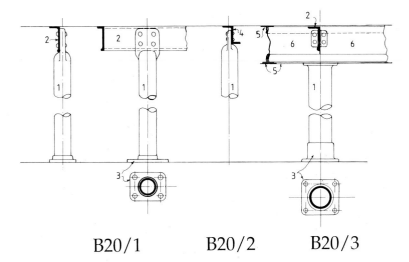

B20/1   B20/2   B20/3

B21 BULKHEADS

The principal watertight bulkheads were continuous from the protective deck to the double bottom or, outside the latter, to the outer bottom. The transverse bulkheads extending unbroken across the full width of the ship, while the longitudinal bulkheads were constructed between them except for the protective sections of longitudinal bulkhead abreast the magazines which were continuous and cut the adjacent transverse bulkheads. Above the protective deck the bulkheads were built between the decks and while several of the transverse bulkheads in these positions passes right across the ship, most of those amidships were cut by either longitudinal bulkheads or the barbettes.

The plating of the watertight bulkheads was laid horizontally with lapped edges and butts and this was stiffened according to the bulkhead's area, the degree of adjacent support structure (*ie* other bulkheads, decks, trunks etc.) and any support they were required to give to the structure above, such as barbettes. The stiffening, provided by various arrangements of I, zed and angle bar, was fitted at various nominal spacings but these distances were adjusted to fit the structure and, where other parts of the ship's structure provided the necessary support, the stiffening bars were omitted. On the principal deep bulkheads the plating was thicker at the bottom to allow for the greater pressure of water in these positions in the event of flooding. The construction of the various bulkheads is listed below.

Main transverse watertight bulkheads below protective deck
Stations 12 (collision bulkhead) 58, 70, 91,100, 142, 149, 183, 206: Of 17lbs plating at bottom reducing to 14lbs at top (station 206 14lbs only) stiffened with 5in zed bars spaced approximately 3ft apart. Two additional 10in zeds were fitted abreast the centre of the bulkhead at station 58 (under A barbette) and four 10in zeds to the bulkhead at station 183 (see B21/19).
Station 121: As above except for large unsupported area between boiler rooms which was stiffened with 12in I bars approximately 8ft apart with intermediate and horizontal 5in zed bars.
Stations 18, 26, 32, 40, 197 (last between platform deck and middle deck): Of 12lbs plating, stiffened with alternate 5in zeds and angle bars, approximately 2ft apart.
Station 200: (from outer bottom to platform deck only) 14lbs plating, stiffened with angle bars.

Main longitudinal watertight bulkheads below protective deck
Inner coal bunker bulkheads and engine room wing bulkheads: Of 17lbs at bottom reducing to 10lbs at top. Stiffened with 8in zeds at beams (4ft apart) and intermediate angle bars.
Wing coal bunker bulkheads: Of 14lbs at bottom reducing to 10lbs at top. Stiffened with 5in zeds at beams and intermediate angle bars.
Middle line engine room bulkhead: Of 17lbs plating, stiffened with 12in I bars spaced 8ft apart, with intermediate and horizontal 5in zed bars.

Main transverse watertight bulkheads above protective deck
Generally of 10lbs plating, stiffened by angle bars spaced about 2ft 6in apart.

Main longitudinal bulkheads above protective deck
Coal bunker bulkhead: Of 10lbs stiffened by angle bars 2ft apart.
Funnel hatch bulkheads: Of 14lbs stiffened by angle bars 2ft apart.

Minor bulkheads
These were generally of light plating of 5 or 7lbs but were increased to 10lbs under the 12in guns to help support the deck against blast.

General
Additional stiffening was fitted to minor bulkheads where necessary under heavy weights. The transverse coal bunker bulkheads were non-watertight and the plating was laid vertically. Around the propeller shafts the bulkhead plating was increased to 20lbs. For details of protective bulkheads see B21/19.

B   Lines and constructional details

B21/1 *Main transverse watertight bulkhead at station 121 (looking aft) (scale ¹/₈in = 1ft)*

B21/2 *Plan view of bulkhead (scale ¹/₈in = 1ft)*

B21/3 *Section at I bar stiffeners (scale ¹/₈in = 1ft)*

B21/4 *Section at zed bar stiffeners (scale ¹/₈in = 1ft)*

1   Zed bar, 5in × 3in × 2.5in × 12lbs (horizontal bars fitted over plating laps)
2   'I' bar, 12in × 6in × 6in × 54lbs
3   Angle bar, 3.5in × 3.5in × 10lbs
4   Angle bar, 3.5in × 2.5in × 6.5lbs
5   14lbs flanged bracket (I bar flange cut-away)
6   Angle bar 3in × 3in × 6.5lbs
7   17lbs plating
8   14lbs plating
9   Lapped butts
10 Lapped edges
11 Inner coal bunker bulkhead
12 Wing coal bunker bulkhead
13 Upper coal bunker bulkhead
14 Funnel hatch bulkhead (14lbs) – continuous
15 10lbs plating
16 Protective (middle) deck
17 6th longitudinal
18 Main deck
19 Double bottom
20 Keel
21 14lbs bracket

B21/2

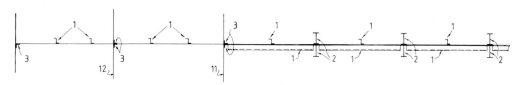

B21/1

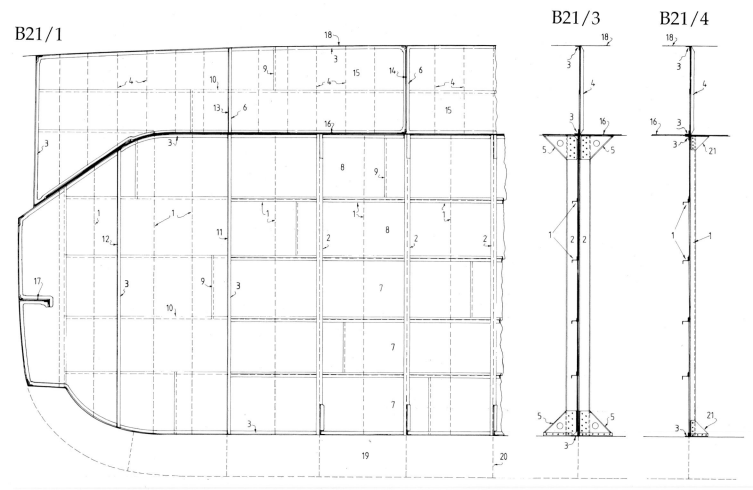

B21/3

B21/4

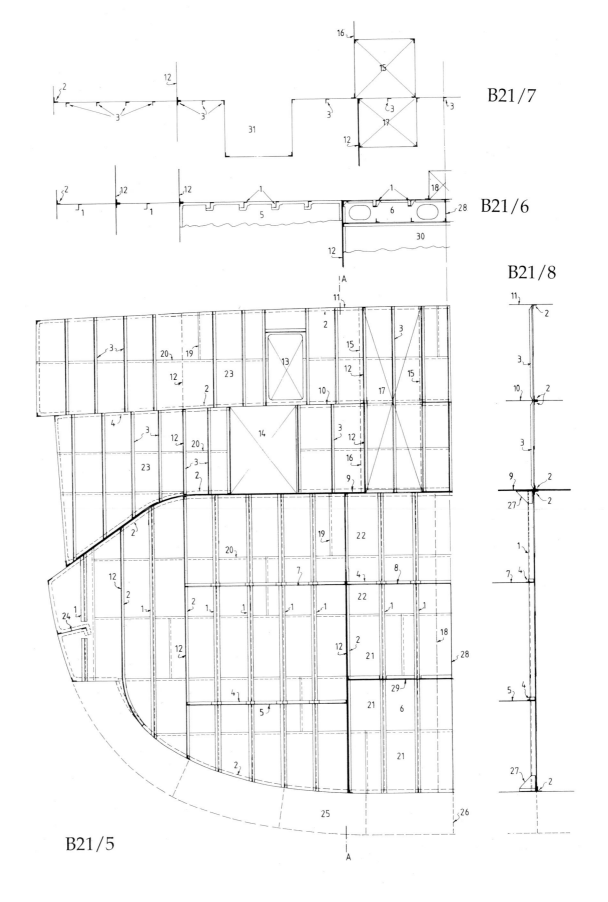

B21/5 *Main transverse watertight bulkhead at station 70 looking aft (scale 1/8in = 1ft)*

B21/6 *Plan view of bulkhead and adjacent structure at platform deck level (scale 1/8 in = 1ft)*

B21/7 *Plan view of bulkhead at middle deck (scale 1/8in = 1ft)*

B21/8 *Section of bulkhead at A-A (scale 1/8in = 1ft)*

1	Zed bar 5in × 3in × 2.5in × 12lbs
2	Angle bar 3.5in × 3.5in × 10lbs
3	Angle bar 3.5in × 2.5in × 6.5lbs
4	Angle bar 3in × 3in × 6.5lbs
5	Dynamo room flat
6	Air space
7	Hydraulic machinery room flat
8	12pdr ammunition working space flat
9	Middle deck
10	Main deck
11	Upper deck
12	Longitudinal bulkhead
13	Watertight door
14	Opening to watertight enclosure around hatch to hydraulic engine room
15	Boiler room vent trunk (on aft side)
16	Funnel hatch bulkhead (on aft side)
17	12pdr ammunition embarkation trunk
18	Ash hoist (on aft side)
19	Lapped butt
20	Lapped edge
21	17lbs plating
22	14lbs plating
23	10lbs plating
24	6th longitudinal
25	Double bottom
26	Keel
27	14lbs bracket
28	Middle line frame in air space
29	Horizontal frame in air space
30	12pdr shell room flat
31	Watertight enclosure around hatch to hydraulic engine room

B21/7

B21/6

B21/8

B21/5

B   Lines and constructional details

B21/9   *Details of watertight boundary angles to 2nd and 6th longitudinals passing through bulkheads outside the double bottom (scale ¼in = 1ft)*

1   Outer bottom plating
2   Longitudinal
3   Angle bar 3.5in × 3.5in × 10lbs
4   Forged angle collar

B21/10   *Detail of method of making bulkheads watertight to keel forward of double bottom (scale ¼in = 1ft)*

1   Keel
2   Angle bar 3.5in × 3.5in × 10lbs
3   Vertical lap joint in bulkhead
4   Hold flat
5   Angle bar 3.5in × 2.5in × 6.5lbs, stiffener on fore side of bulkhead
6   Angle bar 3in × 3in × 6.5lbs

B21/11   *Main transverse watertight bulkhead at station 206 looking forward (scale ⅛in = 1ft)*

1   Zed bar 5in × 3in × 2.5in × 12lbs
2   Longitudinal bulkhead
3   Middle line bulkhead
4   Longitudinal bulkhead on forward side
5   Angle bar 3.5in × 3.5in × 10lbs
6   Cut-up casting
7   Angle bar 3in × 3in × 6.5lbs
8   14lbs plating
9   Watertight door
10   Lower deck
11   Platform deck flat
12   Butt lap
13   Edge lap
14   Propeller shaft recess

B21/12   *Middle line engine room bulkhead, looking to port (scale ¹⁄₁₆in = 1ft)*

B21/13   *Plan view of bulkhead (scale ¹⁄₁₆in = 1ft)*

B21/14   *Section of bulkhead at T bars (scale ¹⁄₁₆in = 1ft)*

1   I bar, 12in × 6in × 6in × 54lbs
2   Intercostal horizontal stiffener fitted over plating edge laps, zed bar 5in × 3in × 2.5in × 12lbs
3   Zed bar 5in × 3in × 2.5in × 12lbs, port side only
4   20lbs bracket
5   Electric lift trunk
6   Transverse bulkhead
7   Deck beam
8   Flanged plate
9   Angle bar 3.5in × 3.5in × 10lbs, starboard side only
10   Middle deck
11   Inner bottom
12   Deep bracket to support bulkhead adjacent to main steam pipe cross connection, starboard side only

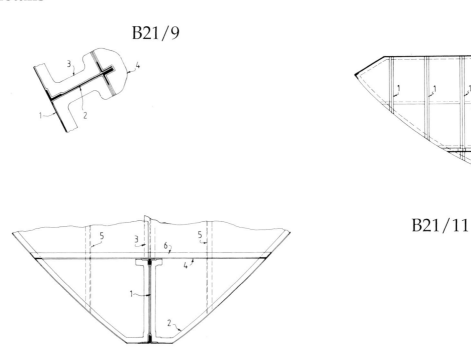

B21/9

B21/11

B21/10

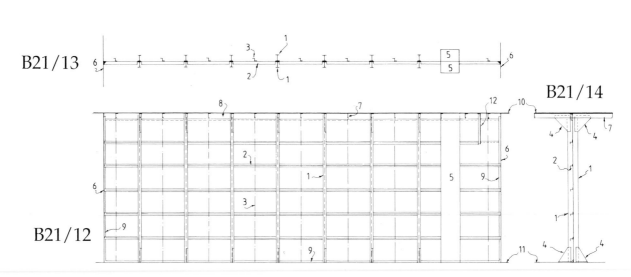

B21/13

B21/14

B21/12

B21/15 *Transverse section at station 102, looking aft (scale ¹/8in = 1ft)*

B21/16 *Plan view of bulkheads at stations 100/102 (scale ¹/8in = 1ft)*

B21/17 *Profile of bulkheads at stations 100/102 (scale ¹/8in = 1ft)*

1 Transverse coal bunker bulkhead (non-watertight) 10lbs plating laid vertically
2 Inner coal bunker bulkhead, 17lbs plating at bottom, 14lbs plating at middle, 10lbs plating at top
3 Wing coal bunker bulkhead, 14lbs plating at bottom, remainder 10lbs
4 Zed bar 5in × 3in × 2.5in × 12lbs
5 Zed bar 8in × 3.5in × 3.5in × 18.2lbs
6 Angle bar 3.5in × 2.5in × 6.5lbs
7 Angle bar 3.5in × 3.5in × 10lbs
8 20lbs bracket
9 14lbs bracket
10 Half beam
11 Stays
12 Middle line frame in cross bunker
13 Position of holes in middle line frame
14 Middle deck
15 Enclosure for pipes
16 Coal bunker door
17 Access lobby to top of cross bunker
18 Opening to platform in boiler room
19 Escape trunk from wing and lower coal bunkers
20 Watertight bulkhead at station 100
21 Intercostal flanged plate
22 Double bottom
23 Keel

B21/18 *Detail of method of making head of longitudinal bulkhead watertight to beams using a flanged plate*

Employed on principal longitudinal bulkheads such as middle line and wing bulkheads in engine room and inner coal bunker bulkhead

1 Flanged plate
2 Bulkhead plating
3 Beam
4 Deck

B21/18

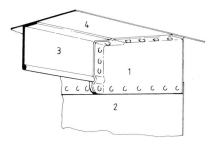

B21/17

B21/16

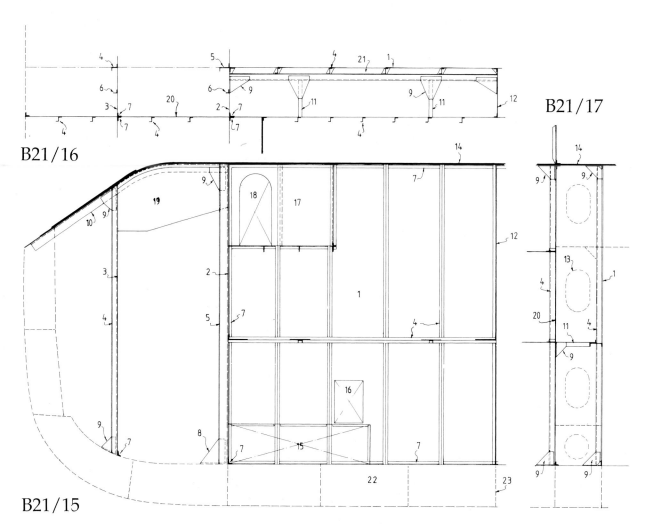

B21/15

B21/19 *Detail of method of making head of longitudinal bulkhead watertight to beams using angle bar*

1 Angle bar
2 Bulkhead plating
3 Beam
4 Deck

B21/19

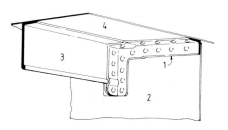

B   Lines and constructional details

B21/20 *Perspective view of hull structure under 'Y' barbette, showing additional stiffening under barbette and to after engine room bulkhead*

1. Zed bar 10in × 3.5in × 3.5in × 21lbs
2. Zed bar 5in × 3in × 2.5in × 12lbs
3. Angle bar 3.5in × 2.5in × 6.5lbs
4. Main transverse watertight bulkhead at station 183 (after end of engine room)
5. Transverse watertight bulkhead at station 197 (platform deck to middle deck only)
6. Transverse watertight bulkhead at station 200 (outer bottom to platform deck only)
7. Longitudinal protective bulkheads
8. Longitudinal middle line bulkhead to engine room
9. Zed bar 8in × 3.5in × 3.5in × 18.2lbs
10. Engine room wing bulkheads
11. Watertight compartment
12. Plate frames
13. Steam dynamo room
14. Compartment for storage of compressed air reservoirs
15. 12in ammunition working space
16. Gunners' stores
17. 12in gun mounting trunk enclosure
18. Watertight door to hydraulic machinery room
19. Line of floor of hydraulic machinery room
20. Hydraulic tank
21. Watertight door to Engineers' store
22. Engineers' store
23. Openings for inner propeller shafts
24. Line of flat of Engineers' store
25. Longitudinal bulkhead
26. Middle line bulkhead
27. Part of supporting structure for propeller shaft bearing
28. Plate frames under (see B11/12)
29. 6th longitudinal
30. Fore end of after submerged torpedo room

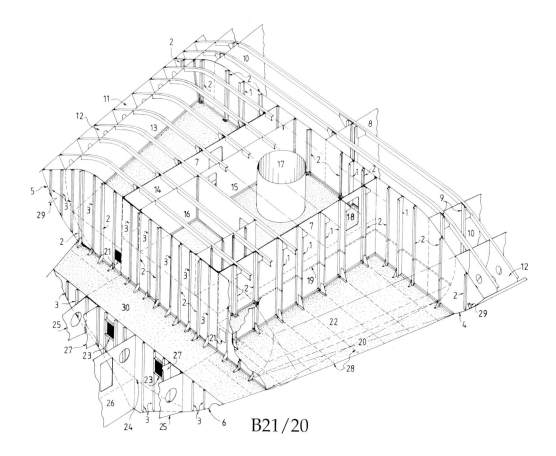

B21/20

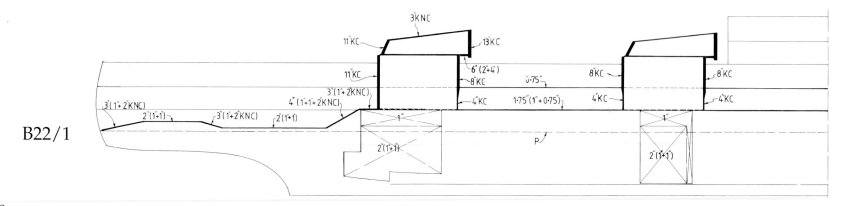

B22/1

B22 ARMOUR LAYOUT (scale ¹/₃₂in = 1ft)

B22/1 Internal profile

Numbers give the nominal thickness of armour and protective plating in inches – the figures normally quoted both officially and unofficially. However almost all of *Dreadnought's* armour and plating was specified by weight, the nominal thickness being derived from the basis that a 1in plate weighed 40lbs/sq.ft. However, as steel actually weighs 40.42lbs/sq.ft. all these thicknesses were slightly less than those given – the 11in main belt, for example was 440lbs KC which would give a true thickness of 10.89in. Armour plate (KC and KNC) of 6in and lesser thickness was the principal exception as most of the armour plate manufacturers supplied these sizes to the specified thickness in inches.
KC = Krupp Cemented (or equivalent)
KNC = Krupp Non-Cemented (or equivalent)
Unspecified thicknesses; mild steel
P = lower edge of slope of protective deck
G = armour gratings in funnel uptakes and machinery ventilation shafts
Thicknesses given for 'Y' gunhouse apply to all mountings. Figures in parentheses give thickness of each layer of plating where total thickness is 'built-up', the inner or lower thickness being given first. The slope of the protective deck for example is 2.75in thick made up of 1in and 0.75in mild steel with a third layer of 1in KNC.

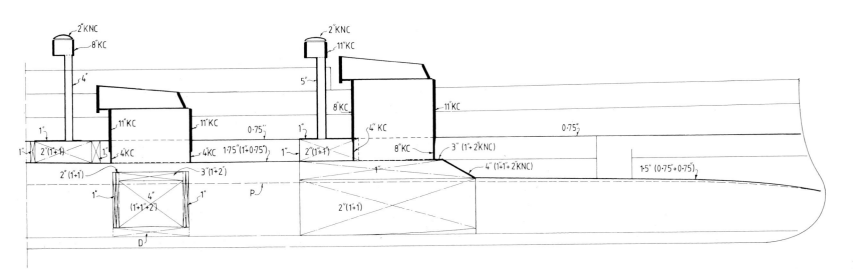

B Lines and constructional details

B22/2 *External profile*

B22/3 *Half plan of main deck*

B22/4 *Half plan of protective deck*

B22/5 *Half plan at level of platform deck*

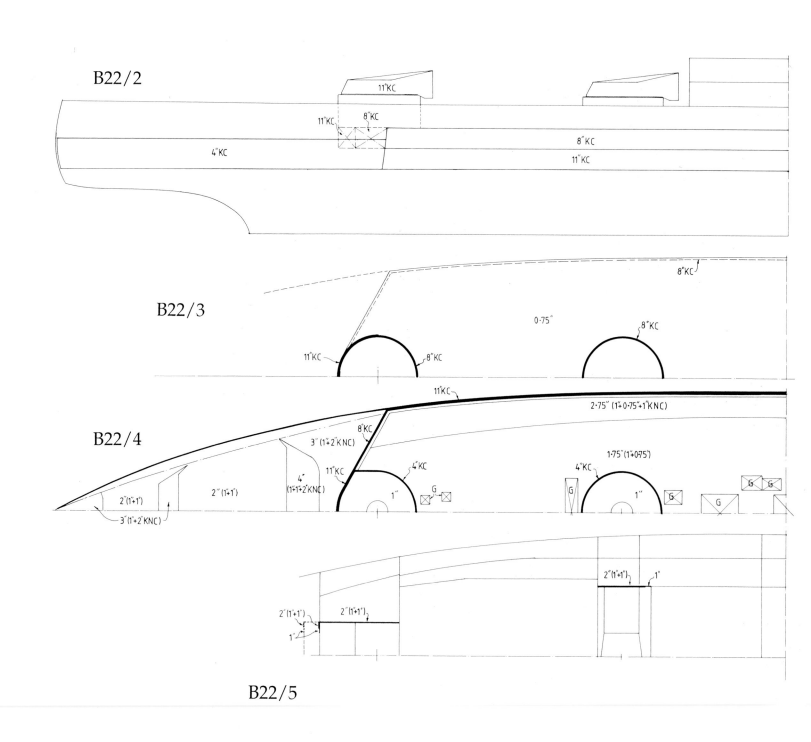

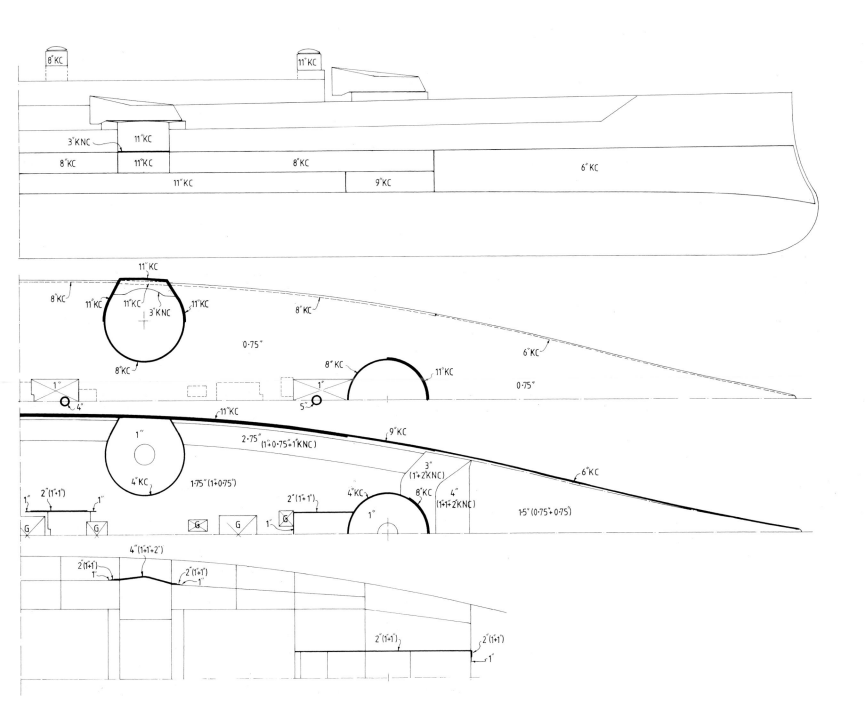

8″KC

11″KC

3″KNC   11″KC

8″KC   11″KC

11″KC

8″KC   6″KC

9″KC

11″KC

8″KC   11″KC   11″KC   3″KNC   11″KC

8″KC

8″KC

0·75″

6″KC

8″KC   11″KC

1″   5″   0·75″

4″

11″KC

1″

9″KC

2·75″
(1″+0·75″+1″KNC)

3″
(1″+2″KNC)

4″KC   1·75″ (1″+0·75″)   2″(1″+1″)   4″KC   8″KC   4″
(1″+1″+2″KNC)   6″KC

2″(1″+1″)   1″   2″(1″+1″)   1″   1″
1·5″ (0·75″+0·75″)

G   G   G   G   1″   G

4″(1″+1″+2″)

2″(1″+1″)
1″   2″(1″+1″)
1″

2″(1″+1″)   2″(1″+1″)
1″

B   Lines and constructional details

B23   BARBETTES

B23/1 *Perspective view of 'X' barbette*

The basic features shown in this view are applicable to all the barbettes. However they differed from each other in general arrangement of armour and in height according to their position in the ship.

1 Framing to plating behind armour. Zed bars 8in × 3.5in × 3.5in × 18.2lbs with reverse angle bar 3in × 3in × 6.5lbs, on inner edge
2 Outer stiffeners to ring bulkhead. Zed bars 6in × 3.5in × 3in × 14lbs
3 Inner stiffeners to ring bulkhead. Zed bars formed of two angle bars, 3in × 3in × 6.5lbs, riveted back-to-back
4 Plating behind armour, two thicknesses of 17lbs

11 Training rack seat
12 Elastic platform
Perforated, 14lbs plating intended to deform if barbette was damaged and thus prevent distortion of the ring bulkhead structure.
13 30lbs plating
14 Keyway for locking upper sections of armour plate together with dovetailed key
15 Upper deck

16 Main deck
17 Middle deck
18 Structure for turret buffer stop and locking bolt housing
19 320lbs KC armour
20 160lbs KC armour
21 Openings for framing behind armour
A Aft

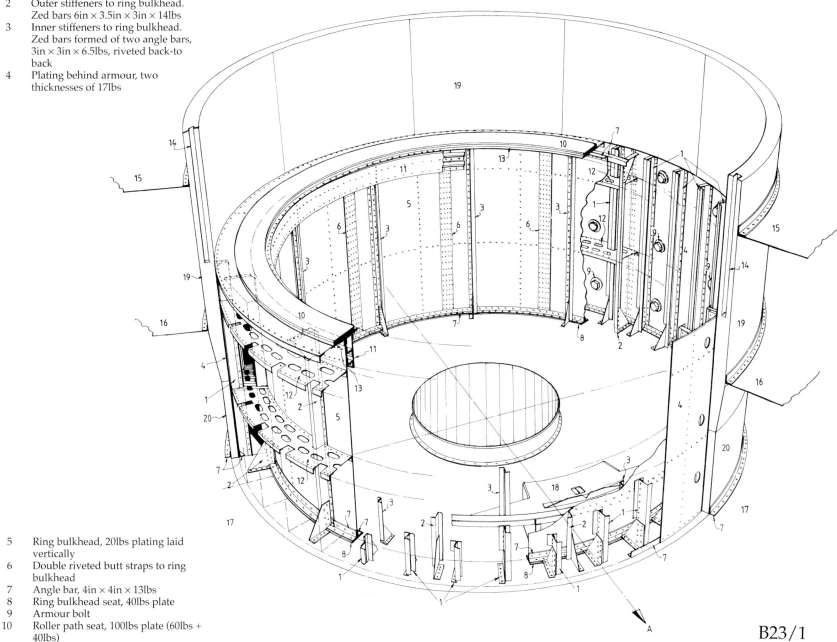

5 Ring bulkhead, 20lbs plating laid vertically
6 Double riveted butt straps to ring bulkhead
7 Angle bar, 4in × 4in × 13lbs
8 Ring bulkhead seat, 40lbs plate
9 Armour bolt
10 Roller path seat, 100lbs plate (60lbs + 40lbs)

B23/1

B23/2 Part plan of 'Y' barbette and screen bulkhead (scale ¹/8in = 1ft)

B23/3 Part plan of 'X' barbette (scale ¹/8in = 1ft)

B23/4 Part plan of 'Q' barbette at main deck (scale ¹/8in = 1ft)

B23/5 Part plan of 'Q' barbette at middle deck (scale ¹/8 = 1ft)

1   Zed bar 8in × 3.5in × 3.5in × 18.2lbs with reverse angle bar, 3in × 3in × 6.5lbs, on inner edge
2   Zed bar 6in × 3.5in × 3in 14lbs
3   Zed bar 8in × 3.5in × 3.5in × 18.2lbs
4   Zed bar, formed of two angle bars, 3in × 3in × 6.5lbs, riveted back-to-back
5   Ring bulkhead
6   Wood backing to armour
7   8in KC armour
8   11in KC armour
9   4in KC armour
10 Bulkhead
11 Outer bottom plating
12 Structure for turret buffer stop and locking bolt housing
13 Stiffeners cut short at buffer stop structure
14 Stiffener cut-away to clear walking pipe
15 Framing behind side armour
16 Ring bulkhead terminated at, and joined to, framing
17 120lbs KC plate
18 6in zed bar and reverse angle
19 Manhole to space below flat
20 Inboard edge of flat
21 Supporting frames to flat (under)

B23/2

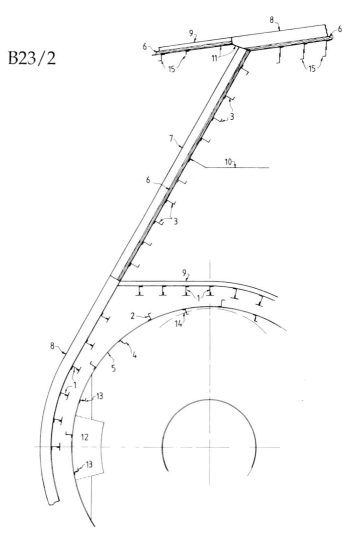

B23/3

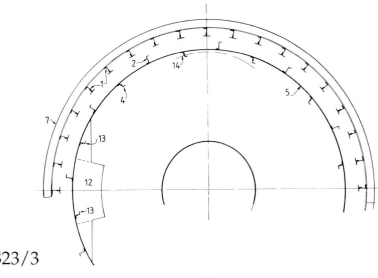

B23/4

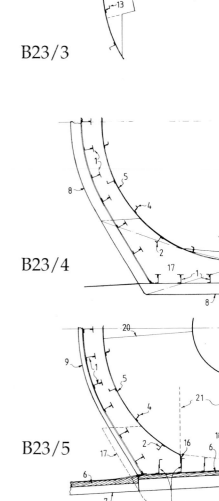

B23/5

B Lines and constructional details

*B23/6 Half section at centreline (station 95.5)
of 'Q' barbette looking forward (scale
¼ in = 1ft)*

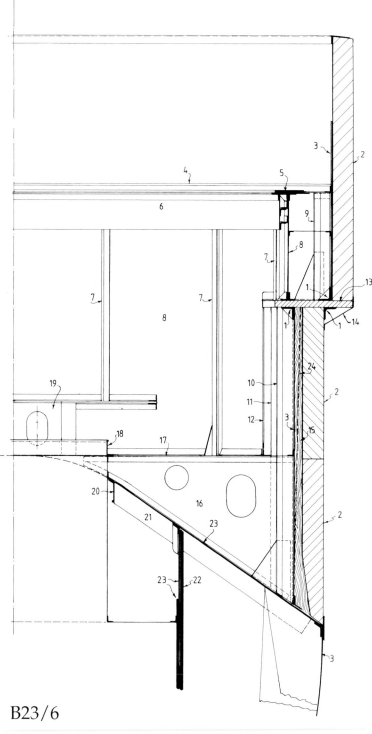

B23/6

1   Angle bar 6in × 6in × 37.4lbs
2   11in KC armour
3   Outer bottom plating
4   Top of plating behind barbette
armour

Note that, unlike the other barbettes, the angle is
above and not below the level of the roller path
seat.

5   Roller path seat
6   Training rack seat
7   Inner stiffeners to ring bulkhead
8   Ring bulkhead
9   Frames to barbette armour, 8in zed
with reverse angle
10 Frame at station 95, 8in zed with
reverse angle
11 Frame at station 94
12 Frame at station 93 and end of ring
bulkhead below 120lbs plate
13 120lbs KNC plate
14 Fashion plate
15 Teak backing
16 Plate frame at station 94
17 Flat
18 Coaming to opening for ammunition
trunk
19 Structure for turret buffer stop and
locking bolt
20 Carling
21 Half beam
22 80lbs plate
23 40lbs plate
24 Line of outer bottom plating outside
barbette

B24   ARMOUR BOLT

The vertical armour was secured by means of
bolts which passed through the backing and
screwed into the rear face of the plate. The bolts
were arranged to give approximately one to
every seven square feet of armour plate. In
exposed areas (such as inside gun mountings) a
steel cup was fitted over the head in case it
should break off if the armour were struck.

1   Armour
2   Teak backing

Bolt was also used on armour without wood
backing, in which case the narrow shank was cut
back closer to the head.

3   Rubber grommet
4   Ship's plating
5   Washer
6   Bolt
7   Hexagonal head
8   Air space

B24

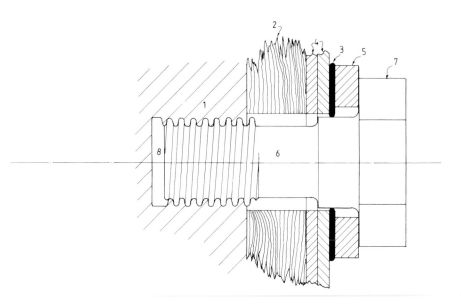

C Machinery

C1 GENERAL ARRANGEMENT OF BOILER ROOMS (scale $^1/_{16}$in = 1ft)

The three boiler rooms were generally similar in layout and, with some small exceptions, each contained the same machinery and fittings. Each boiler group was slightly offset from the middle line, that in 'A' boiler room being 7.5in to port and those in the other two boiler rooms, 7.5in to starboard. The boilers were mounted at the level of the stokehold floor, 2ft above the inner bottom, which allowed space for pipework, inspection, cleaning and painting. It also provided for easier access to the double bottom and reduced the level of corrosion from bilge water.

C1/1   Profile of boiler rooms, shown from outboard of end of boilers

C1/2   Plan at level of lower deck

C1/1

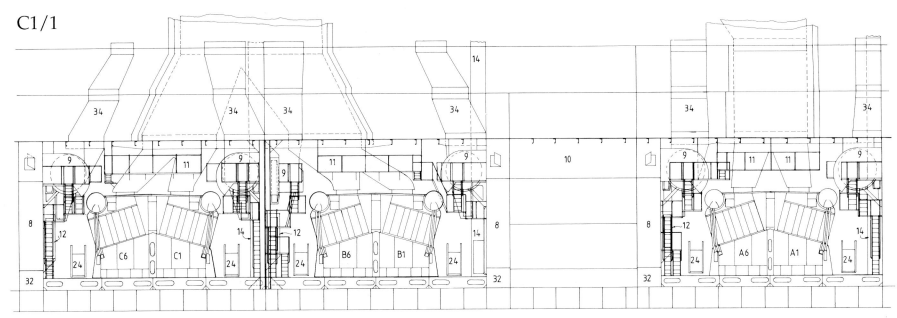

C1/2

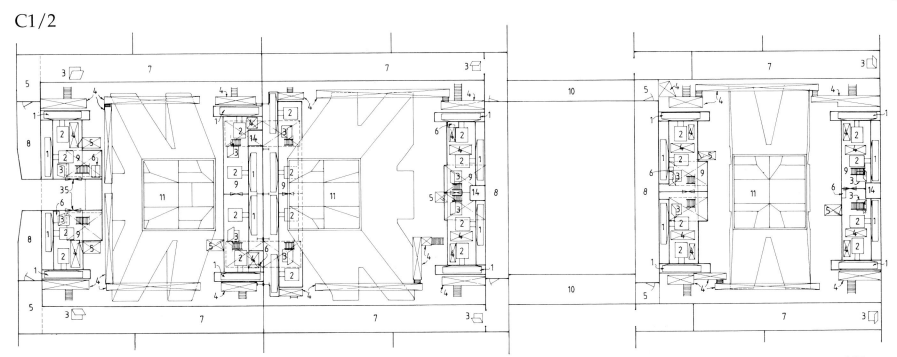

C   Machinery

C1/3   *Plan at level of platform deck*

C1/4   *Plan of hold*

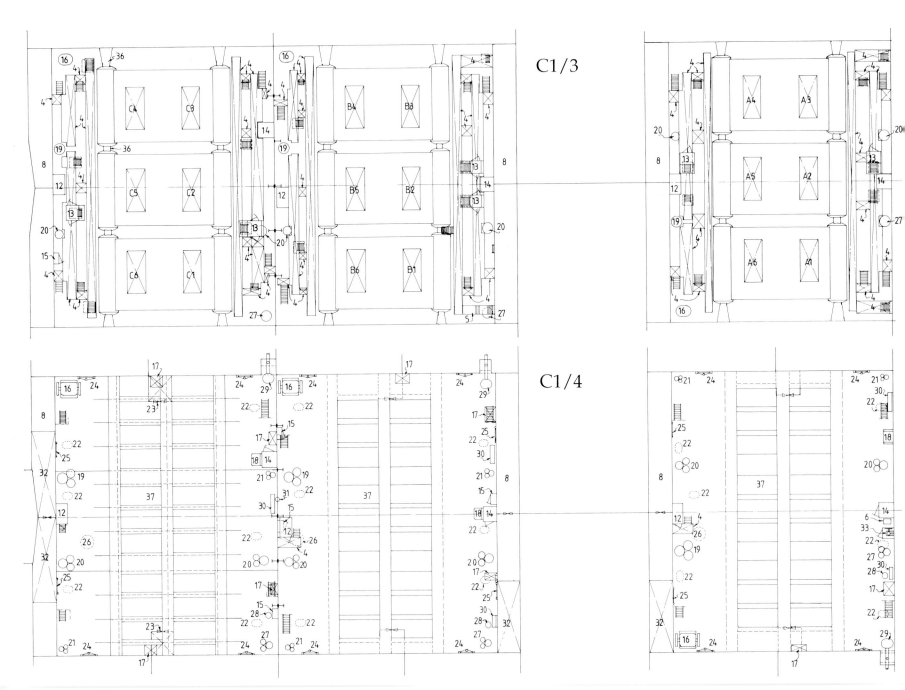

C1/3

C1/4

C1/5 *Section through 'C' boiler room, looking forward from front of boilers*

C1/6 *Section through 'B' boiler room, looking aft at after end*

C1/7 *Section through 'B' boiler room, looking forward at forward end*

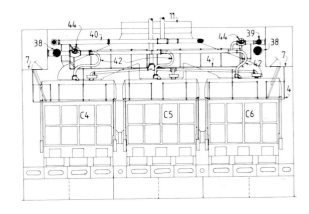

C1/5

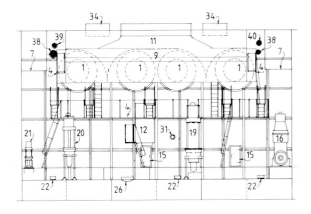

C1/6

1	Fan
2	Fan engine
3	Hatch
4	Grating
5	Platform
6	Lubricating oil tank (over)
7	Platform of perforated plate (access to coal bunkers and temperature tubes)
8	Coal bunker
9	Fan chamber
10	Space for steam pipes
11	Boiler uptakes
12	Telephone cabinet
13	Air lock
14	Ash hoist
15	Locker
16	Air compressor
17	Portable cover to space under floor giving access to valves
18	Vice bench
19	Main feed pump
20	Auxiliary feed pump
21	Oil fuel pump
22	Watertight manhole to double bottom compartment
23	Watertight manhole
24	Vertical sliding watertight door to lower coal bunker
25	Vertical sliding non-watertight door to cross coal bunker
26	Well in inner bottom for bilge suction
27	Fire and bilge pump
28	Air reservoir for ash ejector
29	Ash ejector
30	Valve chest
31	Scuttle

32	Space for pipes
33	Oil-fuel hand pump
34	Vent supply trunks
35	Opening in side of passage (covered with portable plate) for removal of machinery
36	Boiler stays
37	Boiler seats – note that No 3 boiler room is shown without the floor plates
38	Main steam pipe
39	Auxiliary steam pipe
40	Auxiliary exhaust steam pipe
41	Additional branch to auxiliary steam range fitted in 1908 to supply forward steam driven dynamo
42	Connection to main steam valve on boiler
43	Fixed pipe-mounting
44	Screw-lift steam valve
45	Sliding pipe-fitting to bulkhead
46	Auxiliary steam to hydraulic pumping engines
47	Exhaust steam from hydraulic pumping engines
48	Exhaust steam from steam dynamo (fitted 1908)
49	Non-return valve
50	Fixed pipe fitting to bulkhead
51	Steam separator
52	Sliding pipe mounting
53	Connection to boiler safety valve
54	Waste steam pipe
55	Exhaust steam safety valve
56	Waste steam pipes to atmosphere
57	Casing around steam pipes
A1–6, B1–6, C1–6	Boilers

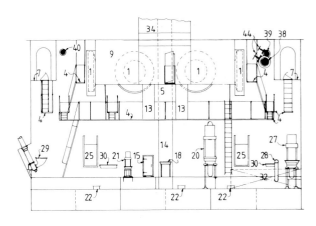

C1/7

149

C Machinery

C1/8   *Plan of main steam pipe arrangements*

C1/9   *Plan of auxiliary steam pipe arrangements*

Note that branches to auxiliary machinery are not shown.

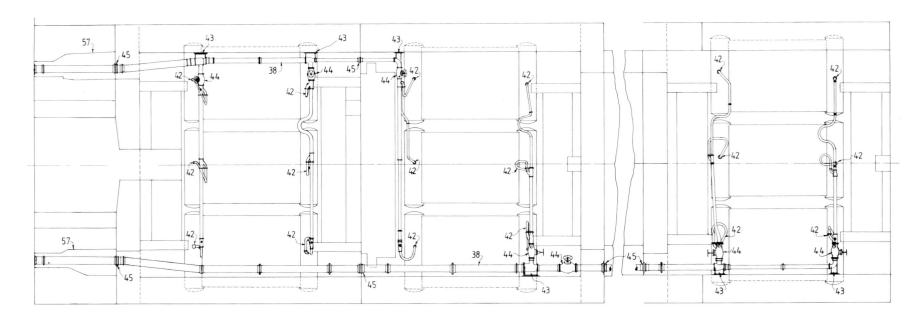

C1/8

C1/9

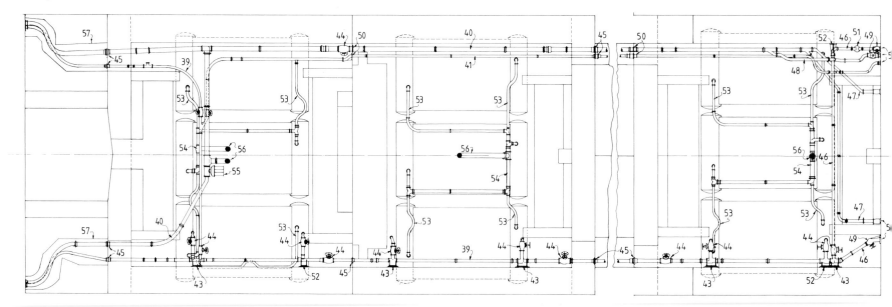

C2 PERSPECTIVE VIEW OF BOILER
ROOM FLOOR – 'C' BOILER
ROOM

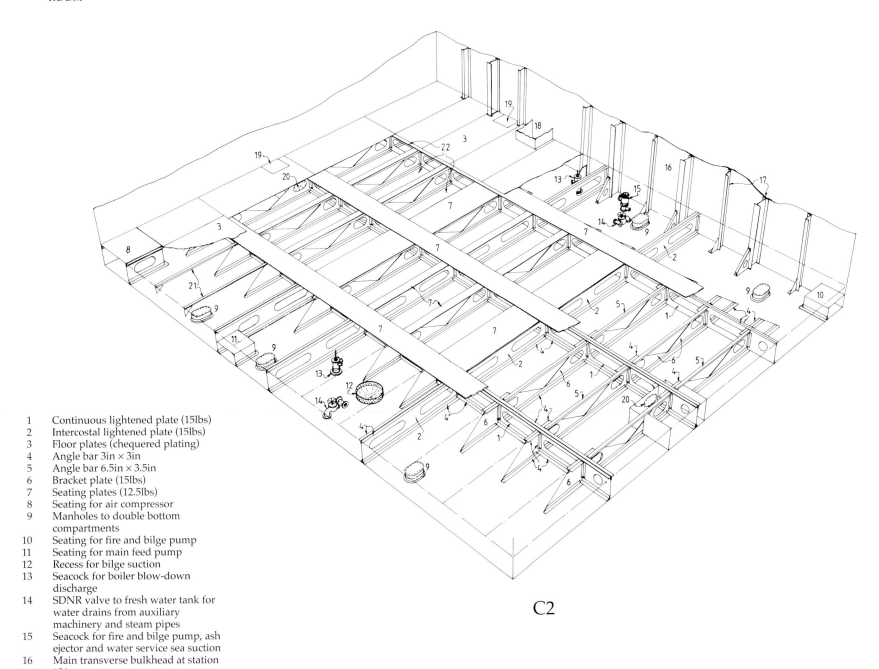

C2

1   Continuous lightened plate (15lbs)
2   Intercostal lightened plate (15lbs)
3   Floor plates (chequered plating)
4   Angle bar 3in × 3in
5   Angle bar 6.5in × 3.5in
6   Bracket plate (15lbs)
7   Seating plates (12.5lbs)
8   Seating for air compressor
9   Manholes to double bottom
    compartments
10 Seating for fire and bilge pump
11 Seating for main feed pump
12 Recess for bilge suction
13 Seacock for boiler blow-down
    discharge
14 SDNR valve to fresh water tank for
    water drains from auxiliary
    machinery and steam pipes
15 Seacock for fire and bilge pump, ash
    ejector and water service sea suction
16 Main transverse bulkhead at station
    121
17 Bulkhead stiffeners (see B21/1)
18 Ash hoist
19 Portable plate giving access to
    valves (under)
20 Watertight manhole
21 Floor supports
22 Openings for boiler ash pans

C Machinery

C3 PERSPECTIVE VIEW OF 'C' BOILER ROOM

This view shows the boiler room looking forward from the after starboard corner. The lagging fitted to the steam pipes and boiler drums has been omitted. The after fan chamber is not shown in order to give a clear view of the boilers and the platforms beyond it.

C3

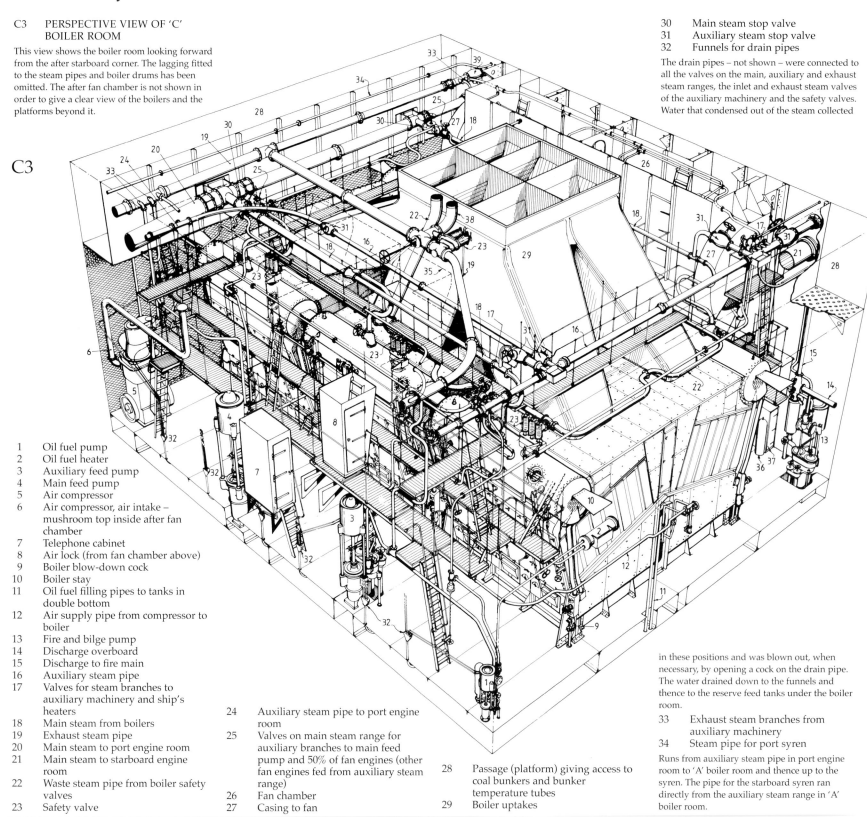

1   Oil fuel pump
2   Oil fuel heater
3   Auxiliary feed pump
4   Main feed pump
5   Air compressor
6   Air compressor, air intake – mushroom top inside after fan chamber
7   Telephone cabinet
8   Air lock (from fan chamber above)
9   Boiler blow-down cock
10 Boiler stay
11 Oil fuel filling pipes to tanks in double bottom
12 Air supply pipe from compressor to boiler
13 Fire and bilge pump
14 Discharge overboard
15 Discharge to fire main
16 Auxiliary steam pipe
17 Valves for steam branches to auxiliary machinery and ship's heaters
18 Main steam from boilers
19 Exhaust steam pipe
20 Main steam to port engine room
21 Main steam to starboard engine room
22 Waste steam pipe from boiler safety valves
23 Safety valve

24 Auxiliary steam pipe to port engine room
25 Valves on main steam range for auxiliary branches to main feed pump and 50% of fan engines (other fan engines fed from auxiliary steam range)
26 Fan chamber
27 Casing to fan

28 Passage (platform) giving access to coal bunkers and bunker temperature tubes
29 Boiler uptakes

30 Main steam stop valve
31 Auxiliary steam stop valve
32 Funnels for drain pipes

The drain pipes – not shown – were connected to all the valves on the main, auxiliary and exhaust steam ranges, the inlet and exhaust steam valves of the auxiliary machinery and the safety valves. Water that condensed out of the steam collected in these positions and was blown out, when necessary, by opening a cock on the drain pipe. The water drained down to the funnels and thence to the reserve feed tanks under the boiler room.

33 Exhaust steam branches from auxiliary machinery
34 Steam pipe for port syren

Runs from auxiliary steam pipe in port engine room to 'A' boiler room and thence up to the syren. The pipe for the starboard syren ran directly from the auxiliary steam range in 'A' boiler room.

35 Outline of after fan chamber
36 Air vessel for discharge to ash ejector
37 Locker
38 Waste steam pipe from exhaust steam range
39 Exhaust steam stop valve

C4 BABCOCK AND WILCOX WATER TUBE BOILER (scale ¼in = 1ft)

These boilers were of a simple and efficient design, comparatively easy to operate and maintain. Those fitted in *Dreadnought* had mixed tubes, the main heating element being of small tubes with large tubes above and below them. The boilers were fitted in groups of six joined back-to-back by the boiler casings and athwartships by common furnace walls. Because of the latter arrangement the midship's boilers had a slightly wider grate than the outboard boilers.

C4/1 *Front view of end boiler*

C4/2 *Side view of end boiler*

See Key on page 155.

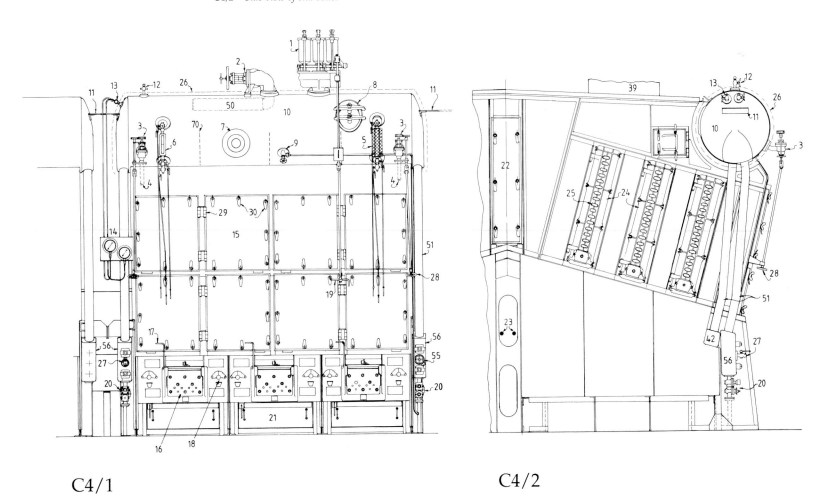

C4/1

C4/2

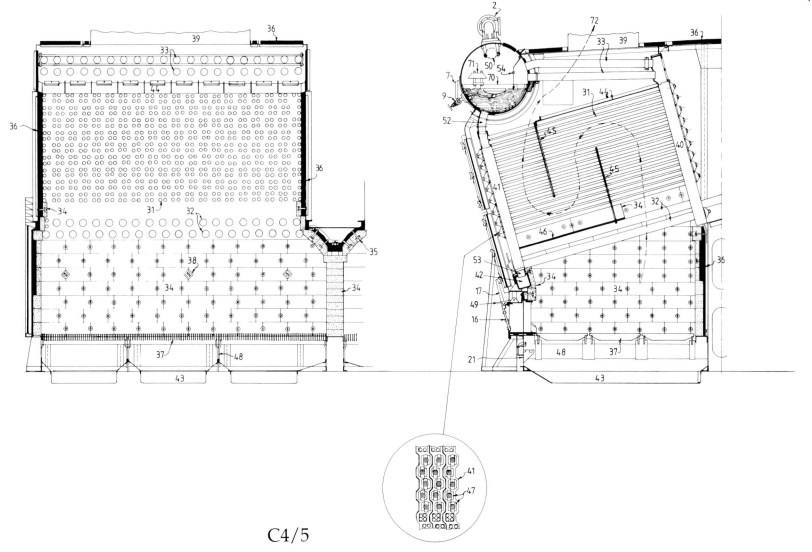

C4/5

C4/3   Section of boiler looking towards rear
       wall

C4/4   Section of boiler looking towards side
       wall

C4/5   Detail of downtake headers viewed from
       boiler front, showing zig-zag form

C4/6   Detail of safety valve

C4/7   Detail of flat glass water-gauge

C4/8   Oil fuel supply arrangement
       (diagramatic)

1   Triple spring safety valve
2   Main steam stop valve

Flange for steam pipe shown at rear applies to boilers C1 and C6, on other boilers steam outlet was at the top of the valve.

3   Feed-water check valve
4   Feed water supply

One from main feed pump and one from auxiliary feed pump.

5   Glass tube water-gauge

Covered with wire mesh protector.

6   Flat glass water-gauge
7   Position for feed water regulator

These do not appear to have been fitted in *Dreadnought*, as the design drawings do not show one and the arrangement is not suitable for its installation, although this could of course have been changed. The boilers could be operated quite satisfactorily with manual feed and at this time this was standard practice in the merchant navy. However, the Admiralty normally specified a feed regulator and it is possible that these were installed at a later date.

8   Manhole
9   Scum valve

Connected to an upturned pan at the water level inside the drum – opening the valve caused the surface water and any oil or other contaminates floating on it to be blown out through the valve. A pipe from this valve was led down to the main blow-down pipe at the bottom left hand side of the boiler.

10   Main steam / water drum
11   Boiler stay
12   Air cock
13   Pressure gauge cocks
14   Pressure gauges

Two fitted in case one should fail.

15   Access doors to downtake headers for inspection, repair and replacement of tubes
16   Furnace door (opens inwards)
17   Furnace door handle
18   Mountings for furnace fuel oil sprayers
19   Handle for easing safety valve springs and blowing-off steam
20   Double blow-down valve

Opened to clear sediment from the auxiliary mud box. The sediment was blown out through a seacock under the boiler room, each boiler being connected to it by pipes under the stokehold floor.

21   Air doors to underside of grate

Also provided access for clearing ashes from ash pit.

22   Access door to rear of boilers
23   Compressed air pipes to rear of furnace
24   Access doors for soot cleaning
25   Access holes for soot cleaning

Covered by small sliding plate.

26   Lagging
27   Salinometer cock
28   Feed water check valve operating wheel
29   Door hinges
30   Door clips (snecks)
31   Generating tubes (small)
32   Generating tubes (large)
33   Return tubes
34   Fire brick
35   Fire brick bolts
36   Insulation
37   Grate
38   Air inlets from compressed air supply
39   Boiler uptake to funnel
40   Uptake header
41   Downtake header
42   Mud box

Extends full width of boiler joining bases of downtake headers.

43   Ash pen
44   Wrought iron baffle plates
45   Cast iron flame plates
46   Fire brick baffle
47   Hand holes, closed by internal plate held in position by a dog and nut
48   Division plate
49   Catch for holding furnace door open
50   Dry pipe
51   Downcomers
52   Short tubes connecting downtake header to steam-and-water drum
53   Short tubes connecting down take headers to mud box
54   Hinged dash plates across ends of return tubes

Served to guide water, carried through tubes with the steam, downwards while the steam passed upward to the dry pipe.

55   Boiler drain valve
56   Auxiliary mud box

Connected at top to main mud box.

57   Drain pipe for safety valve outlet
58   Waste steam pipe to atmosphere
59   Water-gauge steam cock
60   Water-gauge water cock
61   Water-gauge drain cock
62   Water-gauge cock operating handles
63   Fuel oil sprayers
64   Distribution header
65   Fuel pipe to other sprayer
66   Oil filter
67   Oil heater
68   Steam inlet
69   Drain pipe to reserve feed tank
70   Wash plates to limit movement of water in drum when ship was rolling
71   Feed water inlet nozzle
72   Flow of furnace gases

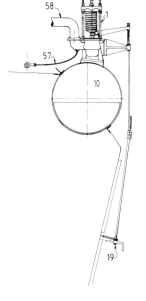

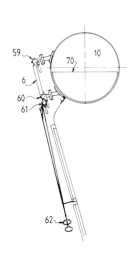

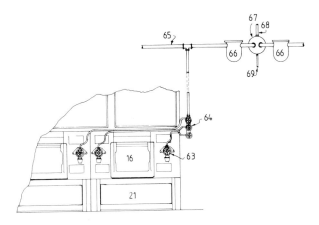

C Machinery

C5   ASH EJECTOR, 'C' BOILER ROOM (scale $^1/_8$in = 1ft)

Each boiler room was fitted with an ash ejector for disposing of ashes from the stokehold directly overboard. Ashes were placed in the hopper, at the bottom of which was a grating connected to an overboard discharge pipe. The bottom of the discharge pipe was connected to the boiler rooms' fire and bilge pump via a valve which was closed until the pressure from the pump reached 200lbs/sq.in. The valve was then opened and the resulting jet of water carried the ashes up the pipe. Once this process had been initiated ashes could be continually shovelled into the hopper until the stokehold was clear.

An ash hoist was also fitted which consisted of a large bucket for raising ashes up a trunk (electric lift) to the upper deck from where they could be disposed of overboard. However, this system was not popular, as it involved moving ashes about on the upper deck, while the ash ejector had the advantage of discharging directly overboard with a minimum amount of mess and effort.

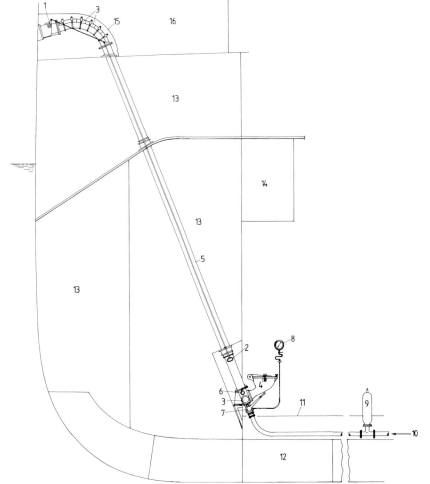

1	Side valve
2	Handle for operating side valve
3	Inspection cover
4	Hopper
5	Discharge pipe
6	Air inlet valve

Open when expelling ashes.

7	Ejector valve
8	Pressure gauge
9	Air vessel

To maintain steady pressure from fire and bilge pump.

10	Pipe from fire and bilge pump
11	Stokehold floor
12	Double bottom
13	Coal bunker
14	Boiler room platform passage
15	Casing to discharge pipe
16	WO's mess

C5

C6 ARRANGEMENT OF AIR COMPRESSOR SYSTEM, 'A' BOILER ROOM (scale $^1/_8$in = 1ft)

C6/1 Profile

C6/2 Plan

Each boiler room was fitted with an air compressor to supply air to the boiler furnaces and for boiler cleaning. The furnace supply consisted of three air jets fitted in the back of each boiler furnace which provided for the control of the combustion of the furnace gases; the jets could be adjusted to suit furnace conditions. For cleaning, flexible hose connections were fitted, the hoses being used to blow soot off the tubes, baffles etc, via the soot doors and openings in the sides of the boilers.

1   Boiler uptakes
2   Fan chamber
3   Air compressor
4   Air compressor air intake pipe
5   Air pipe to boiler furnace air jets
6   Hose connection
7   Furnace air jets
8   Steam inlet valve
9   Steam exhaust valve
10 Coal bunker door
11 Oil fuel filling pipes
12 Coal bunker bulkhead at station 89
13 Air distribution pipe
14 Furnace grate
A1–A6   Boilers

C6/1

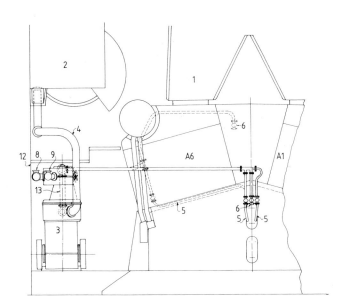

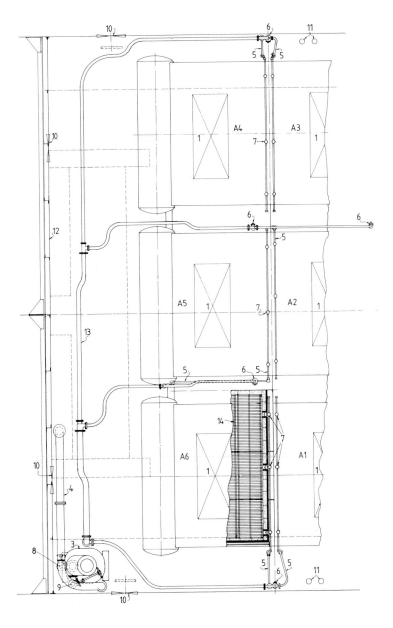

C6/2

C Machinery

C7 GENERAL ARRANGEMENT OF
BOILER UPTAKES AND BOILER
ROOM VENTILATOR SHAFTS

1 'C' boiler room
2 'B' boiler room
3 'A' boiler room
4 Fan chamber
5 Door to boiler room on main deck
6 Ventilator shafts
7 Funnel stays
8 Waste steam pipe from exhaust
steam range
9 Waste steam pipe from 'C' group
boilers

10 Waste steam pipe from 'B' group
boilers
11 Waste steam pipe from 'A' group
boilers
12 Communication tube to signal tower
13 Foremast
14 Foremast strut
15 Ash hoist from 'B' boiler room
16 Boiler uptakes

17 Funnel hatch casing
18 Working space for 12in ammunition
to 'X' magazine and shell room
19 Flying deck
20 Upper deck
21 Main deck
22 Middle deck
23 Extension to casing around waste
steam pipes

24 Funnel stay band
25 Outer funnel
26 Hood
27 Cravat
28 Cage for canvas cover

C7

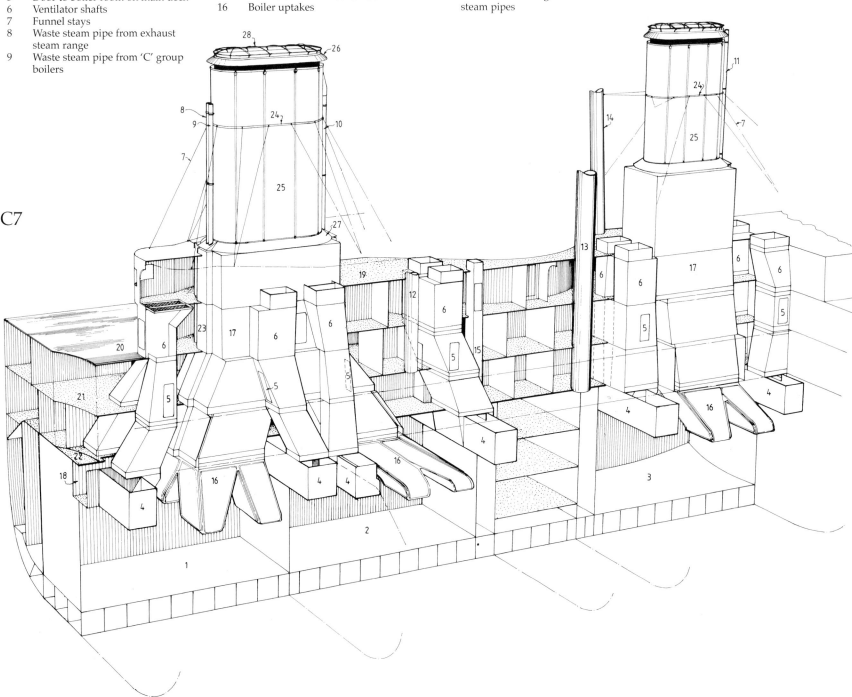

C8 AFTER FUNNEL

C8/1 Profile of funnel top (scale ¹/8in = 1ft)

C8/2 Plan of funnel top (scale ¹/8in = 1ft)

C8/3 Sectional plan of funnel (scale ¹/8in = 1ft)

C8/4 Perspective view of funnel (shown sectioned down middle line)

The exact details of the internal stays, platforms and ladders are not known, the arrangement shown is based on contemporary funnel design.

1 Angle bar stiffeners
2 Division plates
3 Funnel stays
4 Funnel cage (for canvas cover)
5 Cleats for tying down canvas cover
6 Outer funnel casing
7 Inner funnel casing
8 Hood
9 Hood brackets
10 Cravat
11 Waste steam pipe from 'B' boiler room
12 Waste steam pipe from 'C' boiler room
13 Waste steam pipe from exhaust steam range
14 Funnel hatch casing
15 Armour gratings in protective deck
16 Doors on middle deck to space between funnel uptakes
17 Doors on upper deck giving access to interior of funnel

This was a triple door arrangement with openings in the hatch casing and the inner and outer funnels.

18 Short zed bar and· channel bar spacers between inner and outer funnels
19 Air space, 4.5in wide
20 Longitudinal bulkhead between main and middle deck

These provided the outer walls of the funnel hatch casing between these decks.

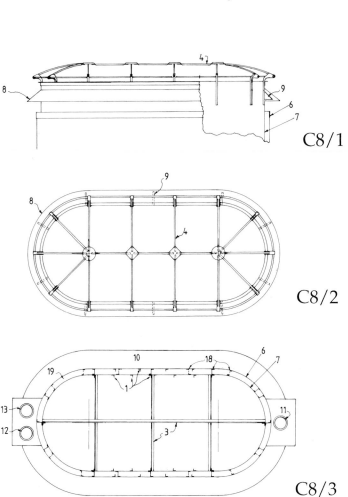

C8/1

C8/2

C8/3

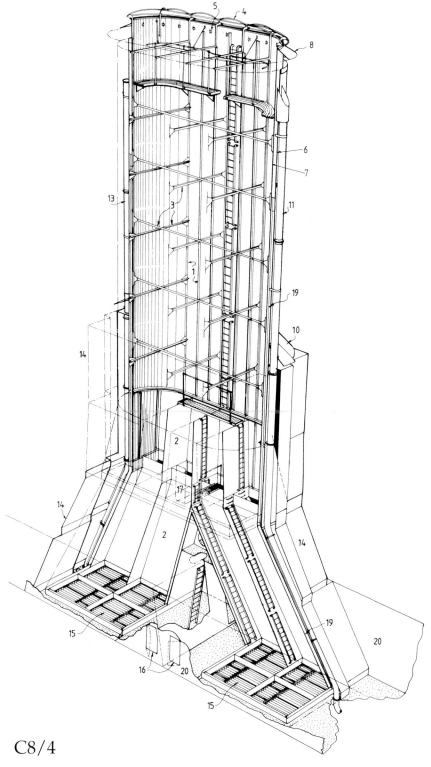

C8/4

C9   PART PERSPECTIVE OF FUNNEL
     HATCH IN PROTECTIVE DECK;
     'B' BOILER ROOM

C9

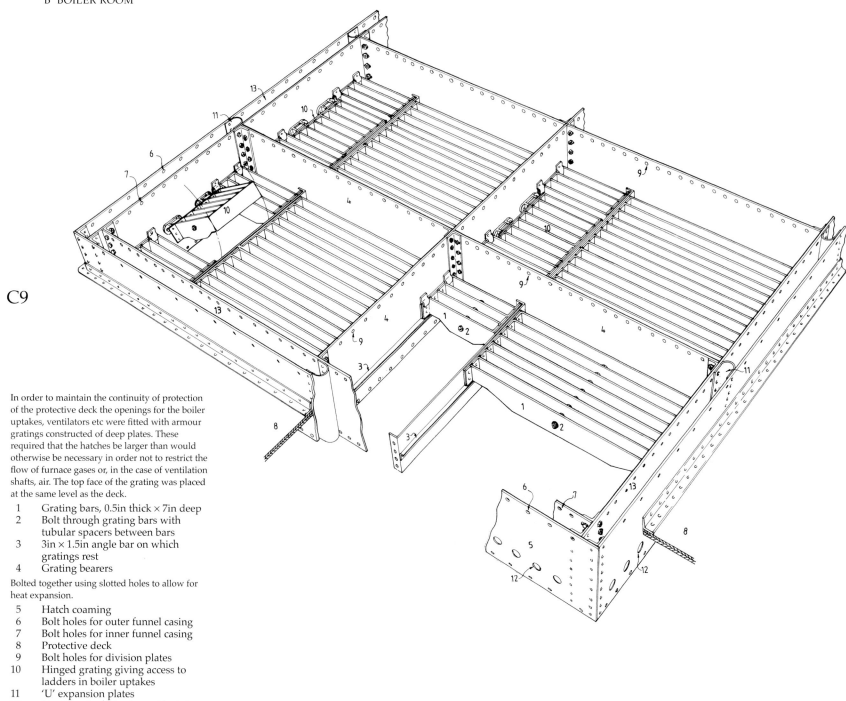

In order to maintain the continuity of protection of the protective deck the openings for the boiler uptakes, ventilators etc were fitted with armour gratings constructed of deep plates. These required that the hatches be larger than would otherwise be necessary in order not to restrict the flow of furnace gases or, in the case of ventilation shafts, air. The top face of the grating was placed at the same level as the deck.

1   Grating bars, 0.5in thick × 7in deep
2   Bolt through grating bars with
    tubular spacers between bars
3   3in × 1.5in angle bar on which
    gratings rest
4   Grating bearers

Bolted together using slotted holes to allow for heat expansion.

5   Hatch coaming
6   Bolt holes for outer funnel casing
7   Bolt holes for inner funnel casing
8   Protective deck
9   Bolt holes for division plates
10 Hinged grating giving access to
    ladders in boiler uptakes
11 'U' expansion plates
12 2in diameter holes to vent hot air
    from boiler room into air space
    between inner and outer funnel
    casing
13 Airspace

C10

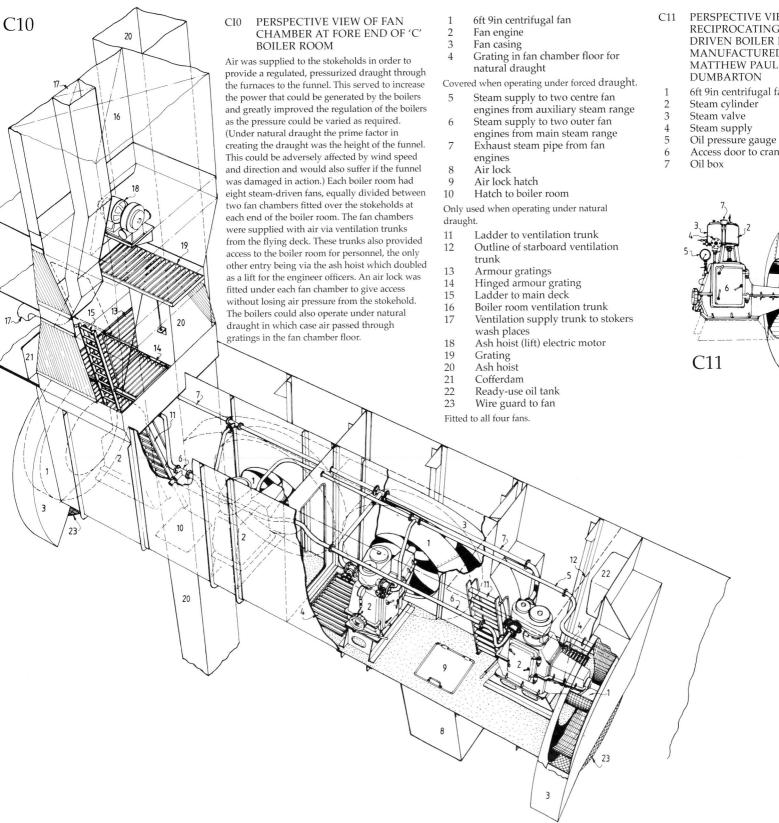

CI0   PERSPECTIVE VIEW OF FAN CHAMBER AT FORE END OF 'C' BOILER ROOM

Air was supplied to the stokeholds in order to provide a regulated, pressurized draught through the furnaces to the funnel. This served to increase the power that could be generated by the boilers and greatly improved the regulation of the boilers as the pressure could be varied as required. (Under natural draught the prime factor in creating the draught was the height of the funnel. This could be adversely affected by wind speed and direction and would also suffer if the funnel was damaged in action.) Each boiler room had eight steam-driven fans, equally divided between two fan chambers fitted over the stokeholds at each end of the boiler room. The fan chambers were supplied with air via ventilation trunks from the flying deck. These trunks also provided access to the boiler room for personnel, the only other entry being via the ash hoist which doubled as a lift for the engineer officers. An air lock was fitted under each fan chamber to give access without losing air pressure from the stokehold. The boilers could also operate under natural draught in which case air passed through gratings in the fan chamber floor.

1   6ft 9in centrifugal fan
2   Fan engine
3   Fan casing
4   Grating in fan chamber floor for natural draught

Covered when operating under forced draught.

5   Steam supply to two centre fan engines from auxiliary steam range
6   Steam supply to two outer fan engines from main steam range
7   Exhaust steam pipe from fan engines
8   Air lock
9   Air lock hatch
10   Hatch to boiler room

Only used when operating under natural draught.

11   Ladder to ventilation trunk
12   Outline of starboard ventilation trunk
13   Armour gratings
14   Hinged armour grating
15   Ladder to main deck
16   Boiler room ventilation trunk
17   Ventilation supply trunk to stokers wash places
18   Ash hoist (lift) electric motor
19   Grating
20   Ash hoist
21   Cofferdam
22   Ready-use oil tank
23   Wire guard to fan

Fitted to all four fans.

C11   PERSPECTIVE VIEW OF STEAM RECIPROCATING ENGINE-DRIVEN BOILER ROOM FAN, MANUFACTURED BY MATTHEW PAUL AND CO, DUMBARTON

1   6ft 9in centrifugal fan
2   Steam cylinder
3   Steam valve
4   Steam supply
5   Oil pressure gauge
6   Access door to crank
7   Oil box

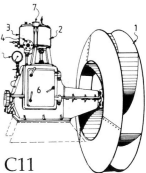

C11

C Machinery

C12 GENERAL ARRANGEMENT OF ENGINE ROOMS (scale $^1/_8$in = 1ft)

The port and starboard engine rooms, apart from being a mirror image of each other in plan view, were almost identical. The principal differences between the two were that the starboard engine room had a larger telephone cabinet and, because of the arrangement of stiffening on the middle line bulkhead, the reserve oil tanks were arranged horizontally in the port engine room and vertically in the starboard engine room.

These drawings are based primarily on the engine room design drawings, modified in reference to the 'as-fitted' drawings of the ship. As the latter only show the locations of the principal equipment there will be differences in the detail of the layout between the ship as designed and as completed, although these will be of a minor nature. Full details of the auxiliary and exhaust steam ranges in the engine rooms do not appear to have survived and cannot therefore be shown in detail.

Notes:

Main steam: This was operated from the valves under the starting platform and had three routes:-
a) Ahead, through the HP ahead turbine to the LP ahead turbine
b) Cruising ahead, through the cruising turbine prior to entering the HP and LP ahead turbines
c) Astern, through the HP astern turbine to the LP astern turbine. In all cases the turbines exhausted into the main condenser.

Auxiliary steam: Supplied steam to all the engine room auxiliaries and the auxiliary steam engines in the after section of the ship. (The steering engine, wet air pumps and circulating pumps were also supplied from the main steam range)

Auxiliary exhaust: This took the exhaust steam from all the ship's steam auxiliaries and normally exhausted into the auxiliary or main condenser. However, the ship could also operate on closed exhaust, an economy measure in which the auxiliary exhaust was isolated from the condensers and the steam used to generate fresh water in the evaporators. In addition any over-pressure in the auxiliary exhaust would lift the piston relief valve at the forward end of the engine room allowing the surplus steam into either the HP or LP turbines (depending on the power being used by the engines). When the latter was not in use, or in the case of a further increase in pressure, a second piston relief valve set at a slightly higher pressure, allowed the surplus to exhaust into the condenser.

1 Floor plates – all steel chequered plates except those marked 'G' which were gratings
2 HP ahead turbine
3 HP astern turbine
4 Cruising turbine
5 LP ahead and astern turbine
6 Exhaust steam from LP turbine to main condenser
7 Air vessel
8 Ahead manoeuvring valves
9 Astern manoeuvring valves
10 Cruising manoeuvring valves
11 Main steam to HP astern turbine
12 Main steam to HP ahead turbine
13 Main steam to cruising turbine
14 Exhaust steam from HP ahead turbine to LP ahead turbine
15 Exhaust steam from HP astern turbine to LP astern turbine
16 Auxiliary exhaust to LP ahead turbine
17 Turbine speed governor gear
18 Oil fuel pump suction
19 Manhole to double bottom
20 Feed water tanks, cross connection
21 Feed water discharge to boiler rooms
22 Fire and bilge pump double bottom compartment suction

These were terminated on flexible hose connections and not directly to the pumps, as they were only required on the rare occasions when it was necessary to pump out the double bottom compartments or to flood them.

23 Overflow feed-water pipe from feed tank to overflow feed tank
24 Valve chest for fire and bilge pump suctions
25 Fire and bilge pump
26 Fire and bilge pump bilge suction
27 Bilge injection.

This could be used to either flood the bilge in case of fire or to pump out the bilge (using the main circulating pumps) in case of flooding.

28 Lubricating oil drain tanks
29 Oil cooling-water pump
30 Oil cooling pump sea suction
31 Forced lubrication pump
32 Wet air pump
33 Oil fuel pump

To transfer oil from the double bottom compartments under the engine room to those under the boiler rooms.

34 Steering engine
35 Guard over steering engine cross connection shaft
36 Main circulating pumps
37 Distiller
38 Evaporator
39 Main circulating pump sea suction
40 Feed water heater
41 Distiller circulating pump
42 Brine pump
43 Distiller circulating pump suction

44 Fire and bilge pump sea suction
45 Main steam from cruising turbine to HP ahead turbine
46 Auxiliary exhaust steam connection to HP ahead turbine
47 Main steam to manoeuvring valves
48 Telephone cabinet
49 Electric lift
50 Vice bench
51 Oil cooler
52 Turbine turning gear

For hand rotation of rotors for inspection, maintenance etc.

53 Air pump suction to main condenser
54 Main condenser bed
55 Sluice valves to main condenser circulating water inlet
56 Sluice valves to bilge injection
57 Auxiliary condenser
58 Dry air pump
59 Auxiliary steam separator
60 Outer shaft
61 Inner shaft
62 Guard over shaft
63 Guard over shaft coupling
64 Torsion meter wheel
65 Shaft bearing
66 Turbine foundation girders
67 Air screen
68 Main condenser
69 Main steam cross connection
70 Main steam cross connection valve
71 Main steam self-closing valve
72 Air pump discharge to feed tank
73 Auxiliary steam
74 Auxiliary exhaust
75 Piston relief valve
76 Grease extractors

For filtering feed water from air pumps.

77 Electric motor for ventilation fan
78 Lime tank
79 Door to engineers stores
80 Oil cooling pump discharge to sea
81 Fire and bilge pump and brine pump discharge to sea
82 Main condenser circulating water discharge to sea
83 Auxiliary condenser circulating water discharge to sea
84 Steam valves to dynamos
85 Auxiliary exhaust to main condenser
86 Auxiliary steam cross connection
87 Girders for turbine cover lifting gear
88 Turbine cover lifting gear
89 Reserve lubricating oil tanks
90 Daily service lubricating oil tanks
91 Brackets to support after edge of 'X' barbette
92 Ramming stay for main condenser
93 Emergency main steam shut-off gear, operated from main deck
94 Auxiliary condenser circulating water inlet
95 Pillars supporting auxiliary condenser bed

96 Fire and bilge pump discharge to fire main
97 Bracket under pillar
98 Pressure gauges
99 Mean speed indicator {from turbines}
100 Counter
101 Chadburn speed and direction indicator
102 Kilroy's stoking indicator
103 Engine telegraph
104 Revolution telegraph
105 Oil fuel tank
106 Overflow feed tank
107 Feed tank
108 Engineers stores
109 Dry air pump suction
110 Scuttle
111 Turbine drains to air pumps
112 To atmosphere via engine room hatch

C12/1 Plan of port engine room hold

C12/2 Plan of port engine room at level of
       starting platform

C12/1

C12/2

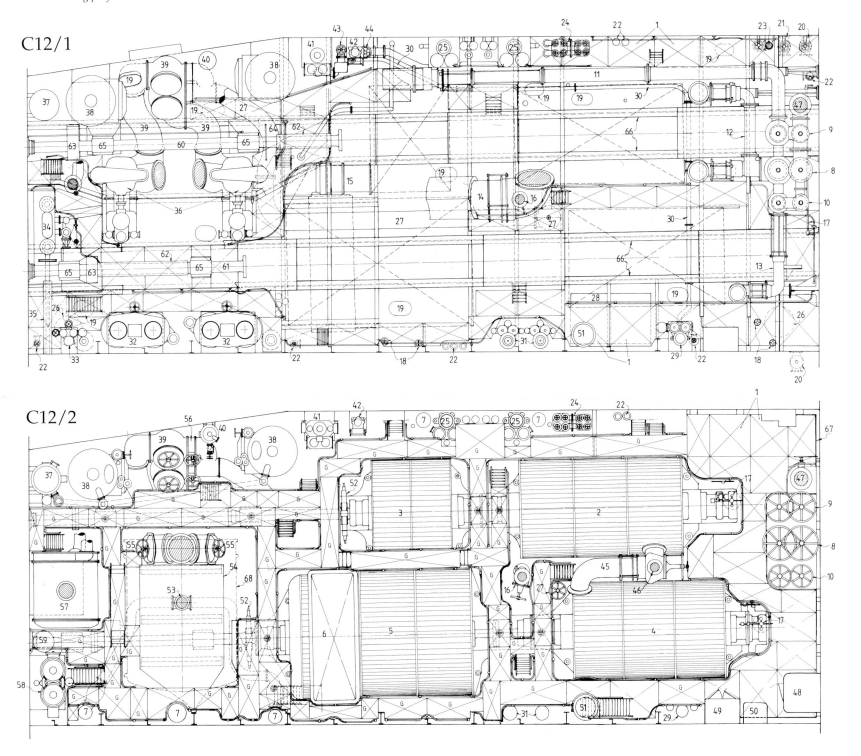

C Machinery

C12/3 *Plan of upper section of port engine room*   See Key on page 162.

C12/4 *Profile of port engine room at inner shaft, looking to port*

C12/3

C12/4

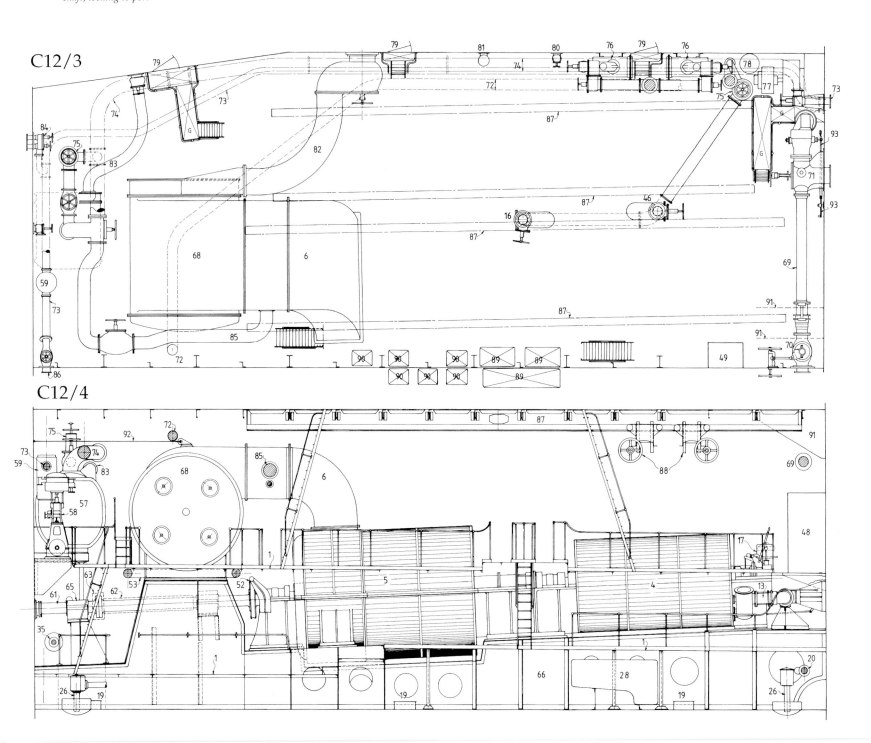

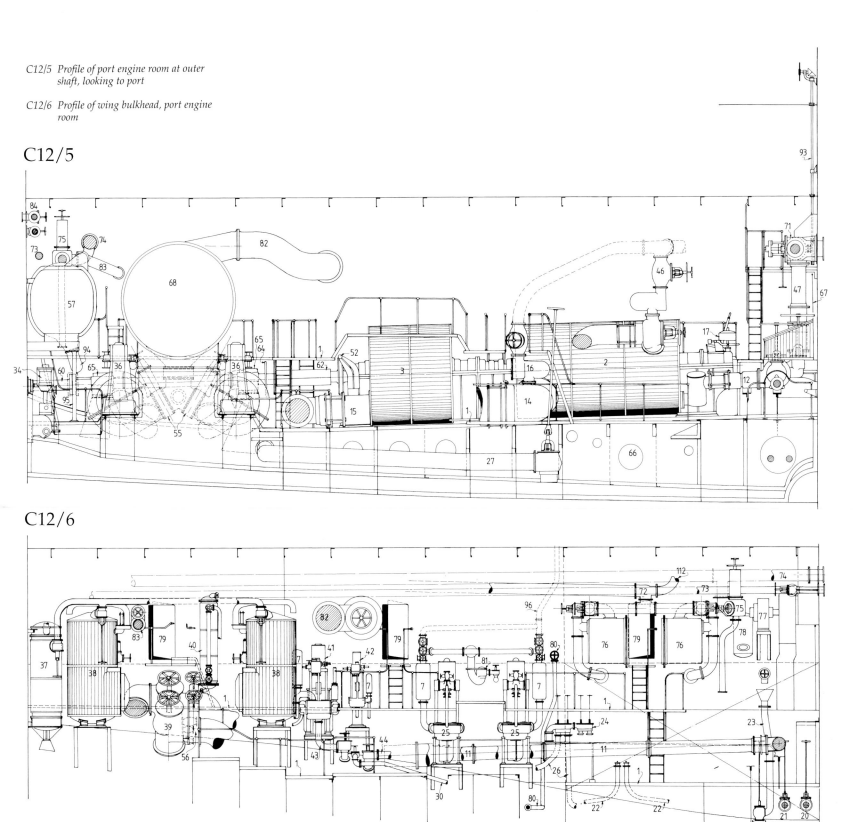

C12/5 Profile of port engine room at outer shaft, looking to port

C12/6 Profile of wing bulkhead, port engine room

C12/5

C12/6

C Machinery

C12/7   *Section at after bulkhead of port engine room, looking aft*   *See Key on page 162*

C12/8   *Section of port engine room at station 152, looking forward*

C12/9   *Profile of middle line bulkhead, starboard engine room, looking to port*

C12/10   *Section of port engine room at station 174 looking aft*

C12/11   *Section of port engine room at station 166 looking forward*

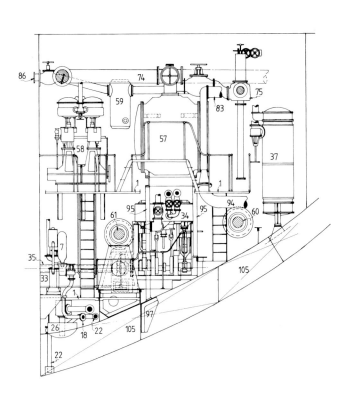

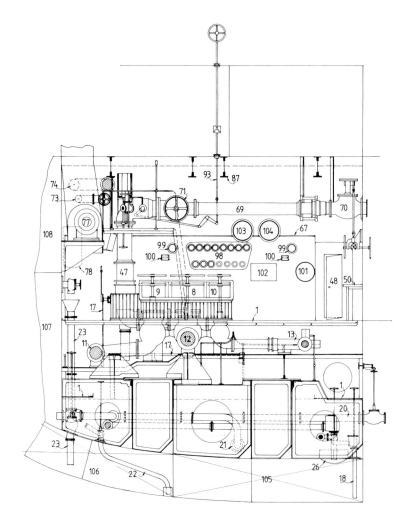

C12/7

C12/8

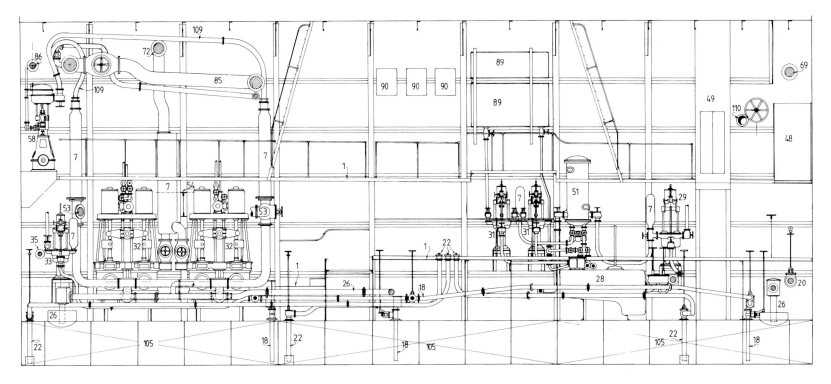

C12/9

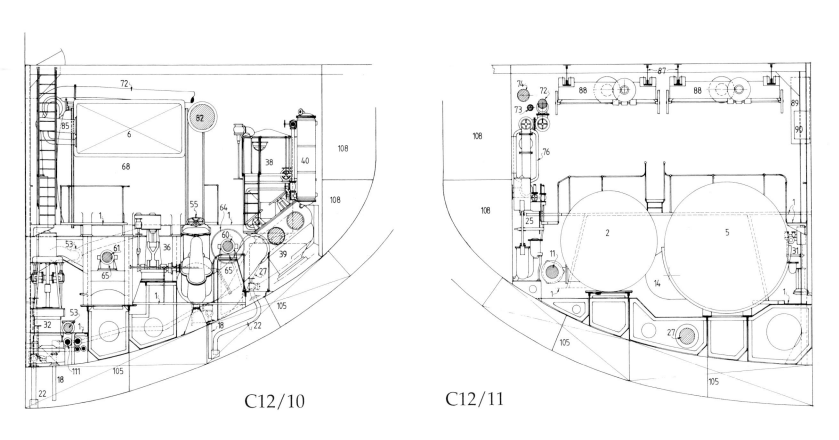

C12/10

C12/11

C Machinery

C13

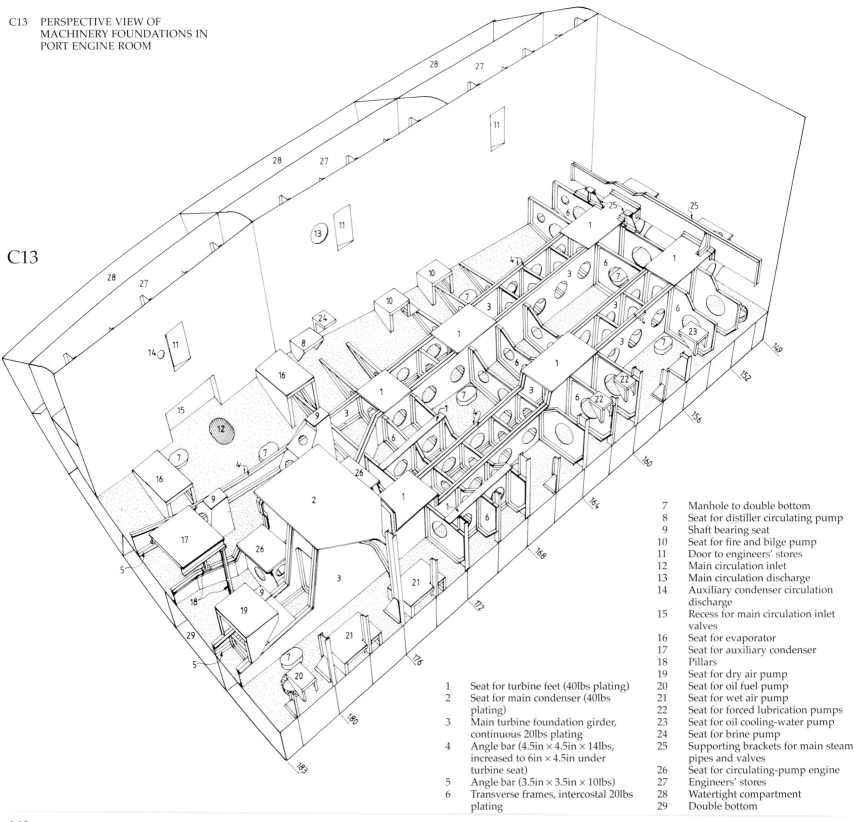

1   Seat for turbine feet (40lbs plating)
2   Seat for main condenser (40lbs plating)
3   Main turbine foundation girder, continuous 20lbs plating
4   Angle bar (4.5in × 4.5in × 14lbs, increased to 6in × 4.5in under turbine seat)
5   Angle bar (3.5in × 3.5in × 10lbs)
6   Transverse frames, intercostal 20lbs plating
7   Manhole to double bottom
8   Seat for distiller circulating pump
9   Shaft bearing seat
10 Seat for fire and bilge pump
11 Door to engineers' stores
12 Main circulation inlet
13 Main circulation discharge
14 Auxiliary condenser circulation discharge
15 Recess for main circulation inlet valves
16 Seat for evaporator
17 Seat for auxiliary condenser
18 Pillars
19 Seat for dry air pump
20 Seat for oil fuel pump
21 Seat for wet air pump
22 Seat for forced lubrication pumps
23 Seat for oil cooling-water pump
24 Seat for brine pump
25 Supporting brackets for main steam pipes and valves
26 Seat for circulating-pump engine
27 Engineers' stores
28 Watertight compartment
29 Double bottom

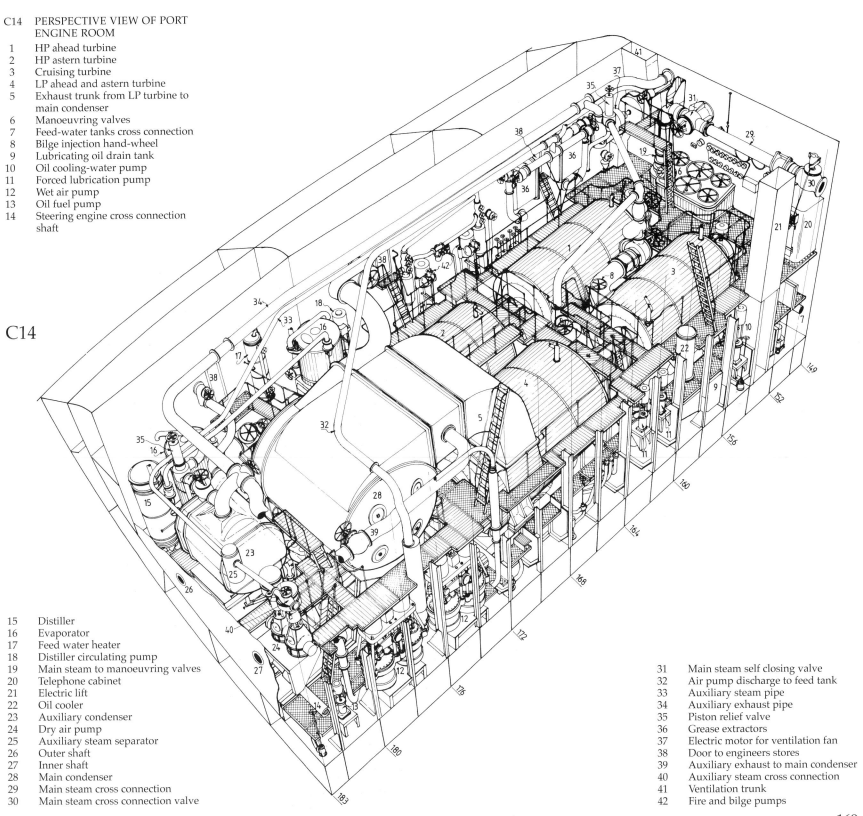

C14 PERSPECTIVE VIEW OF PORT
ENGINE ROOM

1   HP ahead turbine
2   HP astern turbine
3   Cruising turbine
4   LP ahead and astern turbine
5   Exhaust trunk from LP turbine to
    main condenser
6   Manoeuvring valves
7   Feed-water tanks cross connection
8   Bilge injection hand-wheel
9   Lubricating oil drain tank
10 Oil cooling-water pump
11 Forced lubrication pump
12 Wet air pump
13 Oil fuel pump
14 Steering engine cross connection
    shaft

C14

15 Distiller
16 Evaporator
17 Feed water heater
18 Distiller circulating pump
19 Main steam to manoeuvring valves
20 Telephone cabinet
21 Electric lift
22 Oil cooler
23 Auxiliary condenser
24 Dry air pump
25 Auxiliary steam separator
26 Outer shaft
27 Inner shaft
28 Main condenser
29 Main steam cross connection
30 Main steam cross connection valve

31 Main steam self closing valve
32 Air pump discharge to feed tank
33 Auxiliary steam pipe
34 Auxiliary exhaust pipe
35 Piston relief valve
36 Grease extractors
37 Electric motor for ventilation fan
38 Door to engineers stores
39 Auxiliary exhaust to main condenser
40 Auxiliary steam cross connection
41 Ventilation trunk
42 Fire and bilge pumps

169

C   Machinery

C15   TURBINES

C15/1   Longitudinal section of high pressure turbine (scale ¼in = 1ft)

The cruising turbine was of similar construction, while the high pressure astern turbine was a shortened version with only one, central, rotor wheel to the rotor drum.

C15/2   Forward end of high pressure turbine (scale ¼in = 1ft)

C15/3   Longitudinal section of low pressure turbine (scale ¼in = 1ft)

C15/4   Forward end of low pressure turbine (scale ¼in = 1ft)

1   Rotor wheel
2   Rotor drum
3   Thrust block
4   Rotor shaft bearings
5   Dummy piston

Fitted with labarinth rings to reduce leakage of steam to hollow rotor and thence direct to the exhaust side of the turbine.

6   Rotor spindle
7   Rotor shaft glands

To prevent leakage of steam when under pressure or the intake of air when under vacuum.

8   Turbine blades

Alternate rows fixed to rotor – moving, and casing – fixed.

9   Expansion stages
10   Turbine casing
11   Low pressure ahead turbine
12   Low pressure astern turbine
13   Fixed mounting-foot
14   Moving mounting-foot

Bolt holes elongated to allow for heat expansion of turbine.

15   Flange of cruising turbine rotor shaft
16   Exhaust orifice
17   Inlet orifice
18   Steam outlet to low pressure turbine
19   Steam inlet
20   Ahead steam inlet
21   Astern steam inlet
22   Exhaust to condenser

23   Lubricating oil inlet
24   Lubricating oil outlet
25   Position for pressure relief valve
26   Guides for lifting turbine casing
27   Sight holes for inspection of lubricating oil flow, covered with hinged caps
28   Drive for governor gear and revolution counters

The outer casings of the turbines were lagged for insulation purposes, this in turn being covered with an outer layer of wood planking held in place with metal bands. This is not shown in these drawings but can be seen in the general arrangement drawings of the engine room.

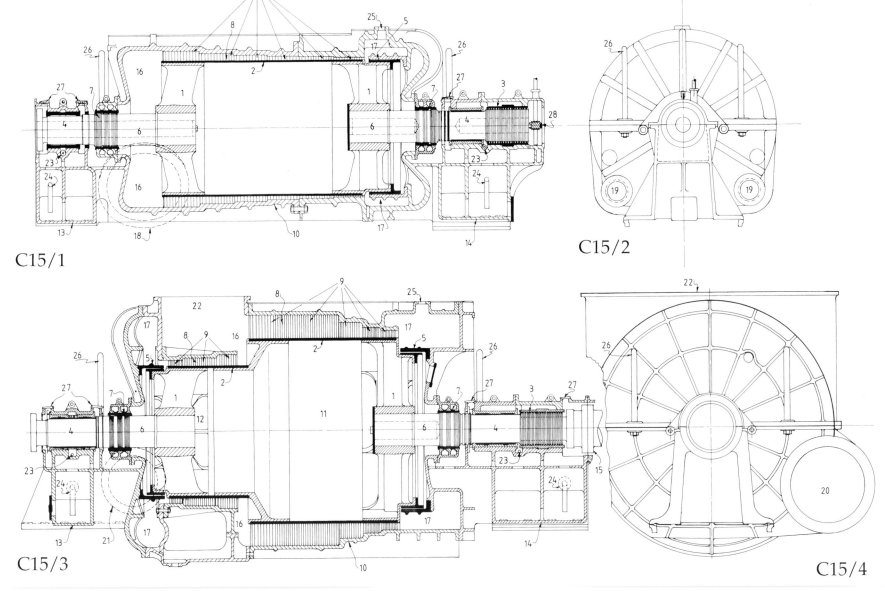

C15/1

C15/2

C15/3

C15/4

C16 GENERAL ARRANGEMENT OF PORT ENGINE ROOM VENTILATION (scale ¹/₈in = 1ft)

Starboard engine room was mirror image of port engine room. Drawings show arrangement for ship as completed.

C16/1 Half section at engine room exhaust trunk (looking forward)

C16/2 Half section at engine room supply trunk (looking aft)

1 Flap valve for redirection of air supply
2 Flap valve to close off air supply
3 Butterfly valve to close off air supply
4 Butterfly valve to control level of air supply
5 Air flaps to exhaust trunk
6 Fan motor
7 30in diameter supply fans
8 35in diameter exhaust fans
9 Supply trunk
10 Hatch for natural air supply (armoured)
11 Opening
12 Sliding door (access to engine room)
13 Wind sail (air scoop) – rotatable
14 Galley skylight
15 'Y' barbette
16 'X' barbette
17 Evaporator
18 Auxiliary condenser
19 Main condenser
20 HP ahead turbine
21 Cruising turbine
22 HP astern turbine
23 LP turbine
24 20in supply fan
25 Flap valve for alternative air intake from main deck
26 Fixed slotted plate with hinged and counter-balanced covers (also slotted)

This arrangement, which was intended to be closed to prevent gun blast from X turret damaging the fan motors was removed in 1907.

27 Access doors to hinged covers and counter-balance weights
28 Access door to engine room
29 Natural supply vent to main deck
30 Seat for electric lift motor
31 Electric lift
32 Upper deck
33 Main deck
34 Middle (protective) deck
35 Issue room
36 Hammock stowage
37 Mainmast
38 Cofferdam
39 Doors (open for natural exhaust only)
40 Girders for turbine cover lifting gear
41 Exhaust trunk
42 Armour gratings
43 Light grating
44 Louvred valve
45 Recess in trunk for air pump discharge pipe
46 Engine room access trunk
47 Door for alternative air supply from main deck and access to supply trunk

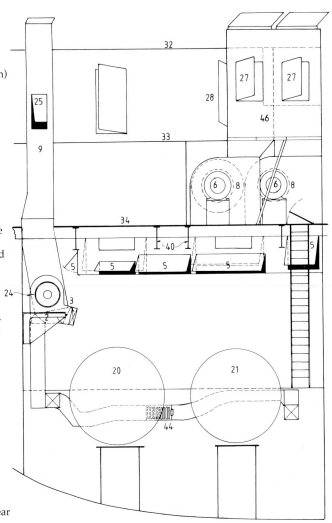

C16/1

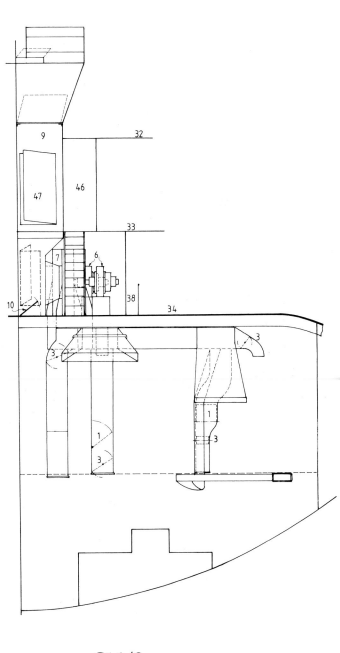

C16/2

C Machinery

C16/3 *Profile of port engine room (looking to port)*

C16/4 *Profile of engine room hatch as modified in Aug–Nov 1907*

C16/5 *Plan of modified engine room hatch (full width shown)*

See Key on page 171.

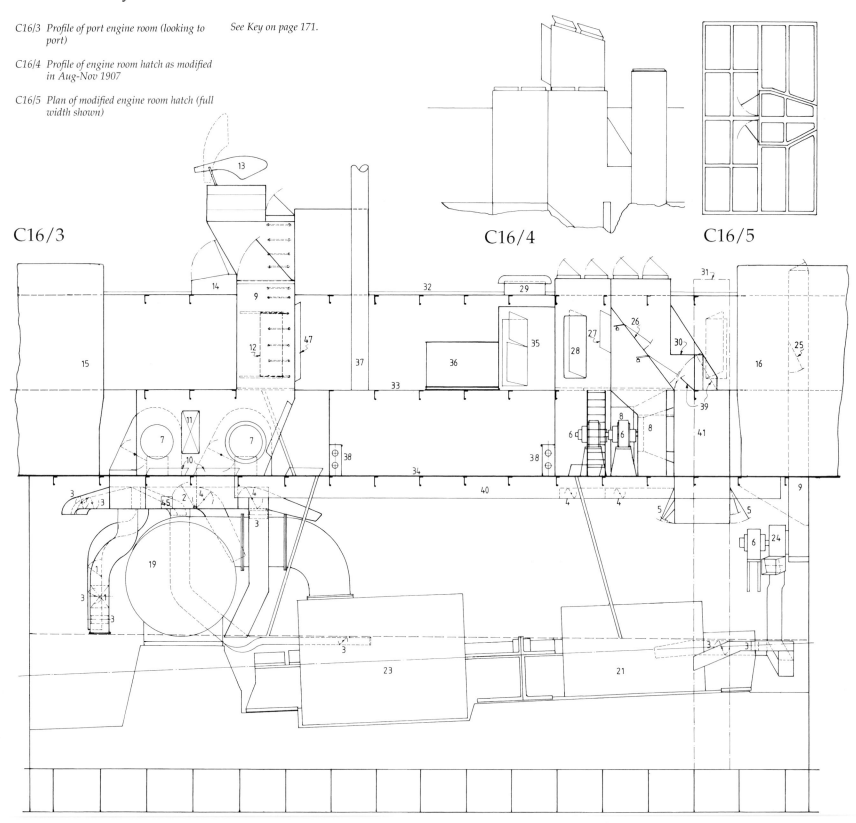

C16/3

C16/4

C16/5

C16/6 Half plan at main deck

C16/7 Half plan at middle deck

C16/8 Plan of port engine room

C16/6

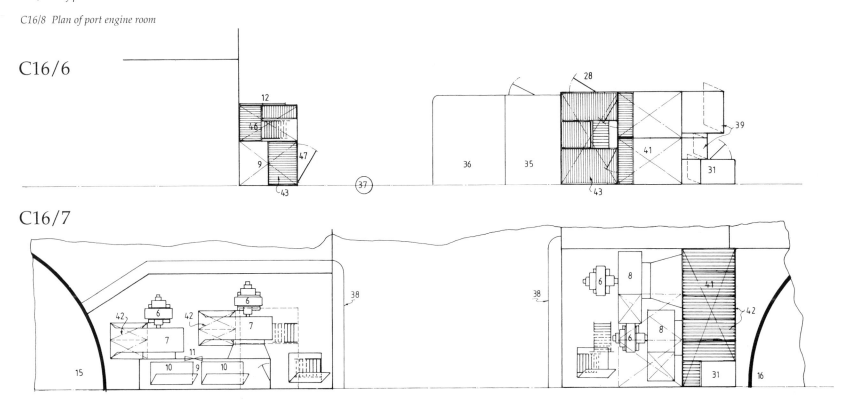

C16/7

C16/8

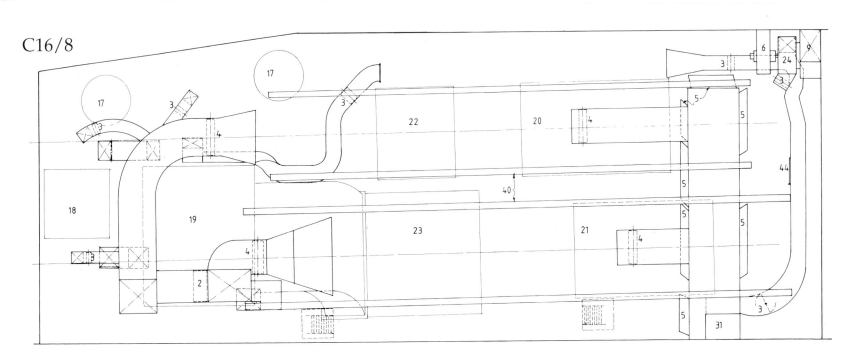

C Machinery

C17 PERSPECTIVE VIEW OF STARBOARD PROPELLER SHAFT ARRANGEMENT

C18 DETAIL OF PROPELLER (scale ¼in = 1ft)

Note starboard propellers (shown) are right hand, port propellers left hand.

C18/1 Propeller boss assembly

C18/2 Propeller viewed from aft

C18/3 Propeller profile

1 Propeller shaft
2 Tapered and keyed end to shaft
3 Screw thread for cone
4 Cone
5 Boss
6 Blades
7 Cone locking bolts
8 Wash plate on shaft bracket

C18/1

C18/2

C18/3

C17

1 Plummer blocks (shaft bearings)
2 Shaft coupling
3 Loose coupling
4 Stuffing box
5 Stuffing box on aft side of bulkhead
6 Recess for steering skew-gear

Note that this is on starboard side only and that on the port side the stuffing box is on the engine room side of the bulkhead.

7 Fixed casing around shaft where it passed through 'Y' shell room
8 Air space
9 Middle line bulkhead
10 Starboard engine room
11 Shaft coupling to turbine rotor shaft
12 'Y' shell room
13 'Y' magazine and handing room
14 Submerged torpedo room
15 Shaft passage
16 Engineers' store
17 Torpedo head magazine
18 Shaft bracket carrying shaft stern bearing
19 Hand steering compartment

C19 DETAIL OF PLUMMER BLOCKS
(scale ¼in = 1ft)

C19/1 Section

C19/2 Profile
1   Shaft
2   Lubricating oil box
3   Cooling water box
4   Hinged cap
5   White metal bearing face on lower
     half only

C20 PROFILE OF STUFFING BOX
(scale ¼in = 1ft)

These were designed to prevent the admission of
sea water past the shaft and into the ship, this
being achieved by compressing a seal around the
shaft. The stuffing box shown here is the
aftermost, and most important, which was deeper
than those fitted to the watertight bulkheads of
the engine room and shaft passages.

1   Shaft seal
2   Adjusting nuts
3   Stuffing box
4   Stuffing gland
5   Watertight bulkhead
6   Shaft

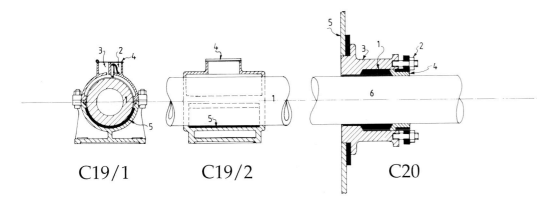

C19/1   C19/2   C20

C21 SHAFT COUPLING (scale ¼in =
     1ft)

C21/1 Profile

C21/2 Section

C22 LOOSE COUPLING (scale ¼in =
     1ft)

In order to allow for the withdrawal of the tail
shaft the aftermost coupling was fitted with a
'loose' coupling, that is, loose in the sense that it
was removable.

C22/1 Profile

C22/2 End view
1   Tail shaft
2   Intermediate shaft
3   Split ring
4   Keys
5   Bolt holes

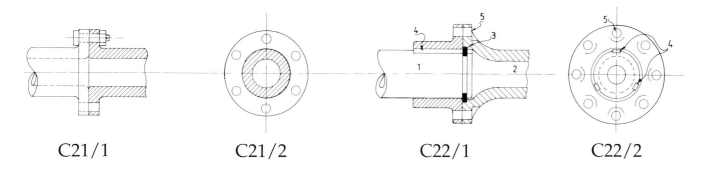

C21/1   C21/2   C22/1   C22/2

C Machinery

C23 STEERING ARRANGEMENTS

Dreadnought had five steering positions – the standard position on the bridge and protected positions in the conning tower, lower conning tower, signal tower and lower signal tower. All these positions could be connected to the control shafting which operated the steering engines fitted on the after bulkhead of the port and starboard engine rooms. Two sets of control shafting were provided, one down each side of the ship, which could control either steering engine, the latter being clutched so that only one could be engaged with the steering gear at any one time. These complex arrangements allowed for system back-up in case of disablement due to action damage, accident or maintenance requirements. If the entire system broke down the steering could be operated by the hand steering gear in the after part of the ship. The steering engine operation was controlled by a steam valve which was opened by the control shaft and then returned to a closed position by the running of the engine. Thus the further the helm was put over, the more the valve opened, the longer the engine ran and the further the rudders moved.

C23/1 Profile of steering controls as completed (scale $^1/_{32}$in = 1ft)

C23/2 Plan of steering gear drive shaft as completed (scale $^1/_{32}$in = 1ft)

C23/3 Plan of helm indicator gear (scale $^1/_{16}$in =1ft)

C23/4 Profile of modified steering gear arrangements fitted in late 1907 (scale $^1/_{32}$in = 1ft)

C23/5 Plan of new steering gear drive shaft arrangements fitted in late 1907 (scale $^1/_{32}$in = 1ft)

C23/6 Plan of upper part of engine room, late 1907 (scale $^1/_{32}$in = 1ft)

1   Hand steering compartment
2   Telemotor valve for helm signal gear
3   Telemotor pipes
4   Steering shaft
5   Bevel gear drive to steering gear
6   Helm signals
7   Helm signal gear
8   Cover over propeller shaft
9   Engine room
10   Steering engine
11   Steering engine control shafts
12   Skew gear
13   Navigating platform
14   Conning tower
15   Signal tower
16   Lower conning tower
17   Lower signal tower
18   New position of after evaporator
19   New position of distiller
20   New and modified platforms
21   Original platforms
22   Recess in wing bulkhead for evaporator

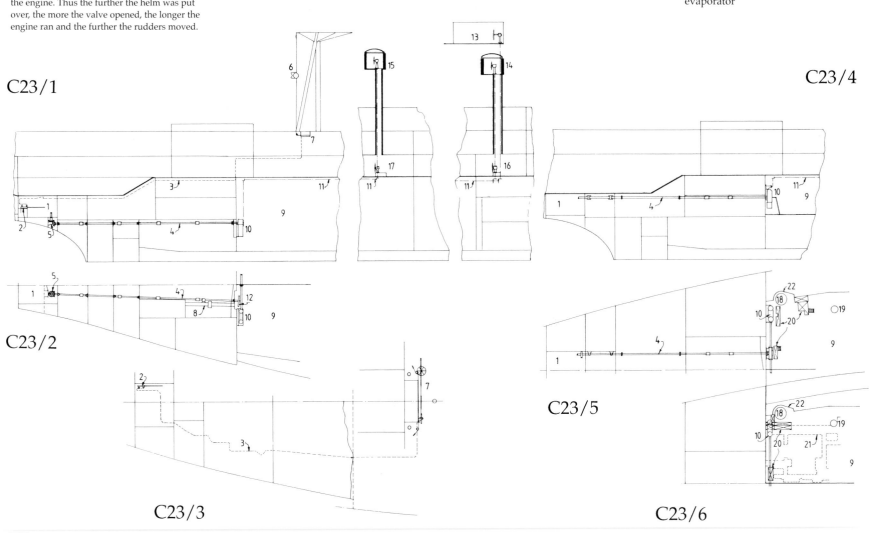

C23/1

C23/2

C23/3

C23/4

C23/5

C23/6

C24 SECTION OF STEERING WHEEL AND PEDESTAL (scale ½in = 1ft)

1 Wheel
2 Bevel drive gear to control shaft
3 Shaft end stop gear
4 Pointer for helm angle indicator
5 Helm indicator drive gear
6 Control shaft to steering engine control valve

The arrangement shown is for conning tower positions; that on the navigating platform was similar but the wheel projected further from the pedestal, while those in the lower positions were mounted on platforms and therefore had shorter pedestals.

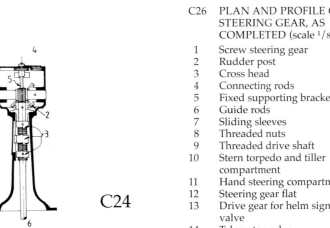

C24

C25 DIAGRAMMATIC LAYOUT OF HELM SIGNAL GEAR

This equipment was provided to indicate to accompanying ships the direction in which the helm was being moved.

1 Red flag (port)
2 Green ball (starboard)
3 Blocks on spurs to mainmast starfish
4 Spring box
5 Bottle screw
6 Opening in upper deck for wire
7 Steel wire
8 Pulleys
9 Rack and pinion drive to steel wire drive wheel
10 Telemotor piston
11 Telemotor pipes from hand steering compartment

C25

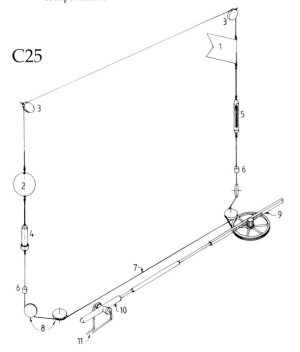

C26 PLAN AND PROFILE OF STEERING GEAR, AS COMPLETED (scale ⅛in = 1ft)

1 Screw steering gear
2 Rudder post
3 Cross head
4 Connecting rods
5 Fixed supporting brackets
6 Guide rods
7 Sliding sleeves
8 Threaded nuts
9 Threaded drive shaft
10 Stern torpedo and tiller compartment
11 Hand steering compartment
12 Steering gear flat
13 Drive gear for helm signal telemotor valve
14 Telemotor valve
15 6in dia drive shaft
16 Bevel gears
17 Hand steering wheels
18 Portable plates giving access to palm compartment (under)
19 Ladder
20 Hatch (over)
21 Electric compass receiver
22 Telemotor pipes to helm signal gear
23 Drive shaft from steering engines
24 Upper rudder head bearing
25 Lower rudder head bearing
26 Rudder head
27 Rudder head casting
28 Cast steel rudder frame
29 Prefabricated zed frames
30 Prefabricated channel frame
31 Butt straps for covering plates
32 Outline of covering plates (20lbs)
33 Lifting hole
34 Rudder stop
35 Contour plate
36 Interior of rudder filled with wood (fir)

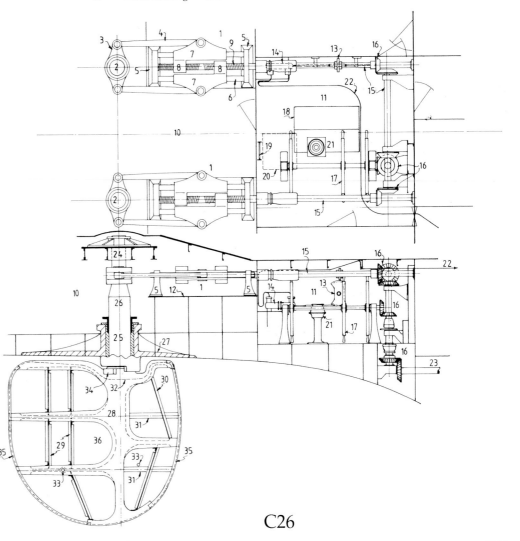

C26

C Machinery

C27   PLAN AND PROFILE OF HAND
STEERING COMPARTMENT AS
MODIFIED IN LATE 1907 (scale
$\frac{1}{8}$in = 1ft)

C27

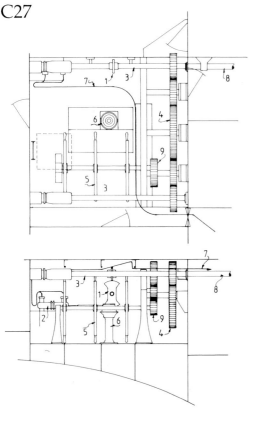

1   Drive gear for helm signal telemotor
valve
2   Telemotor valve
3   6in dia drive shaft
4   Spur gear cross connection drive
5   Hand steering wheels
6   Electric compass receiver
7   Telemotor pipes to helm signal gear
8   Drive shaft from steering engines
9   Drive from hand steering wheels

C28   PERSPECTIVE VIEW OF
STEERING GEAR AS
COMPLETED

1   Stern torpedo tube
2   Stern casting
3   Rudder head casting
4   Starboard rudder
5   Port rudder
6   Screw steering gear
7   Stern torpedo and tiller
compartment
8   Hand steering compartment
9   Store
10   Telemotor pipe
11   Telemotor valve drive gear
12   Steering gear flat
13   Hand steering wheels
14   Electric compass receiver

C29   ARRANGEMENT OF STEERING
ENGINES AS BUILT (scale $\frac{3}{16}$in =
1ft)

C29/1   *After engine room bulkhead looking aft*

C29/2   *Plan of arrangement in starboard engine
room*

C29/3   *Profile of steering engine*

1   Middle line bulkhead
2   Drive shaft
3   Steering shaft
4   Skew gear
5   Worm and worm wheel drive gear
6   Clutch
7   Clutch cross connection shaft
8   Inner propeller shaft
9   Drive shaft from steering wheels
10   Steering engine control-valve gear
11   Connecting rods and cranks to
steering engine steam pistons
12   Steering engine valve eccentrics
13   Steam inlet valve
14   Steam exhaust valve
15   Recess in bulkhead for skew gear

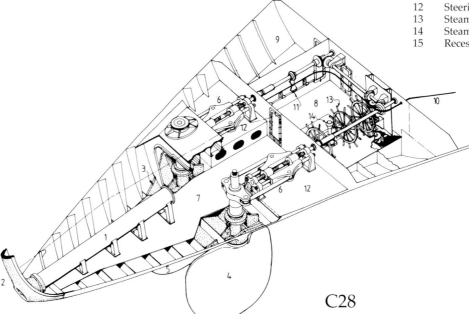

C28

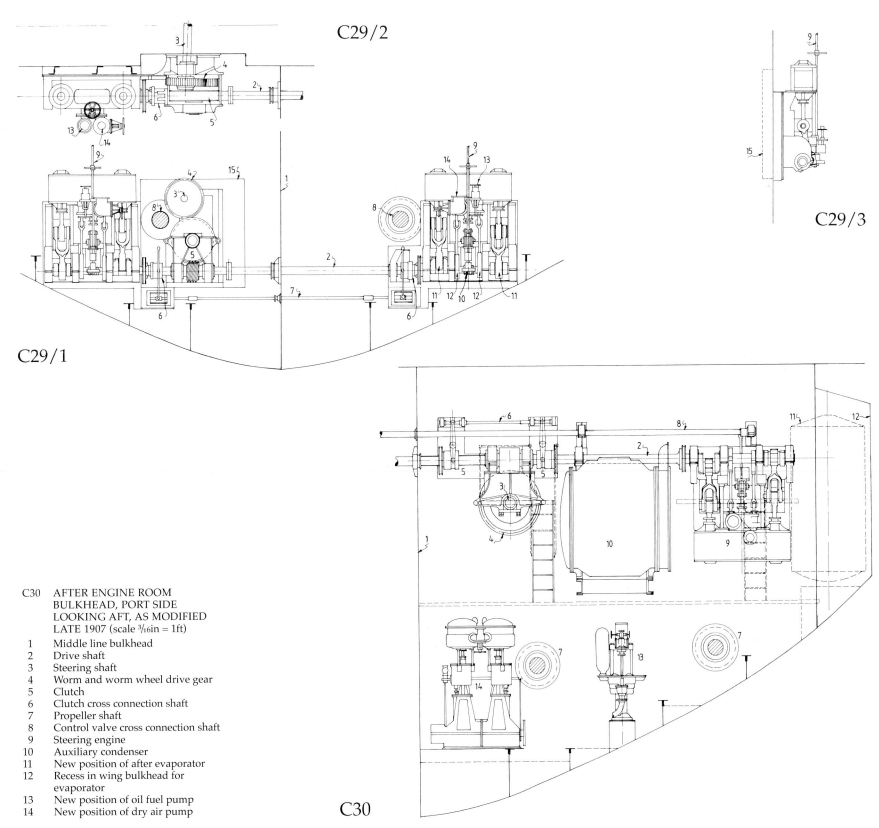

C29/2

C29/3

C29/1

C30 AFTER ENGINE ROOM
     BULKHEAD, PORT SIDE
     LOOKING AFT, AS MODIFIED
     LATE 1907 (scale $^3/_{16}$in = 1ft)

1   Middle line bulkhead
2   Drive shaft
3   Steering shaft
4   Worm and worm wheel drive gear
5   Clutch
6   Clutch cross connection shaft
7   Propeller shaft
8   Control valve cross connection shaft
9   Steering engine
10 Auxiliary condenser
11 New position of after evaporator
12 Recess in wing bulkhead for
    evaporator
13 New position of oil fuel pump
14 New position of dry air pump

C30

C   Machinery

C31   DISTRIBUTION OF AUXILIARY MACHINERY OUTSIDE ENGINE AND BOILER ROOMS (scale $^1/_{32}$in = 1ft)

C31/1   *Hold, aft*

C31/2   *Platform deck, aft*

C31/3   *Platform deck, forward*

C31/4   *Port dynamo room as modified 1908–09*

C31/5   *Lower deck, abreast 'Y' turret*

C31/6   *Lower deck, abreast 'X' turret*

C31/7   *Lower deck, abreast 'P' & 'Q' turrets*

C31/8   *Lower deck, abreast P & Q turrets, as modified up to April 1910*

C31/9   *Lower deck, forward*

C31/10   *Lower deck, forward, as modified up to April 1910*

C31/11   *Middle deck, aft*

1   Ventilation supply fan
2   Ventilation air chamber (distribution box for air trunks)
3   Magazine cooling fan (fitted 1907–08)
4   Cooler
5   Valve chest (for 50 ton electric pump)
6   Seacock
7   Flat
8   Evaporator
9   Water tank
10   Electric motor pumps for fresh water
11   Engineers' store
12   'G' 50 ton electric pump
13   'F' 50 ton electric pump
14   'E' 50 ton electric pump
15   'D' 50 ton electric pump
16   'C' 50 ton electric pump
17   'B' 50 ton electric pump
18   'A' 50 ton electric pump
19   Ready use oil tank
20   Air compressor
21   Air reservoirs
22   Diesel engine operating valves
23   Diesel dynamo
24   12pdr dredger hoist motor
25   Capstan engine
26   Vice bench
27   Hose rack
28   Steam dynamo
29   Bench (cupboard under)
30   Steps
31   Hydraulic pumping engine
32   Low power switchboard

33   Motor-generator
34   Switchboard room
35   Main switchboard
36   Motor alternator for turret danger signals
37   Motor alternator (added 1910)
38   Motor alternators for wireless transmitter (added 1910)
39   Motor alternator for wireless transmitter
40   Motor generator (new position 1910)
41   Switchboard
42   Motor generators (added 1908–09)
43   Motor alternator for telephone exchange
44   Motor alternator for telephone exchange (new position 1908–09)
45   Working space for 12pdr ammunition
46   Control telephone exchange
47   Telephone exchange
48   Telephone cabinet
49   Transmitting station
50   Magazine cooling machinery compartment (added 1907–08)
51   Evaporator
52   Brine tank
53   Brine pump
54   CO_2 machine (compressor)
55   Condenser
56   Vent trunk (added)
57   Refrigerating machinery
58   Battery box
59   Heater

60   Downton hand pump (added 1907 as backup to electric pumps for fresh water tanks)
61   Shelf
62   Tool box
63   Electricians' and Armourers' workshop
64   Engineers' workshop
65   Ventilation fan for dynamo room (added 1907–08)
66   Vice bench (removed when '65' added)
67   Cupboard
68   Tank
69   Workshop motor
70   Shaping machine
71   Lathe
72   Drilling machine
73   CO_2 storage flasks
74   Storage bins
75   Storage racks
76   Boring machine
77   Steam pipe space
78   Planing machine
79   Grindstone
80   Oil tank
81   Sanitary pump
82   Hand shearing machine
83   Hydraulic topping machinery for main boat boom
84   Hydraulic lifting machinery for main boat boom
85   Lift motor
86   Electric capstan motor

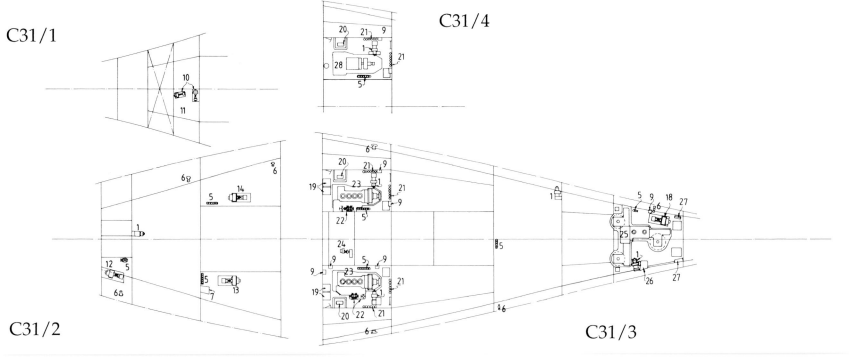

C31/1

C31/4

C31/2

C31/3

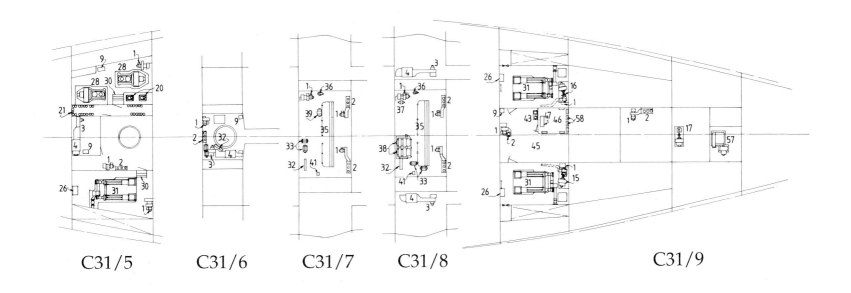

C31/5 C31/6 C31/7 C31/8 C31/9

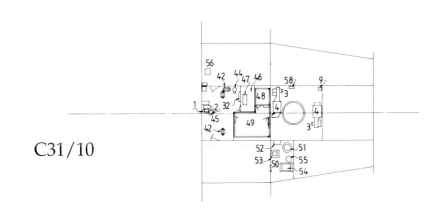

C31/10

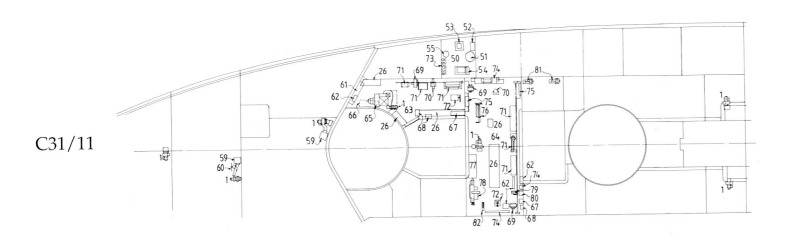

C31/11

181

C   Machinery

C31/12   *Middle deck, forward*   *See Key on page 180.*

C31/13   *Main deck, aft*

C31/14   *Main deck, forward*

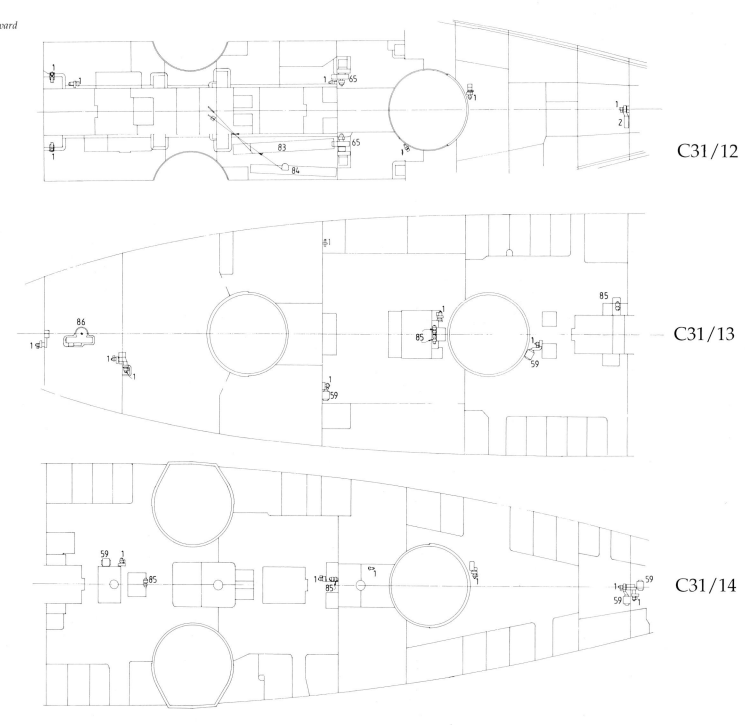

C31/12

C31/13

C31/14

C32 SIEMENS DYNAMO DRIVEN BY
A HIGH SPEED, 400rpm,
BROTHERHOOD STEAM PISTON
ENGINE

The entire unit weighed about 8½ tons.

C33 SIEMENS DYNAMO DRIVEN BY
A FOUR CYLINDER DIESEL
ENGINE CONSTRUCTED BY
MIRRLEES, BICKERTON AND
DAY LTD

The engines ran at 400rpm, developed 160 bhp
and were equipped with a forced lubrication
system. The entire unit weighed about 17 tons.

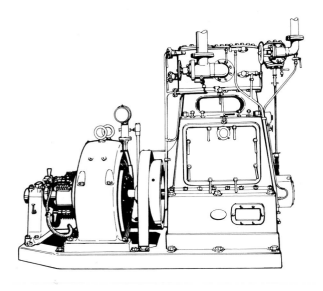

C32

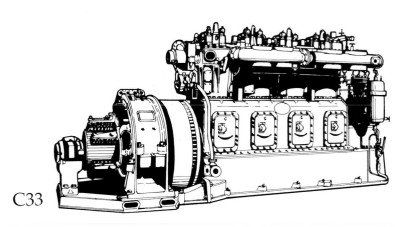

C33

C Machinery

C34 GENERAL ARRANGEMENT OF AFTER MAGAZINE COOLING MACHINERY FITTED IN 1907–8 (scale $^1/_4$in = 1ft)

C34/1 *Plan*

C34/2 *Equipment on port side, looking to port*

C34/3 *Equipment on starboard side looking to starboard*

1   Brine tank
2   Evaporator
3   Distiller
4   Brine pump
5   Compressor
6   Ladder
7   Hatch (over)
8   Spare CO_2 bottles
9   Auxiliary steam pipe in port engine room
10 Auxiliary exhaust steam pipe in port engine room
11 Steam supply to compressor and brine pump
12 Steam exhaust from compressor and brine pump
13 Circulation pump sea water suction
14 Connection to rising main of fire and bilge pump in port engine room
15 Connection to sea inlet valve (for port engine room distiller circulation pump) in port engine room
16 Circulation pump discharge to sea
17 Circulation pump discharge to condenser
18 Steam inlet to brine pump
19 Steam exhaust from brine pump
20 Steam inlet to compressor
21 Steam exhaust from compressor
22 Brine pump discharge from brine tank
23 Brine pump suction to brine tank
24 Supply to 'X' magazine cooler
25 Supply to 'Y' magazine cooler
26 Discharge from brine pump to coolers via evaporator
27 Suction from coolers to brine pump
28 CO_2 discharge to condenser
29 CO_2 suction from evaporator
30 CO_2 supply from condenser to evaporator
31 Discharge from port engine room distiller circulating pump
32 Screen
33 Middle deck
34 Main deck
35 Protective deck
36 Port engine room wing bulkhead (under)

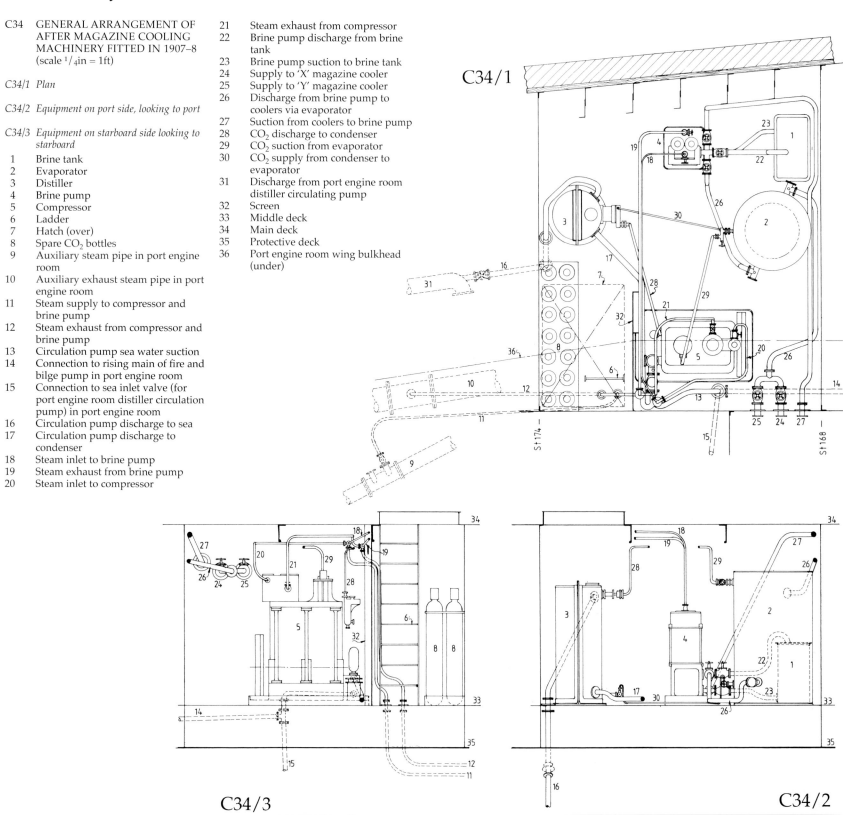

C34/1

C34/3

C34/2

184

C35 DIAGRAMMATIC ARRANGEMENT
OF MAGAZINE COOLER

1 Supply trunk
2 Exhaust trunk
3 Watertight slide valve
4 Throttle valve
5 Spindle to main deck for remote
  closing of valves
6 Magazine
7 Cooler
8 Temperature tube
9 12½in electrically driven fan
10 Brine supply pipe from cooling
   machinery
11 Brine discharge pipe to cooling
   machinery

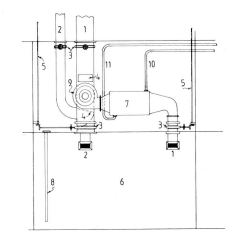

C35

C36 PUMPING AND FLOODING
SYSTEM AT FORE END (scale ¹/₈in
= 1ft, drawing is semi-diagramatic)

Each main watertight section was provided with
separate pumping and flooding arrangements but
all the pumps were connected to the main fore-
and-aft fire mains. The electrically driven
centrifugal pumps were connected to one fire
main and the steam driven pumps in the main
machinery compartments to another but these
were also inter-connected so that any pump could
supply any part of the system.

1 Screw-down non-return and flood
  valve
2 Non-return valve
3 Screw-down valve
4 Flood valve for spirit room
5 Deck plate
6 Valve control rod
7 Hose connection
8 To hose connections on upper and
  forecastle decks
9 Air escape pipe
10 5in fire main
11 4in overboard discharge
12 4in sea suction
13 4in bilge suction
14 'B' pump seacock, 15in diameter
15 'B' pump discharge, 5in diameter
16 Valve chest
17 Electric motor
18 'B' 50 ton centrifugal pump
19 Mud box
20 Slide valve
21 Spirit room
22 Bread room
23 Submerged torpedo room
24 Torpedo lobby
25 4in rising main
26 Screw-down non-return drain valve

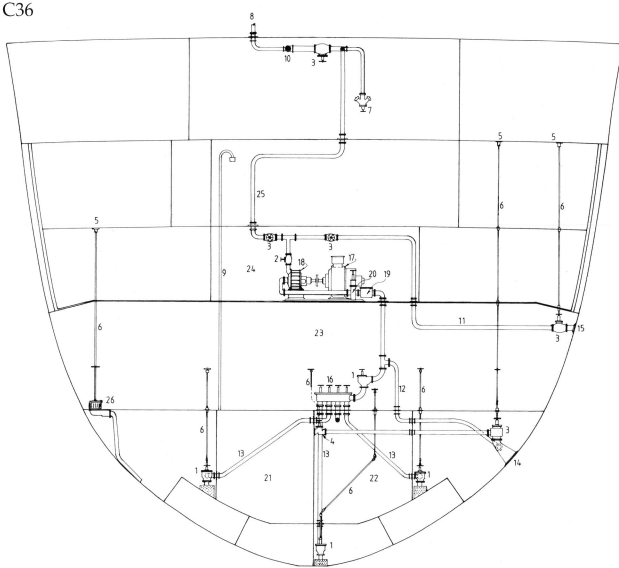

C36

185

C Machinery

C37 PLAN OF MAIN DECK
SHOWING ARRANGEMENT OF
FIRE MAINS

1 'A' 50 ton pump
2 'B' 50 ton pump
3 'C' 50 ton pump
4 'D' 50 ton pump
5 'A' boiler room 50 ton fire and bilge
   pump
6 'B' boiler room 50 ton fire and bilge
   pump
7 'C' boiler room 50 ton fire and bilge
   pump
8 75 ton fire and bilge pumps in
   engine rooms
9 'E' 50 ton pump
10 'F' 50 ton pump
11 'G' 50 ton pump
12 To gooseneck vent on forecastle
13 To officers' heads
14 To officers' heads and bath ejectors
15 Bath ejector
16 To heads
17 To ash shoot
18 To upper deck gravity tank
M Hose connections on main deck
U Hose connections on upper deck
L Hose connections on lower deck
F Hose connections on forecastle
S Hose connections in superstructure

The open circles are screw down valves. The solid
circles are hose connections.

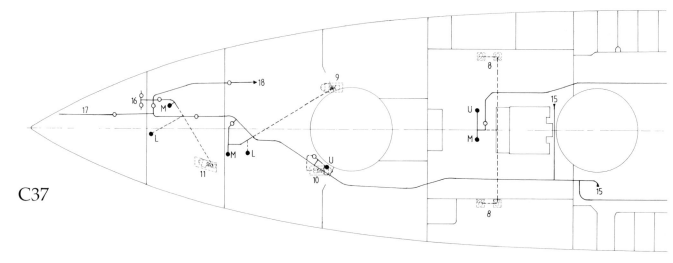

C37

C38 DETAILS OF VALVES ETC

C38/1 Typical arrangement of scupper

C38/2 Typical seacock

C38/3 Screw-down valve

*C38/4 Foot valve (screw-down, non-return and
flood valve)*

C38/5 Flood valve

C38/6 Screw-down, non-return drain valve

*C38/7 Arrangement of seacock in double
bottom*

*C38/8 Arrangement of seacock outside double
bottom*

C38/9 Slide valve

1 Upper deck
2 Spurnwater
3 7in drain pipe
4 Inspection cover
5 Lip (replaced pipe covers originally
   fitted)
6 Open-close indicator
7 Stuffing gland
8 Machined face
9 Leather sealing pad
10 Stop
11 Non-return flap
12 Flood pipe
13 Sea suction
14 Distance piece
15 Seacock

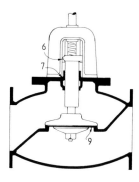

C38/1

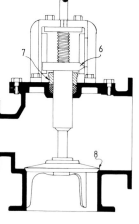

C38/2

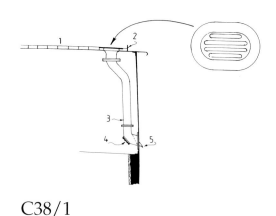

C38/3

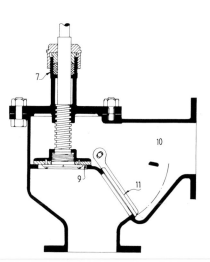

C38/4

186

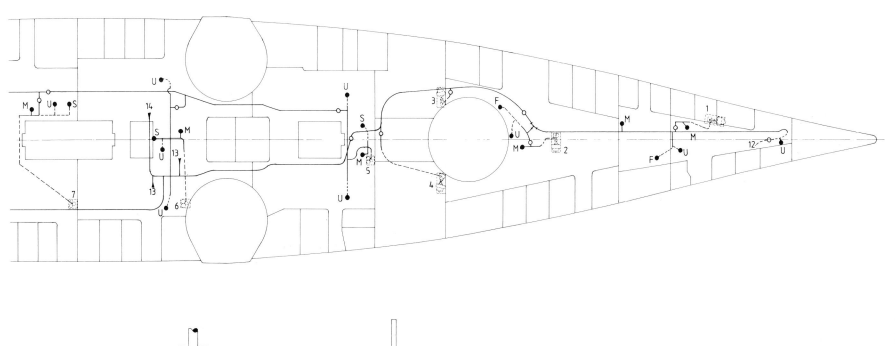

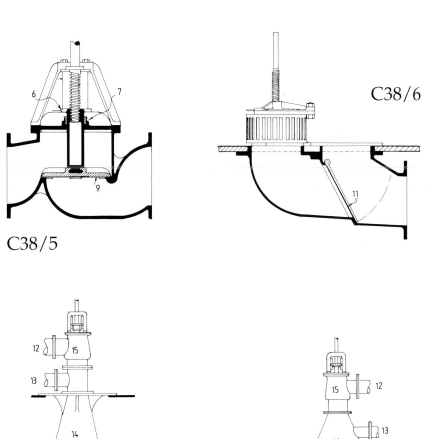

C38/6

C38/5

C38/7

C38/8

C38/9

C Machinery

C39 COAL BUNKERS

The main coal bunkers were arranged amidships abreast the boiler rooms but the upper bunkers also extended aft over the engine rooms as far as station 174. Each boiler room had its own group of bunkers and there was no intercommunication between these groups in order to avoid piercing the main watertight bulkheads. However, the coal in the upper bunkers abreast the engine rooms could be moved aft through watertight doors in 149 bulkhead on the middle deck and thence down to the lower bunkers abreast 'X' barbette. From here the coal could be moved aft to the bunkers abreast 'C' boiler room through watertight doors in bulkhead 142. This arrangement gave an uneven distribution of coal, particularly as the bunkers abreast 'A' boiler room were smaller than those aft due to the ship's form. Direct access to coal was 669 tons for 'A' boiler room, 905 tons for 'B' boiler room and 1256 tons (including the bunkers over the engine rooms) for 'C' boiler room. There were, however, emergency coaling trunks from the upper bunkers abreast the engine rooms to the upper deck which allowed for coal being hauled up to the upper deck, transported forward and tipped into the forward bunker coaling chutes. These emergency trunks, fitted back-to-back on the division bulkhead between the bunkers, terminated on the upper deck at rectangular covers positioned abreast the engine room hatch. One of the innovations in *Dreadnought* was the provision of fixed coaling chutes between the upper and main decks. In earlier ships these were portable canvas chutes which allowed coal dust to escape onto the messdecks.

C39/1 General arrangement of coal bunkers amidships

C39/1

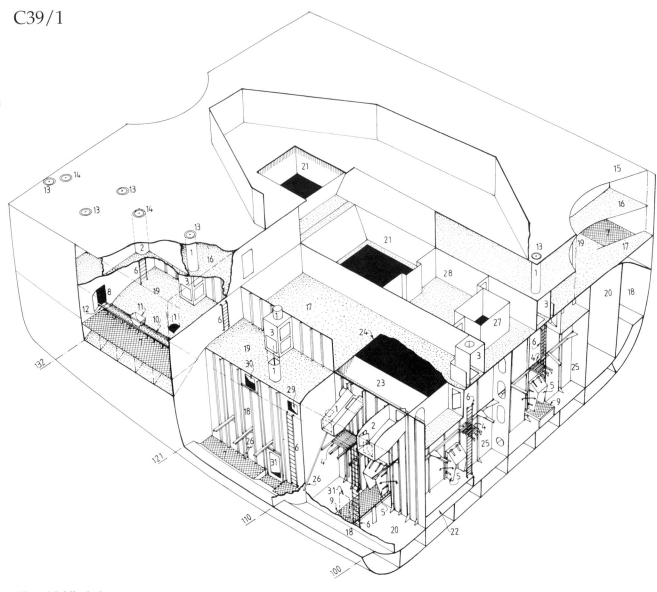

1	Coal chute	17	Middle deck
2	Escape trunk	18	Wing bunker
3	Coaling trunk	19	Upper bunker
4	Coal break	20	Inner bunker
5	Hinged screen to stokehold doors	21	Funnel hatch
6	Ladder to escape trunk	22	Space for pipes
7	Flat (chequered plating)	23	Passage abreast boiler room giving access to escape trunks and temperature tubes
8	Watertight door between intermediate bulkheads only	24	'B' boiler room
9	Shovelling flat	25	Cross bunker
10	Coal skid rails	26	Temperature tube
11	Coal skid	27	'B' boiler room vent trunk
12	Portable rails to pass through watertight door when open	28	Lower signal tower
13	Coal scuttle	29	Door to escape trunk
14	Escape scuttle	30	Door to coaling chute
15	Upper deck	31	Door between inner and wing bunkers
16	Main deck		

C39/2 *Transverse section of coal bunkers amidships (scale ⅛in = 1ft)*

1   Coal chute
2   Coal scuttle
3   Escape trunk
4   Escape ladder
5   Coal trunk
6   Watertight door 4ft 6in × 2ft 3in between upper bunkers
7   Coal skid rails
8   Doors for coaling upper bunkers (open inward)
9   Flat
10   Doors to direct coal from upper bunkers to lower bunkers (open inward)
11   Armoured hatch for coaling lower bunkers
12   Hatch for coaling inner bunker
13   Watertight door, 3ft × 2ft, for coaling wing bunker
14   Watertight door, 3ft × 2ft 6in
15   Vertical sliding watertight door, 3ft 6in × 2ft 3in
16   Screen to door
17   Coal break
18   Temperature tube
19   Access to temperature tubes
20   Platform in boiler room
21   Upper bunker
22   Wing bunker
23   Lower bunker
24   Shovelling flat

C39/3 *Plan of coal scuttle in upper deck*

1   Deck rim
2   Cover
3   Holes for spanner
4   Lifting handle

C39/4 *Detail of temperature tube (scale 1½in = 1ft)*

1   Cap
2   Eye for hanging thermometer
3   2½in diameter tube

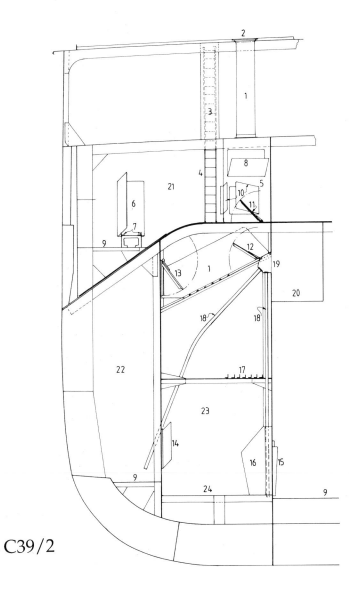

C39/2

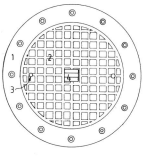

C39/3

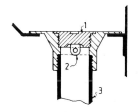

C39/4

189

C Machinery

C39/5 Coaling trunk (scale ¼in = 1ft)

1 Portable angle
2 Doors for coaling upper bunkers
   (shown in position for coaling upper
   bunkers)
3 Doors for coaling lower bunkers
4 Portable bars
5 Door clips
6 Longitudinal bulkhead
7 Main deck
8 Middle deck

C39/6 Plan of railway for coal skid (scale ¼in = 1ft)

C39/7 Vertical sliding watertight door to inner bunker, viewed from stokehold side

1 Door in raised position
2 Door frame (recess for door was of
   wedge form)
3 Door clip
4 Chain wheel
5 Bevel gears
6 Pulley
7 Door operating chain
8 Screwed shaft for lifting door
9 Threaded bush
10 Clearance holes
11 Screen
12 Shovelling flat

The cross bunkers, being non-watertight, had a simpler arrangement with light covers lifted vertically to a chain run over a pulley.

C39/8 Detail of screen to coal bunker door (scale ¼in = 1ft)

1 Top screen
2 Side screen
3 Chain for lifting top screen
4 Cleat for chain
5 Portable 'T' bars
6 Stowed position for T bars
7 Vertical sliding watertight door
8 Shovelling flat

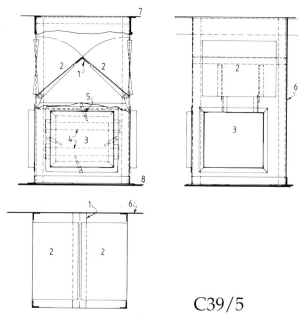

C39/5

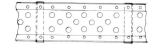

C39/6

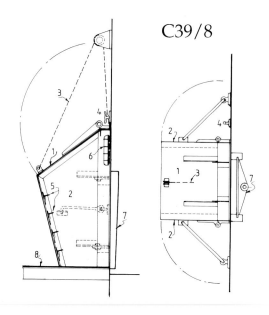

C39/8

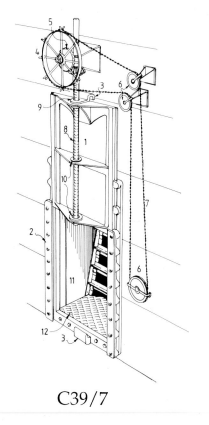

C39/7

D   Accommodation

1	Bin	40	Water tank
2	Kit bag rack	41	Seat with lockers under
3	Wash stand	42	Prisons
4	Chest of drawers	43	Seat (and in other cells)
5	Table with drawers or cupboards (under)	44	Table (and in other cells)
6	Shelf (over)	45	Master-at-Arms
7	Hinged table	46	Dwarf wall
8	Ice chest	47	Letter box
9	Bath (over)	48	Drinking water tank
10	Admiral's domestics' mess	49	Marines' helmets
11	Ladderway to domestics' mess	50	Sergeants of Marines' mess
12	Electric pump	51	Bank instrument room
13	Coal box	52	Steam cooker
14	Admiral's steward (cabin arranged as starboard side)	53	Hot over
15	Admiral's cook	54	Boiling copper
16	Surgeon's cabin	55	Hot water tank
17	Washing-up trough	56	Boiler
18	Tiled area	57	Cooking range
19	Sink	58	Ship's galley
20	Cooking range	59	Dresser
21	Officers' smoking room	60	Cooks' kitchen
22	Gun room galley	61	Test tank (for checking quality of drinking water)
23	Ward room galley	62	Tanks
24	Gun room	63	Issue room
25	Ward room	64	ERAs' mess
26	Card table	65	CPOs' mess
27	Bookcase	66	Sick bay
28	Tank (over)	67	Dispensary
29	Passage	68	Bath
30	Heater	69	Cots (two levels)
31	Ventilation supply fan	70	Cabin for two WOs
32	Ward room ante-room	71	Stool
33	Gun room pantry	72	Engineers' office
34	Ward room pantry	73	WOs' mess
35	Wash deck locker	74	Engineer Lieutenant's cabin
36	Seamen's heads	75	Engineer Commander's cabin
37	Urinals	76	WOs' pantry
38	WCs	77	Desks
39	Chief and 1st class POs' WCs	78	Hose reel (port and starboard)
		79	Hatch to CO_2 machinery room

80	Cap box	119	Secretary's office (converted to Fleet Surgeon's cabin 1908–09)
81	Chaplain's cabin	120	Cabin for two officers (converted to Signal Officer's cabin 1908–09)
82	Navigating officer's cabin	121	Flag Lieutenant's cabin (converted to Commander's cabin 1908–09)
83	Commander's cabin	122	Cabin for two officers
84	Chief of staff's office	123	Bathing cubicles (removed by 1910)
85	Ship's office	124	Washing basins
86	Paymaster's cabin	125	Footboard
87	Fleet Surgeon's cabin	126	Cabin for two officers
88	Armament office	127	Junior officers' bathroom
89	Police office	128	Bin (added by 1910)
90	Safe	129	Domestics' mess (converted to domestics' baggage room by 1910)
91	Pistol rack	130	Vertical ladder
92	Pouches for pistols	131	Oil tanks
93	Secretary's office	132	Paint store
94	Secretary's cabin	133	Ship's corporals
95	New side scuttle	134	Dry canteen
96	Flag commander's cabin	b	Bunk
97	Chief of Staff's day cabin	c	Cupboard
98	Chief of Staff's sleeping cabin	d	Sideboard
99	Chief of Staff's WC and bathroom	dk	Desk
100	Admiral's pantry	e	Seat
101	Dressing table	h	Hammock stowage
102	Plate rack	k	Kneehole table
103	Dresser with drawers under	L	Locker
104	Captain's day cabin	m	Mess table and benches
105	Captain's sleeping cabin	n	Bath
106	Captain's pantry	p	Rifle rack
107	Captain's WC and bathroom	Q	Officers' cabin
108	Watertight door (5ft 6in × 3ft) with wood door on inside	r	Rack (over)
109	Admiral's dining cabin	s	Settee
110	Admiral's saloon	T	Table (T^1 table added 1908–09)
111	Admiral's sleeping cabin	v	Stove (solid fuel)
112	Admiral's WC and bathroom	w	Wardrobe
113	Wood grating platform	x	Mess shelf
114	Step		
115	Towel rack		
116	Curtain		
117	Midshipmen's study		
118	Admiral's secretary's cabin (converted to officer's cabin 1908–09)		

D1/1

D1   GENERAL ARRANGEMENT OF ACCOMMODATION SPACES
(scale ¹⁄₃₂in = 1ft)

D1/1   Upper deck forward, January 1907

D1/2   Upper deck forward, as modified up to April 1910

D1/2

D Accommodation

D1/3   *Main deck aft, January 1907*   *See Key on page 191.*

D1/4   *Modifications to main deck aft, 1907–08*

D1/5   *New Masters-at-Arms' mess, 1907*

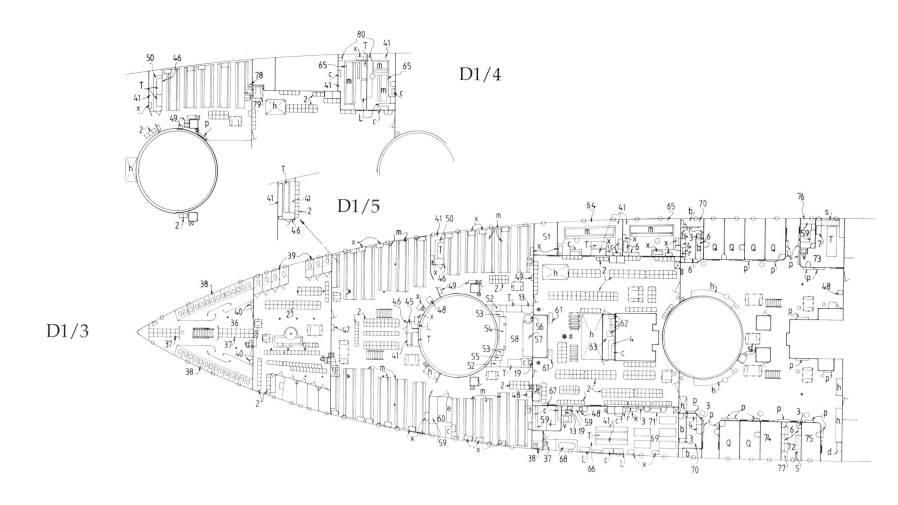

D1/4

D1/5

D1/3

D1/6   Main deck forward, January 1907

D1/7   Modified arrangement of cabins on
        starboard side of main deck, 1908–09

D1/8   Modified arrangement of cabins on port
        side of main deck, 1908–09

D1/9   Middle deck, aft, January 1907

D1/8

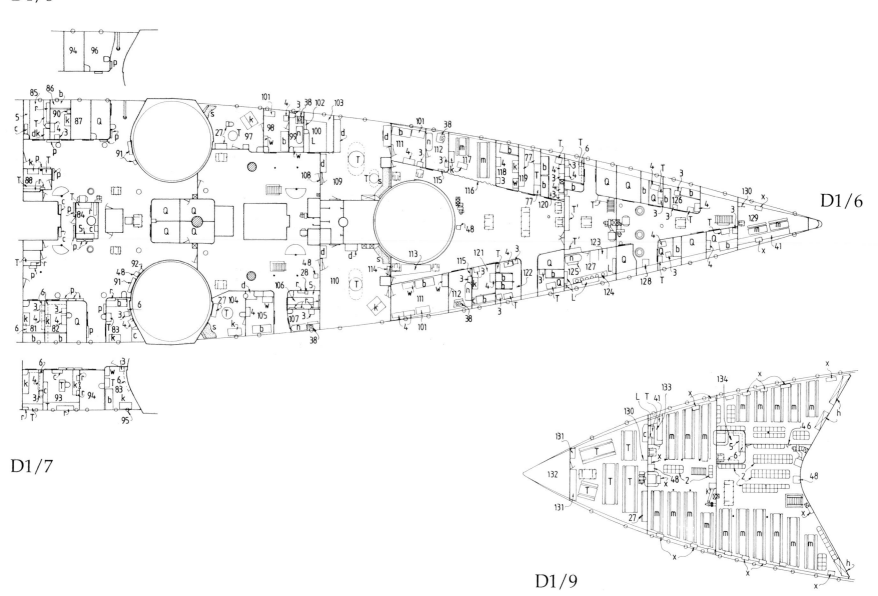

D1/7

D1/9

D1/6

D Accommodation

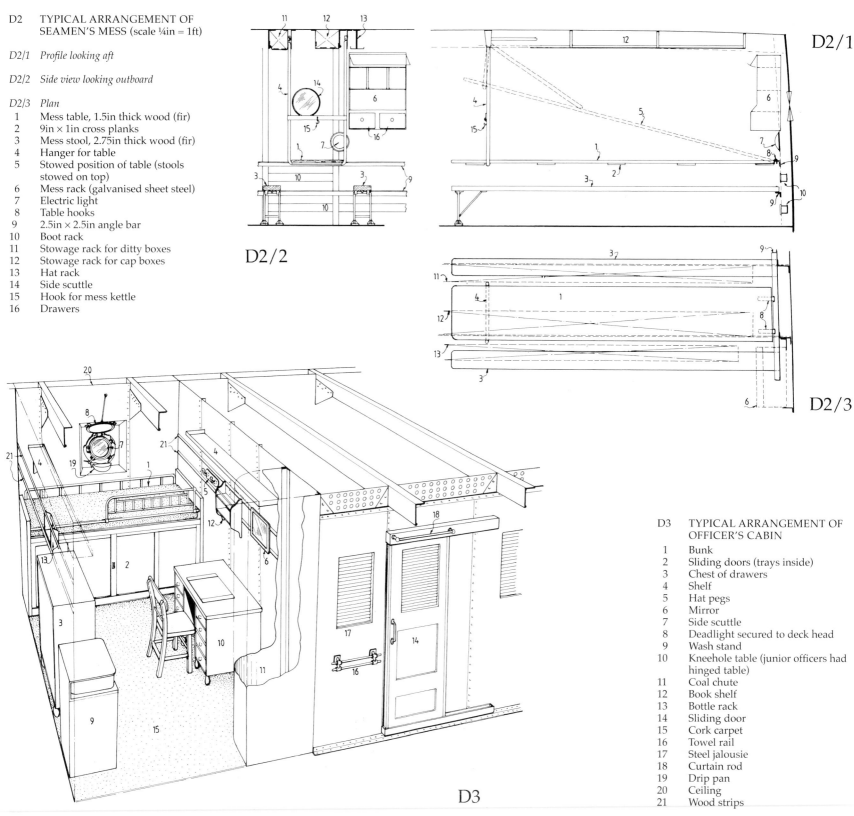

D2 TYPICAL ARRANGEMENT OF
SEAMEN'S MESS (scale ¼in = 1ft)

D2/1 Profile looking aft

D2/2 Side view looking outboard

D2/3 Plan

1   Mess table, 1.5in thick wood (fir)
2   9in × 1in cross planks
3   Mess stool, 2.75in thick wood (fir)
4   Hanger for table
5   Stowed position of table (stools
    stowed on top)
6   Mess rack (galvanised sheet steel)
7   Electric light
8   Table hooks
9   2.5in × 2.5in angle bar
10 Boot rack
11 Stowage rack for ditty boxes
12 Stowage rack for cap boxes
13 Hat rack
14 Side scuttle
15 Hook for mess kettle
16 Drawers

D2/1

D2/2

D2/3

D3 TYPICAL ARRANGEMENT OF
OFFICER'S CABIN

1   Bunk
2   Sliding doors (trays inside)
3   Chest of drawers
4   Shelf
5   Hat pegs
6   Mirror
7   Side scuttle
8   Deadlight secured to deck head
9   Wash stand
10 Kneehole table (junior officers had
    hinged table)
11 Coal chute
12 Book shelf
13 Bottle rack
14 Sliding door
15 Cork carpet
16 Towel rail
17 Steel jalousie
18 Curtain rod
19 Drip pan
20 Ceiling
21 Wood strips

D3

E Superstructure

E1 PROFILE OF SUPERSTRUCTURE
January 1907 (scale $\frac{1}{16}$in = 1ft)

Starboard foremast strut is omitted.

1 Watertight door, 4ft 6in × 2ft 6in to boiler room vent
2 Watertight door, 5ft × 2ft
3 Mushroom top exhaust vent from seamen's wash place
4 Mushroom top exhaust vent from CPOs' washplace
5 Skylight to main deck
6 Hawser reel
7 Coaling derrick
8 Derrick stump mast
9 36in searchlight
10 Watertight door 6ft 3in × 4ft
11 Screen to main W/T aerial
12 400 gallon sanitary tank
13 Signal tower
14 After control platform

15 9ft FQ2 rangefinder
16 Flag lockers
17 Stove funnel from WOs' galley
18 Boat crutches
19 Hinged plate
20 Hydraulic gear and controls for main derrick
21 Platform for passing 12pdr ammunition to roof of 12in turret
22 Mast stay
23 Engine room telegraph
24 Control rod from engine room telegraph
25 Admiral's shelter
26 Bow light
27 Light and vent to main deck
28 Watertight door, 5ft 6in × 4ft

29 Mushroom top exhaust vent from Admiral's pantry
30 Ship's bell
31 Siren
32 Steaming light
33 Conning tower
34 Chart table
35 Searchlight controls
36 Compass
37 Semaphore
38 Breakwater
39 Non-watertight door
40 Hinged grating
41 Position of sides of control platform when hinged up

E1

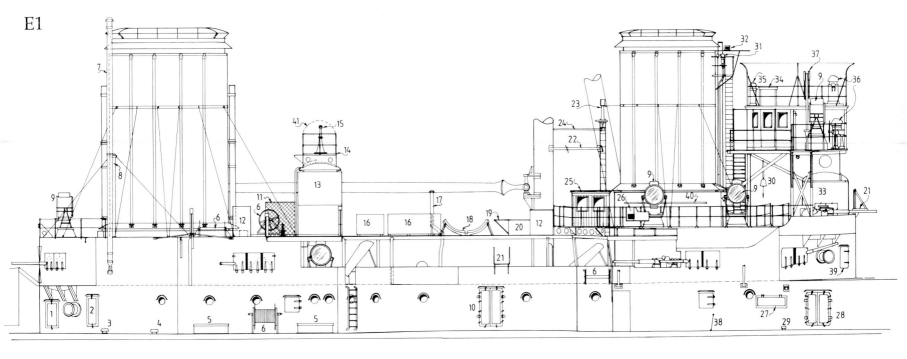

E Superstructure

E2 PROFILE OF SUPERSTRUCTURE WITH SIDE OMITTED January 1907 (scale $^1/_{16}$in = 1ft)

1. Boiler room vent
2. 12pdr gun pedestal
3. Hoods to boiler room vents (removed 1907)
4. Door to funnel uptakes
5. Bakery
6. Light and vent trunk to bakery
7. Flag locker
8. Signal tower
9. Pillar
10. Channel bar pillar
11. Fairlead for boat hoist wires
12. Ash hoist from 'B' boiler room
13. Wire mesh
14. WOs' galley
15. Stove funnel from WOs' galley
16. Electric coaling winch

17. Vent supply trunk to switchboard room
18. Passage
19. Admiral's shelter
20. Hydraulic gear and controls for main derrick
21. Admiral's walk
22. Hinged grating
23. Vent supply trunk
24. Silencer for diesel engine exhaust
25. Shelf
26. 12pdr dredger hoist trunk
27. Locker for searchlight screens
28. Conning tower
29. Wireless office
30. Signal house

E6 PROFILE OF SUPERSTRUCTURE June 1915 (scale $^1/_{16}$in = 1ft)

Only differences from January 1907 are indicated.

1. Rope reel (fitted between 1907 and 1910)
2. W/T aerial screen (fitted 1910)
3. Fresh water tank (fitted 1907)
4. Hot water tank for Admiral's, Chief of Staff's and Captain's bath rooms (fitted 1907)
5. Compass (fitted 1909)
6. Admiral's sea cabin (fitted 1909)
7. 36in searchlight (moved from bridge wings 1915)
8. 9ft FQ2 rangefinder (fitted 1913)
9. Flag lockers (moved from original positions 1907–08)
10. Gyro compass repeater (fitted 1915)
11. Searchlight controls

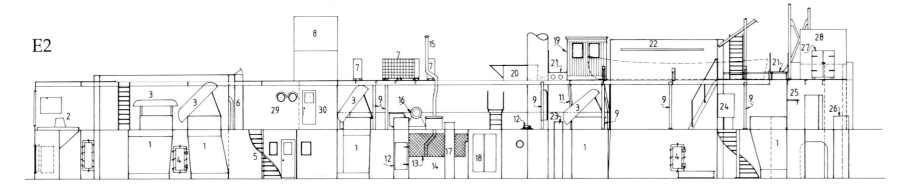

E2

E3 AFTER END OF SUPERSTRUCTURE, LOOKING FORWARD January 1907 (scale $^1/_{16}$in = 1ft)

1. Arched opening
2. Watertight doors, 4ft 6in × 2ft 6in, to boiler room vent (blanked off 1907)

E4 PROFILE OF ADMIRAL'S SEA CABIN March 1909 (scale $^1/_{16}$in = 1ft)

1. Compass
2. Profile of signal house on port side

E5 SECTION AT ADMIRAL'S SEA CABIN, LOOKING FORWARD March 1909 (scale $^1/_{16}$in = 1ft)

1. Compass
2. Admiral's sea cabin
3. Signal house
4. Flag locker
5. Hot water tank to supply Admiral's, Chief of Staff's and Captain's bathrooms
6. Boiler room vent
7. Hawser reel
8. Stable door
9. Engine room telegraph
10. Step
11. Channel bar pillar
12. Mast stay

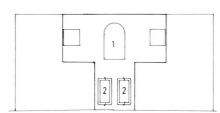

E3

E4

E5

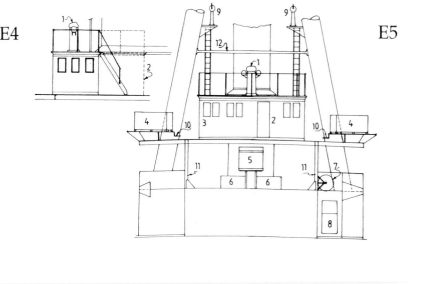

E6

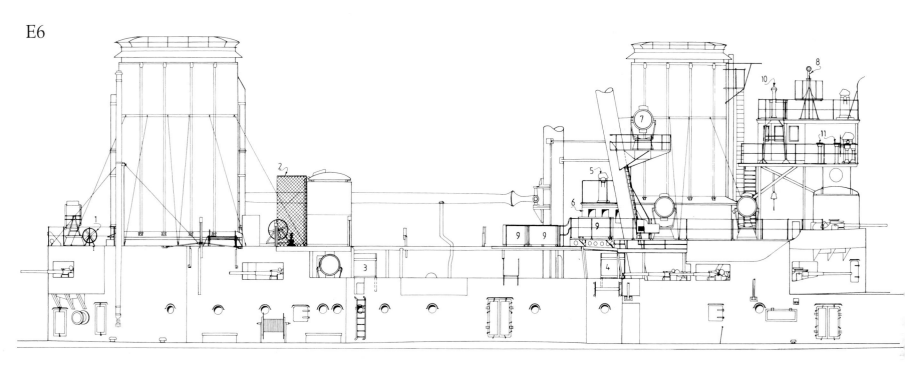

E7   SECTIONS OF BRIDGE
SHOWING SUPPORTING
STRUCTURE January 1907 (scale
$^1/_{16}$in = 1ft)

E7/1   *After end of bridge looking forward*

E7/2   *Section at fore side of chart house
looking aft*

E7/3   *Section at aft side of CT looking forward*

1	Captain's cabin	7	Pillar
2	Chart house	8	Awning stanchions
3	Door to Captain's cabin	9	Conning tower
4	Extended guardrail stanchion for canvas wind screen	10	Ship's bell
5	Channel bar	11	Locker for searchlight screens
6	Stay (2½in dia.)	12	Admiral's walk
		13	Pedestal for 12pdr gun

E7/1

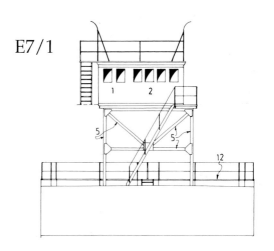

E7/2

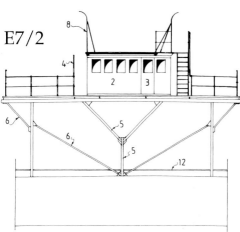

E7/3

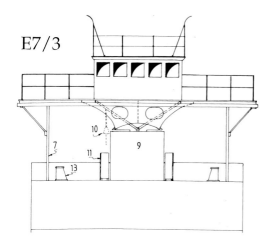

E Superstructure

E8/1 PLAN OF SUPERSTRUCTURE AT UPPER DECK June 1915 (scale $^1/_{16}$ in = 1ft)

1 Electric coaling winch
2 Boiler room vent
3 Vent trunk
4 Mushroom top exhaust vent from stokers' wash place
5 Mushroom top exhaust vent from leading stokers' wash place
6 Mushroom top exhaust vent from seamen's wash place
7 Mushroom top exhaust vent from CPOs' wash place
8 Rack
9 Officers' WCs
10 Skylight to main deck
11 Hawser reel
12 Painted canvas room (enlarged during 1907–10)
13 Spiral staircase
14 Stable door
15 Bakery
16 Oven
17 Table (drawers under)
18 Coal box
19 Electric kneading machine
20 Ash hoist

21 Square side port
22 Window
23 12pdr ammunition hand-up
24 Tank
25 Officers' urinal
26 Flour store
27 Shelves
28 Table (bins under)
29 Hinged table
30 Bin
31 Boatswain's ready-use store
32 Carpenters' ready-use store
33 Chest of drawers
34 Locker
35 Shelf (over)
36 Communication tube
37 Gunners' ready-use store
38 Cupboard (drawers under)
39 Hammock stowage
40 Coal scuttle
41 WOs' galley
42 Cooking stove
43 Coal box
44 Table (cupboard under)
45 Sink

46 Passage
47 Foremast
48 Holes for boat hoist wires
49 Distributing station
50 Heater
51 Galley scullery (added after completion)
52 Table
53 Washing-up trough
54 Store
55 Cupboard with drawers under for surgical dressings
56 Drinking water tank
57 Quartermaster's locker
58 Cutting-up table
59 Admiral's galley
60 Cooking range
61 Settee
62 Sideboard
63 Ladderway
64 Table
65 Cupboard
66 Exhaust vents to auxiliary machinery room (added 1907–08)
67 Light and vent to main deck

68 Mushroom top exhaust vent to Admiral's pantry
69 Bench
70 Food lift
71 Ice chest
72 Cupboard (original position of ice chest at time of completion)
73 Wash deck cupboard
74 Cupboard for diving gear
75 Diving pump
76 Wood door
77 Electric motor fan
78 Embarkation scuttle for 12in ammunition
79 Grating
80 Foremast strut
81 Metal locker
82 Bread store (added after completion)
83 Frame
84 Store
S Scupper
L Vertical ladder
C Cordage reel
D Sliding door
O Opening in bulkhead

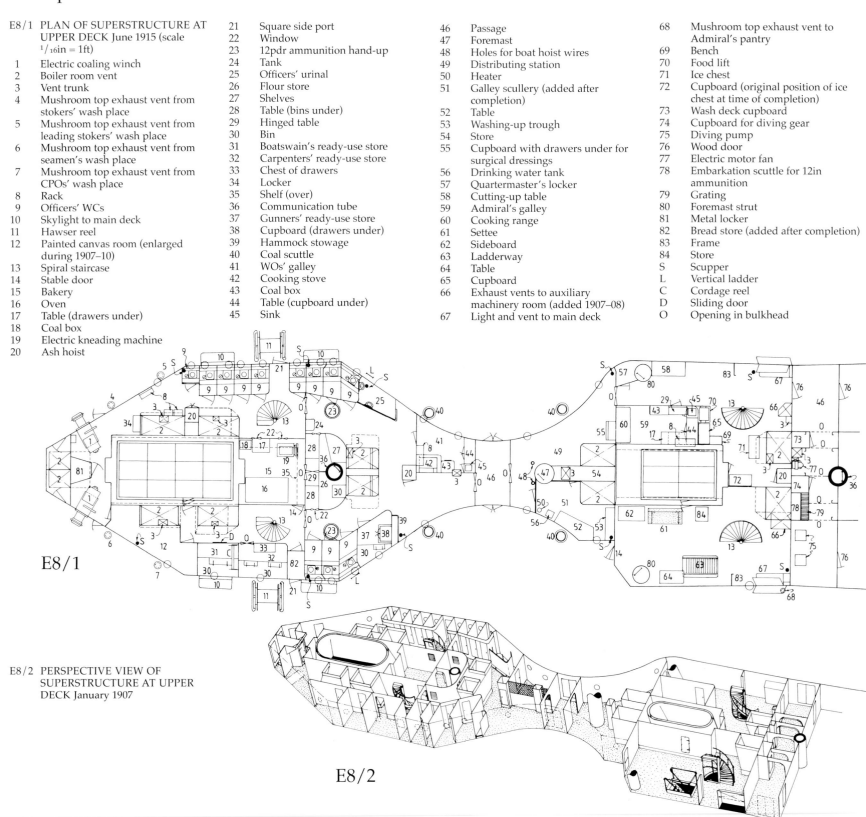

E8/1

E8/2 PERSPECTIVE VIEW OF SUPERSTRUCTURE AT UPPER DECK January 1907

E8/2

E9/1 PLAN OF FLYING DECK June 1915 (scale ¹/₁₆in = 1ft)

1. Boiler room vent
2. Pedestal for 12pdr gun
3. Vent trunk
4. Mushroom top exhaust vent to WC
5. 36in searchlight
6. Channel bar pillar
7. Pillar
8. Bakery oven funnel
9. Ash hoist
10. Kneehole table
11. Light and vent to bakery
12. Light and vent trunk to bakery
13. Silent cabinet for W/T set
14. Condenser (capacitor in modern terminology)
15. Transformer
16. Cupboard
17. Hinged table
18. 12pdr ammunition hand-up
19. Mushroom top exhaust vent from WOs' bath room
20. Fresh water tank (fitted 1907)
21. Hot water tank for Admiral's, Chief of Staff's and Captain's bath rooms (fitted 1907)
22. Platform for passing 12pdr ammunition to 12in turret roof
23. Foremast
24. Foremast strut
25. Electric coaling winch
26. Vent to WOs' galley
27. Stove funnel
28. Signal house
29. Communication tube
30. Expansion joint
31. Fairleads for boat hoist wires
32. Skylight to Admiral's galley
33. Mushroom top exhaust vent from bath room
34. Stowage for torpedo dropping gear (for steam pinnaces)
35. Silencer for diesel exhaust (port silencer removed 1908)
36. Locker for 12pdr ready-use ammunition
37. 12pdr dredger hoist
38. 12pdr dredger hoist trunk
39. Shelf (over)
40. Exhaust vent from auxiliary machinery (added 1907–08)
41. Insulator for short range W/T aerial
42. Ladder to roof of 'X' turret for passing 12pdr ammunition
43. Derrick stump mast
44. W/T office
45. Extension to W/T office added 1910
46. Locker (over)
47. Brackets (under)
S. Scupper
L. Vertical ladder
C. Cordage reel
O. Opening in bulkhead

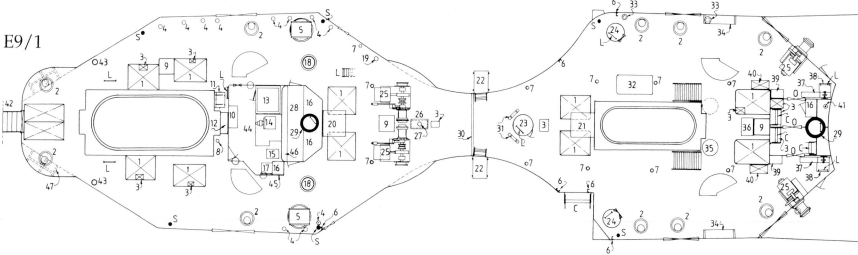

E9/1

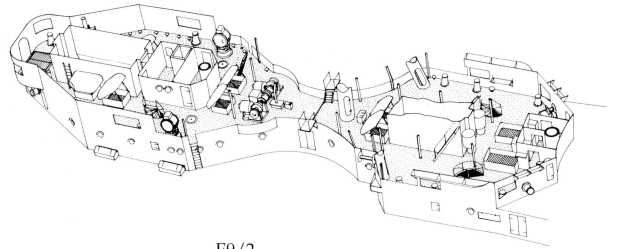

E9/2 PERSPECTIVE VIEW OF FLYING DECK January 1907

E9/2

199

E   Superstructure

E10/1 PLAN OF BOAT DECK January 1907 (scale $\frac{1}{16}$in = 1ft)

1	36in searchlight	18	36ft sailing pinnace	36	Admiral's sea cabin
2	36in searchlight, electrically controlled from compass platform	19	27ft whaler	37	Settee
		20	40ft Admiral's barge	38	Kneehole table
3	Hawser reel	21	Drip pan for oil service	39	Door
4	Flag locker	22	Screen to W/T aerial	40	Hole for boat wires
5	Ladder	23	W/T aerial flight	41	Hinged grating (over)
6	Guardrail stanchion	24	Vent and light to bakery	42	Bow light
7	400 gallon sanitary tank	25	Signal tower	43	32ft galley
8	15cwt Martins anchor	26	Hatch	44	30ft gig
9	Beams (under)	27	43cwt Martins anchor	45	Hand-up for 12pdr ammunition
10	Coaling derrick	28	Flag deck	46	Conning tower
11	Stump mast	29	13ft 6in balsa raft (under)	47	Searchlight screen locker
12	27ft whaler (under)	30	32ft cutter	48	Platform for supplying 12pdr ammunition to roof of 'A' turret
13	16ft skiff dinghy (under)	31	Hinged plate		
14	27ft whaler (under), alternative position	32	Hydraulic gear and controls for main derrick	49	Stove funnel
				50	Pedestal for 12pdr gun
15	16ft skiff dinghy (under), alternative position	33	Foremast	C	Cordage reel
		34	Foremast strut	S	Scupper
16	45ft steam pinnace	35	Admiral's walk (fitted with wood gratings)	P	Pillar
17	42ft launch				

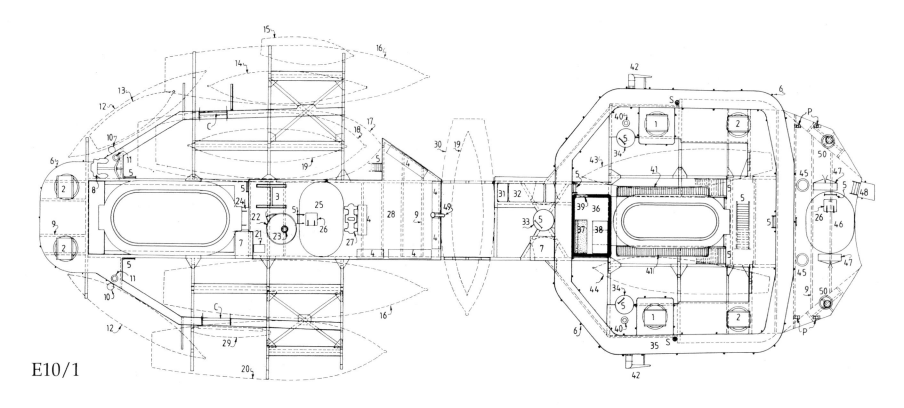

E10/1

E10/2 PLAN OF BOAT DECK June 1915
Only differences from January 1907 are indicated.

1 36in searchlight
2 36in searchlight, electrically controlled from bridge
3 Flag locker
4 Beams (under)
5 Rope reel
6 Screen to W/T aerial (fitted in new position 1910)
7 Extra spark-gap scuttle (fitted 1910)
8 43cwt Martins anchor (moved to new position in 1907)
9 50ft steam pinnace (replaced 45ft pinnace in 1908)
10 27ft Montague whaler
11 Fairlead bracket
12 Roof of extended W/T office
13 30ft gig
14 32ft cutter
15 Flag deck
16 Hole for hydraulic pipes
17 Step
18 Admiral's sea cabin
19 Stove
20 Bunk
21 Kneehole table
22 Signal house
23 Table
24 Door
25 Platform moved from port side in 1910
26 Wash deck locker
27 Short range W/T aerial insulator (fitted 1910)
28 Aerial screen
S Scupper

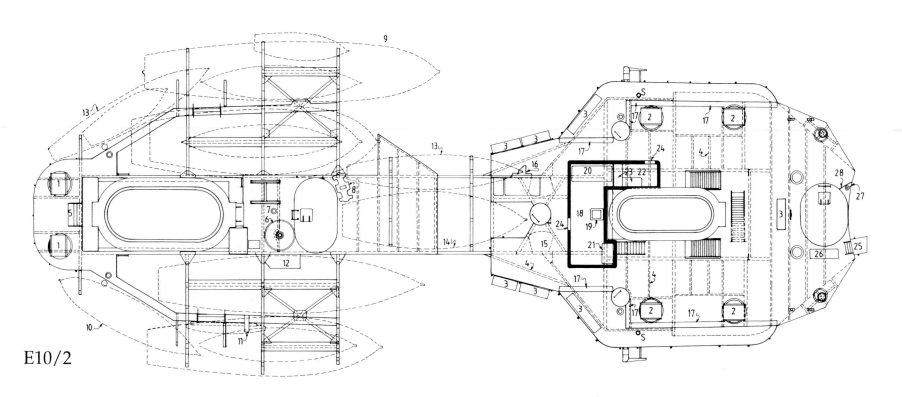

E10/2

E Superstructure

E11/1 PLAN OF NAVIGATING
PLATFORM January 1907 (scale
$^1/_8$in = 1ft)

1   Guardrail stanchion
2   Scupper
3   Ladder
4   Gravity flashing lantern
5   Sounding machine
6   36in searchlight
7   Engine room telegraph
8   Revolution telegraph
9   Compass
10   Steering wheel
11   Door
12   Chart house
13   Captain's cabin
14   Settee
15   Chart table
16   Kneehole table
17   Semaphore
18   Scuttle to conning tower
19   Beams (under)
20   Outline of compass platform (over)

E11/2 PLAN OF NAVIGATING
PLATFORM June 1915 (scale $^1/_8$in =
1ft)

1   Guardrail stanchion
2   Scupper
3   Ladder
4   Engine room telegraph
5   Revolution telegraph
6   Compass
7   Steering wheel
8   Chart house
9   Searchlight control
10   Captain's cabin
11   Scuttle to conning tower
12   Fore end of platform removed from
     this point 1916

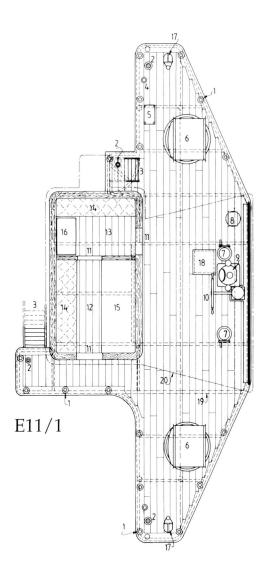

E11/1

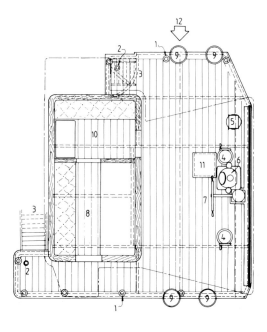

E11/2

202

E12/1 PLAN OF COMPASS PLATFORM
January 1907 (scale $^1/_8$in = 1ft)

1 Guardrail stanchion
2 Awning stanchion
3 Searchlight signals
4 Searchlight controls
5 Helm indicator (over)
6 Scupper
7 Chart table
8 Compass
9 Ladder

E12/2 PLAN OF COMPASS PLATFORM
June 1915 (scale $^1/_8$in = 1ft)

1 Guardrail stanchion
2 Awning stanchion
3 Searchlight signals
4 Searchlight controls
5 Semaphore (removed from starboard side 1915)
6 Position of semaphore 1908–1915
7 Extension to platform fitted 1908
8 Extension to platform fitted 1915
9 Scupper
10 Helm indicator (over)
11 Chart table
12 Compass
13 Ladder
14 9ft FQ2 rangefinder (fitted 1913)
15 Gyro compass receiver (fitted 1915)
16 Position of steaming light post 1910–1913

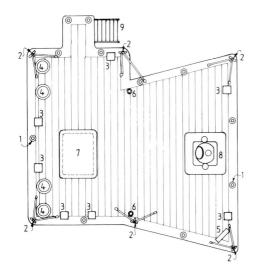

E12/1

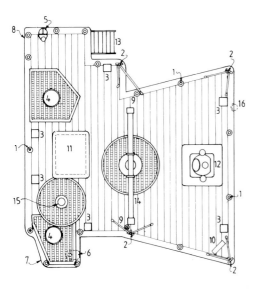

E12/2

E   Superstructure

E13   PLAN OF SEARCHLIGHT
PLATFORM ON FOREMAST (scale
$^1/_8$in = 1ft)

1   Guardrail stanchion
2   Foremast
3   Mast struts (under)
4   Manholes to ladders in mast struts
5   Ladder
6   24in searchlight (removed 1910)
7   Locker for Scott's signal flasher
(removed 1910)
8   Ladder to foretop
9   Siren (fitted 1907)
10 Steaming light
11 Centre bracket with arched opening
fitted 1915

E14   PLAN OF SEARCHLIGHT
PLATFORM FITTED ON
STARBOARD STRUT OF
FOREMAST June 1915 (port
platform similar but handed) (scale
$^1/_8$in = 1ft)

1   36in searchlight, electrically
controlled from compass platform
2   Manhole to access ladder
3   Guardrail stanchions
4   Mast strut
5   Drain
6   Support brackets (under)
7   Line parallel to middle line

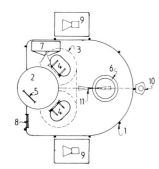

E13

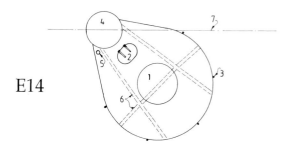

E14

E15   PLAN OF ROOF OF ADMIRAL'S
SEA CABIN, 1909 (scale $^1/_8$in = 1ft)

1   Guardrail stanchion
2   Ladder
3   Compass
4   Chart table
5   Engine room telegraph platform
(over)

E15

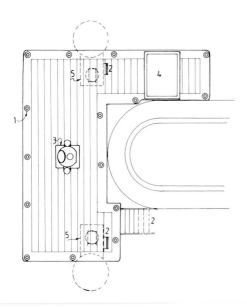

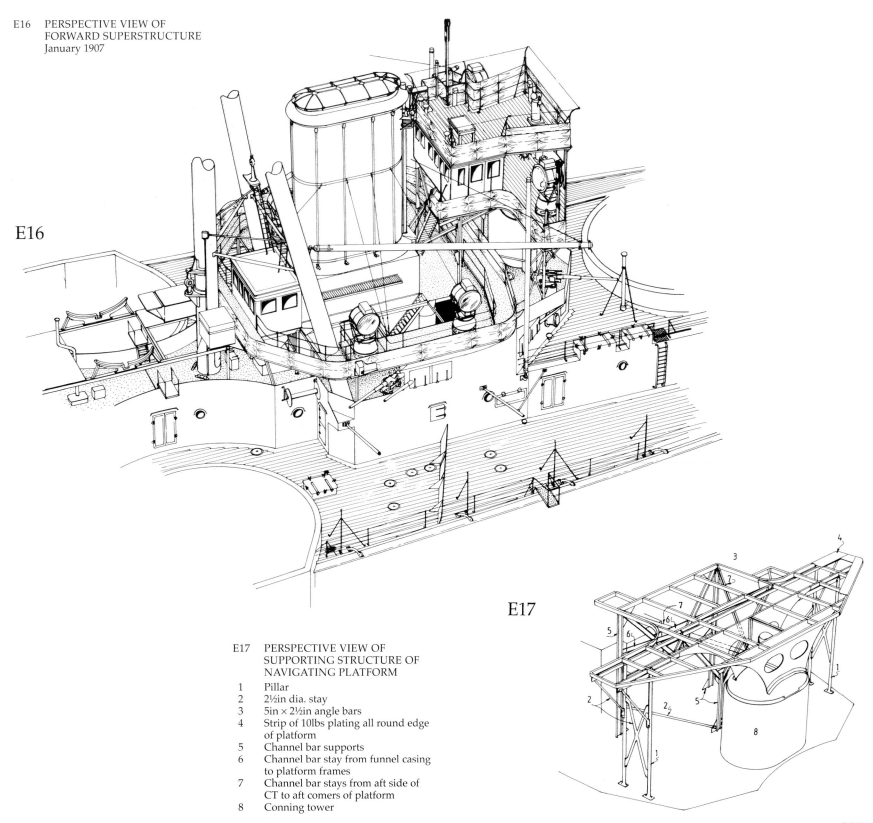

E16　PERSPECTIVE VIEW OF
FORWARD SUPERSTRUCTURE
January 1907

E16

E17

E17　PERSPECTIVE VIEW OF
SUPPORTING STRUCTURE OF
NAVIGATING PLATFORM

1　Pillar
2　2½in dia. stay
3　5in × 2½in angle bars
4　Strip of 10lbs plating all round edge
of platform
5　Channel bar supports
6　Channel bar stay from funnel casing
to platform frames
7　Channel bar stays from aft side of
CT to aft comers of platform
8　Conning tower

F   Rig

F1   COALING RIG (scale $^1/_{32}$in = 1ft)
1   Coaling jackstay
2   Guy
3   Coaling whips (taken to coaling winches)
4   Downhauls
5   Coaling derrick
6   Main derrick

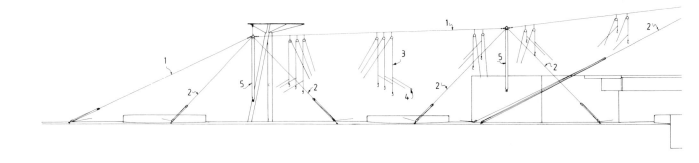

F1

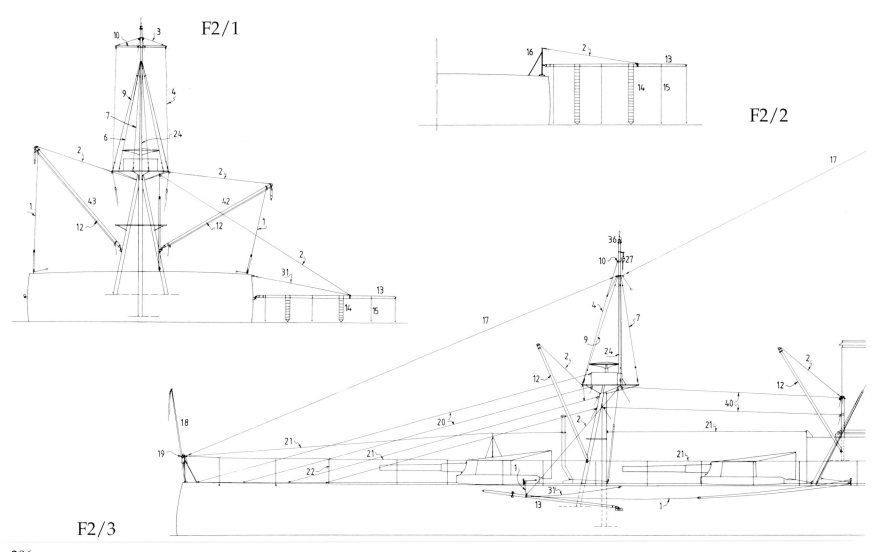

F2/1

F2/2

F2/3

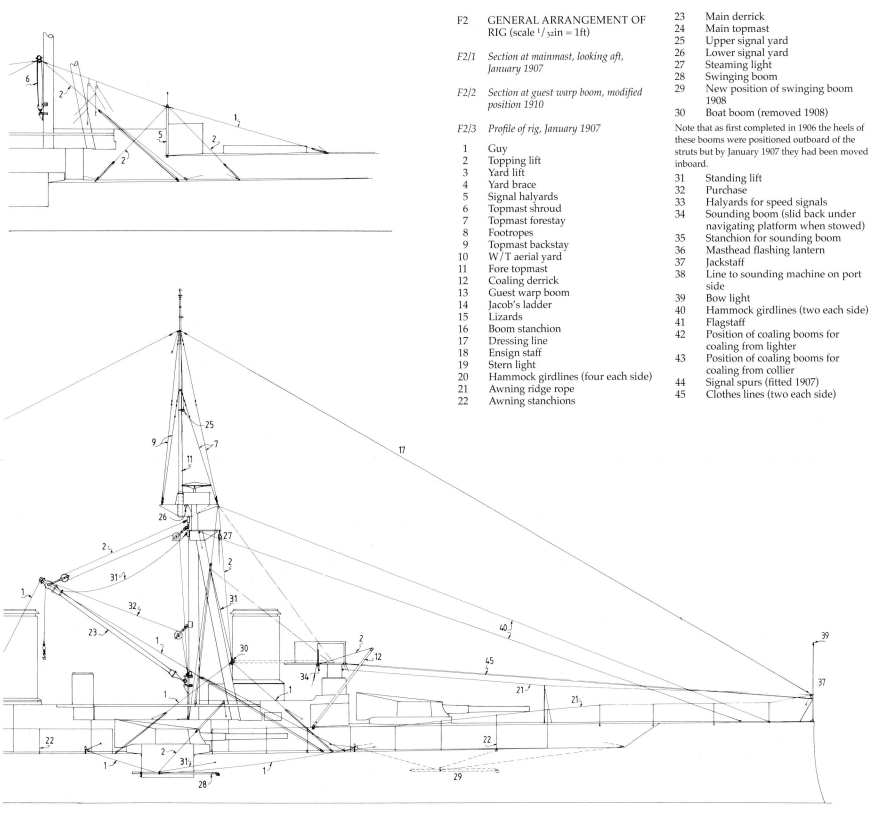

F2 **GENERAL ARRANGEMENT OF RIG** (scale ¹⁄₃₂in = 1ft)

F2/1 *Section at mainmast, looking aft, January 1907*

F2/2 *Section at guest warp boom, modified position 1910*

F2/3 *Profile of rig, January 1907*

1 Guy
2 Topping lift
3 Yard lift
4 Yard brace
5 Signal halyards
6 Topmast shroud
7 Topmast forestay
8 Footropes
9 Topmast backstay
10 W/T aerial yard
11 Fore topmast
12 Coaling derrick
13 Guest warp boom
14 Jacob's ladder
15 Lizards
16 Boom stanchion
17 Dressing line
18 Ensign staff
19 Stern light
20 Hammock girdlines (four each side)
21 Awning ridge rope
22 Awning stanchions

23 Main derrick
24 Main topmast
25 Upper signal yard
26 Lower signal yard
27 Steaming light
28 Swinging boom
29 New position of swinging boom 1908
30 Boat boom (removed 1908)

Note that as first completed in 1906 the heels of these booms were positioned outboard of the struts but by January 1907 they had been moved inboard.

31 Standing lift
32 Purchase
33 Halyards for speed signals
34 Sounding boom (slid back under navigating platform when stowed)
35 Stanchion for sounding boom
36 Masthead flashing lantern
37 Jackstaff
38 Line to sounding machine on port side
39 Bow light
40 Hammock girdlines (two each side)
41 Flagstaff
42 Position of coaling booms for coaling from lighter
43 Position of coaling booms for coaling from collier
44 Signal spurs (fitted 1907)
45 Clothes lines (two each side)

F Rig

F2/4 *Section at foremast, looking forward, January 1907*

F2/5 *Section at topmast after addition of flagstaff, 1907*

F2/6 *Section at bridge showing sounding boom*

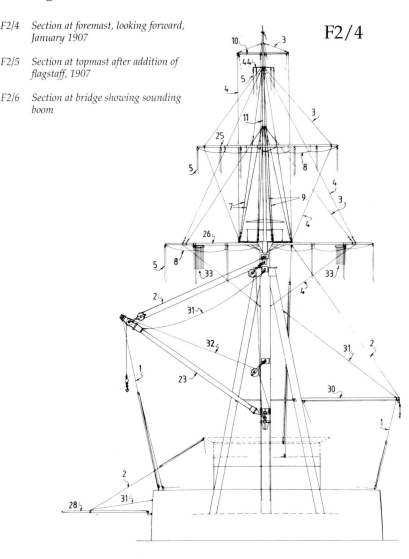

F2/4

F3/1 PROFILE OF BASE OF FOREMAST (scale ¼in = 1ft)

F3/2 SECTION OF FOREMAST (scale ¼in = 1ft)

The foremast and mainmast were similarly constructed except that the mainmast and its struts, being of smaller diameter, did not have internal ladders.

1 Deck beam
2 Doubling fitted where mast passed through decks
3 'T' bar cross stay, 5in × 3in, spaced approximately 8ft apart on each quarter and shifted approximately 2ft from quarter section to quarter section
4 Angle bar connecting mast to deck
5 Butt strap, spaced approximately 22ft 6in apart
6 'T' bars, 6in × 4in
7 Main deck
8 Upper deck
9 Ladder

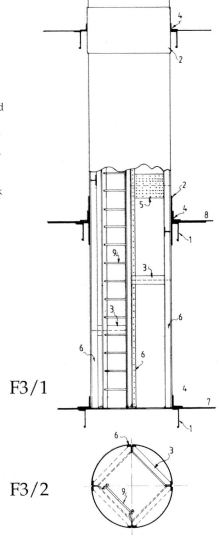

F3/1

F3/2

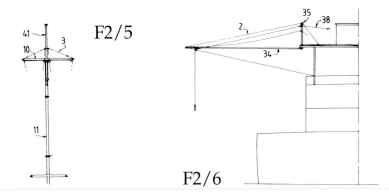

F2/5

F2/6

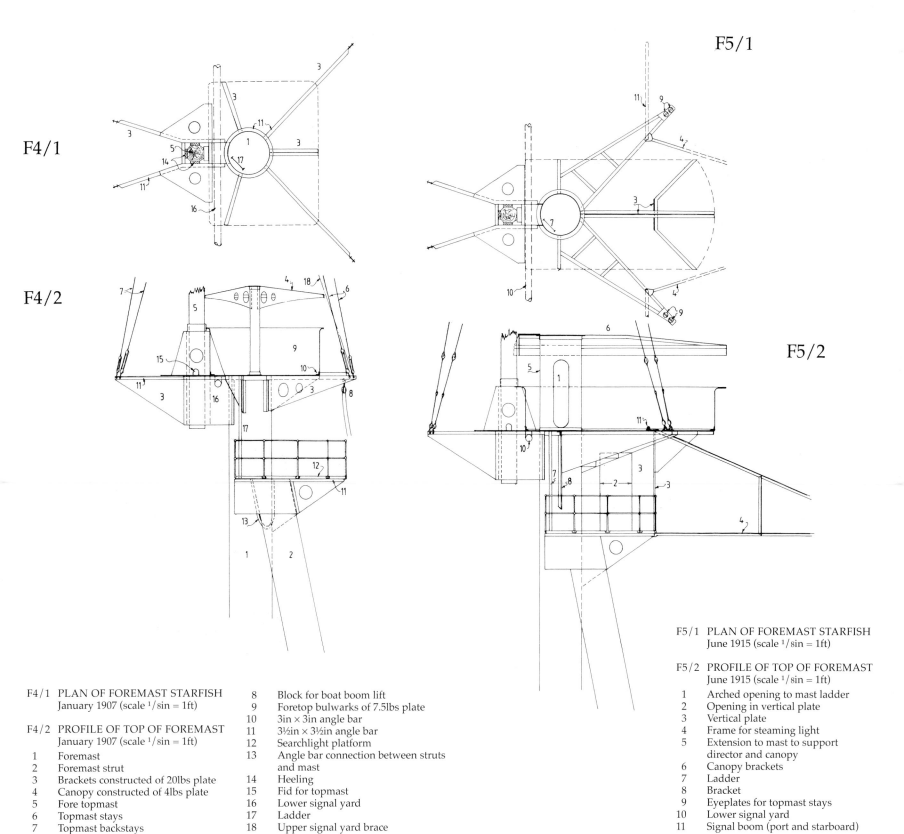

F5/1

F4/1

F4/2

F5/2

F5/1 PLAN OF FOREMAST STARFISH
June 1915 (scale $^1/_8$in = 1ft)

F5/2 PROFILE OF TOP OF FOREMAST
June 1915 (scale $^1/_8$in = 1ft)

1   Arched opening to mast ladder
2   Opening in vertical plate
3   Vertical plate
4   Frame for steaming light
5   Extension to mast to support
     director and canopy
6   Canopy brackets
7   Ladder
8   Bracket
9   Eyeplates for topmast stays
10   Lower signal yard
11   Signal boom (port and starboard)

F4/1 PLAN OF FOREMAST STARFISH
January 1907 (scale $^1/_8$in = 1ft)

F4/2 PROFILE OF TOP OF FOREMAST
January 1907 (scale $^1/_8$in = 1ft)

1   Foremast
2   Foremast strut
3   Brackets constructed of 20lbs plate
4   Canopy constructed of 4lbs plate
5   Fore topmast
6   Topmast stays
7   Topmast backstays
8   Block for boat boom lift
9   Foretop bulwarks of 7.5lbs plate
10   3in × 3in angle bar
11   3½in × 3½in angle bar
12   Searchlight platform
13   Angle bar connection between struts
     and mast
14   Heeling
15   Fid for topmast
16   Lower signal yard
17   Ladder
18   Upper signal yard brace

F Rig

F6   PERSPECTIVE VIEW OF
FORETOP, 1913

1   New foretop fitted 1912
2   Searchlight platform
3   Steaming light
4   Frame for steaming light fitted 1913
5   Lower signal yard
6   Topmast stays
7   Topmast backstays
8   Lower signal yard lift
9   Lower signal yard brace
10   Upper signal yard brace
11   Signal halyards
12   Footrope
13   Signal booms fitted 1912
14   Halyards for speed signals (removed
     1914)
15   Jackstay

1   Main topmast
2   Heeling
3   Fid for topmast
4   Jacobs' ladder to top
5   Searchlight platform
6   Platform support struts
7   Block for helm signals
8   Mainmast
9   Mainmast struts

F7/1   PLAN OF MAINMAST STARFISH
(scale $^1/_8$in = 1ft)

F7/2   PROFILE OF MAINTOP (scale $^1/_8$in
= 1ft)

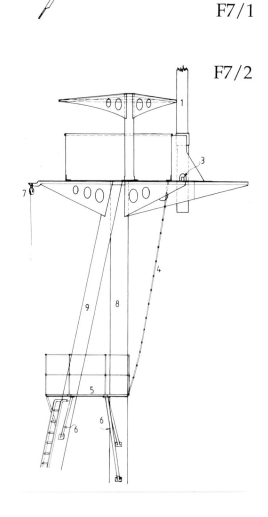

F7/1

F7/2

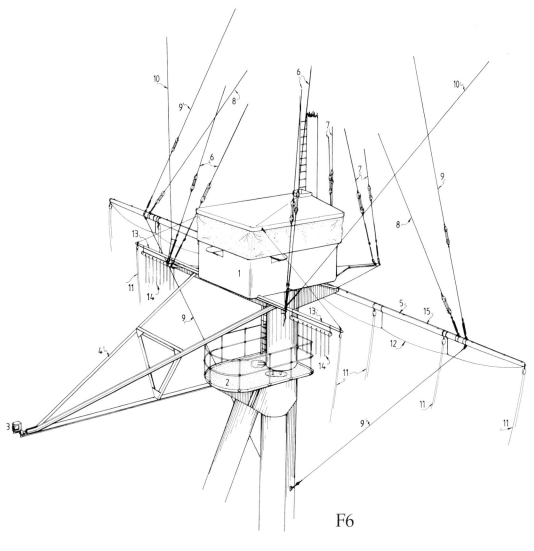

F6

F8 DETAILS OF MASTS, SPARS AND
    BOOMS (Unless otherwise stated
    scale $^1/_8$in = 1ft)

The lower masts and the main derrick were
constructed of steel, all other masts, spars etc
were of wood.

F8/1 *Foremast*

F8/2 *Detail of signal arms (scale $^1/_4$in = 1ft)*

F8/3 *Flagstaff fitted to foretopmast in 1907*

F8/4 *Masthead flashing lantern (scale $^1/_4$in =
      1ft)*

As first completed this was fitted on the head of
the main topmast only. Later it was also provided
at the foremast flagstaff head.

F8/5 *Main topmast*

F8/6 *Wireless aerial yard*

F8/7 *Half profile of lower signal yard*

1   Sheaves for striking topmast
2   Fid hole (for locking mast in place)
3   Pawl rack
4   Sheave
5   Band for stays and lower signal yard
    lifts
6   Signal arm
7   Eye for Jacobs ladder
8   Band for stays and signal yard lifts
9   Band for wireless aerial yard lifts
10 Lightning conductor
11 Wind vane
12 Truck
13 Fore topmast
14 Arm for steaming light
15 Band for stays and shrouds
16 Heeling
17 Masthead flashing lantern
18 Aerial wire halyards
19 Band for yard lifts and braces
20 Eyes for jackstay
21 Signal halyards
22 Footrope
23 Band for yard sling
24 Band for topping lift and guys
25 Eyes for topping lift
26 Links for guys
27 Links for coaling stay
28 Link for block

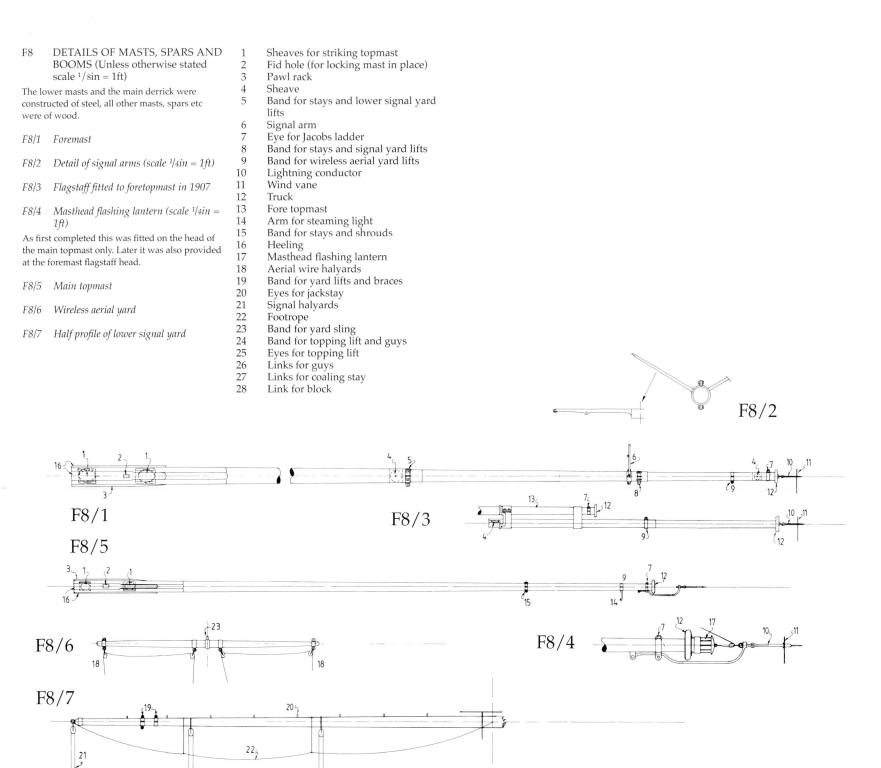

F8/2

F8/1

F8/3

F8/5

F8/6

F8/4

F8/7

F Rig

F8/8   *Profile of upper signal yard*

F8/9   *Plan of upper signal yard*

F8/10   *Profile of 50ft guest warp boom*

F8/11   *Profile of 30ft swinging boom*

F8/12   *Detail of heel fitting for guest warp
         boom (scale ¼in = 1ft)*

Heel of swinging boom was similar.

F8/13   *Profile of coaling derrick*

F8/14   *Plan of coaling derrick*

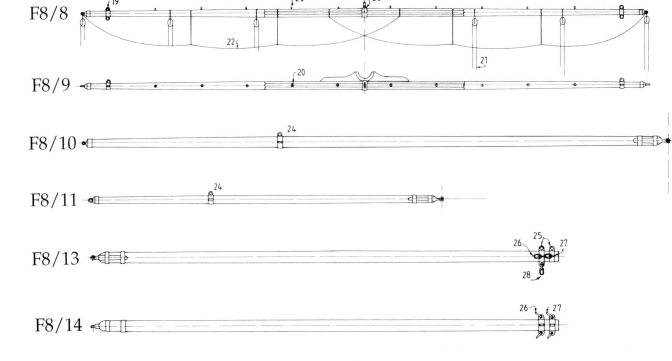

F8/8

F8/9

F8/10

F8/11

F8/13

F8/14

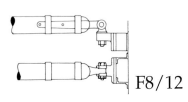

F8/12

F9   DETAIL OF STERN (scale $\frac{1}{16}$in =
        1ft)

F9/1   *Profile of stern*

F9/2   *Plan of after end of quarterdeck*

F9/3   *Profile and plan of original stern
         platform*

1   Ensign staff
2   Tray for stern light
3   Gallows for stern light
4   Bracket for ensign staff
5   Eyes for awning ridge ropes
6   Stern platform (as fitted during
     May–June 1907)
7   After boat booms (added May-June
     1907)
8   Ensign staff stanchion
9   Roller for speed log hawser
10   Original stern platform (carried
     1906–07)
11   Frame for roller

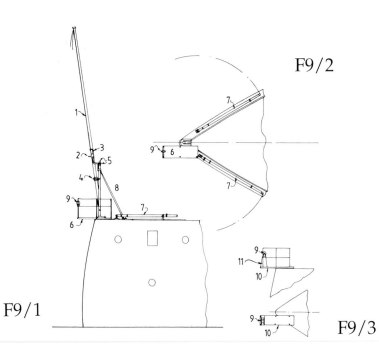

F9/2

F9/1

F9/3

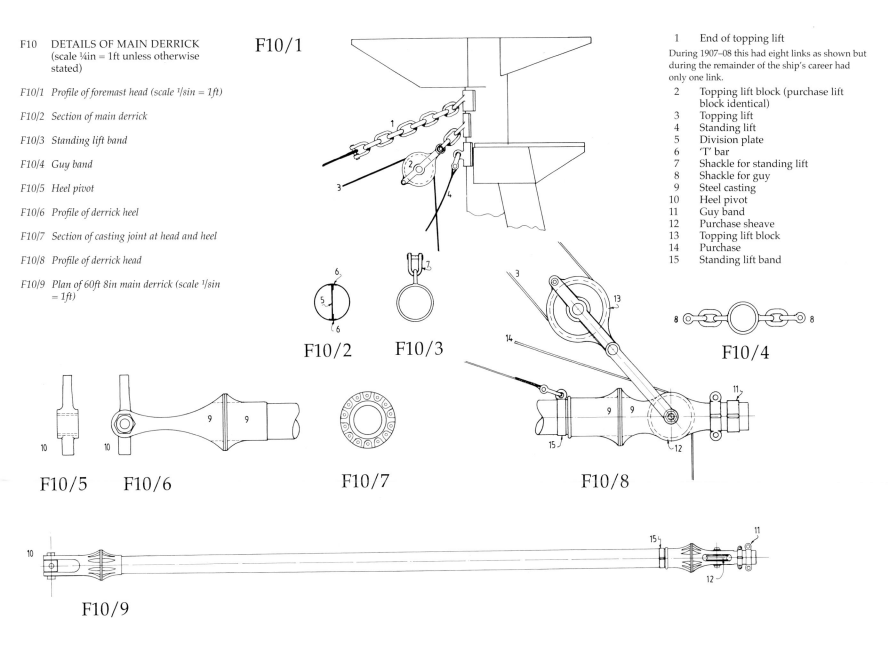

F10 DETAILS OF MAIN DERRICK
(scale ¼in = 1ft unless otherwise
stated)

F10/1 Profile of foremast head (scale ⅛in = 1ft)

F10/2 Section of main derrick

F10/3 Standing lift band

F10/4 Guy band

F10/5 Heel pivot

F10/6 Profile of derrick heel

F10/7 Section of casting joint at head and heel

F10/8 Profile of derrick head

F10/9 Plan of 60ft 8in main derrick (scale ⅛in
= 1ft)

1 End of topping lift
During 1907–08 this had eight links as shown but
during the remainder of the ship's career had
only one link.
2 Topping lift block (purchase lift
block identical)
3 Topping lift
4 Standing lift
5 Division plate
6 'T' bar
7 Shackle for standing lift
8 Shackle for guy
9 Steel casting
10 Heel pivot
11 Guy band
12 Purchase sheave
13 Topping lift block
14 Purchase
15 Standing lift band

F10/1

F10/2   F10/3   F10/4

F10/5   F10/6   F10/7   F10/8

F10/9

F11 PLAN OF 38ft BOAT DERRICK
(scale ⅛in = 1ft)

Two of these derricks served the boats fitted
abreast the forefunnel during 1906–07. As
originally built in October 1906 the heels of these
derricks were outboard of the foremast struts –
they were moved inboard of the struts in late
1906. Both derricks were removed in August–
November 1907.

1 Foremast strut
2 Heel bracket
3 Topping lift, guy and purchase band
4 Standing lift band

F11

F   Rig

F12   TORPEDO NET DEFENCE

The nets were lowered by releasing them from
the net shelves and dropping them over the side
where they automatically unrolled. The booms
were then swung out, using the working guys,
and secured. To stow the nets the reverse
procedure was adopted except that the brails
were used to haul up the net.

F12/1   *Profile of hull with torpedo nets rigged*
         (scale 1/32in = 1ft)

F12/2   *Half plan of hull with torpedo net rigged*
         (scale 1/32in = 1ft)

1	Electric coaling winch
2	Brails
3	Brailing davit
4	30ft net defence boom
5	12ft net defence boom
6	Boom topping lifts
7	Working guy
8	Leech brail (for automatically hauling up rear end of net when booms are moved to stowed position)
9	Standing guy
10	Jackstay
11	Capstan
12	Standing part of brail
13	Boom stowage chocks
14	Second stowage chock for 2nd boom only
15	Riding bitt
16	Net defence fairlead
17	Whip brails (later when net shelf extended around wing barbettes)
18	Roller
19	Net
20	Net shelf
s	Bottle screw and slip
b	Block secured to eyeplate
B	Block

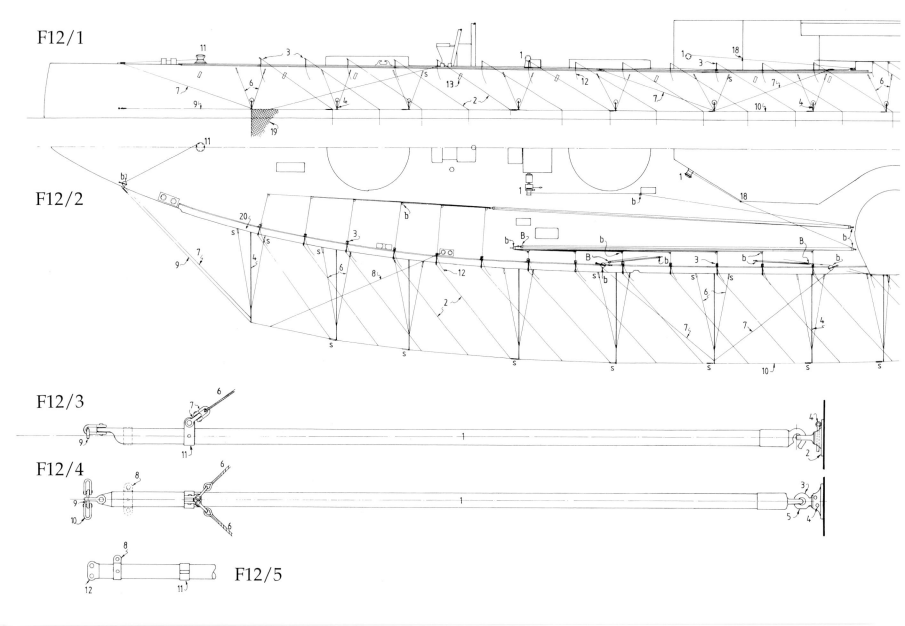

F12/1

F12/2

F12/3

F12/4

F12/5

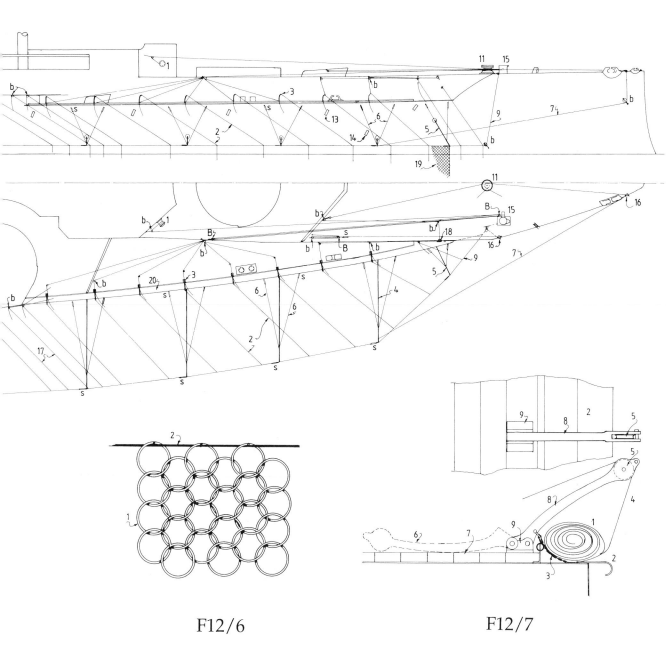

F12/3 *Profile of 30ft torpedo net boom (apart from length, 12ft boom identical) (scale ¼in = 1ft)*

F12/4 *Plan of 30ft torpedo net boom (scale ¼in = 1ft)*

F12/5 *Plan of head of aftermost boom (scale ¼ in = 1ft)*
1   7½in diameter steel tube (aftermost boom 8½in diameter)
2   Socket attached to ship's side
3   Swivel eye
4   Pins for locking swivel eye to socket
5   Flat in eye to allow for shipping and unshipping boom (flat on forward edge)
6   Topping lift
7   Shackles for topping lifts
8   Lugs for working guys (fitted only on those booms with working guys)
9   Long link
10 Shackles for jackstay
11 Band for topping lifts
12 Eyeplate for jackstay shackles

F12/6 *Detail of Bullivant torpedo net*
1   2½in dia interlocking steel rings
2   Wire head rope (connected to jackstay by lacing with steel wire)

F12/7 *Profile and plan of brailing davit (scale ³/₃₂in = 1ft)*
1   Net, rolled up
2   Net shelf
3   Standing part of brail, runs from base of davit to bottom of net on inboard side of net
4   Working part of brail, runs from davit through thimble on jackstay to bottom of net on outboard side to join standing part of brail
5   Sheave
6   Davit, hinged back position
7   Deck planking
8   Davit
9   Davit shoe

F12/8 *Detail of stowage chock for booms*
1   Angle bar connection to ship's side
2   Wood block
3   Hinged hoop to hold boom in place

F12/8

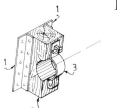

F12/6

F12/7

G1/1

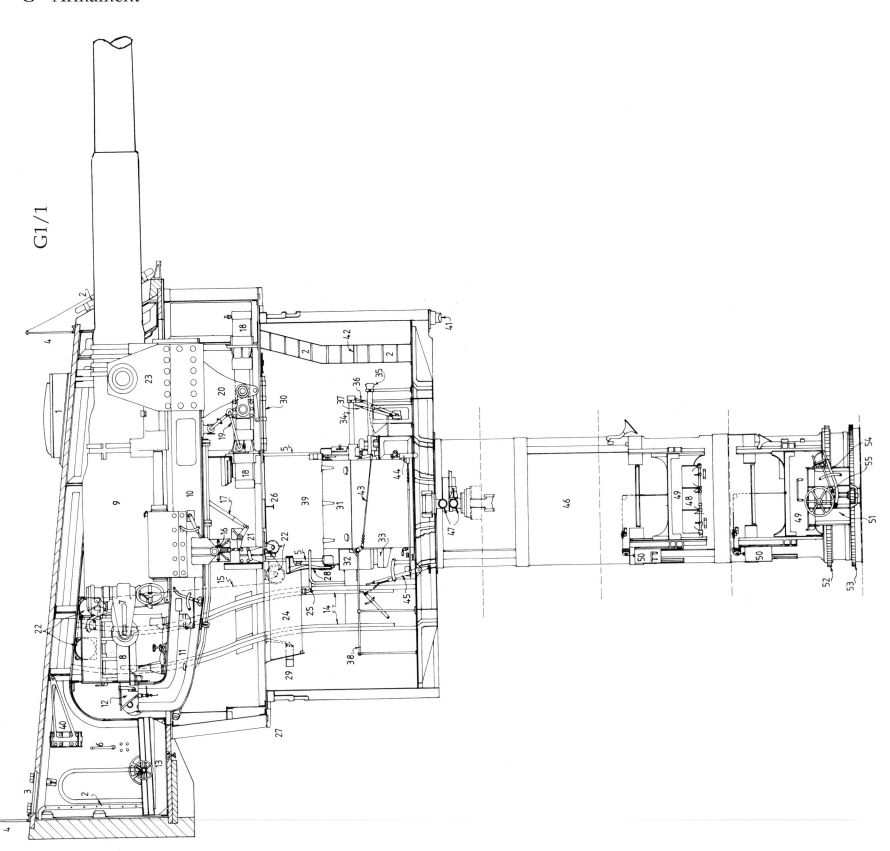

G1/1   Profile of 12in mounting, section at right gun (scale 3/16in = 1ft)

Mounting shown is 'X'. 'P' and 'Q' mountings were the same but 'Y' mounting had a trunk 6 inches longer and' A' mounting a trunk 9ft longer. Items in background in working chamber have been omitted.

1   Centre sighting hood
2   Ladder
3   Hatch
4   Stanchion
5   Pillar
6   Shell winch handle
7   Breech (open)
8   Gun loading cage in raised position
9   12in MK X gun
10 Gunslide
11 Gun loading arm
12 Chain rammer
13 Shell hand-loading bogie
14 Gun loading cage hoist rails
15 Gun loading cage lifting wire
16 Gunslide locking bolt
17 Gunslide locking bolt operating gear
18 Gunslide elevating cylinders
19 Walking pipes to transfer hydraulic power from rotating structure to elevating structure
20 Stop bracket (for gun at full elevation)
21 Elevating bracket
22 Gun loading cage lifting wire pulleys
23 Trunnion arm
24 Gun washout tank (collects water used to spray breech)
25 Drain pipe from washout tank
26 Traversing rail
27 Upper roller path
28 Gun loading cage cam
29 Shell transporting rail
30 Gun loading cage hoist compensating gear
31 Hinged top to central hoist
32 Cordite tray
33 Shell tray
34 Cordite rammer
35 Shell rammer
36 Central hoist control lever
37 Rammer control lever
38 Guardrail
39 Working chamber
40 Crane
41 Turret locking bolt
42 Platform
43 Shell door opening gear
44 Locking bolt for gun loading cage
45 Lever for gun loading cage bolt, tell-tale and relief valve
46 Trunk
47 Walking pipes for transferring hydraulic power from fixed to revolving structure
48 Cordite loading tray
49 Lifting door
50 Counter-balance weight for lifting door
51 Revolving shell bogie
52 Shell bogie rack on trunk
53 Shell bogie rack on fixed structure
54 Clutch lever for moving shell bogie drive from fixed to revolving structure
55 Handwheel for training shell bogie

G1/2

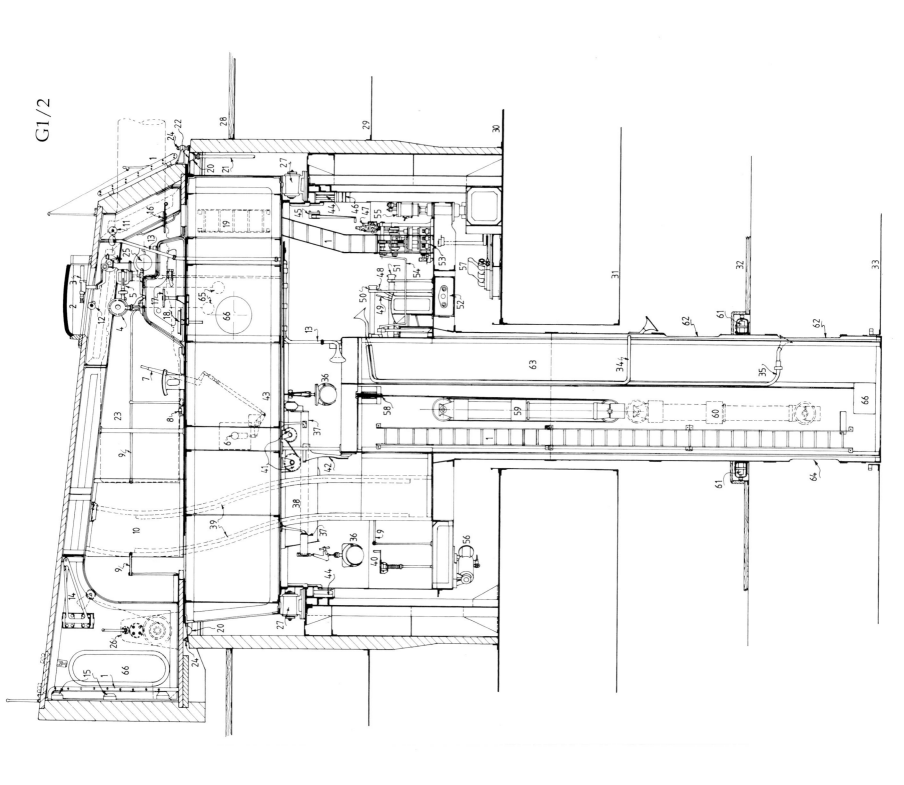

G1/2 *Profile of 12in mounting, section at centreline (scale $^3/_{16}$in = 1ft)*

Note that the gun cradle and items on the far side of the working chamber and gunhouse have been omitted. The mounting shown is 'X' mounting.

1 Ladder
2 Centre sighting hood
3 Telescopic sight
4 Elevation control handwheel
5 Training control lever
6 Gunslide locking bolt
7 Gunslide locking bolt operating lever
8 Locking bolt indicator
9 Guardrail
10 Plate for gun loading cage rails
11 Voice pipe from centre sight setter to left sight setter
12 Voice pipe from centre sighting hood to left sighting hood
13 Voice pipe from centre sight setter to shell hand up in working chamber
14 Shell crane
15 Armour bolts
16 Sight setter's stool
17 Hand wheel for adjusting height of gunlayer's stool
18 Gunlayer's stool
19 Ladder on right side
20 Gutter
21 Drain pipe

22 Leather apron
23 Pillar
24 Apron adjusting screws
25 Trunnion
26 Shell hoisting winch
27 Turret rollers
28 Upper deck
29 Main deck
30 Middle deck
31 Lower deck
32 Platform deck
33 Shell room flat
34 Voice pipe from handing room to working chamber
35 Voice pipe from shell room to working chamber
36 Shell grab
37 Overhead shell transporting rail
38 Gun washout tank
39 Gun loading cage rails
40 Training stop operating lever
41 Pulleys for gun loading cage wire
42 Cam for gun loading cage
43 Ready-use shell transversing press
44 Training rack
45 Pump for automatic brake cylinder

46 Rails for automatic safety depression gear
47 Automatic brake
48 Central hoist control lever
49 Rammer control lever
50 Cordite rammer
51 Shell rammer
52 Hand pump tank
53 Hand pump
54 Hand pump handle
55 Turret locking bolt
56 Training buffer
57 Training stop
58 Pulley for central hoist wire
59 Hydraulic press for left central hoist
60 Hydraulic press for right central hoist
61 Rollers
62 Openings in trunk for hand transfer of ammunition with central hoist out of action
63 Shell hand-up for use with central hoist out of action
64 Access opening
65 Elevation control valves (right side)
66 Opening

G Armament

G1/3 *Profile of 12in gunhouse and working chamber, section at left side (scale ³/₁₆in = 1ft)*

1   Left sighting hood
2   Pillar
3   Trunnion bracket
4   Handrail
5   Armour bolts
6   Platform
7   Ladder
8   Ready-use shell
9   Opening
10 Gun loading cage operating lever
11 Run in and out valves operating lever
12 Voice pipe from gun loading position to shell chamber
13 Elevation scale (fixed to pillar)
14 Rear platform
15 Gun platform
16 Gun well
17 Hydraulic press for gun loading hoist
18 Locking bolt for gunslide
19 Elevation limit stop
20 Hand traversing winch (for ready use shell)
21 Shell bin (ten 12in ready-use shell)
22 Hydraulic lifting press for ready-use shell
23 Training engine brake cylinder
24 Training pinion
25 Training rack
26 Opening giving access to training rack (normally secured with cover plate)
27 Three cylinder hydraulic training engine
28 Training engine bed

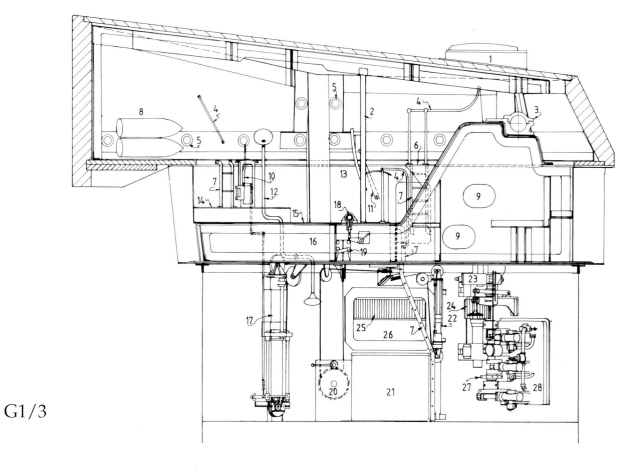

G1/3

G2   TRANSVERSE SECTION OF 12in GUN MOUNTING (scale ³⁄₁₆in = 1ft)

The gunhouse shell chamber and trunk are
sectioned at the centreline. The gun, gunslide, etc
have been omitted from the right side and the
training gear has been omitted from the left side.

1 Sighting hood
2 Elevation control wheel
3 Guardrail
4 Ladder
5 Training creep control wheel
6 Gun loading cage in raised position
7 Gunslide locking bolt
8 Walking pipes for hydraulic power
   to chain rammer
9 Walking pipes for hydraulic power
   to run-in and run-out cylinders
10 Cross connection rod for slide
    locking bolts
11 Sighting gear (attached by bracket to
    trunnion arm)
12 Gun loading cage rails
13 Lever on gun loading cage to drop
    cordite charges into ramming
    position after shell had been
    rammed into gun – this was done in
    two stages of two quarter charges
    each
14 Gun wash-out tank
15 Drain pipe from wash-out tank
16 Three cylinder hydraulic training
    engine
17 Training pinion
18 Training rack
19 Shell bin
20 Working chamber
21 Central hoist
22 Shell hoist in raised position
23 Cordite hoist in raised position
24 Shell hoist in lowered position
25 Cordite hoist in lowered position
26 Gun loading cage in lowered
    position
27 Training engine clutch hand wheel
28 Training rollers
29 Turret locking bolt
30 Hydraulic traversing press
31 Run in and out control valve
32 Traversing winch
33 Lifting winch
34 Shell transporting rail
35 Shell grab
36 Hand pump for automatic brake
37 Hydraulic lifting press
38 Main walking pipes
39 Cordite tray
40 Roller ring
41 Rotating shell-bogie
42 Lifting door
43 Shell and cordite hoist rails
44 Shell tray
45 Handing room
46 Shell room
47 Training control lever
48 Loading cage cam
49 Ring bulkhead

G2

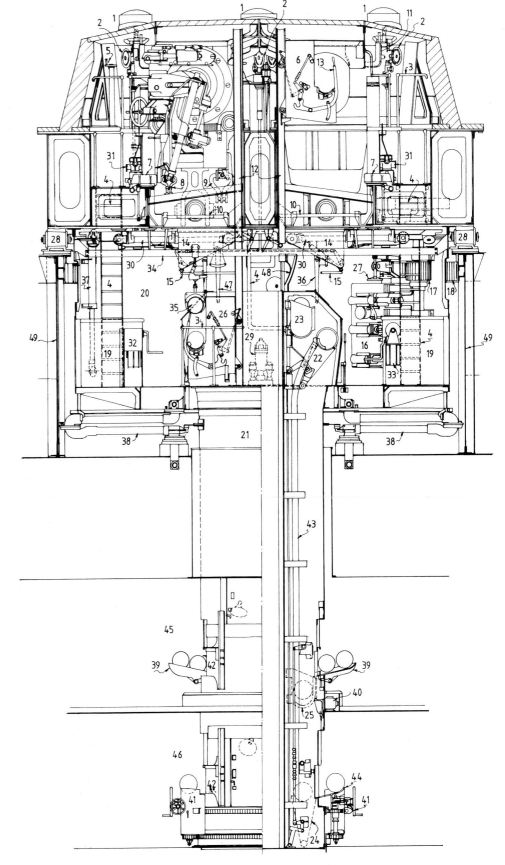

221

G   Armament

G3   12in GUNHOUSE

G3/1   Plan of 12in gunhouse (scale $^3/_{16}in = 1ft$)
The right hand side of the gunhouse is shown
with the roof removed, the left side is shown with
the roof supports omitted and the armour cut
down to the gunhouse floor.

1   Gun loading hoist lever
2   Cordite hand-up*
3   Shell lifting winch*
4   Hand loading bogie*
5   Screws for leather apron to barbette
6   Brackets and screws for leather
    apron
7   Leather apron (to make barbette
    watertight)
8   Metal strip on upper edge of leather
    apron
9   Barbette armour
10 Gunhouse rear plate (13in KC)
11 Gunhouse side and front armour
    (11in KC)
12 Breech mechanism
13 Chain rammer
14 Gun loading arm
15 Gun loading hoist rails

16 Ventilation shaft
17 Ladder to turntable floor and
    passage to shell chamber
18 Controls and valves for run-in and
    run-out gear
19 Elevating control wheel
20 Hand wheel for creep valve of
    training gear
21 Trunnions
22 Shell hand-up*
23 Pillar
24 Sight setter's seat
25 Gunlayer's stool
26 Ladder to working chamber
27 Lever for operating gun cradle
    locking bolt
28 Telescopic sights
29 Locking bolt indicator
30 Cradle locking bolt bracket

31 Ladder to gun platform
32 Ladder to gunhouse roof (hatch-
    over)
33 Caps over armour bolts
34 Breech block (open)
35 Wheel for hand operation of breech
36 Gun loading cage in raised position
37 Shell crane*
38 Ventilation fan
39 Ladder to gunhouse roof
40 Armour key
41 Brackets supporting gunhouse walls
42 Hole in roof for extraction of breech
    pin
43 Ready-use shell rack
44 Voice pipe from gun loading
    position to working chamber
45 Voice pipe from central sight setter
    to shell hand-up
46 Voice pipes between sight setters
47 Voice pipes between sighting hoods
*Items used for auxiliary loading with gun
loading cage out of action

G3/1

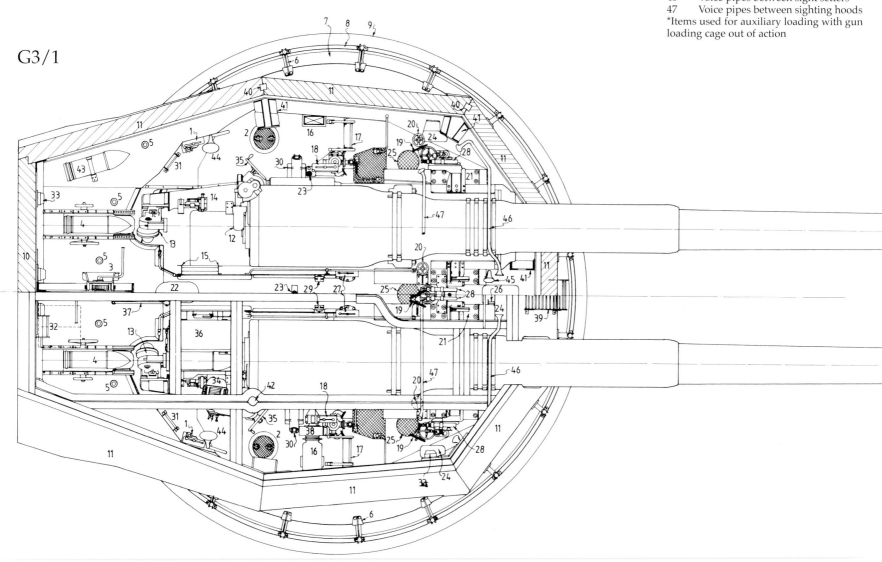

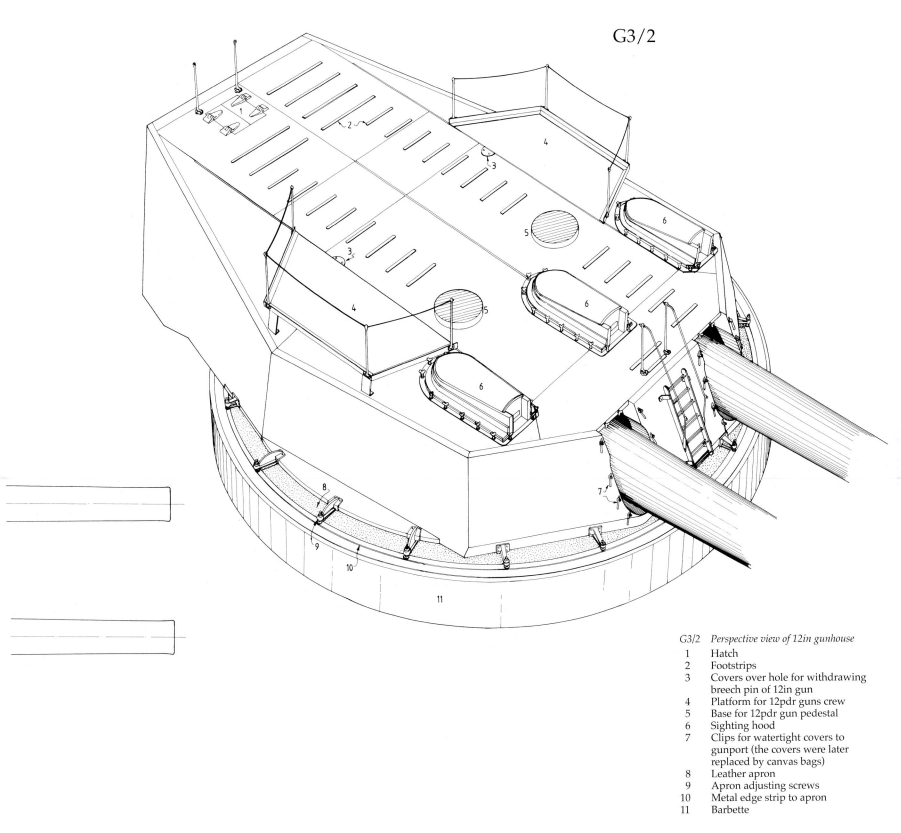

G3/2

G3/2 *Perspective view of 12in gunhouse*
1   Hatch
2   Footstrips
3   Covers over hole for withdrawing
      breech pin of 12in gun
4   Platform for 12pdr guns crew
5   Base for 12pdr gun pedestal
6   Sighting hood
7   Clips for watertight covers to
      gunport (the covers were later
      replaced by canvas bags)
8   Leather apron
9   Apron adjusting screws
10   Metal edge strip to apron
11   Barbette

G Armament

G4 PLAN OF TURNTABLE (scale $^3/_{16}$in = 1ft)

Left side shows top of turntable, right side shows base of turntable.

1   Top of turntable
2   Gun platform
3   Rear platform
4   Trunnion bearing
5   Ladder and passage to working chamber
6   Gun well
7   Opening for gun loading hoist
8   Bracket
9   Elevation cylinders
10 Opening for cordite hand-up
11 Gun loading hoist rails
12 Ladder
13 Brackets for locking bolts
14 Pinion on training engine shaft
15 Wheel on training pinion shaft
16 Ladder to working chamber
17 Opening for shell hand-up
18 Elevation cylinder mountings

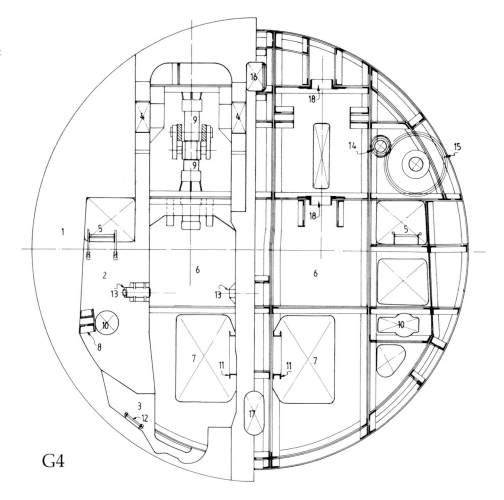

G4

G5 PLAN OF WORKING CHAMBER
(scale $^3/_{16}$in = 1ft)

Left side shows gear on roof of chamber, on right side gear on roof is omitted. All items are fitted on both sides unless otherwise stated.

1 Shell bin
2 Shell and cordite hoist
3 Gun loading hoist
4 Gun loading hoist rails
5 Ladder to turntable
6 Gun loading hoist hydraulic press
7 Compensating gear pulleys for gun loading hoist wire
8 Transporting rail for ready-use shell
9 Hydraulic press for transversing ready-use shell
10 Hand winch for traversing ready-use shell (left side only)
11 Hand lifting winch for ready-use shell (right side only)
12 Platform
13 Training stop lever
14 Lift and traverse hydraulic press control valves and levers
15 Hydraulic press for lifting ready-use shell (left side only)
16 Hydraulic press for central hoist
17 Telegraph to shell room
18 Cordite rammer
19 Shell rammer
20 Rammer and hoist control valves and levers
21 Access door to area under working chamber
22 Hand pump handle
23 Hand pump
24 Brake drum for training gear
25 Brake cylinder
26 Three cylinder hydraulic training engine
27 Training pinion (engages rack on fixed structure)
28 Turret locking bolt
29 Automatic brake valve
30 Automatic brake cylinder pump
31 Guardrail
32 Lever for operating gun loading hoist locking bolt
33 Cordite tray
34 Shell tray
35 Voice pipe to shell room
36 Voice pipe to handing room
37 Voice pipe to centre sight setter (right side only)
38 Voice pipe to gun loading position in gunhouse
39 Gun washout tank

Bottom plate hinges clear for passage of gun loading hoist.

40 Overhead trolley rail for ready-use shell
41 Cross connection rod for training control
42 Training control lever (left side only)

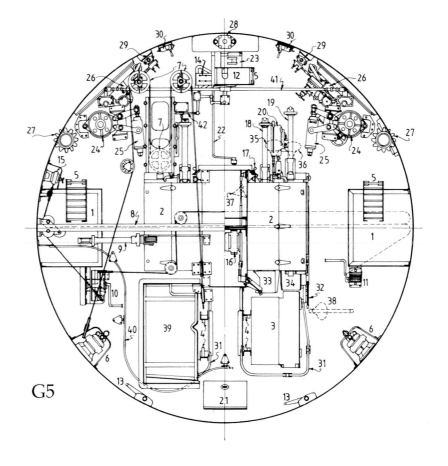

G5

G   Armament

G6   12in BL Mk X GUN

G6/1   Section on centreline (scale ¼in = 1ft)

G6/2   Profile (scale ¼in = 1ft)

G6/3   Breech end (scale ½in = 1ft)

G6/4   Muzzle end (scale ½in = 1ft)

1   Inner' A' tube (nickel steel)
2   'A' tube (nickel steel)
3   Wire
4   'B' tube
5   Jacket
6   Shrunk collar
7   Breech ring (screwed to jacket)
8   Breech bush (screwed to 'A' tube)
9   Chamber
10   Ribs for locating gun in cradle
11   Grooves for locking gun to cradle
12   Breech carrier hinge lugs on breech ring
13   Fixing screws for hydraulic mechanism for operating breech
14   Wellin stepped screw for breech block (30º turn to lock or unlock breech block)

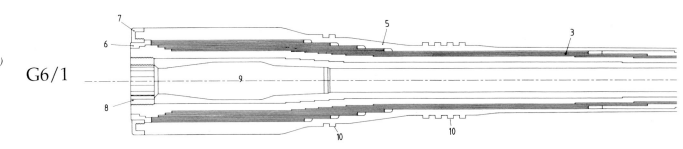

G6/1

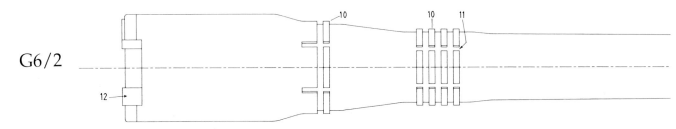

G6/2

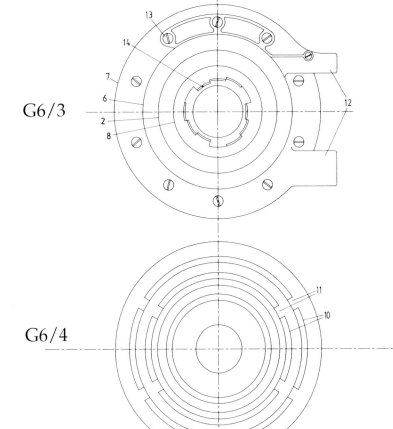

G6/3

G6/4

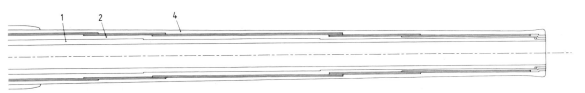

G7 PURE-COUPLE BREECH MECHANISM FOR 12in Mk X GUN (scale ½in = 1ft)

The mechanism is shown for the right hand gun. The left gun was handed – that is, the hinge of the carrier was on the left hand side. However the gun was universal and could be mounted either way up, while the breech block, carrier and internal mechanism were the same as for the right gun but fitted on the opposite side and therefore the other way up. The breech ring, hydraulic breech operating mechanism and breech handwheel were handed.

G7/1   End view

G7/2   Plan

G7/3   Side view

1   Hydraulic cylinder
2   Cylinder piston rod
3   Drip tray
4   Breech carrier
5   Breech retaining catch
6   Breech catch release
7   Breech block
8   Rack for operating breech by hydraulic power
9   Handwheel for hand operation of breech
10   Gun firing lock
11   Handwheel for engaging / disengaging clutch for breech mechanism handwheel
12   Hydraulic supply pipe
13   Hydraulic exhaust pipe
14   Breech ring

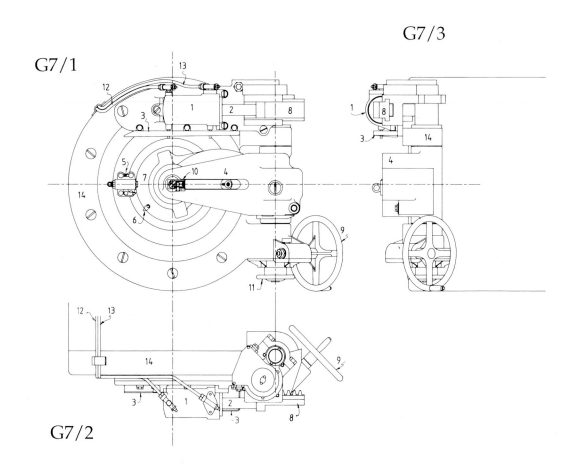

G7/1

G7/3

G7/2

G Armament

G8 GENERAL ARRANGEMENT OF GUNSLIDE AND LOADING ARM

G8/1 *Rear of gunslide (scale ¼in = 1ft)*

G8/2 *Profile of gunslide and loading arm (scale ¼in = 1ft)*

G8/3 *Front of gunslide (scale ¼in = 1ft)*

G8/4 *Section of gunslide at 'A' (scale ¼in = 1ft)*

G8/5 *Section of gunslide at 'B' (scale ¼in = 1ft)*

G8/6 *Plan of gunslide and loading arm (scale ¼in = 1ft)*

1 Trunnion
2 Trunnion arm
3 Cradle (recoils with gun)
4 Elevating arm
5 Gunslide
6 Recoil cylinder
7 12in Mk X gun
8 Auto leakage pump filling pipe
9 Locking bolt bracket
10 Chain rammer chain casing
11 Walking pipe end box for hydraulic power to chain rammer
12 Walking pipe end box for run-in and run-out cylinders
13 Pointer for elevation scale
14 Auto leakage pump lever

15 Hydraulic pipes for breech operating mechanism
16 Run-in cylinder
17 Run-out cylinder
18 Oil box
19 Intercepting valve (under)
20 Rubbing piece
21 Loading tray, shown in loading position

Lifted to loading position by cam on gun loading cage.

22 Loading tray in lowered position
23 Loading tray return spring
24 Gun loading cage stops
25 Loading arm
26 Loading arm bracket

27 Breech operating lever
28 Breech mechanism control valve
29 Chain rammer operating lever
30 Rammer motor control valve
31 Rammer interlock

Prevents rammer from operating unless cage is raised.

32 Chain rammer motor (3 cylinder hydraulic)
33 Chain rammer
34 Rammer head
35 Auto leakage pump
36 Air connections for run-in and run-out cylinders
37 Gun wash-out spray
38 Wash-out operating lever

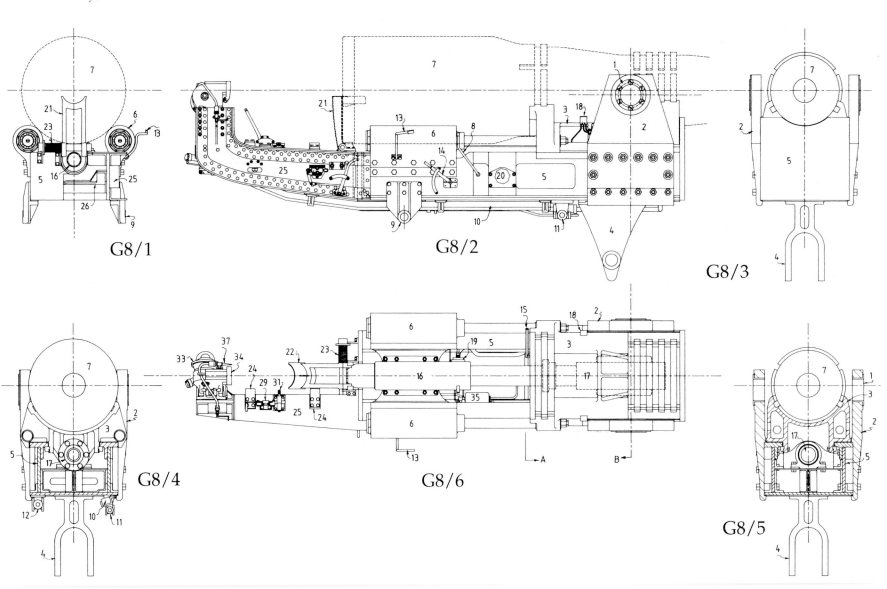

G8/1

G8/2

G8/3

G8/4

G8/6

G8/5

G8/7   *Rear of loading arm and chain rammer (scale ½in = 1ft)*

G8/8   *Profile of loading arm (scale ½in = 1ft)*

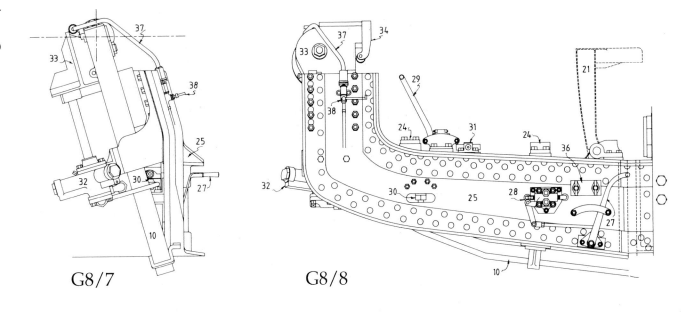

G8/7

G8/8

G9   **GENERAL ARRANGEMENT OF 12pdr 18cwt GUN ON PIV* MOUNTING (scale ½in = 1ft)**

G9/1   *Rear view*

G9/2   *Profile of right side*

1	Gun (maximum elevation 20°, maximum depression 10°)	9	Dummy (auxiliary contact) for breech in case of failure of main circuit
2	Interceptor		
3	Pilot lamp	10	Night sight switch
4	Electricity supply from low power system	11	Dial lamp switch
		12	Trunnion
5	Auxiliary firing pistol	13	Sighting gear
6	Main firing pistol	14	Layer's shoulder rest
7	Main firing circuit	15	Trainer's shoulder rest
8	Auxiliary firing circuit	16	Pedestal

17	Training stops
18	Recoil and run-out cylinder
19	Training rack
20	Terminal box
21	Elevating hand wheel
22	Training hand wheel
23	Cradle
24	Carriage
25	Recoil spring box

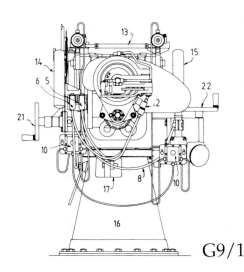

G9/1

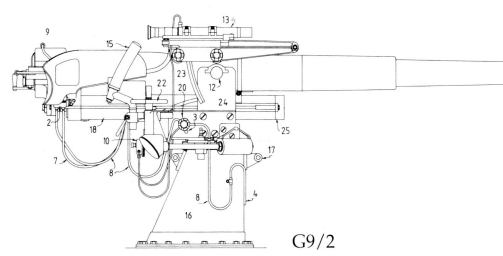

G9/2

229

G   Armament

G9/3   *Front view*

G9/4   *Profile of left side*

G9/5   *Plan*

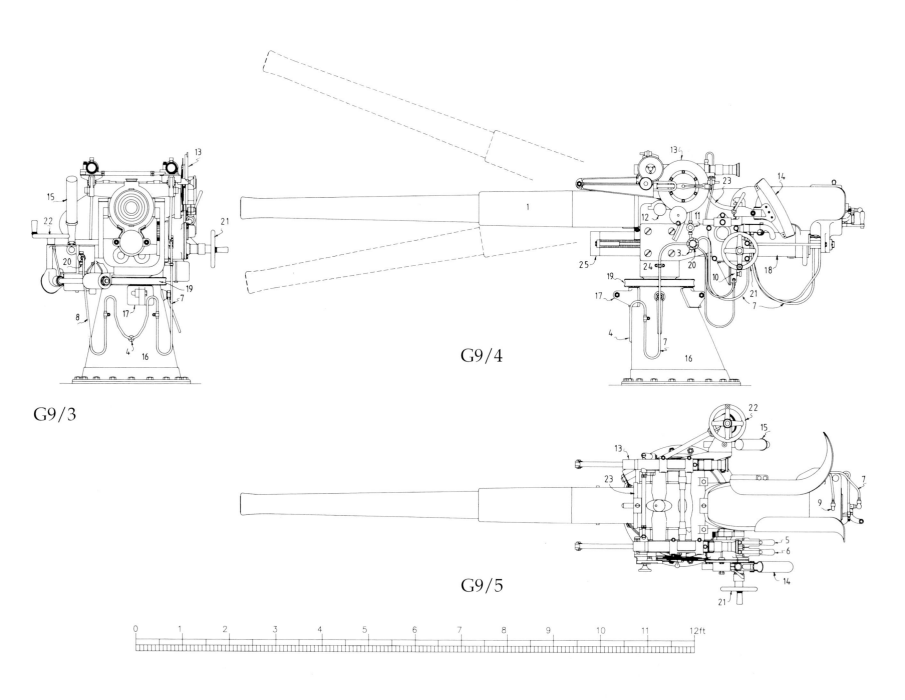

G9/3

G9/4

G9/5

12pdr 18cwt Mk1 QF GUN (scale
½ in = 1 ft)

G10/1 Section

G10/2 Plan

G10/3 Profile

G10/4 End view of breech
1   'A' tube
2   'B' tube
3   Breech piece
4   Breech bush
5   Wire
6   Jacket
7   Breech ring
8   Lug for recoil cylinder piston rod
9   Key for location in cradle
10 Ejector
Operated by cam on rear of breech pivot;
knocked out empty cartridge when breech was
opened.
11 Breech carrier hinge

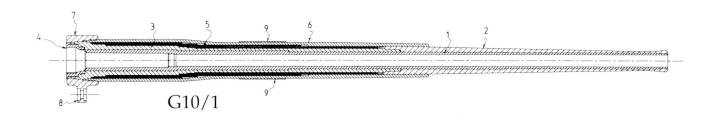

G10/1

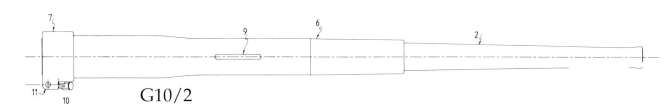

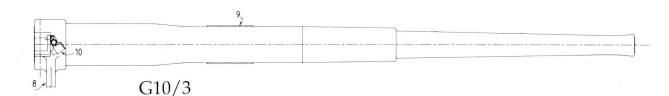

G10/2

G10/4

G10/3

G11 12pdr GUN CRADLE (scale ½in =
1ft)

G11/1 Front view

G11/2 Left side

G11/3 Rear view

G11/4 Right side

G11/5 Plan

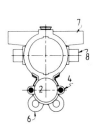

G11/1

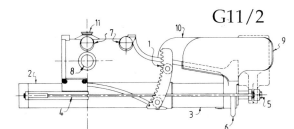

G11/2

G11/3

G11/4

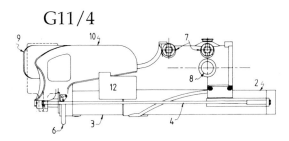

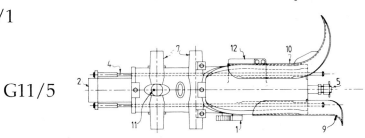

G11/5

1   Elevation rack
2   Recoil spring box
3   Recoil and run-out cylinder
4   Rods connecting front end of recoil
    spring to lugs on breech of gun
5   Recoil piston rod
6   Lifting rings
7   Pillars for mounting sighting gear
8   Trunnion
9   Shield to protect layer from gun
    recoil
10 Shield to protect trainer from gun
    recoil
11 Lubricator
12 Recoil cylinder tank (water and
    glycerine mixture)

G Armament

G12 12pdr GUN CARRIAGE (scale ½in = 1ft)

G12/1 *Front view*

G12/2 *Left side*

G12/3 *Rear view*

G12/4 *Right side*

G12/5 *Plan*

1	Pivot post (fits inside pedestal)
2	Trunnion arms
3	Trunnion cap
4	Elevation gear arm
5	Training gear arm
6	Training hand wheel
7	Elevating hand wheel
8	Elevating pinion (engages with rack on cradle)
9	Training gearbox
10	Training worm case
11	Training worm
12	Firing pistols
13	Adjustments for shoulder rest
14	Layer's shoulder rest
15	Trainer's shoulder rest
16	Night sight switch
17	Elevation gearbox

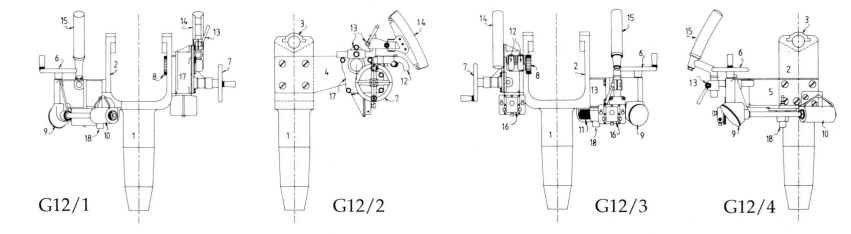

G12/1   G12/2   G12/3   G12/4

G12/5

18   Training stop

G13   12pdr GUN PEDESTAL (scale ½in = 1ft)

G13/1   *Plan*

G13/2   *Front view*

G13/3   *Left side*

G13/4   *Rear view*

G13/5   *Right side*

1   Training rack

2   Training stops

Position of stop brackets vary according to position of mounting; no stops were fitted to the 12pdr guns on the turret roofs.

3   Training clamp handle

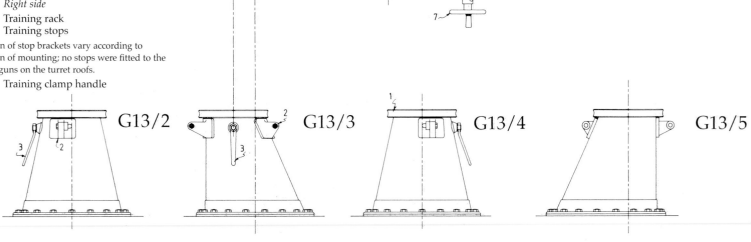

G13/1   G13/2   G13/3   G13/4   G13/5

G14   12pdr 18cwt MkI GUN BREECH
       MECHANISM (scale 1in = 1ft)

G14/1 *Left side*

G14/2 *Rear*

G14/3 *Right side*

G14/4 *Plan*
   1   Electric and percussion lock
   2   Firing circuit cable
   3   Auxiliary firing circuit cable
   4   Dummy, for stowing auxiliary firing
       cable
   5   Breech operating lever
   6   Breech block
   7   Carrier
   8   Breech catch housing
   9   Breech catch recess
  10   Breech actuating link
  11   Shell case extractor
  12   Extractor buffer
  13   Interceptor
  14   Carrier hinge
  15   Breech operating lever hinge
  16   Lug for percussion firing lanyard

G14/1

G14/2

G14/3

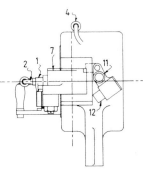

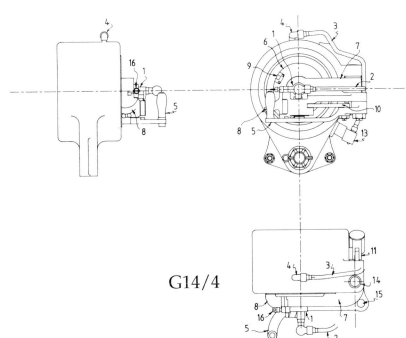

G14/4

G15/1

G15   12pdr GUN SIGHTING GEAR
       (scale ½in = 1ft)

G15/1 *Plan*

G15/2 *Front view*

G15/3 *Left side*

G15/4 *Rear view*

G15/5 *Right side*

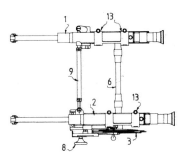

   1   Trainer's telescope
   2   Layer's telescope
   3   Range dial
   4   Range setting hand wheel
   5   Elevation rack
   6   Elevation rack cross connection
       spindle
   7   Deflection dial

   8   Deflection setting hand wheel
   9   Deflection cross connection rod
  10   Telescope rear pivot
  11   Elevation pivot
  12   Sight bar
  13   Telescope clamps
  14   Night sight connection

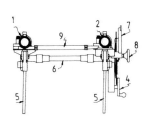

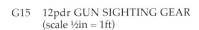

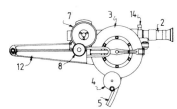

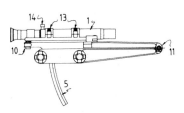

G15/2

G15/3

G15/4

G15/5

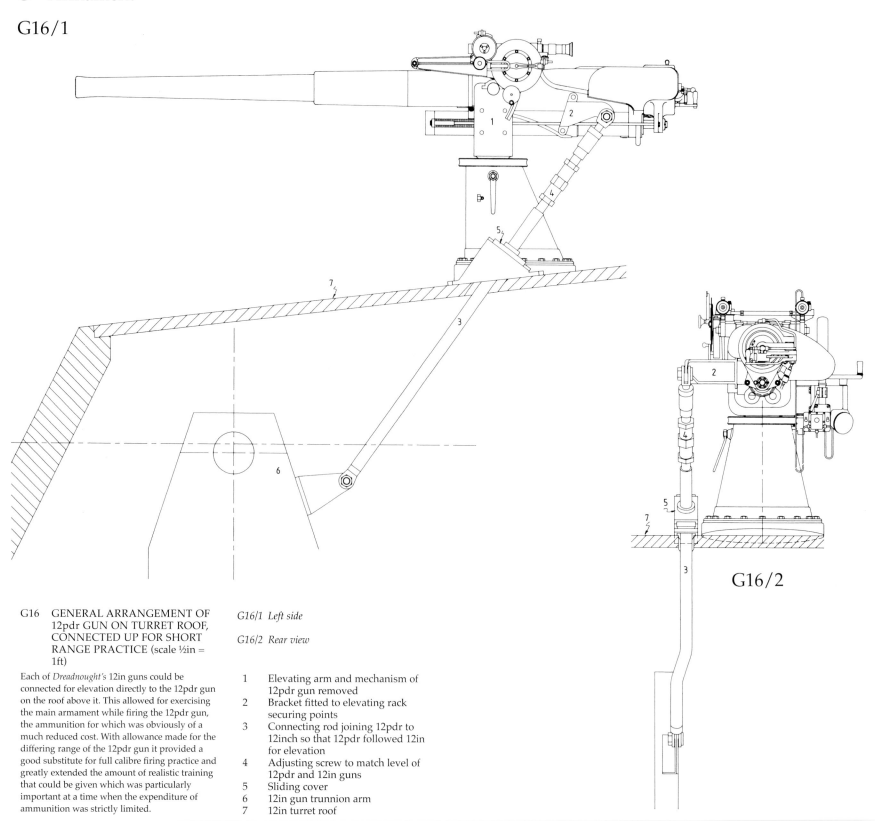

G16/1 *Left side*

G16/2 *Rear view*

G16   GENERAL ARRANGEMENT OF 12pdr GUN ON TURRET ROOF, CONNECTED UP FOR SHORT RANGE PRACTICE (scale ½in = 1ft)

Each of *Dreadnought's* 12in guns could be connected for elevation directly to the 12pdr gun on the roof above it. This allowed for exercising the main armament while firing the 12pdr gun, the ammunition for which was obviously of a much reduced cost. With allowance made for the differing range of the 12pdr gun it provided a good substitute for full calibre firing practice and greatly extended the amount of realistic training that could be given which was particularly important at a time when the expenditure of ammunition was strictly limited.

1   Elevating arm and mechanism of 12pdr gun removed
2   Bracket fitted to elevating rack securing points
3   Connecting rod joining 12pdr to 12inch so that 12pdr followed 12in for elevation
4   Adjusting screw to match level of 12pdr and 12in guns
5   Sliding cover
6   12in gun trunnion arm
7   12in turret roof

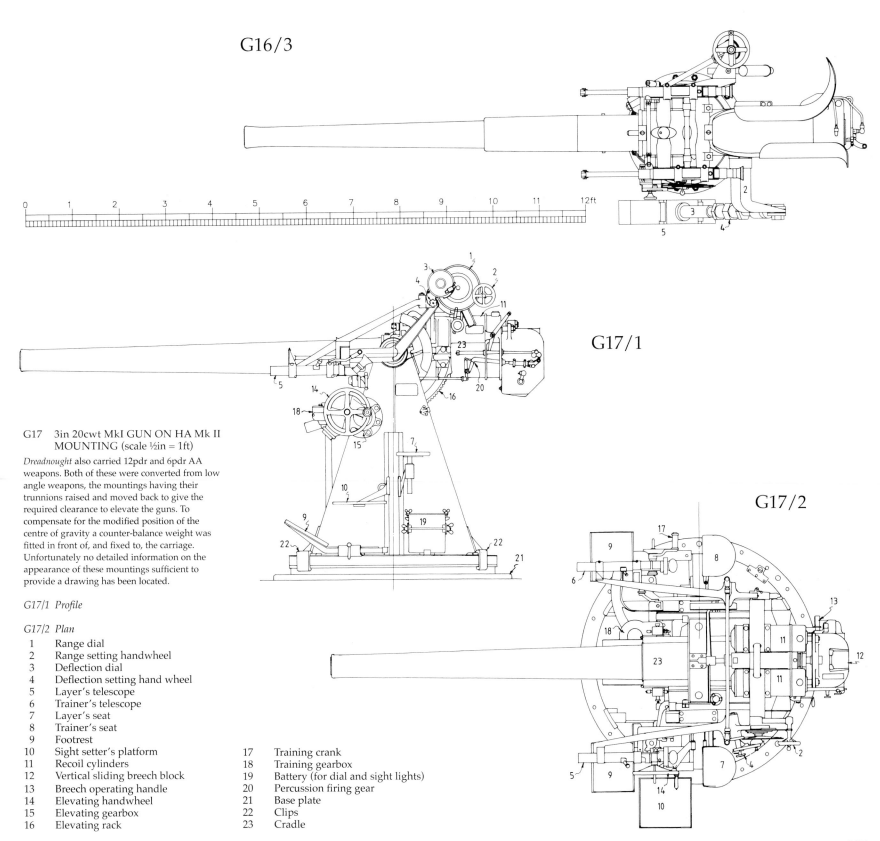

G16/3

0 1 2 3 4 5 6 7 8 9 10 11 12ft

G17/1

G17/2

G17   3in 20cwt MkI GUN ON HA Mk II
MOUNTING (scale ½in = 1ft)

Dreadnought also carried 12pdr and 6pdr AA
weapons. Both of these were converted from low
angle weapons, the mountings having their
trunnions raised and moved back to give the
required clearance to elevate the guns. To
compensate for the modified position of the
centre of gravity a counter-balance weight was
fitted in front of, and fixed to, the carriage.
Unfortunately no detailed information on the
appearance of these mountings sufficient to
provide a drawing has been located.

G17/1 Profile

G17/2 Plan

1	Range dial
2	Range setting handwheel
3	Deflection dial
4	Deflection setting hand wheel
5	Layer's telescope
6	Trainer's telescope
7	Layer's seat
8	Trainer's seat
9	Footrest
10	Sight setter's platform
11	Recoil cylinders
12	Vertical sliding breech block
13	Breech operating handle
14	Elevating handwheel
15	Elevating gearbox
16	Elevating rack
17	Training crank
18	Training gearbox
19	Battery (for dial and sight lights)
20	Percussion firing gear
21	Base plate
22	Clips
23	Cradle

G   Armament

G18   PLAN OF FORWARD
SUBMERGED TORPEDO ROOM
(scale ⅟₁₆in = 1ft)

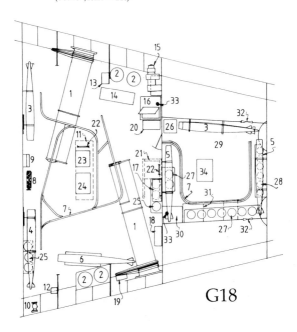

G18

G19   18in BROADSIDE SUBMERGED
TORPEDO TUBE, TYPE 'B' (scale
¼in = 1ft)

G19/1   *End view showing rear 'chopper' door*

G19/2   *Section at door opening gear*

G19/3   *Section at firing gear*

G19/4   *Section at side door (door shown open)*

G19/5   *Plan*

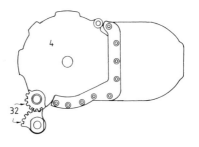

G19/1

1   18in torpedo tube
2   Firing air-reservoirs
3   Four 18in torpedo bodies
4   Two 18in torpedo bodies
5   Three 14in torpedo bodies
6   18in torpedo body on trolley
7   Torpedo transport rails (over)
8   Valve chest
9   Hose rack
10 Seacock
11 Torpedo hatch (over)
12 Tank
13 Tool chest
14 Bench
15 Ventilation fan
16 Torpedo pistol tank
17 Cupboard for gyroscopes
18 Cupboard for gyroscope table
19 Tool box
20 Transporting trolley
21 Escape trunk (over)
22 Ladder
23 Hatch to spirit room
24 Hatch to bread room
25 Torpedo collision heads
26 Wet gun-cotton
27 18in torpedo heads
28 14in torpedo heads
29 Torpedo head and dry gun-cotton
    magazine
30 Dry gun-cotton magazine
31 Stowage for wet gun-cotton (over)
32 Watertight manhole in bulkhead
33 Scupper
34 Hatch to submarine mine store

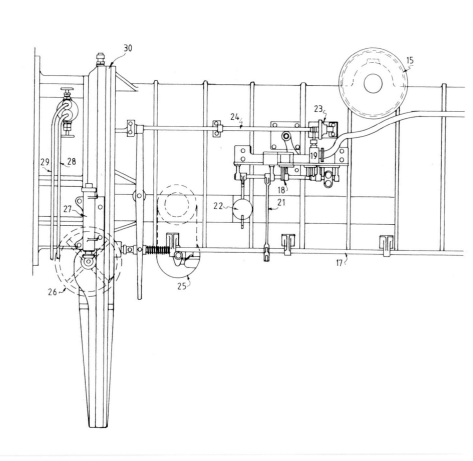

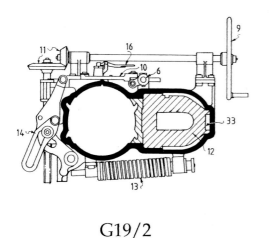

G19/2

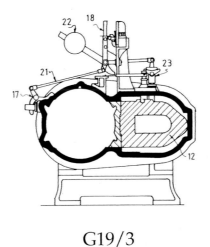

G19/3

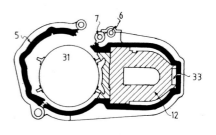

G19/4

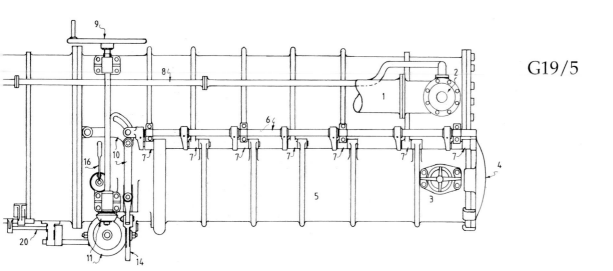

G19/5

1 Pipe from firing reservoirs
2 Large firing valve
3 Air escape valve (for filling and draining tube)
4 Rear 'chopper' door
5 Side door
6 Door locking rod
7 Door locking bolts
8 Pipe between small and large firing valves
9 Door operating handwheel
10 Locking rod operating levers
11 Bevel gears
12 Bar
13 Buffer for side door
14 Side door operating levers
15 Worm wheel driven by electric motor (not shown) for operating bar
16 Tripper
17 Firing gear rod
18 Firing lever
19 Small firing valve
20 Interlock bar
21 Firing rod connecting rod
22 Dropping ball
23 Bar stop
24 Bar stop rod
25 Drain valve (to clear tube of sea water prior to opening)
26 Sluice valve operating hand wheel
27 Sluice valve indicator
28 Flood pipe from Kingston valve
29 Exhaust air pipe from sluice valve box
30 Sluice valve casing
31 Torpedo
32 Rear door operating gears (rear door opens double distance of side door)
33 Rack on bar for engaging with pinion for driving bar in and out

H Fire control

H1 PLAN OF TRANSMITTING STATION ON LOWER DECK FORWARD, AS FITTED DURING 1908–09 (scale ¹⁄₁₆in = 1ft)

1 Telephone cabinet
2 Transmitting station
3 Motor generator
4 Telephone exchange
5 12pdr dredger hoist
6 Hatch to 12pdr shell room
7 Ammunition embarkation hatch (over)
8 Overhead rail for transporting 12in ammunition
9 Drinking tank
10 Longitudinal protective bulkhead
11 Armoured door
12 Sound insulated walls
13 Manhole
14 Ventilation fan
15 Air chamber
16 Vent trunk
17 12pdr ammunition working space

H2 PLAN OF LOWER CONNING TOWER, AS MODIFIED DURING 1908–10 (scale ¹⁄₁₆in = 1ft)

1 Short range W/T silent cabinet (fitted 1910)
2 W/T aerial trunk (over)
3 12pdr dredger hoist
4 Vent trunk
5 Main plotting table
6 Auxiliary plotting table
7 Ladder
8 Hatch (over)
9 Range clock
10 Engine room telegraphs
11 Revolution telegraph
12 Electric compass repeat
13 Steering wheel
14 Ventilation fans to auxiliary machinery spaces
15 Ventilation fan for silent cabinet
16 Ammunition embarkation trunk
17 Communication tube (over)
18 Board for instruments

H3 PLAN OF LOWER SIGNAL TOWER AND SECONDARY PLOTTING STATION AS FITTED DURING 1908–10 (scale ¹⁄₁₆in=1ft)

1 Lockers (over)
2 Rack (over)
3 Basins
4 Chief and leading seamen's wash place
5 Gunner's store
6 Plotting station
7 Main plotting table
8 Auxiliary plotting table
9 12pdr hand up (over)
10 Range clock
11 Hatch (over)
12 Navyphone silent cabinet
13 Lower signal tower and transmitting station
14 Board for instruments
15 Electric compass
16 Engine room telegraph
17 Steering wheel
18 Communication tube (over)
19 Ladder to communication tube
20 Locker

H4 PLAN OF FORETOP January 1907 (scale ¹⁄₈in = 1ft)

1 9ft FQ2 rangefinder
2 Range clock
3 Canopy support
4 Manhole to searchlight platform
5 Manhole to mast ladderway
6 Rangefinder clamping rail

H5 PLAN OF FORETOP June 1915 (scale ¹⁄₈in = 1ft)

1 9ft FQ2 rangefinder on Argo mounting
2 Gyro stabilising unit for Argo mounting
3 Shelf
4 Dumaresq table
5 Screen
6 Cupboard for storage of instruments etc
7 Manhole to platform under
8 Support to canopy and director
9 Ladder to manhole (over)
10 Opening for access to mast ladder
11 Manhole to mast ladder
12 Evershed bearing indicator

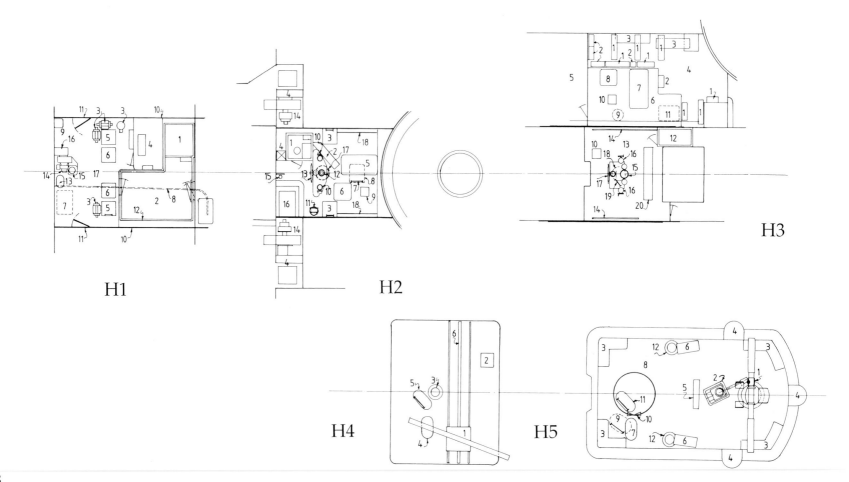

H1

H2

H3

H4

H5

H6 PLAN OF AFTER CONTROL PLATFORM (scale ¹/8in = 1ft)

1 Hinged wings to platform
2 Hinged grating giving access to hatch in roof of signal tower
3 9ft FQ2 rangefinder
4 Rangefinder clamping rail
5 Guardrail stanchions

H7 PLAN OF SIGNAL TOWER (scale ¹/8in = 1ft)

1 Torpedo directors
2 Steering wheel
3 Hatch (over)
4 Communication tube
5 Ladder
6 Engine room telegraph
7 Helm indicator (over)

H8 PLAN OF CONNING TOWER (scale ¹/8in = 1ft)

1 Junction box (over)
2 Hatch (over)
3 Ladder
4 Engine room telegraph
5 Helm indicator (over)
6 Combined receiver (Vickers – range and deflection)
7 Communication tube
8 Steering wheel

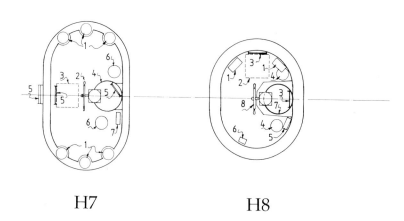

H7　　　　　H8

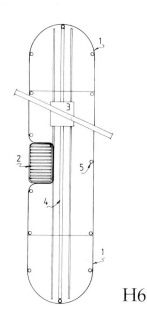

H6

H9 9ft FQ2 BARR AND STROUD RANGE FINDER ON MP2 MOUNTING (scale ½in = 1ft)

The MNI mounting also carried by *Dreadnought* was generally similar but had a fixed base without the traversing rail.

H9/1　Rear view

H9/2　Left side view

1 Left eye piece
2 Elevation handle
3 Height adjustment handwheel
4 Finger rest
5 Pedestal
6 Lamp switch
7 Right eye piece
8 Rangefinder eye piece
9 Arm rest
10 Chest bracket
11 Adjusting screw for arm rest
12 Training clamp
13 Sunshade
14 Pedestal clamping hand wheels
15 Rollers
16 Traversing rail
17 Roller track

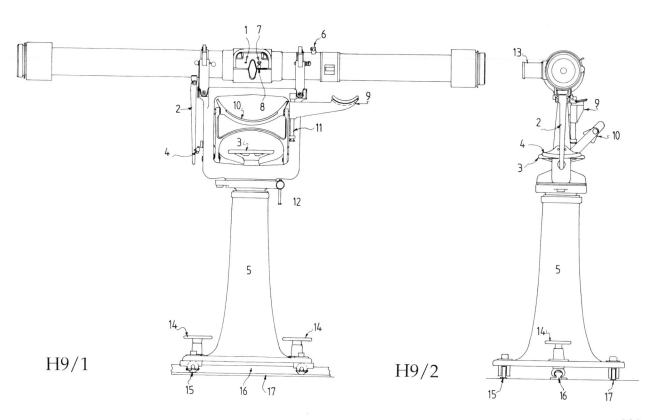

H9/1　　　　　H9/2

H Fire control

H10 9ft FT8 BARR AND STROUD RANGEFINDER ON MG3 TURRET MOUNTING (scale ½in = 1ft)

The FT24 rangefinder, which replaced the FT8 in *Dreadnought's* 'A' turret in 1918, was of generally similar appearance.

H10/1 Rear view

H10/2 Left side view

1   Periscope
2   Eye pieces
3   Coincidence adjustment scale
4   Rotating bracket
5   Elevation handle
6   Auxiliary training hand wheel
7   Finger rest
8   Bracket fixed to centre division plate in turret
9   Training handwheel
10 Periscope clamp
11 Rangetaker's seat
12 Seat locking clamp
13 Rear wall of turret
14 Seat bracket

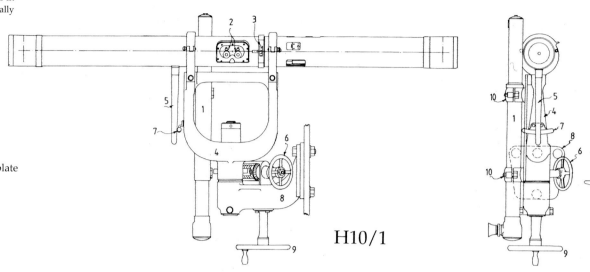

H10/2

H10/1

H11 PROFILE OF GUN DIRECTOR TOWER, WITH TOWER SECTIONED ON CENTRELINE (scale ½in = 1ft)

1   Canopy (rotates with director)
2   Canopy rollers
3   Director
4   Door
5   Door clips
6   Lookout windows
7   Sighting ports
8   Apron
9   Canopy rotating arms
10 Tripod mounting
11 Circular base
12 Director tower (fixed)

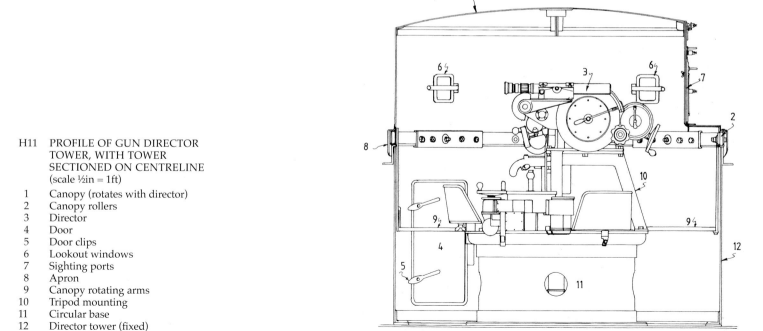

H11

H12   PERSPECTIVE VIEW OF TRIPOD TYPE DIRECTOR

1   Trainer's telescopic sight
2   Layer's telescopic sight
3   Range setting handwheel
4   Telescope arm pivot
5   Elevation hand wheel
6   Range dial
7   Deflection handwheel
8   Deflection dial
9   Phone man's seat
10   Sight setter's seat
11   Trainer's seat
12   Layer's seat
13   Slewing handwheel
14   Training handwheel
15   Training repeater
16   Ring frame (revolves)
17   Tripod
18   Gun ready board
19   Base (fixed)
20   Gun firing pistols

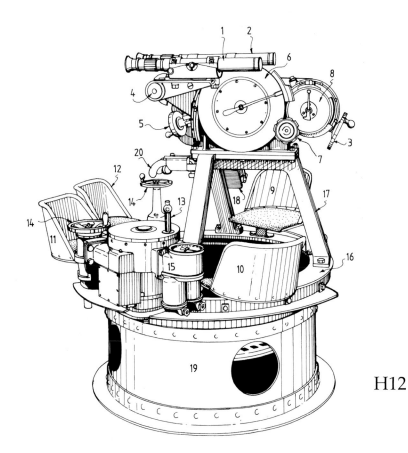

H12

H13   PERSPECTIVE VIEW OF HENDERSON GUN DIRECTOR FIRING GEAR

Fitted to *Dreadnought's* director in 1918: The Henderson firing gear contained a gyro stabilised switch that only closed the gun firing circuits with the ship vertical, thereby eleminating the possibility of elevation errors occurring when the guns were fired with the ship rolling. The gear included a stabilised gunsight, the stabilisation being achieved by a prism operated by the same gyro mechanism as operated the gun firing switch.

1   Telescopic sight
2   Brackets for standard trainer's telescopic sight
3   Telescope ring containing stabilised prism
4   Adjusting key
5   Adjusting wheel
6   Casing of gyroscope and firing mechanism
7   Bracket for fixing to director
8   Inspection window

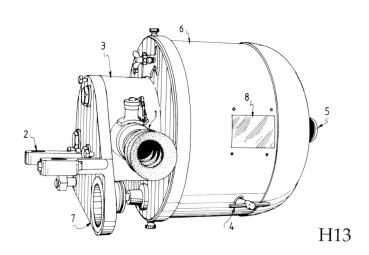

H13

H Fire control

H14   DREYER FIRE CONTROL TABLE MkI

H14/1 *Rear view*

H14/2 *Front view*

H14/3 *Plan*

The Dreyer table was a mechanical calculating machine which processed all the information necessary to provide the guns with the corrected range and deflection necessary to bring them onto the target. Information was supplied from the control positions on the course, bearing and speed of the target together with spotting information. In addition corrections were made for own ship's course and speed, wind speed etc. The table also plotted the progress of information and corrections on a continuously moving sheet of paper which allowed the control officer to observe the pattern of a developing action and whether the predicted fall of shot was in line with the observed fall of shot. Unlike later types the MkI table was entirely hand operated, including the drive for the plot; the only mechanical drive was from the clockwork-driven range clock.

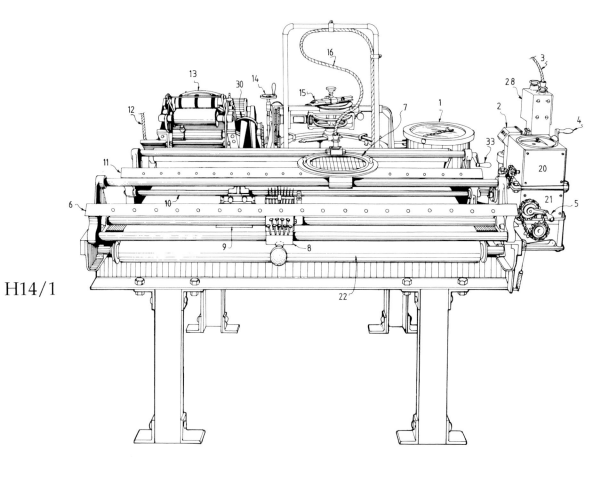

H14/1

1	Range clock	14	Own course setting handle	29	Watch box
2	Gun range counter	15	Dumaresq	30	Bearing indicator
3	Flexible drive to gun range counter on bulkhead	16	Flexible drive to rate grid	31	Range clock key
		17	Gun range screw	32	Rate handle
4	Spotting handle	18	Deflection totaliser	33	Handle for taking up slack in plot paper
5	Tuning handle	19	Gun range pencil holder		
6	Typewriter scale	20	Spotting corrector gearbox	34	Drive from gun range to bearing plot
7	Rate grid	21	Tuning gearbox		
8	Typewriter	22	Paper roller	35	Paper drive handle
9	Clock range pencil holder	23	Dumaresq deflection drum	36	Dumaresq deflection corrected for range
10	Clock range screw	24	Corrected deflection drum		
11	Range clock scale	25	Chasing handle	37	Wind correction
12	Flexible drive from totaliser to deflection master transmitter	26	Bearing handle	38	Uncorrected drift
		27	Deflection transmitting handle	39	Spotting
13	Bearing rate grid	28	Commutator	40	Total gun deflection

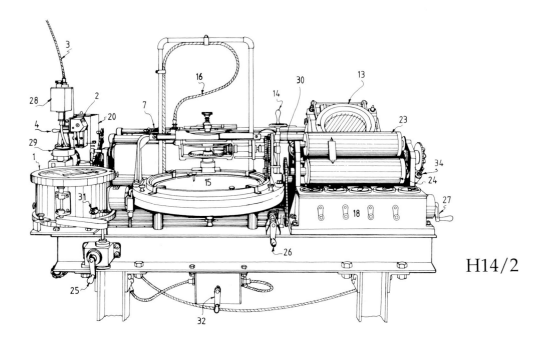

H14/2

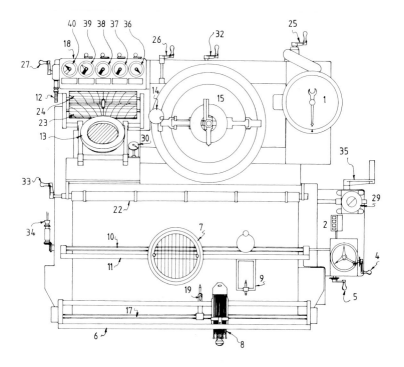

H14/3

I   Fittings

I1   HATCHES (scale ¼in = 1ft)

Hatches fell into two basic groups, standard watertight hatches and armoured hatches.

Standard hatches: these were fitted on top of coamings which were 12in above the upper surface of the deck on all decks above the protective deck and 6in above the surface of the deck on all decks below the protective deck. As with all warships the size of these hatches was kept to a minimum, the largest being those for embarking torpedoes. Some hatches were purely for personnel access, some for the embarkation of stores, ammunition etc, while others served both purposes. There were considerable variations in the hatch dimensions.

Armoured hatches: these were fitted on the protective deck, the covers being the same thickness as the deck and overlapping the hatchway at the edge. Six inch coamings were fitted outside the hatch unless it was already closely bounded by a watertight compartment. The weight of these hatches necessitated the provision of lifting gear and all those which served as escapes from occupied compartments were fitted with permanent counter-balance weights. They were also fitted with clips which allowed them to be open from either side. Hatches to compartments which were not occupied, such as store rooms, were lifted by means of a purchase and could only be opened from above. Clips were normally fitted to the deck but on hatches without coamings any clip that might be tripped over was fitted to the hatch cover.

I1/1   Typical ammunition hatch

That shown is for 'Q' turret – upper deck station 86 starboard.

1   Davit socket
2   Davit
3   Hinges
4   Clips
5   Cover stay
6   Coaming
7   Cleat

I1/2   Typical ladderway hatch

That shown is at station 166 on the upper deck, port and starboard.

1   Clips
2   Hinge
3   Stanchion for holding hatch open
4   Stanchion brackets
5   Coaming
6   Angle bar stiffener on cover
7   Handrail stanchions
8   Plan with hatch open
9   Profile of hatch in section showing ladder

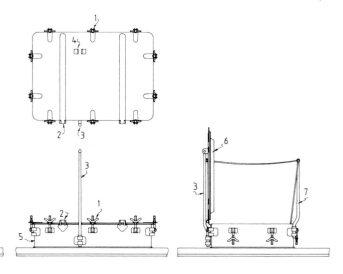

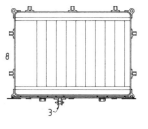

I1/2

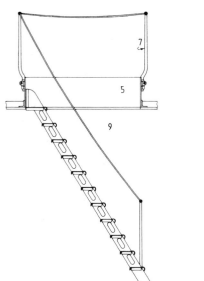

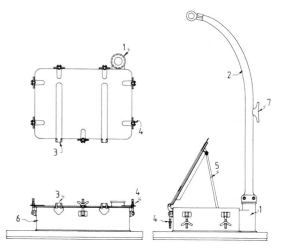

I1/1

I1/3 *Typical ladderway hatch*

Variation on I1/2 with hinge on narrow edge –
that shown is at station 132 on the upper deck,
port and starboard.

1   View of underside of cover showing
    angle bar stiffeners
2   Cover stay
3   Ladder
4   Angle bar stiffener
5   Rubber sealing strip

I1/4 *Plan of torpedo hatch*

That shown is at station 200, upper deck,
starboard.

1   Cover in two sections
2   Hinge
3   Clips
4   Stanchion for cover
5   Davit socket
6   Portable 'T' bar between covers

I1/5 *Typical armoured hatch with coaming*

1   Hinge
2   Clips
3   Clip handle on underside for
    escapes only
4   Coaming
5   Eye for lifting gear

I1/6 *Typical armoured hatch without*
    coaming

1   Hinge
2   Clip on deck
3   Clip on cover
4   Opening for clip in carling
5   Eye for lifting gear

I1/7 *Arrangement of counter-balance gear for*
    armoured hatch

1   Wire rope
2   Pulley
3   Guide rod
4   Counter-balance weight

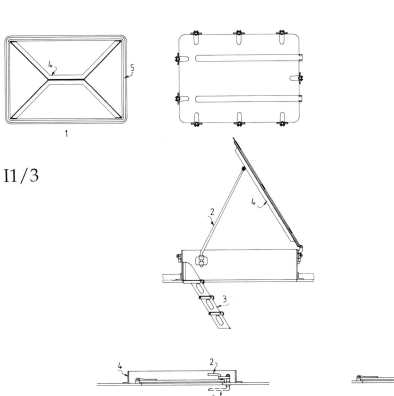

I1/3

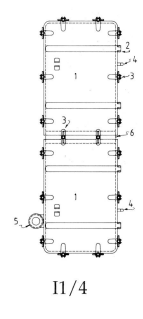

I1/4

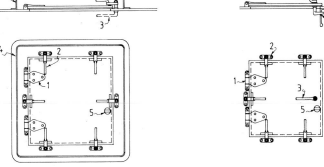

I1/5

I1/6

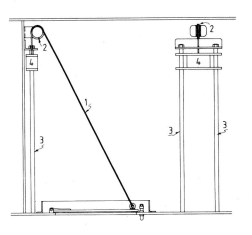

I1/7

I Fittings

I2   ESCAPE TRUNK (scale ¼in = 1ft)

Escape trunks were fitted to the auxiliary machinery compartments and the submerged torpedo rooms. They gave direct access to the main deck and were intended to limit the possibility of the compartment being flooded from above and to provide a means of escape and ventilation. (Trunk shown is for capstan machinery compartment.)

I2/1   *Section looking forward*

I2/2   *Profile*

I2/3   *Plan of sliding shutter, viewed from underside*

1   Hatch coaming
2   Ladder
3   Escape trunk
4   Cofferdam
5   Counter-balance weight for armour grating
6   Grating clip
7   Armour grating
8   Sliding watertight shutter
9   Chain for closing watertight shutter
10   Chain sprocket wheel
11   Shutter frame
12   Angle bar supporting armour grating
13   Deck plate for closing shutter from main deck
14   Bevel gears
15   Screwed shaft
16   Main deck
17   Middle deck
18   Lower deck

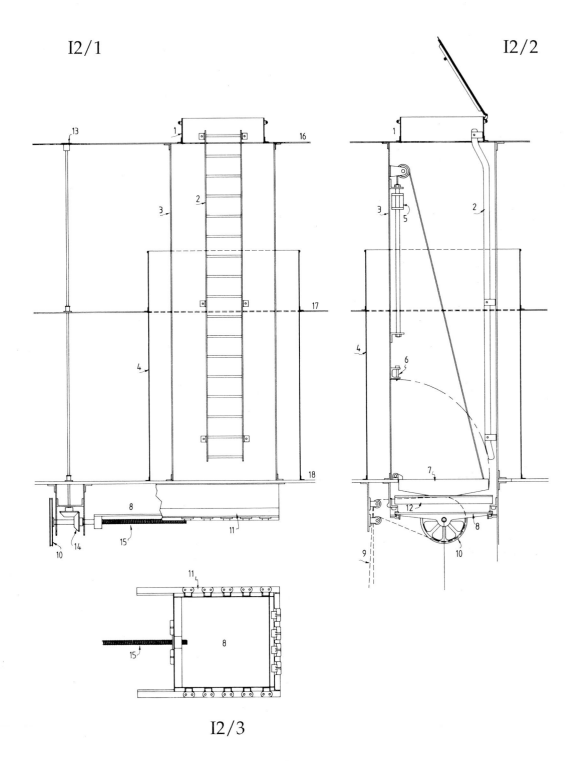

I2/1

I2/2

I2/3

246

I3   SKYLIGHTS (scale ¼in = 1ft)

The following do not illustrate all skylights but cover the majority of variations. The key for I3/1 is generally applicable to all drawings.

I3/1   *Ward room skylight*

1   Clips
2   Hinges
3   Cover (closed)
4   Cover (open)
5   Window sashes
6   Rubber sealing strip
7   Angle bar stiffener on cover
8   Division plate
9   Lightening holes in division plates
10   Deck beams
11   Longitudinal girder under forecastle deck
12   Portable stanchion for securing covers open
13   Adjustable bar for supporting window sash

I3/2   *Plan of gun room skylight*

I3/3   *Plan of skylight to main deck – fitted on forecastle deck*

Skylight to sick bay similar.

I3/4   *Plan of skylight to Admiral's galley*

This skylight was not sloped and was generally similar in construction to a hatchway.

I3/5   *Skylights to main deck*

Three fitted on upper deck around 'Y' turret.

I3/6   *Skylights to main deck fitted against superstructure on upper deck*

1   Clip to hold cover open
2   Bulkhead of superstructure

I3/1

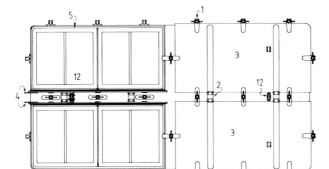

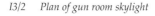

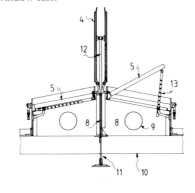

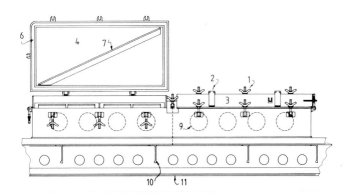

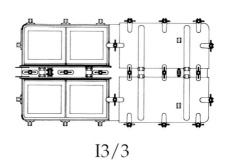

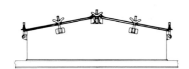

I3/2

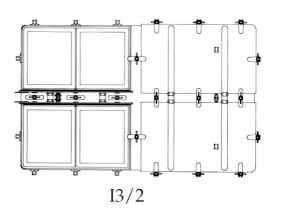

I3/3

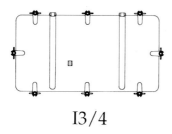

I3/4

I3/5

I3/6

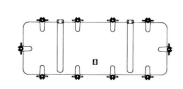

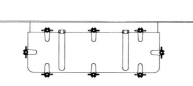

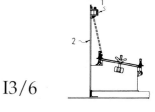

I   Fittings

I3/7   *Skylight to gun room galley*
1   Stove funnel
2   Funnel stays

I3/8   *Skylight to main deck at station 140 on upper deck, port and starboard*
1   Stiffening angle to cover
2   Rubber sealing strip
3   Window sash
4   Stanchion for cover
5   Bar for holding sash open

I4   LIGHT AND VENT TRUNK TO MAIN DECK (scale ¼in = 1ft)
1   Forecastle side
2   Forecastle deck
3   Upper deck
4   Watertight cover
5   Trunk
6   Hinges

I5   SIDE SCUTTLE (scale ½in = 1ft)
1   Scuttle or port
2   Frame
3   Clips
4   Deadlight
5   Rubber sealing strip
6   Clip lug
7   Sidelight glass
8   Hinge of deadlight (has two positions – one for closing over sidelight glass, one for closing over port with glass hinged inboard)
9   Hinge of sidelight glass
10   Rigol

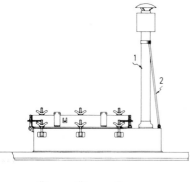
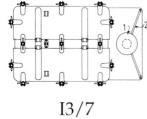

I3/7

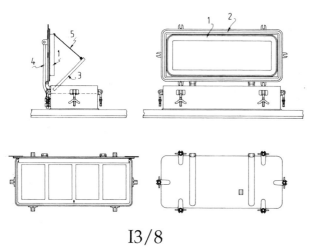

I3/8

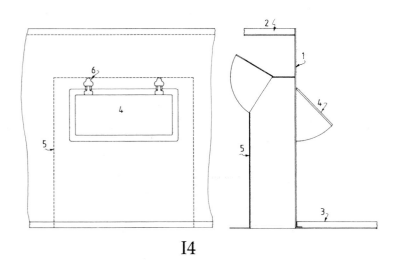

I4

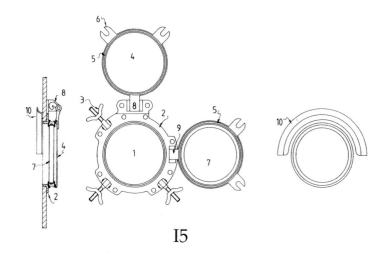

I5

I6   SQUARE PORTS

These were fitted at the sides of the main deck and superstructure for light and ventilation purposes. Where the ship's frames were 4ft apart, most of these ports were made 2ft 6in × 2ft 6in, but at the fore and after ends, where the frames were 3ft apart, the port width was reduced to 1ft 11in. There were also two narrow ports on the midships section, both on the port side, at stations 76 and 128 – the former to the Chief of Staff's sleeping cabin and the latter in a position restricted by an adjacent cabin bulkhead.

I6/1   Square port 2ft 6in × 1ft 11in. Interior and exterior view (scale ¼in = 1ft)

I6/2   Square port 2ft 6in × 2ft 6in. Interior and exterior view (scale ¼in = 1ft)

I6/3   Plan view in section of 2ft 6in × 2ft 6in port showing opening gear

I6/4   Plan view in section of 2ft 6in × 2ft 6in port showing strongback

1   Hinges
2   Rigol
3   Clips
4   Angle bar for strongback
5   Zed frames
6   Window operating handle
7   Window frame
8   Strongback (portable)
9   Butterfly clips securing strongback to angle on window
10   Window in fully open position
11   Worm and wormwheel drive
12   Channel bar

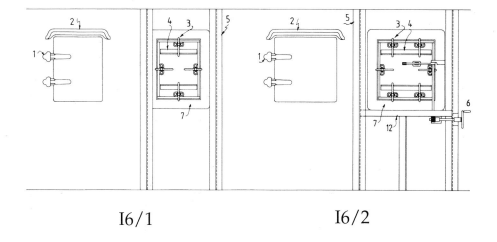

I6/1   I6/2

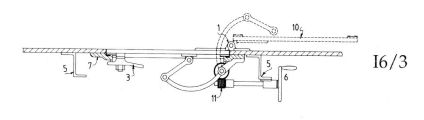

I6/3

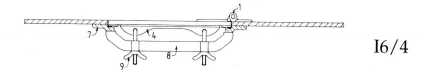

I6/4

I Fittings

I7 WATERTIGHT DOORS (scale ¼in = 1ft)

I7/1 Standard watertight door, 5ft 6in × 2ft 6in

The majority of *Dreadnought*'s watertight doors were of this size, including all those on the main deck, except for the larger doors noted below. A few doors were of smaller dimensions, mainly those to coal bunkers and stores, etc., but were of similar design.

1. Door frame
2. Clips
3. Clip wedge
4. Hinge
5. Handle
6. Angle bar stiffener

I7/2 Watertight door 5ft 6in × 3ft

These were fitted on the main deck in bulkhead 70 and gave access to the Admiral's dining cabin and Admiral's saloon. Like other watertight doors in the Admiral's compartments the opening was also fitted with a cosmetic wood door.

I7/3 Double watertight door 5ft 6in × 4ft

Doors of this type were fitted on each side of the forecastle at upper deck level at station 68 and in bulkhead 32 on the main deck. Two larger versions of 6ft 3in × 4ft were also fitted on each side of the superstructure inboard of P and Q turrets.

1. Clips on doors
2. Portable 'T' bar

I7/4 Typical superstructure door 5ft × 2ft

That shown is at after end of superstructure at station 130.

1. Clips on frame
2. Clips on door
3. Handle
4. Hinge

I7/5 Section of door clip (scale ½in = 1ft)

I7/6 Section of door hinge (scale ½in = 1ft)

I8 TYPICAL VENTILATION SUPPLY TRUNK TOP ON WEATHER DECK (scale ¼in = 1ft)

I9 TYPICAL MUSHROOM TOP EXHAUST VENT (scale ¼in = 1ft)

I10 MUSHROOM TOP EXHAUST VENTS TO AFTER DYNAMO ROOM AND HYDRAULIC ENGINE ROOM (abreast 'Y' turret). (scale ¼in = 1ft)

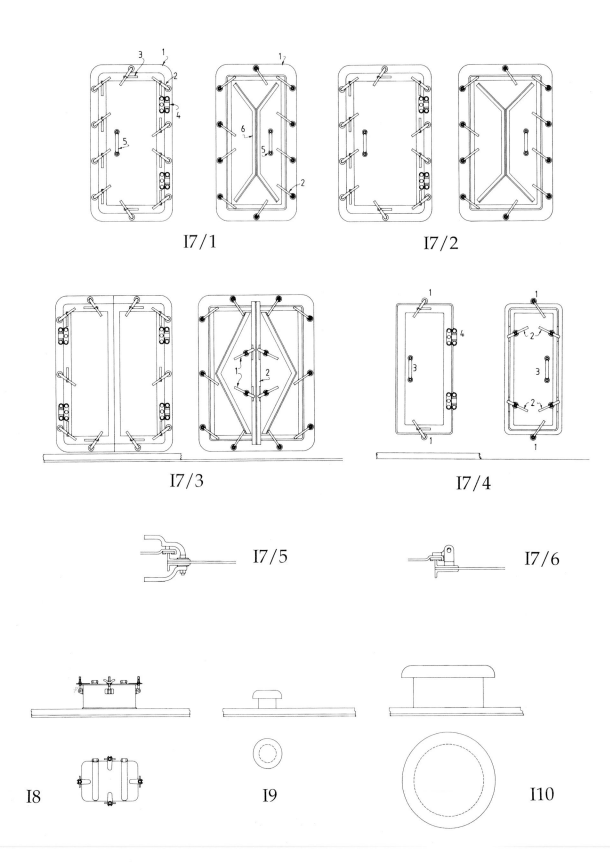

I7/1

I7/2

I7/3

I7/4

I7/5

I7/6

I8

I9

I10

GUARDRAILS (scale ¼in = 1ft)

I11/1 Guardrails and stanchions around upper and forecastle decks

1 Wire rope guardrails
2 Shoe
3 Chain link
4 Bottle screw for adjustment of length
5 Slip
6 Stay (joggled to clear guardrails) fitted at regular intervals for lateral support
7 Stanchion
8 Heel fitting
9 Position of stanchion when guardrails cleared for action
10 Wood deck

I11/2 Fixed guardrails to compass platform, navigating platform and Admiral's bridge

1 Stanchion
2 Tubular metal guardrails
3 Fixed heel
4 Wood platform

I11/3 Guardrails to superstructure platforms

1 Stanchion
2 Tubular metal guardrails
3 Heel riveted to angle of platform
4 Steel platform

I12 TYPICAL STOVE FUNNEL (scale ¼in = 1ft)

1 Stay band
2 Stay (normally fitted with two spaced at 90°)
3 Funnel
4 Funnel casing
5 Cap (replaced by cowl tops by 1916)

I13 AWNING STANCHIONS (scale ¼ in = 1ft)

I13/1 Arrangement of awning stanchions in way of torpedo net shelf

I13/2 Arrangement of awning stanchions on forecastle deck and on upper deck abaft torpedo net shelves

1 Stanchion
2 Stay
3 Hook for awning shackle
4 Heel fitting (similar to that for guardrails but larger)
5 Spurnwater
6 Torpedo net shelf
7 Wood deck
8 Heel fitting riveted to ship's side

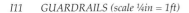
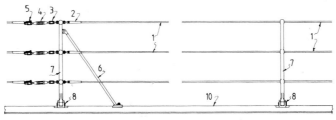
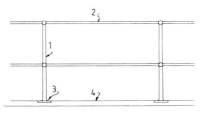

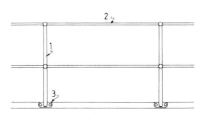
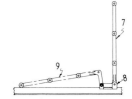

I11/1

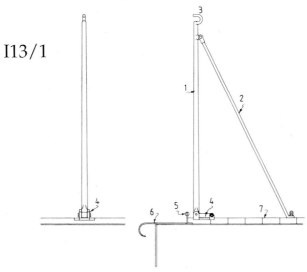

I11/2

I11/3

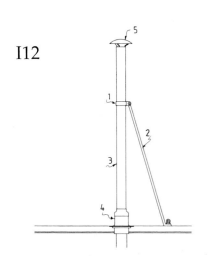

I12

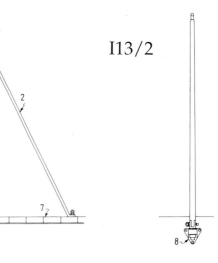

I13/1

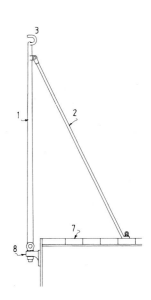

I13/2

J Ground tackle

J1   MAIN ANCHOR GEAR (scale ¹⁄₁₆in = 1ft)

J1/1   *Plan of forecastle*

J1/2   *Profile*

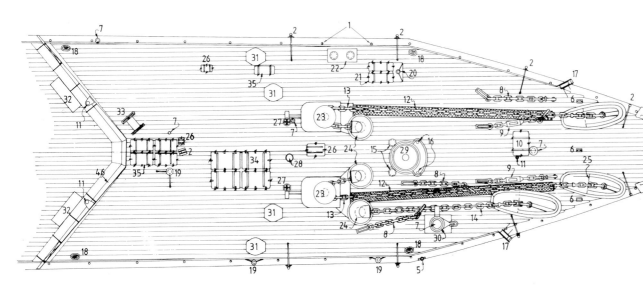

J1/1

J1/2

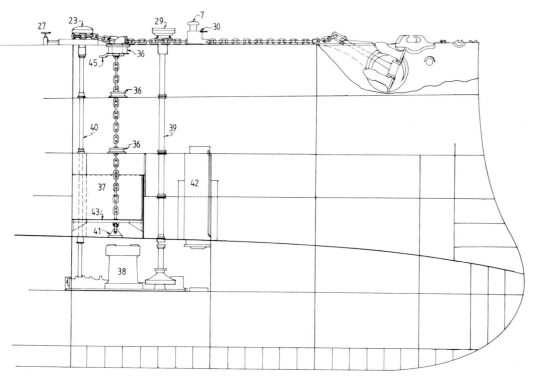

1	Guardrail stanchions
2	Awning stanchion
3	Jackstaff
4	Fairlead
5	Fairlead for torpedo net defence
6	Eyeplate
7	Mushroom top vent
8	Blake's stopper
9	Screw stopper
10	Ladderway
11	Davit socket
12	Ribbed chaffing plate for cable
13	Bower anchor cable
14	Sheet anchor cable
15	Roller
16	Alternative positions for rollers
17	Cathead
18	Scupper
19	Stove funnel
20	Galley funnel
21	Skylight to officers' galley
22	Bollard
23	Napier cable holder
24	Deck pipe with watertight bonnet
25	Hawse pipe cover plate
26	Vent trunk
27	Cable holder brake handwheel
28	Deck plate
29	Capstan
30	Riding bitt
31	Deck plates for 12pdr mountings
32	Wash deck lockers (new positions – fitted about 1907–08)
33	Hawser reel
34	Gun room skylight
35	Skylight to main deck
36	Deck pipe
37	Cable locker
38	Capstan engine
39	Capstan drive spindle
40	Cable holder drive spindle
41	Cable clench
42	Escape trunk from capstan engine room
43	Cable locker flat
44	Spurnwater
45	Cable stopper
46	Breakwater

J2   ANCHORS

Dreadnought carried the following anchors:

Port bower: 128cwt, 2qtr, 14lbs Wasteney Smith stockless

Starboard bower: 128cwt, 2qtr Wasteney Smith stockless

Sheet: 127cwt, 7lbs Wasteney Smith stockless

Stream: 43cwt, 1qtr, 18lbs Martin's close-stowing

Kedge: 15cwt, 1qtr, 6lbs Martin's close-stowing

Kedge: two 5cwt, 3qtr, 2lbs Admiralty pattern

   The bowers were the main anchoring and mooring anchors while the sheet anchor was a spare bower for use in emergencies. The stream anchor, stowed on the fore side of the signal tower, served to hold the ship in a temporary position and as a stern anchor. The kedge anchors were used for general work such as manoeuvring the ship and its main anchors. The Martin's kedge anchor was originally stowed at the after end of the boat deck, and the Admiralty pattern anchors one on each side of the mainmast on the upper deck.

J2/1   *Wasteney Smith stockless anchor (scale ¼in = 1ft)*

1   Shank
2   Ring
3   Crown
4   Arms
5   Flukes
6   Bill
7   Gravity band
8   Tripping palms
9   Stop, to prevent flukes moving beyond 45°

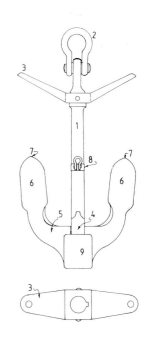

J2/2

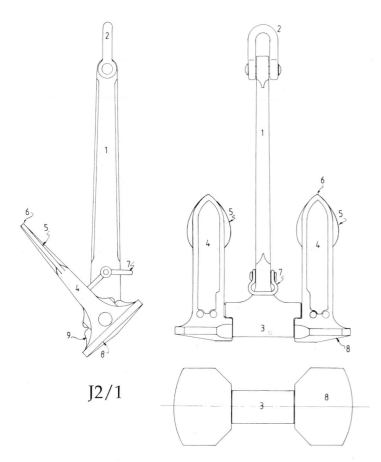

J2/1

J2/2   *Martin's close stowing anchor (scale ¼in = 1ft)*

Stream anchor shown, kedge anchor was 5ft long.

1   Shank
2   Ring
3   Stock
4   Crown
5   Arm
6   Fluke
7   Bill
8   Gravity band
9   Tripping palms

J2/3   *Admiralty pattern anchor (scale ¼in = 1ft)*

1   Shank
2   Ring
3   Stock
4   Crown
5   Arm
6   Fluke
7   Bill
8   Gravity band
9   Stowed position of stock

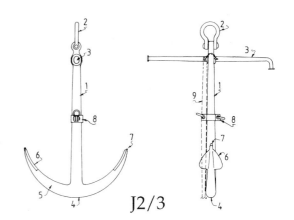

J2/3

K   Boats

K1   50ft STEAM PINNACE (scale $^1/_8$in = 1ft)
1   Cleat
2   Skylight to engine room
3   Vent to engine room
4   Vent to boiler room
5   Hatch to engine room
6   Hatch to boiler room
7   Gun mounting
8   Coal chute
9   Vent to fore cabin
10   Stern benches
11   Steering wheel
12   Compass
13   Deck lights

K2   40ft ADMIRAL'S BARGE (scale $^1/_8$in = 1ft)
1   Cleat
2   Skylight to engine room
3   Vent to engine room
4   Vent to boiler room
5   Hatch to engine room
6   Hatch to boiler room
7   Coal chute
8   Hatch and skylight to fore cabin
9   Stern benches
10   Portable cabin top (occasionally replaced with canvas cover)
11   Deck lights

K1

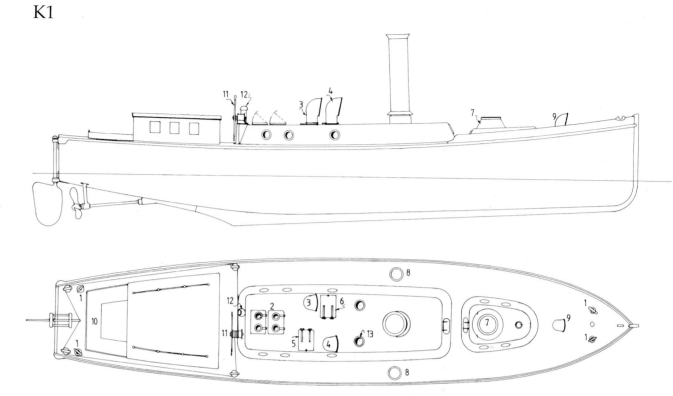

K2

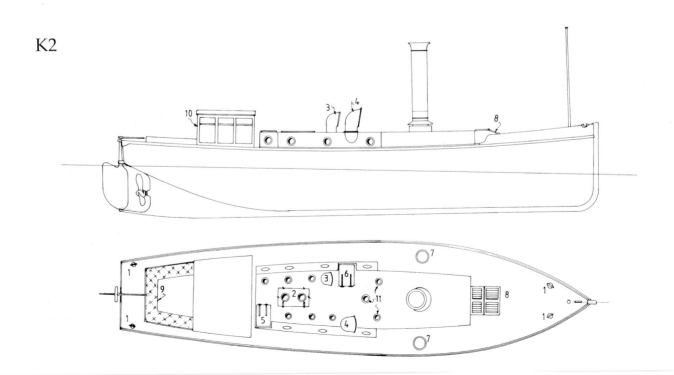

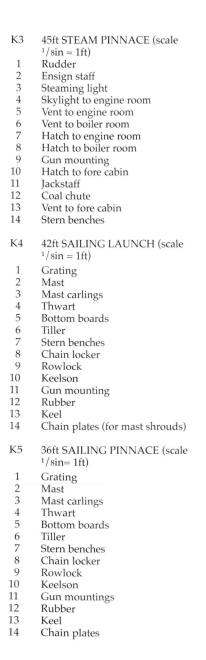

K3   45ft STEAM PINNACE (scale
      ¹/8in = 1ft)
 1   Rudder
 2   Ensign staff
 3   Steaming light
 4   Skylight to engine room
 5   Vent to engine room
 6   Vent to boiler room
 7   Hatch to engine room
 8   Hatch to boiler room
 9   Gun mounting
10   Hatch to fore cabin
11   Jackstaff
12   Coal chute
13   Vent to fore cabin
14   Stern benches

K4   42ft SAILING LAUNCH (scale
      ¹/8in = 1ft)
 1   Grating
 2   Mast
 3   Mast carlings
 4   Thwart
 5   Bottom boards
 6   Tiller
 7   Stern benches
 8   Chain locker
 9   Rowlock
10   Keelson
11   Gun mounting
12   Rubber
13   Keel
14   Chain plates (for mast shrouds)

K5   36ft SAILING PINNACE (scale
      ¹/8in= 1ft)
 1   Grating
 2   Mast
 3   Mast carlings
 4   Thwart
 5   Bottom boards
 6   Tiller
 7   Stern benches
 8   Chain locker
 9   Rowlock
10   Keelson
11   Gun mountings
12   Rubber
13   Keel
14   Chain plates

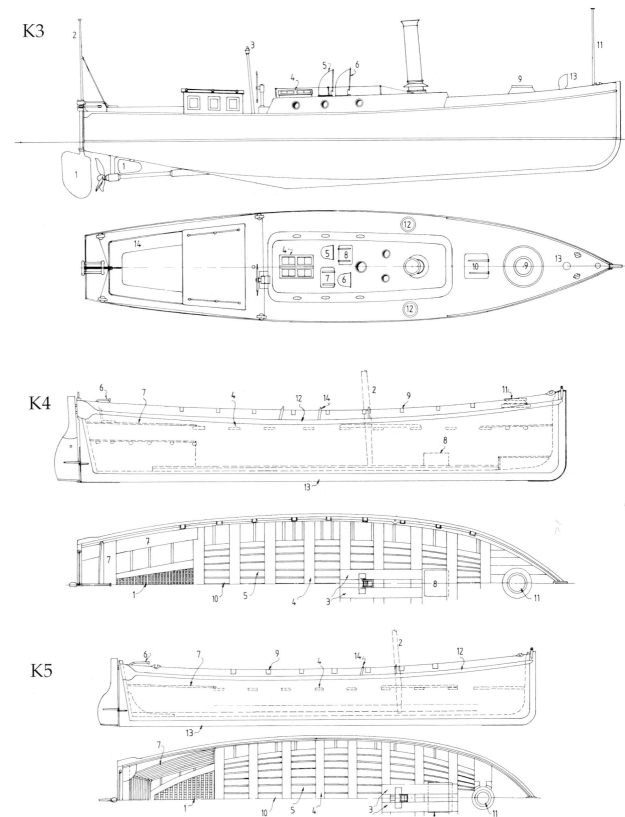

K Boots

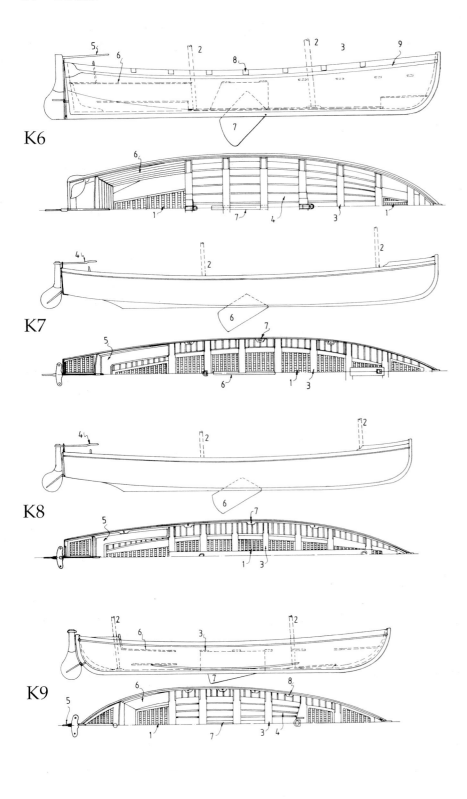

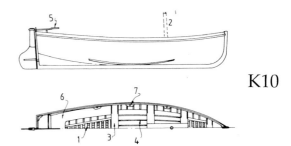

K6

K7

K8

K9

K10

K6	32ft CUTTER (scale $\frac{1}{8}$in = 1ft)
1	Grating
2	Mast
3	Thwart
4	Bottom boards
5	Tiller
6	Stern benches
7	Dropping keel or centre board
8	Rowlocks
9	Rubber

K7	32ft GALLEY (scale $\frac{1}{8}$in = 1ft)
1	Grating
2	Mast
3	Thwart
4	Tiller
5	Stern benches
6	Dropping keel or centre board
7	Rowlocks

K8	30ft GIG (scale $\frac{1}{8}$in = 1ft)
1	Grating
2	Mast
3	Thwart
4	Tiller
5	Stern benches
6	Dropping keel or centre board
7	Rowlocks

K9	27ft WHALER (scale $\frac{1}{8}$in = 1ft)
1	Grating
2	Mast
3	Thwart
4	Bottom boards
5	Rudder
6	Stern benches
7	Dropping keel or centre board
8	Rowlocks

K10	16ft DINGHY (scale ½in = 1ft)
1	Grating
2	Mast
3	Thwart
4	Bottom boards
5	Tiller
6	Stern benches
7	Rowlocks